To
John Barnard

...ntury. Her fiction charts new female versions of epic

WILLA CATHER
A LIFE SAVED UP

HERMIONE LEE

VIRAGO

ACKNOWLEDGEMENTS FOR ILLUSTRATIONS

For Charles Cather, Virginia Cather, dug-out home, Annie Pavelka and family,
Willa Cather and Louise Pound, riding handcar in Wyoming, with Isabelle in
Wyoming, at *McClure's*, Olive Fremstad, Bishop Lamy, at Grand Manan, and
Cather family group, to the Willa Cather Pioneer Memorial and Educational
Foundation, Nebraska State Historical Society.
For Willa Cather as a child, Willa Cather Collection, Barrett Library, University
of Virginia Library.
For attic bedroom, © Lucia Woods, 1973.
For Willa Cather at *Nebraska State Journal* office, 1890s, Bailey/Howe Library,
The University of Vermont.
For Ethelbert Nevin, The Carnegie Library of Pittsburgh.
For Sarah Orne Jewett and Annie Fields, The Boston Athenaeum.
For Sam McClure, The Lilly Library, The University of Indiana.
For Willa Cather at Mesa Verde, and Willa Cather and Isabelle in France, Helen
Cather Southwick.
For Wetherills, and Cliff Palace, The Mesa Verde Museum Association.
For Quebec, The National Archives of Canada.
For Willa Cather and Menuhin, Sir Yehudi Menuhin.

Published by VIRAGO PRESS Limited 1989
20–23 Mandela Street, Camden Town, London NW1 OHQ

*A CIP Catalogue record for this book
is available from the British Library*

Typeset by Goodfellow & Egan Cambridge Ltd
Printed and bound in Great Britain by Billings & Sons Ltd

CONTENTS

ACKNOWLEDGEMENTS

I AM grateful to the British Academy for a personal research grant in 1987 which enabled me to visit Nebraska, and to the Department of English at the University of York for its invaluable provision of research terms. I thank the following librarians for their help in providing access to Cather materials: Inge Dupont at the Pierpont Morgan, Robert Hall at the Clifton Waller Barrett Library at the University of Virginia, Elsie Thomas, Lynn Porn and Joseph Svoboda at the Love Library, University of Nebraska, and Sue Fintel and Ann Billesbach at the Willa Cather Pioneer Memorial Museum. I am grateful for assistance and for materials sent by mail to the William Perkins Library at Duke University, the Huntington Library, the Houghton Library at Harvard, the Newberry Library at Chicago, the Nebraska State Historical Society, and The Bailey/Howe Library at Vermont. The resources of the Brotherton Library at Leeds have been of enormous value to me.

The author gratefully acknowledges permission to reprint the following: Julian Barnes © 1988, for quotation from 'The thunderous presence of l'homme-plume', TLS, Oct 7–13 1988; Elizabeth Bayd and the Willa Cather Pioneer Memorial Museum for Annie Pavelka's letter; Jonathan Cape Ltd and the Estate of C. Day Lewis for quotation from Virgil's Georgics, translated by C. Day Lewis; Victor Gollancz Ltd for quotation from The Fischer-Dieskau Book of Lieder, Victor Gollancz Ltd, English translation © George Bird and Richard Stokes, 1976; Houghton Mifflin Company for quotations from My Ántonia, © 1918, 1926, 1946 Willa Sibert Cather, © 1949 Houghton Mifflin Company, renewed 1954 by Edith Lewis, renewed 1977 by Bertha Handlam, reprinted by permission of Houghton Mifflin Company; for quotations from O Pioneers!, © 1913 and 1941 Willa Sibert Cather, reprinted by permission of Houghton Mifflin Company; for quotations from The Song of the Lark, © 1915 and 1943 Willa Sibert Cather, reprinted by permission of Houghton Mifflin Company; and for quotations from Alexander's Bridge, © 1912, 1922 Willa Sibert Cather, renewed 1950 by Edith Lewis, reprinted by permission of Houghton Mifflin Company; Alfred A. Knopf, Inc., for quotations from Death Comes for the Archbishop, © 1927 Willa Sibert Cather, renewed 1955 by the Executors of the Estate of Willa Cather, reprinted by permission of Alfred A. Knopf, Inc.; for quotations from My Mortal Enemy, © 1926 Willa Sibert Cather, renewed 1954 by Edith Lewis and the City Bank Farmers'

Trust Company, reprinted by permission of Alfred A. Knopf, Inc.; for quotations from *Not Under Forty*, © 1936 Willa Sibert Cather, renewed 1964 by Edith Lewis and the City Bank Farmers' Trust Company, reprinted by permission of Alfred A. Knopf, Inc.; for quotations from *Obscure Destinies*, © 1930, 1932 Willa Sibert Cather, renewed 1958, 1960 by the Executors of the Estate of Willa Cather, reprinted by permission of Alfred A. Knopf, Inc.; for quotations from *One of Ours*, © 1922 Alfred A. Knopf, Inc., renewed 1950 by Edith Lewis and the City Bank Farmers' Trust Company, reprinted by permission of Alfred A. Knopf, Inc.; for quotations from *The Professor's House*, © 1925 Willa Sibert Cather, renewed 1953 by Edith Lewis and the City Bank Farmers' Trust Company, reprinted by permission of Alfred A. Knopf, Inc.; for quotations from *Sapphira and the Slave Girl*, © 1940 Willa Sibert Cather, renewed 1968 by Edith Lewis and the City Bank Farmers' Trust Company, reprinted by permission of Alfred A. Knopf, Inc.; quotations from *Willa Cather on Writing: Critical Studies on Writing as an Art*, © 1949 the Executors of the Estate of Willa Cather, reprinted by permission of Alfred A. Knopf, Inc.; for quotations from *Youth and the Bright Medusa*, © 1920 Willa Sibert Cather, renewed 1948 by the Executors of the Estate of Willa Cather, reprinted by permission of Alfred A. Knopf, Inc.; Karl Miller, © 1985, for quotation from *Doubles*, Oxford University Press, 1985, 1987; Charles P. Olson Estate, © 1947, for quotation from *Call Me Ishmael*, 1947, Jonathan Cape 1967; Penguin Books Ltd for quotation from *Sketches from a Hunter's Album* by Ivan Turgenev, translated Richard Freeborn, Penguin Classics 1967, © Richard Freeborn 1967; University of Nebraska Press for quotations from *Willa Cather's Short Fiction, 1892–1912*, © 1965, 1970, University of Nebraska Press.

Personally, I am indebted for help, inspiration, advice and encouragement of very various kinds to: Julian Barnes, Mildred Bennett, Jacques Berthoud, Christopher Butler, A.S. Byatt, Portia Dadley, Maura Dooley, Ruth Ellison, Nicky Grene, Hugh Haughton, Tom Heacox, Robert Heyder, Ernest Hofer, Pat Kavanagh, Benjamin Lee, Josephine Lee, Alan Mac-Donald, Sharon O'Brien, Ursula Owen, Susan Rosowski, Joan Scanlon, Alistair Stead, Richard Verdi, Hugo Vickers, and, most of all, Jennifer Uglow. Anne Tindall typed with unfailing patience and efficiency. My greatest debt is expressed in the dedication.

LIST OF ILLUSTRATIONS

1

JOURNEYS

Soto! Explore thyself!
Therein thyself shalt find
The 'Undiscovered Continent' –
No Settler had the Mind.[1]

Emily Dickinson, c. 1864

WILLA CATHER said, late in life, that she seemed fated to send people on journeys.[2] She was always getting letters from readers who had set off for Nebraska or the Mesa Verde, New Mexico or Quebec, in the footprints of her characters. In fact the managers of the Bishop's Lodge Hotel at Santa Fé had done so well out of the Archbishop that they had offered her unlimited free accommodation. But, she added, she did not want to go back to the places she had written about; they had all changed. This suggests one of the paradoxes of Cather's writing. In her life, her journeys, and her writing, she is an original, adventurous explorer, like the pioneers in the title of her early novel, energetically making her mark on an 'undiscovered continent'. But she is also a historian; her imagination works through memory, distance, and loss. She translates her landscapes, and the figures in them, into landscapes of the mind.

This makes the journey in pursuit of Cather a complicated one. Since she died in 1947, her admirers have continued to retrace her tracks, westward from Virginia to Red Cloud, east from Lincoln, Nebraska, to Pittsburgh and New York, down through the Southwest, across the ocean to Paris and Provence, and up to Canada and Maine and New Hampshire. They find recognizably impressive landscapes, but utterly transformed environments. Anyone writing on Cather also has to make journeys to numerous American libraries, to read the letters which survived her attempts to reclaim and destroy all her correspondence, and which her will ensured could not be quoted or published. Just as she wanted no visitors spoiling the places she had loved, so she wanted no tourists inspecting her life. Cather resists her pursuers: she would prefer to be an 'undiscovered continent'.

A Cather pilgrimage – to her home town, for instance – can be interesting, but, like most literary pilgrimages, has ultimately not much to do with a reading of her novels. It is an inner, not an outer, journey that's required. Certainly I found my own visit (my first to the mid-West) to the small, subdued crossroads town of Red Cloud, 130 miles west of Lincoln, a curious experience, full of vivid impressions. Summoned by the noon-time siren to the beef and noodles diet of the Corral Café, I listen to an unflagging stream of local jocularity (very old lady with no teeth: 'I'd have given him a piece a my mind cepn I wouldn have had none left', and so on). On a wet Sunday evening, I watch well-behaved, overweight families consuming huge pizzas and cokes in the non-alcoholic Prairie Pizza, a large brown-carpeted room with wooden benches and tables down the sides and a big space in the centre. It has gold-framed paintings of Indian pow-wows, *two* pianos covered in wicker baskets of plastic flowers, a (real) old black Ford without wheels on a platform above the door; and on the end wall a large American flag surrounded by models of a plane, a car, a cross, and an Indian head-dress, captioned 'First Americans' Right to Worship – Right to be Free'. Driving out on mud roads to the little fenced-in French and Czech graveyards on the high farmland of the 'Divide', or to the 600 acres reclaimed by the Nebraska State Nature Conservancy to revert to 'Willa Cather Memorial Prairie', I can hear woodlarks calling over miles of space on a warm April evening (two weeks after a blizzard, with snow still on the low slopes). Crossing the Kansas–Nebraska border, I see two wooden signs on the long empty road (one reading 'Leaving Kansas – Come Again', the other 'Nebraska – The Good Life'). I am shown the large ugly bungalow built by 'Ántonia's' grand-daughter, and the neatly reconstructed 'depot' building where no more trains come in. I hear from the waitress in the Palace Bar about the alcoholism and hard times of the local farmers, the merits of the death penalty and the lack of anything to do in Red Cloud since the 'show building' closed down, and I answer her astounding questions ('Do they have cancer in London? Do you have nigras in England?'). I am told that an aged local used to refer to Cather as 'that morpheedite', or that when the Czech descendants promised to lay on a Czech picnic for the 'Cather Spring Conference' they offered to dress in national costume and provide Kentucky Fried Chicken. And then I go into the back of the red-brick Garber Bank, a tall incongruity in a street of one-story food marts, now the 'Willa Cather Pioneer Memorial Museum', to read, in the wake of European and Chinese and American researchers, letters that Cather didn't want read. I couldn't help feeling the extraordinary contrast between the immense landscape and the little, claustrophobic, provincial town, or notice, even at a glance, the signs of cultural assimilation and stagnation Cather had anticipated. But being led by kindly guides around the 'Cather Childhood Home' or the 'Cather Memorial Prairie' did not unlock, though it might illustrate, 'Old Mrs Harris' or My Ántonia, any more than a trip to the Mesa Verde could explain The Professor's House.

It is another of the contradictions of Cather's work that although she draws intensely on her personal experience, her fiction is not satisfactorily accounted for in biographical terms. Like the image of the rock which she places at the centre of many of her books, she is a resistant subject, even an obstructive one. When you set out to write about her, you feel she would not have liked what you are doing, and would not have liked you either. At times, reading yet more of her grumpy repudiations of the modern world, the dislike is reciprocated. And she does not invite interpretation. Her apparent simplicity, her authenticity and authority, her deep connection to places, her specific cultural histories, make her look straightforward and available. But she is no public monument, no laureate of rural America. The journey for Cather must be through her language, her obsessions, and her evasions; like the title of one of her best books of stories, *Obscure Destinies*, she makes an 'obscure' destination. The memorial signposts helpfully put up all over 'Catherland' by the State of Nebraska are misleading markers.

The Cather trail, forty years on, is well trodden, though not noticeably by British readers: like other great women American writers of the twentieth century such as Ellen Glasgow, Flannery O'Connor or Eudora Welty, Cather has never been widely read or much studied in the UK.[3] In America, since *One of Ours* won the Pulitzer Prize and made her famous in 1922, she is high-school reading, alongside Twain, Hemingway and Thoreau. Like Robert Frost (whom she greatly admired and was influenced by) her fame centres on her celebration of rural America and her nostalgia for pioneering values. Scott Fitzgerald, for instance, who wrote *The Great Gatsby* under the spell of *A Lost Lady*, could nevertheless joke about her 'History of the Simple Inarticulate Farmer turned Swede'.[4] Though she fell out of favour with the New Critics of the 1930s, who found her reactionary and escapist, and though she is regarded as old-fashioned and unexciting by a contemporary American novelist such as Philip Roth, she still, like Frost, has a devoted popular following. Cather hagiography is thriving in Lincoln, Nebraska, culminating last year in James Woodress's huge, adulatory biography. And, within the last ten years, feminist criticism has launched some vigorous raids on Cather territory, resulting in inspired new readings (notably by Sharon O'Brien and Judith Fryer). Less subtle attempts than theirs, however, to appropriate Cather as a spokesperson for feminism, in particular for lesbian feminism, run into as many difficulties as readings which identify her as a Catholic, an agrarian, or a romantic. She evades identification, and resembles no one else.

*

Cather is unique, first of all, in being the only woman of her time to have appropriated a 'great tradition' of male American writing. When she turns herself into male narrators and gives them Virgil to read, when she calls her first Nebraskan novel after Whitman's poem of pioneers, she is not only acting out a desire to transcend, imaginatively, expected sexual roles (though she *is* doing that); more impersonally, she is intervening in a masculine language of epic pastoral. The western frontier was a man's world, subjected to masculine pioneering and male speech. In the Whitman poem of 1865, the penetration of the West is erotically apotheosized as an all-male Olympiad:

> O you youths, Western youths,
> So impatient, full of action, full of manly pride and friendship,
> Plain I see you Western youths, see you tramping with the
> foremost,
> Pioneers! O pioneers!

The women ('O you mothers and you wives!') are following along behind with the pack-horses. Figuratively speaking, they are the earth itself, either as a maiden lying ready for productive defloration ('we the virgin soil upheaving') or as 'the eloquent dumb great mother' in another of Whitman's pioneering poems, 'A Song of the Rolling Earth'. Or else they give inspiration as the Muse/flag, at once heavenly and martial:

> Raise the mighty mother mistress,
> Waving high the delicate mistress, over all the starry mistress,
> (bend your heads all,)
> Raise the fang'd and warlike mistress, stern, impassive,
> weapon'd mistress
> Pioneers! O pioneers![5]

In the later literature of immigrant heroes – Frank Norris's *The Octopus*, or Upton Sinclair's *The Jungle*, Ole Rölvaag's Norwegian epic trilogy, or William Carlos Williams's novel of immigrants in New York, *White Mule* – the female characters are always dependent and subsidiary. Tough though they had to be, in life as in literature, the struggle for the frontier is essentially a male story,[6] with the land as a woman (or a female troll, in Rölvaag's *Giants in the Earth*) who must be penetrated and fertilized.[7]

The activity of the pioneers, and the voice of their poet, is rendered in muscular, strenuous language:

> The great poem of the West. It's that which I want to write. Oh, to put it all into hexameters; strike the great iron note; sing the vast, terrible song; the song of the People. . . Ah, to get back to that first clear-eyed view of things, to see as Homer saw, as Beòwulf saw, as the Nibelungen poets saw. The life is here, the same as then; the Poem is here; my West is here; the primeval, epic life is here. . . It is the man who is lacking, the poet.[8]

Norris's virile, ambitious language intends to master the 'vast, terrible' material of formless American space: the task requires the poet to be 'the man'. This male conquest of space is seen by Charles Olson (writing brilliantly on Melville, in 1947, the year Cather died) as the essential drive of American writing:

> I take SPACE to be the central fact to man born in America. . . . It is geography at bottom, a hell of wide land from the beginning. That made the first American story [Parkman's]: exploration. . . .
>
> Some men ride on such space, others have to fasten themselves like a tent stake to survive. As I see it Poe dug in and Melville mounted. They are the alternatives. . . .
>
> Space has a stubborn way of sticking to Americans, penetrating all the way in, accompanying them. It is the exterior fact. . . . We must go over space, or we wither.[9]

All the great writing of nineteenth-century America could be read, in Olson's terms, as different ways of mastering space. Melville's Ahab tries to blast through it, crash through the wall of impenetrable whiteness. Cooper's pioneers, Twain's Huckleberry Finn, adventure into it; Hawthorne's puritans enclose themselves in rigid self-protective communities; Poe buries himself under it, in what D.H. Lawrence calls his 'horrible underground passages of the human soul'.[10] The American Romantics, Thoreau, Emerson, Whitman, try to live in harmony with it, to expand the 'self' to be commensurate with the space, and feel, in Emerson's hopeful words, 'the currents of the Universal Being circulate through me'.[11] A lone woman writer, Emily Dickinson, made a project, unread in her own time, for mastering space by creating a new geography of the imagination. 'My business is circumference',[12] she wrote, constructing a poetry that encompasses a vast 'circumference' in a tightly contained form.

In all these writings there is a tension between romantic identity with, and fearful opposition to, the imagined 'continent' of undiscovered space, a tension acutely emphasized by the traumatic carving up, in the Civil War, of the actual continent. (And in all these white male writers there is an assumption that American space is there to be colonized, in spite of its aboriginal occupants.) By the turn of the century, infinite space was getting distinctly constricted. The pioneering ideal was turning itself into a nostalgic retrospect for a lost Eden, as in Scott Fitzgerald's lament, at the end of *The Great Gatsby*, for the 'fresh, green breast of the new world' as it might once have looked to the explorer, holding his breath, 'face to face for the last time in history with something commensurate to his capacity for wonder',[13] or Robert Frost's later chauvinistic, retrospective sentiments for 'the gift outright', of the 'unstoried' female land: 'The land was ours before we were the land's.'[14]

The historian Frederick Jackson Turner's influential 1893 essay on the closing of the American frontier celebrated the creation of the American democratic character (strong, energetic, practical, exuberant) through the conquest of the wilderness, and struck an ominous note on the ending of this 'Edenic myth': 'And now, four centuries from the discovery of America . . . the frontier has gone, and with its going has closed the first period of American history.'[15] A less idealized version of the American conquest of space would be constructed in the 1920s by D.H. Lawrence and William Carlos Williams, both of whom saw the history of the New World as one of fatal aggression and repression, producing a morbid split in the American psyche.[16] Alien though these interpretations are from Turner's celebration of the democratic character, the idea of a split or fracture is common to both.

Cather's fiction is obsessed with this idea of fracture, both in the secret lives of her characters and in her public sense of American history. The popular, obvious side of her writing, her memorializing of the pioneers and immigrants of the Western states and her disenchantment with the America of the 'closed frontier', is very much of its time, and is strongly in sympathy with Turner's thesis. She wrote an essay in 1923 called 'Nebraska: the End of the First Cycle', which restates that thesis in the context of her home state:

> In Nebraska, as in so many other States, we must face the fact that the splendid story of the pioneers is finished, and that no new story worthy to take its place has yet begun. The generation that subdued the wild land and broke up the virgin prairie is passing, but it is still there, a group of rugged figures in the background which inspire respect, compel admiration. With these old men and women the attainment of material prosperity was a moral victory, because it was wrung from hard conditions, was the result of a struggle that tested character. They can look out over those broad stretches of fertility and say: 'We made this, with our backs and hands'. The sons, the generation now in middle life, were reared amid hardships, and it is perhaps natural that they should be very much interested in material comforts, in buying whatever is expensive and ugly. Their fathers came into a wilderness and had to make everything, had to be as ingenious as shipwrecked sailors. The generation now in the driver's seat hates to make anything, wants to live and die in an automobile, scudding past those acres where the old men used to follow the long corn-rows up and down. They want to buy everything ready-made: clothes, food, education, music, pleasure. Will the third generation – the full-blooded, joyous one just coming over the hill – will it be fooled? Will it believe that to live easily is to live happily?[17]

The closing of the frontier, with all that that implied in terms of urbanization, political change and foreign policy, naturally involved the American writers. What was to

become of the imaginative mastering of space? Coinciding
with Turner's thesis, a literary battle was raging between
American writers arguing for an epic national literature,
robust, virile and democratic (like those mythical frontier
pioneers), and more Europeanized novelists such as William
Dean Howells and Henry James, intent on social and psychological exactitude. Terms like 'romance' and 'realism',
'naturalism' and 'veritism', were hurled around, notably by
Frank Norris:

> Romance – I take it – is the kind of fiction that takes
> cognizance of variations from the type of normal life. Realism
> is the kind of fiction that confines itself to the type of normal
> life. According to this definition, then, Romance may even
> treat of the sordid, the unlovely – as for instance, the novels
> of M. Zola. . . . Also, Realism . . . need not be in the remotest
> sense or degree offensive, but on the other hand respectable
> as a church and proper as a deacon – as, for instance, the
> novels of Mr Howells. . . . Let Realism do the entertaining
> with its meticulous presentation of teacups, rag carpets, wall
> paper and haircloth sofas, stopping with these, going no
> deeper than it sees, choosing the ordinary, the untroubled,
> the commonplace.
>   But to Romance belongs the wide world for range, and the
> unplumbed depths of the human heart, and the mystery of sex,
> and the problems of life, and the black, unsearched penetralia
> of the soul of man.[18]

Cather drew the line at Zola, but she too liked the idea of a
fiction that would 'plumb' and 'range' and be unconfined,
and when she reviewed Norris's *McTeague* admiringly in
1900, she praised him in his own terms:

> He is big and warm and sometimes brutal, and the strength of
> the soil comes up to him with very little loss in the transmis-
> sion. His art strikes deep down into the roots of life and the
> foundations of Things as They Are – not as we tell each other
> they are at the tea-table.[19]

Cather would not begin to write her own novels for some
years after that review – my first chapters describe her long
'apprenticeship' – and when she did, they were not at all like

Frank Norris's, or any of the male writers from whom she learned so much. She made her own version of the never-concluded struggle in the American imagination between romance and realism, space and confinement, pioneering energy and elegiac memorializing.

Her appropriation of a male tradition – an appropriation which had everything to do with her sexual alienation from conventional femininity – made her work unique. Virginia Woolf's well-known ideal of an artist with an androgynous, 'man-womanly' mind, in *A Room of One's Own* (contemporaneous with Cather's great novels of the 1920s), finds its best illustration, in an American context, in Willa Cather's writing.

Cather's 'cross-dressing', in her life as in her writing, was a complicated matter.[20] She outgrew her (now notorious) youthful phase of calling herself 'William Cather Jr', dressing as a boy, and having passionate erotic crushes on other girls, and on actresses and opera singers, and created for herself a well-controlled, increasingly 'private' life as an independent professional woman, not explicitly or even admittedly homosexual, but emotionally defined by her deep feeling for one woman and her lasting companionship with another. Her own self-concealments made for a euphemistic tone in the early books on Cather. E.K. Brown, Cather's first biographer, spoke of her 'warm friendship'[21] with Isabelle McClung; the shorter, earlier version of Woodress's biography said that 'she was married to her art';[22] and as late as the 1970s and '80s critics were still referring obliquely to Cather and McClung's 'special relationship' or 'close friendship'.[23] An unpublished letter from Virginia Faulkner (who, with Bernice Slote, was the pioneering Cather scholar in Nebraska) to one of Cather's nieces, shows a vigorous rearguard action being fought against lesbian interpretations of Cather's life and work.[24]

Such inexplicit approaches now seem squeamish. On the other hand, blithe appropriations of Cather as a lesbian-feminist are anomalous and inappropriate – as here:

Thirty years after her death, . . . at a public hearing on gay rights, a speaker would cite Willa Cather as one of the homosexuals whose presence in New York had enriched the city's cultural and intellectual life.[25]

Cather looks uncomfortable under this banner. She did not call herself a lesbian,[26] would not have thought of herself as such, wrote disapprovingly of Oscar Wilde's 'infamy'[27] even when she was enthusiastic for 1890s decadence, obscured her sexual feelings in her fictions, and may not have had sexual relationships with the women she loved. Nor did she have the slightest interest in political support among women, or in what Adrienne Rich, in her attempt to extend the definition of the word lesbian, calls 'the bonding against male tyranny'.[28]

None of this means, of course, that we are not allowed to describe her, now, as a lesbian writer. If we can't say anything about writers which they would not have said about themselves, then there is no use in writing about them. But it is important not to collapse Cather's imaginative life into a simple matter of repression, nor to condescend to her for her lack of 'openness'. This mistake seems to me to be made in the description of Cather by one feminist American critic as

a lesbian who could not, or did not, acknowledge her homosexuality and who, in her fiction, transformed her emotional life and experience into acceptable, heterosexual forms and guises.[29]

and by another, arguing that

Cather may have adopted her characteristic male persona in order to express safely her emotional and erotic feelings for other women.[30]

These approaches display the disadvantages of openness. To account for Cather's fiction by reading it as an encoding of covert, even guilty, sexuality, is, I think, patronizing and narrow. It assumes that the work is written only in order to express homosexual feeling in disguise; it makes her out to be a coward (which was certainly not one of her failings);

and it assumes that 'openness' would have been preferable. If the argument is that 'Cather never dealt adequately with her homosexuality in her fiction', that *My Ántonia* is 'a betrayal of female independence and female sexuality', and that *The Professor's House* and *Death Comes for the Archbishop* retreat into 'a world dominated by patriarchy',[31] then Cather is diminished by being enlisted to a cause. She was a writer who worked, at her best, through indirection, suppression, and suggestion, and through a refusal to be enlisted.

That refusal to be co-opted marked, from early on, her attitude to other women writers. Not unlike George Eliot (whom Cather greatly admired), beginning her career as a novelist under a male pseudonym with a castigation of false and trashy versions of femininity in 'Silly Novels by Lady Novelists',[32] Cather too defined herself as a writer against the standards of female writing.

> I have not much faith in women in fiction. They have a sort of sex consciousness that is abominable. They are so limited to one string and they lie so about that. They are so few, the ones who really did anything worth while; there were the great Georges, George Eliot and George Sand, and they were anything but women, and there was Miss Brontë who kept her sentimentality under control, and there was Jane Austen who certainly had more common sense than any of them and was in some respects the greatest of them all. Women are so horribly subjective and they have such scorn for the healthy commonplace. When a woman writes a story of adventure, a stout sea tale, a manly battle yarn, anything without wine, women and love, then I will begin to hope for something great from them, not before.[33]

One of her most ferocious attacks, also written in her twenties, was on Kate Chopin's *The Awakening*. Cather detested it for the 'Emma Bovaryisme' of its heroine, the emotional, dissatisfied Edna Pontellier; her critique of Edna and of women like her sounds like Lawrence's attacks on neurotic modern American women 'battening on love':[34]

> With them everything begins with fancy, and passions rise in the brain rather than in the blood, the poor, neglected, limited one-sided brain that might do so much better things than

badgering itself into frantic endeavours to love. . . . They have driven the blood until it will drive no further, they have played their nerves up to the point where any relaxation short of absolute annihilation is impossible. . . . And in the end, the nerves get even.[35]

These rejections of the 'feminine' in Cather's early critical writings are part of her dedication to classical, heroic forms of narrative with hard clear lines, strong stories and epic simplicity. The project to take over a male tradition of writing meant, at this stage, that she also had to appropriate the dominant male critique of female weakness and emotionalism. It is revealing that one of the few poems by women writers Cather admired was Christina Rossetti's extraordinary 'Goblin Market',[36] a preference which suggests her sense of alarm at setting out to steal the 'goblin fruits' of male art, and, at the same time, her need to remain sexually chaste – even repressed – in order to become an artist. In her essay on the poem, Cather quotes its most startlingly erotic verse. The strong sister Lizzie, who has refused to eat the goblin fruits and has had them smeared all over her, returns to the weak sister Laura, who is pining away for the fruit, and says:

> Never mind my bruises
> Hug me, kiss me, suck my juices
> Squeezed from goblin fruit for you,
> Goblin pulp and goblin dew,
> Eat me, drink me, love me,
> Laura, make much of me.

The sister eats, is poisoned, bitterly regrets her addiction, swoons, and wakes up saved and recovered. Cather gives this a stern puritanical reading (which sounds like her attack on Oscar Wilde): 'Never has the purchase of pleasure, its loss in its own taking, the loathsomeness of our own folly in those we love, been put more quaintly and directly.' She goes on to pity Rossetti for the weakness of her gift ('the divine fire was not given to her lavishly . . . there was . . . only a spark which wasted the body and burnt out the soul') and to ask 'whether women have any place in poetry at all'.

Ten years later, she would preface her first volume of

stories, *The Troll Garden*, several of them about aspiring artists, with a quotation from 'Goblin Market':

> We must not look at Goblin men
> We must not buy their fruits:
> Who knows upon what soil they fed
> Their hungry thirsty roots?

These fruits seem for Cather to be artistic fruits, the arcane property of the male world, at once frightening and desirable to the woman writer. But the powerful unexamined sexual dread in Rossetti's poem also suggests the connection between Cather's sexuality and her writing. If she was to steal the goblin fruits she would have to have more than a spark of the divine fire, would need to be strong – possibly through a refusal of the sexual knowledge proffered by the goblin men to the two sisters.

Cather's reservations towards other women writers made her a solitary figure. Though some of her few close friends, such as Dorothy Canfield Fisher and Zoë Akins, were writers, she did not meet, or admit much interest in, the other great women writers of her time, Edith Wharton or Ellen Glasgow or Gertrude Stein, and was dismissive about the only other well-known Nebraskan woman writer, Mari Sandoz. The one exception to this isolation was her brief friendship, of great formative importance for Cather's life and writing, with the New England writer Sarah Orne Jewett, which came when Jewett was in her late fifties and Cather had not yet begun to write novels. Jewett gave Cather crucial advice about the concentration and single-mindedness needed to become a good writer. But it was her example, as well as her advice, which was important for Cather. In an essay she wrote about Jewett, she tried to define that indefinable effect – 'a cadence, a quality of voice that is exclusively the writer's own' – which she got from her New England stories. What she liked was Jewett's instinctive preference for 'everyday people who grow out of the soil', her ear for her 'native tongue', and the way the sketches in *The Country of the Pointed*

Firs 'melt into the land and the life of the land until they are not stories at all, but life itself'.[37] She was able to make her 'local' materials repay observation in a way which greatly appealed to the younger writer. And these materials were not just quietly and tenderly domestic. Cather appreciated the 'austere and unsentimental'[38] qualities of a book like *A Country Doctor*, with its feminist heroine aspiring to a medical career like her guardian's. Above all, she warmed to Jewett's unselfconscious, matter-of-fact love stories between women, in the sad and beautiful story 'Martha's Lady', or in the novel *Deephaven*. ' "I think I should be happy in any town" ', says the girl narrator of *Deephaven* simply, about her friend, ' "if I were living there with Kate Lanchester." '[39] That innocent, idealized intimacy between women, which enabled Jewett to tell Cather that she did not need to use a male narrator to describe feelings of love for a woman,[40] was not open to the more self-conscious and self-concealing Cather. But the example Jewett gave her, at the time when she most needed it, was of a woman's writing that was strong, truthful, and authentic, and could not be dismissed as 'merely' feminine.

Cather's writing about women in her fiction is complex and rich, and it will be one of the main subjects of this book. Though she is best known, I suppose, for the strong immigrant women heroes of her earlier novels, these semi-mythical figures are in sharp contrast to her dangerously seductive, theatrical 'ladies', and to the obstructive matriarchs who play such persistent and alarming roles in her writing. (At the same time that she gives her female characters such various power, allure and force, she invents male 'heroes' who are contemplative, passive, sensitive and withdrawn.) From the first, too, Cather is interested in groups of women whose stoical domestic labour is a form of narration, and who provide inspiration for an American writing which can be at once heroic and female. This female epic is eloquently established in an early story called 'The Bohemian Girl':

The older women, having assured themselves that there were twenty kinds of cake, not counting cookies, and three dozen fat pies, repaired to the corner behind the pile of water-melons, put on their white aprons, and fell to their knitting and fancywork. They were a fine company of old women, and a Dutch painter would have loved to find them there together, where the sun made bright patches on the floor and sent long, quivering shafts of gold through the dusky shade up among the rafters. There were fat, rosy old women who looked hot in their best black dresses; spare, alert old women with brown, dark-veined hands; and several of almost heroic frame. . . . Nils . . . watched them as they sat chattering in four languages, their fingers never lagging behind their tongues.

'Look at them over there,' he whispered, detaining Clara as she passed him. 'Aren't they the Old Guard? I've just counted thirty hands. I guess they've wrung many a chicken's neck and warmed many a boy's jacket for him in their time.'

In reality he fell into amazement when he thought of the Herculean labours those fifteen pairs of hands had performed: of the cows they had milked, the butter they had made, the gardens they had planted, the children and grandchildren they had tended, the brooms they had worn out, the mountains of food they had cooked. It made him dizzy. [CSF, pp. 28–9]

The description is not only a celebration of a particular culture, but also a programme for a writing that will be appropriate to it (like classical pastoral or Dutch painting), and which Cather then goes on to invent.

But this is not her only kind of writing, nor her only subject matter. Cather's work gets its energy from contraries. She is pulled between the natural and the artificial, the native and the European. She is a democrat and an élitist. She relishes troll-like energy and primitivism as much as delicacy and culture. She is religious, and fatalistic. She is equally interested in renunciation and possessiveness, in impersonality and obsession. Her fictions are of split selves and doublings. Above all, there is a paradox for Cather in the act of writing itself.

Cather uses language with extreme deliberation, and is very interested in linguistic processes: translation, sign-reading, orderings. At the same time, she is trying to invent a fictional language which will be as invisible, as transparent, as close as possible to what it speaks of. To this end, she excises and eliminates as much as she can, and depends (in her own words) on the force of 'the thing not said' for her effect. This isn't just a matter of making a sophisticated narrative read like the story-tellings of an oral culture. It is a communication (more 'modernist', ambiguous and strange than it looks at first sight) which can find a way into the incommunicable; the silent; the obscure. And so it makes a new — and, perhaps, androgynous — version of the old American desire to master the 'undiscovered continent'.

My approach to this writing is not a biographical tour of 'Catherland'. When, in the middle of her life, she at last begins to write novels, I turn away, to a great extent, from what happens in her life to what happens in her language. So I make the journey she invited her readers to take, into the fictional life stories, which she wanted to seem 'not stories at all, but life itself'.

2

HOME

Back out of all this now too much for us,
Back in a time made simple by the loss
Of detail, burned, dissolved, and broken off
Like graveyard marble sculpture in the weather,
There is a house that is no more a house
Upon a farm that is no more a farm
And in a town that is no more a town.

Robert Frost, 'Directive', 1946

WILLA CATHER'S fiction is full of life stories, the recounting of autobiographies and biographies. Her characters review their own 'destinies', or that of the person who has most influenced their own lives. As in classical narratives, with their competing pastoral song-makers, or figures encountered on epic voyages with a crucial tale to tell, the stories are set inside one another, pieces sewn into the larger pattern. Sewing is repeatedly used as an analogy for this female appropriation of a male story-telling tradition. There is a late story, 'Neighbour Rosicky', in which the Czech immigrant, a New York tailor turned Nebraskan farmer, still tailors and patches his own clothes and his children's. 'While he sewed, he let his mind run back over his life.' [OD, p.27] Thea Kronborg, the opera singer heroine of *The Song of the Lark*, first learns music – her kind of story-telling – in a Colorado German household which has on the wall a wonderful 'piece-picture' made of different stuffs, 'a kind of mosaic', representing Napoleon's retreat from Moscow. Old Mrs Lee with Alexandra Bergson in *O Pioneers!*, patching and piecing and quilting while she meshes together the stories she's read in the Swedish papers and the stories of her youth, sometimes forgetting 'which were the printed stories and which were the real stories', is like the narrator, translating the immigrant voices into her own language, piecing the 'many little rolls' of story patterns into her own narrative form, interpenetrating 'real stories' and 'printed stories' in 'a kind of mosaic'.

All Cather's writing is a kind of memorizing and memorializing, her subject matter is 'learned by heart'. There is a scene in a 1925 story, 'Uncle Valentine', in which a gifted American composer, predestined to die young, returns to his childhood landscape. The narrator of the story is herself evoking her own childhood, in which her 'Uncle Valentine' was a glamorous occasional revenant. So a double memory is pieced together: the adult narrator's recollection of her past youth centres on the composer-hero's memory of *his* lost innocence. Here she remembers him, with her family, watching the sun set: 'We sat hushed and still, living in some strong wave of feeling or memory that came up in our visitor.' [UV, p.14] Feeling and memory are indistinguishable: they are the identical source of the story, which takes its inspiration, like almost all her writing, from someone Cather knew.

But the story of 'Uncle Valentine' is not literal autobiography, or biography, and the relation between 'feeling and memory' in her work has to be treated with care. Cather is a writer who draws very intensely and minutely on her life, on people and places she knew and stories she had been told, most especially on the material accumulated in childhood. Even when her subject is based on historical research – the life of Father Machebeuf for *Death Comes For the Archbishop*, or Parkman's history of Canada for *Shadows on the Rock* – her own experiences in New Mexico and Quebec are given to the historical characters.

In her letters and interviews she is always insisting on the relation of her writing to memory − her own and other people's. Her writing 'spontaneously' recreates the people and places she has known; the story is essentially 'simple'[1] and personal. Whenever she is asked about a particular book she gives it some personal identification. My Ántonia is a 'faithful picture'[2] of people she knew in and around Red Cloud in the 1880s. She was 'destined' to write it, she says, from the moment she came to Nebraska at the age of eight, and kept hearing details of an old Czech immigrant's recent suicide.[3] Marian Forrester, the 'lost lady', 'is' Lydia Garber, 'a woman I loved very much in my childhood'.[4] The model for the not-so-lovable Myra Henshawe in My Mortal Enemy is somebody Cather knew well and whose friends all recognized her when the novella was published.[5] Claude Wheeler, the young Nebraskan soldier in One of Ours, is based on her cousin G.P. Cather, a farmboy who died in the war in 1918. Lucy Gayheart 'is' Sadie Becker, a girl she remembers vividly from childhood − but by 1939 she can't be sure if her eyes were grey or golden-brown.[6] When an American artist writes wanting to know if the 'piece-picture' in the Kohlers' house is an invention, she takes particular pleasure in explaining that it was an exact description of something she 'cared about' long ago − though she also notes that she had moved it from its real setting. Her writing thus makes a 'piece-picture' of her past, taking bits of stuff from different places for its heroic histories.

As she gets older, she likes to feel that she is confirming or reactivating others' memories, and many of her letters are written in response to these recognitions, as though the readers with the same fund of recollections are her true audience,[7] for whom the books are 'meant'. She insists increasingly on the personal, non-literary nature of her work, in such formulations as these: All she is doing is coming into a room to tell you about some people she used to know and love[8] . . . She doesn't invent so much as rearrange her memories, and the memories come to her unconsciously, as though written in her mind[9] . . . By the time she is writing her last novel, Sapphira and the Slave Girl, about her family's

Virginian history and her first childhood recollections, she is drawing so heavily on tales she has been told that she can hardly distinguish between history, legend, early memories and invention.

This myth, which she does her best to encourage in later years, of Cather as the simple vehicle of spontaneous recollection (and which Edith Lewis perpetuated in her memoir, saying for instance that 'Old Mrs Harris' might as well have been called 'Family Portraits')[10] is counteracted elsewhere by frequent warnings against literal or autobiographical readings. Writing to a student admirer in 1943 about 'Paul's Case',[11] her marvellous 1905 story of the dissatisfied, pretentious, sensitive provincial boy who becomes besotted with the theatre, steals from the firm's till and runs away for a few ecstatic days in the Waldorf Astoria before committing suicide, she says that she drew the character from a boy she once had in a Latin class in her Pittsburgh teaching days, a restive, nervous show-off, always trying to attract attention. But the story also reflected her own early emotions about New York City. (Of course, she adds, she never did jump under a train, and nor did the original Paul.) That is how stories are made, by the 'grafting' of some other 'outside' person onto the writer's own life. Her characters are 'composites',[12] not individual portraits; their models 'coalesce' as she works on the story.

In a letter about the late story 'Two Friends',[13] she complains that her acquaintances are always looking for the legs and arms and faces of people they know in her fiction. But this story, of a Red Cloud banker and a cattleman from Buffalo whose friendship breaks up over Populist politics, is not a picture of the two men, she says, but *of the memory* of the two men. As so often it is told in the first person, retrospectively, by a narrator remembering herself as a child observer. Their 'feeling' and her 'memory' coalesce in the story.

In spite of such explanations, the search for 'legs and arms and faces' proved irresistible. Cather may have repudiated biographical readings in the interests of privacy, with which she became increasingly obsessed. But her writing invites such readings, since it gives the effect of simple, true memorializing, and since she insists on that as the essence of her art. Of course the literal-minded approach can lead to pitfalls. *A Lost Lady* was serialized before publication, and, in a late letter to an old friend,[14] Cather recalls with glee that Lydia Garber's daughter-in-law had gone round boasting of her relationship to the 'model' for Marian Forrester, until, in later episodes of the serialization, Marian's adultery began to emerge. At this point Mrs Fred Garber became very indignant, and told Cather's brother Douglass that the book should have been stopped. Cather sets this anecdote against a conversation she once had with her father about *My Ántonia*. He had reminded her that several of the episodes in the book were things that they had seen or done together. Until then, Cather believed she had invented them: the scenes had come to her 'unsought'.

The two juxtaposed anecdotes, absurd and serious versions of the same theme, point to the challenge for Cather's interpreters. Her life is in every page of her writing, but she makes of the material 'a fiction so realistic that it would not seem like art'.[15] The key to this process is in the advice from Sarah Orne Jewett which Cather took so much to heart:

> I want you to be sure of your backgrounds . . . you don't see
> them yet quite enough from the outside, – you stand right in
> the middle of each of them when you write, without having
> the standpoint of the looker-on who takes them each in their
> relation to letters, to the world. . . . You must find your own
> quiet centre of life, and write from that to the world.[16]

This negotiation between a centred self rich in 'backgrounds' and an objective onlooker in touch with a wider world of reading, culture and history is what produces Cather's extraordinary literary assurance and power. Indeed, it is the subject of much of her writing, as the distanced traveller, acculturated into a world elsewhere, finds his or her 'destination' and 'destiny' in a return home.

Home itself was, for Cather, the central stage for that

tension – which was to be so fruitful for the writer – between belonging and separateness, involvement and individualism. She describes the struggle in a very beautiful, perceptive and famous passage about Katherine Mansfield's family stories, 'Prelude' and 'At the Bay', a wonderful example of one woman writer recognizing her own experience in the work of another:

> I doubt whether any contemporary writer has made one feel more keenly the many kinds of personal relations which exist in an everyday 'happy family' who are merely going on living their daily lives, with no crises or shocks or bewildering complications to try them. Yet every individual in that household (even the children) is clinging passionately to his individual soul, is in terror of losing it in the general family flavour. As in most families, the mere struggle to have anything of one's own, to be one's self at all, creates an element of strain which keeps everybody almost at the breaking-point.
>
> One realizes that even in harmonious families there is this double life: the group life, which is the one we can observe in our neighbour's household, and, underneath, another – secret and passionate and intense – which is the real life that stamps the faces and gives character to the voices of our friends. Always in his mind each member of these social units is escaping, running away, trying to break the net which circumstances and his own affections have woven about him. One realizes that human relationships are the tragic necessity of human life; that they can never be wholly satisfactory, that every ego is half the time greedily seeking them, and half the time pulling away from them. In those simple relationships of loving husband and wife, affectionate sisters, children and grandmother, there are innumerable shades of sweetness and anguish which make up the pattern of our lives day by day, though they are not down in the list of subjects from which the conventional novelist works.[17]

In Cather's lifelong fictions of the family, that 'double life' is always felt. It is summed up by an image drawn from her own life, of a talented girl, ruthlessly committed to her own ambitions, shutting out the family from her own room. When Thea Kronborg in *The Song of the Lark* makes herself a bedroom, like the young Cather in Red Cloud, out of a tiny unheated attic, she evolves 'a double life' for herself: day-times full of 'tasks' and 'clamour' as 'one of the Kronborg children', nights of reading and solitude when 'she thought things out more clearly'. [SL, p.73]

Homes where the intelligent aspiring child (Thea, Claude, Vickie) has to resist family pressures are frequently and feelingly contrasted with big, intelligent, musical house-holds, dominated by an understanding hostess/mother/manager figure, where the children are well and widely educated, but given their own space: the energetic Harling household in *My Ántonia*, Aunt Charlotte's musical bringing-up of her four daughters and two adoptive nieces in 'Uncle Valentine', the busy, civilized Erlichs in *One of Ours*, all constantly reading and talking, with 'none of the poisonous reticence' of Claude's home. From her childhood, Cather was enormously attracted to such families for their Euro-peanized, unprovincial culture. Her own family was a rich storehouse of native history, and its powerful personalities influenced her whole life. But it did not give Cather the window on the outside world for which, from early youth, she had such furious desires.

What was the Cather family like? We can summon up a genealogy, a landscape, and a strong atmosphere. Willa Cather's first childhood memories were of her paternal grandparents' big farm, Willow Shade, in Frederick County, Virginia. The Shenandoah Valley near the Blue Ridge moun-tains and the border with West Virginia, though not very rich farming country, was a sympathetic, picturesque land-scape of willows and dogwood and azaleas, sheepfolds and streams and winding, wooded hill roads. Her ancestors were colonial settlers from Ireland who had built up what Cather called (in an anonymous biographical sketch written for Knopf)[18] an 'old conservative society'. The land passed down from father to son – a secure patrilineal inheritance[19] – and 'generations of Cathers already filled the graveyards in the valley'.[20] Just a few years before her birth, the area had been

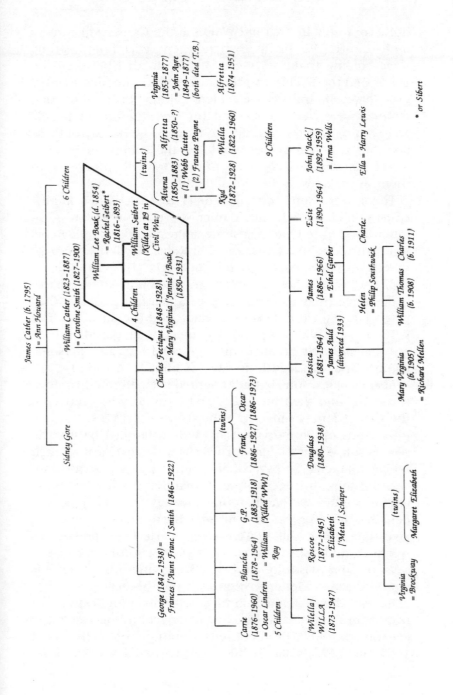

hotly contested in the Civil War, and the Cathers, like many back-country Virginians, where there was not a strong slave-holding tradition, were bitterly divided between the Union and the Rebels. But the society, as Cather described it, was 'ordered and secure', hierarchical: 'People in good families were born good, and the poor mountain people were not expected to amount to much.' The history of these divisions and hierarchies would be the subject of her last novel, *Sapphira and the Slave Girl*, and I will come back to them, as she does, at the end of her life.

There were some strong fathers in the Cather family. Great-grandfather James Cather, born in 1795, was an intelligent farmer and magistrate, a Presbyterian and a Rebel sympathizer, with a house on Flint Ridge, Frederick County, where people liked to go for good talk. His son William (1823–1887), Cather's grandfather, who built Willow Shade, is described by her biographers as 'a taciturn, strong-willed patriarch', with the 'face of a zealot' and the air of an 'Old Testament prophet'. (Jim Burden, meeting his grandfather in *My Ántonia*, 'felt at once his deliberateness and personal dignity, and was a little in awe of him' [MA, pp.11–12]). William's eldest son George inherited the paternal firmness: it was he, and then his father and mother, who pioneered the Cather family move to Nebraska in the 1870s. But like many sons of strong patriarchs, Willa's father Charles, the second son, a law student turned sheep-farmer, was a much milder character, an easygoing, gentle, Virginian gentleman, with his 'boyish, eager-to-please manner, his fair complexion and blue eyes and young face' [OD, p.112] as she describes his likeness in 'Old Mrs Harris'. (The name she gives him there, Hillary Templeton, perfectly expresses his weakness and charm.) He was just a sweet Southern boy, she says of him wistfully and fondly, giving him back his youthfulness in a letter written soon after his death.[21]

But in this extended family, with its ramifications of neighbouring in-laws, its close connections between the generations and its proliferations of young Cathers (between 1873 and 1892 Willa Cather's parents had seven children, their brother George and his wife five), the outstanding, influential characters were women.

Great-aunt Sidney Gore, William's sister, a devout evangelical and a powerfully competent woman, was in her early fifties when Willa Cather was a child. She had single-handedly turned her husband's farm, after his death, into a big health resort called Valley Home, which she managed, and where during the war she looked after the wounded of both sides. She was also a postmistress and teacher, and an eloquent diarist and letter-writer. The village where she lived was renamed after her when she died.

Grandmother Caroline Cather, William's wife, was a tough, efficient farming housewife and pioneer (the grandmother in *My Ántonia* is 'quickfooted and energetic in all her movements ... a strong woman, of unusual endurance' [MA, p.10]). She upped and left for Nebraska with her husband in her mid fifties, and her letters to her daughter (who died young) are full of resilient advice against life's trials. But Caroline herself was getting advice from her old mother-in-law back on Flint Ridge, here (in 1875) sending a wonderfully wry message to Caroline and William via their daughter-in-law, George's wife: this ironical old lady, though not a prominent figure in the Cather story, eloquently suggests the powerful assurance of the Cather matriarchs, and the firm family lines stretching between Virginia and Nebraska:

> I suppose they think that they are such *large* children that they can take the liberty of running abroad as far as they please and staying away as long as they please; but *never mind* there is some very good hickory switches still growing on Flint Ridge and we will try to have some of them in soak for them by the time they get back to Virginia. Why I never learnt William to hunt squirrels and now he aspires to be a buffalo hunter; but it is often the case when children get from under the eye of their parents that they run a little wild![22]

It was Willa Cather's maternal grandmother, though, whose house she was born in, and who moved with the family to Nebraska and lived with them until her death in

1893, who was of most importance to her. She is very touchingly 'drawn', late in Cather's writing, as Rachel Blake in *Sapphira and the Slave Girl* and as 'Old Mrs Harris'. And Cather's early volume of poems began with a sentimental dialect poem (naively indebted to Robert Burns, whom Cather adored at the time) called 'Grandmither, think not I forget'. Rachel Seibert, who grew up in Virginia, was married at fourteen and went to live with her husband in Washington. After he died she returned to Back Creek Valley with five children. She was known locally for her nursing skills, and she taught Willa Cather to write and to read – from the Bible, *The Pilgrim's Progress*, and *Peter Parley's Universal History*. In Red Cloud she was cook, housekeeper, and something of a drudge, for the big Cather family. 'Old Mrs Harris' dwells on her self-denial, stoicism, and kindness to her grandchildren.

Willa Cather's mother is noticeably absent from her daughter's pleasant early memories, which are of helping to herd sheep with her father, or listening to the talk of the family's many visitors and guests, or going up to Timber Ridge to hear local stories from gossipy old Mrs Anderson (whose daughter Marjorie went with the Cathers to Nebraska as houseservant, and was fondly memorialized in the novels). But in spite of all the strong, alternative 'mothering' figures in Cather's childhood, her real mother, as O'Brien is at pains to establish in her biography, was Cather's main challenge, and would be one of her main subjects. She had to separate herself from her, to come to terms with her, and to recognize their likeness.

Virginia Cather was a well-bred, imperious, handsome Southern belle, fussy about dress and social graces in the old genteel tradition, strong-willed (she reconciled the Civil War division in the family) and dominating over her indulgent husband and numerous children, whom she is said to have disciplined with a raw-hide whip.[23] But, like many Southern ladies turned housewives, she was subject to prolonged bouts of depression and illness. (Similar cases are fictionalized by Harriet Beecher Stowe in *Uncle Tom's Cabin*, and in the character of Mrs Birdsong in Ellen Glasgow's *The Sheltered Life*.) This may have made her a difficult mother, resented by her children. But Cather seems to have come to terms with her, imaginatively. In her late work, alarming mature women like Myra Henshawe and Sapphira, who bitterly resent their loss of beauty and authority through illness, are very well understood. And in 'Old Mrs Harris' Cather poignantly imagines her mother's frustration and homesickness in Nebraska.

Cather owed a great deal to the women who brought her up: her own ruthless drive towards independence, her ambitiousness, her resilience and adventurousness, her competence in organizing the shape of her life, her great capacity for work, her impatience with the illnesses she suffered in later years. And those strong nurturing female figures with, at the centre, the difficult mother whose approval was hard to gain, must in part have shaped Cather's lifelong emotional dependency on, and affectionate comradeship with women. Above all, her childhood gave her a sense of possibilities for women. Witness to the negotiation, for all her 'mothers', between fulfilling conventional female roles and asserting great powers, it was no wonder that her youthful admiration — and identification — went to exceptional women playing larger-than-life roles on an elevated stage, women as heroes rather than women as mothers.

> O, yes; of course it's unwomanly to do anything well, and it's shockingly unwomanly to be great. But it would be a dull old world if a few women were not unwomanly to that degree. And while these strong women, these Brünnhildes, go out and fight with fate, and with art that is so much more relentless than fate, their amiable sisters sit back behind a fortification of cradles and tea-towels and carp at them![24]

In all her writing there was to be a see-saw between the epic and the quotidian, the heroic and the domestic, the 'unwomanly' and the 'womanly', which derived from her earliest relationships.

*

'The only thing very noticeable about Nebraska was that it was
still, all day long, Nebraska.' [MA, p.5] So thinks the orphaned
Jim Burden, making his first train journey from Virginia to a
country 'where there was nothing but land: not a country at
all, but the materials out of which countries are made' [MA,
p.7]. Dramatic early dislocations often make a writer – Conrad's from Poland to the sea, Kipling's from India to Southsea,
Elizabeth Bowen's from Ireland to Kent. In the spring of 1883,
when Willa Cather was nine, she made the most important
formative journey of her life. The Cather family – Charles and
Virginia, four children and a niece, grandmother Boak and
Margie Anderson – followed the older brother and the grandparents to Webster County, recently settled territory halfway
across Nebraska and just north of the Kansas line. Charles,
typically, was bowing to his grandfather's pressure. But there
were more positive reasons for the move. Like many other
Virginian farmers, they went in search of better air (tubercu-
losis was rife in their part of Virginia and the Cathers were
susceptible to it), richer and flatter farmland, and escape from
the post-War South. To the nine-year-old migrant, it seemed
a pioneering into nowhere:

> We drove out from Red Cloud to my grandfather's homestead
> one day in April. I was sitting on the hay in the bottom of a
> Studebaker wagon, holding on to the side of the wagon box to
> steady myself – the roads were mostly faint trails over the bunch
> grass in those days. The land was open range and there was
> almost no fencing. As we drove further and further out into the
> country, I felt a good deal as if we had come to the end of
> everything – it was a kind of erasure of personality.
>
> I would not know how much a child's life is bound up in the
> woods and hills and meadows around it, if I had not been jerked
> away from all these and thrown out into a country as bare as a
> piece of sheet iron.[25]

No marks, no boundaries, no signposts, hardly any wooden
houses – mostly sod houses made from the earth or dug-outs
buried in the flanks of the hills or 'draws' – red grass running
everywhere, faint cart tracks, larks singing, and endless undu-
lating prairie: out of this frighteningly formless 'material', like

the settlers digging in and making their marks, Cather would make the shape of her writing.

When the first telegraph wire was brought across the Missouri river at Brownville (Cather recounts, in *The Song of the Lark*, and again in her 1923 essay on Nebraska), 'the first message flashed across the river into Nebraska was not a market report, but a line of poetry: "Westward the course of empire takes its way". The old West was like that'.[26] This chauvinist romanticizing of expansionism will strike us dubiously now: the unstoppable 'course' of any 'empire' seems less of a self-evident good to us, probably, than it did to Bishop Berkeley, whose line of poetry that is. As Edwin Fussell says of Whitman's late pioneering poetry, this sort of language could easily become 'the merest sentimentality or empty rhetoric'.[27] But, in fact, the settling of the 'old West' was an amazing process. When the Territory of Nebraska was created in 1854, a census recorded 2,732 inhabitants — squatters, soldiers, hunters, teamsters. (The Indians, presumably, were not counted.) Then, with the silver-mining boom in Colorado, the 'freighters' came through, taking supplies six hundred miles from the Missouri to the camps at Denver, long trails of oxen and wagon crossing the north-south buffalo tracks. After the Homestead Act of 1862, which meant that settlers could claim up to 160 acres as their own if they farmed the land they had 'staked' for five years, thousands of Americans and immigrants poured into the state. Through the '70s and '80s, the uncounted Indians of the Great Plains fought desperate battles for their territories (one of the Sioux chieftains was called 'Red Cloud'); there were blizzards and droughts and plagues of grasshoppers; farmers tangled with cowboys and ranchers over land-claims.

Willa Cather's family arrived in comparative luxury. They didn't spend their first night, as her Aunt Franc did a few years earlier, in a tent which burnt down in a sudden prairie fire. They were not going to live in a cave in the ground, and they had not had to cross Nebraska on foot, like some of the first immigrant pioneers, or in a 'prairie schooner', as the covered horse-drawn wagons were called. The railways had made all the difference. The Union Pacific lines had been opening up this great flat central plain, between the Missouri and the Rocky Mountains, since the 1860s, and by 1879 the Burlington branch, following the line of the Republican River valley, had reached Red Cloud. The great transcontinental trains and the men who planned and laid their tracks inspired Willa Cather from the first. 'All our great West has been developed from such dreams,' muses the old railroad man in *A Lost Lady*. 'We dreamed the railroads across the mountains.' [ALL, p.51] From early poems and stories to nostalgic late works like *Lucy Gayheart* and 'The Best Years', the 'night express' was remembered as one of the excitements of childhood:

> On Saturdays the children were allowed to go down to the depot to see Seventeen come in. It was a fine sight on winter nights. Sometimes the great locomotive used to sweep in armoured in ice and snow, breathing fire like a dragon, its great red eye shooting a blinding beam along the white roadbed and shining wet rails. When it stopped, it panted like a great beast. After it was watered by the big hose from the overhead tank, it seemed to draw long deep breaths, ready to charge afresh over the great Western land. [OB, pp.109–10]

Trains hardly ever stop at Red Cloud nowadays, and the population is down to 1,300 and falling. But in the 1880s, when it had about 2,500 inhabitants, Red Cloud was a busy stop-off for the Burlington, and a shopping centre for the outlying farmers. It had a school, an opera house, and a tall ugly red building (now the Cather Museum), the Farmers' and Merchants' bank, built by Silas Garber, the State Governor who founded the town in 1870.

For the first eighteen months, Charles Cather tried to farm. By 1884, he and Virginia had four children – Willa, Roscoe (born in 1877), Douglass (born in 1880), and Jessica (born in 1881) – and the family lived on the grandfather's homestead, up on the 'Divide', the high prairie land between the Republican and the Little Blue River. Cather would idealize this landscape, but in reality it seemed, at first, extremely

bleak. Her early Nebraskan experiences, she says in a letter of
1905, were of 'discovering ugliness'.[28] Anything remotely
resembling a landmark – a small muddy creek, a few poplars
– would be hailed with cries of wild enthusiasm by her and
her brothers. But as she rode around this unpromising
scenery on her pony, she discovered what was, to her, a
completely new cultural world.

The Germans had come first to Nebraska, fleeing the
revolutions of 1848. Then the Czechs, or Bohemians – more
of them than to any other American state – from feudal
villages where they had no experience at all of isolated
farming. From the '60s, the Scandinavians began to come in,
hearing of cheap farming land from countrymen in Wisconsin and Minnesota. There were also French communities,
and, by the end of the century, a large number of Russo-
Germans in Lincoln. In her 1923 article on Nebraska, Cather
regretted the Americanization of these distinct ethnic
groups:

> The county in which I grew up, in the south-central part of the
> State, was typical. On Sunday we could drive to a Norwegian
> church and listen to a sermon in that language, or to a Danish
> or a Swedish church. We could go to the French Catholic
> settlement in the next county and hear a sermon in French, or
> into the Bohemian township and hear one in Czech, or we
> could go to church with the German Lutherans.

In 1910, she estimates, the proportion of foreign to native
stock was nine to three. A local Czech historian, Rose
Rosicky, described these people's lives in the *Omaha World
Herald* for October 27, 1929:

> The first home was a dugout. These dugouts preceded the sod
> houses. They were built about four feet in the ground by
> excavating that much, and were very common. Sometimes
> they were built in the side of a bank. For the roof, rafters
> were laid, a few boards or poles placed over them and the
> whole covered with sod. If the homesteader came by wagon,
> the interior furnishing usually consisted of what he had
> brought in that vehicle. . . . Sometimes even a bed was lack-
> ing. . . . Featherbeds, those prized possessions of immigrant

housewives, did valiant service. . . . There was a scarcity of shelter, food, wells, fuel – in fact everything was scarce except the great outdoors.

Five acres were usually broken the first year and the price charged was five dollars. Settlers did not have money to pay for more, nor were there enough teams in the neighbourhood to break more ground. Corn was planted by cutting cracks in the sod with an ax, dropping two or three kernels in each and closing the cracks by stepping on them. Fuel was lacking . . . [so] sunflowers growing along creeks and ravines were gathered and stacked for winter use – a pathetically poor protection against blasts and snow. Such were the beginnings of thousands of immigrants.

The story of the Shimerdas in *My Ántonia* is from the life: there is even a letter from Annie Pavelka, the model for Ántonia, written in 1955 at the age of 86 to a schoolgirl. It is worth quoting from this painstaking letter, since it touchingly corroborates what Annie Pavelka calls 'the Book', and sums up the hundred-year-old history of the Czech immigrants:

Thought I would please you and answer your quastions about our coming to this country from Bohemia 75 years ago last November 5. We started from our vilage Mzizovic 16th of October 1880 and got to Red Cloud in November 5 we were on the water 11 days, there was another Bohemia family came with us, rest on the ship were pollish, my father wanted to bring us to this country so we would have it better here as he used to hear how good it was hear as he had letters from here how wonderfull it was out here that there were beutifful houses lots of trees and so on, but how disapointed he was when he saw them pretty houses duged in the banks of the deep draws. You couldnt see them untill you came rite to the door just steel chimmeny in the roof. there were no roads just tracks from wagon wheels people cut across land to get anywhere at all well we came to Joe Polnickys by hiring a man at Red Cloud, and from there Mr Polnicky took us out to Charlie Kreick . . . and behold our surprise in sieng such beutifful building and our first meal there was corn meal mush and molasses that was what the people lived on and wild fowls and rabbits well my father boght 10060 [i.e. 160] acker farm,

there was nothing on it except sod shack it had just a board bed
and 4 lid stove, no well just 5 aikers of land broken that much
the first homsteder had to on when he didnt live there all time
just so many months so he could realy own it but the folks
didnt live there they moved in with some German family and
that was a bad winter lots of snow not much to cook nothing to
burn no place to go nothing to read people had to burn corn
stalk sunflowers and cow chips it was lucky mother brought
feather beds as we had to sleep on the dirt floors with hay for
mattres, that was hard on father in the old country he had
weaved when it was cold and in the evening he would sit and
make linens and any kind of wearing material allways and was
allways joking and happy he was a man in a millon allways had
lots of friends I was allways with when there was anything to
do allways called me maminka, and mother maminka he never
swore or used dirty words like other men nor he niver drank or
play cards he was a clean man in everyway. then one nice
afternoon it was 15 of feb he told mother he was going to hunt
rabbits he brought a shot gun from the old country he never
used it there nobody dared to shoot there that was all rich
peoples property when he didnt return by five oclock mother
older brother and the man we lived with went to look for him
it was dark when they found him halfsiting in that old house
back of the bed shot in the head and allready cold nearly
frozen. the sherif said it was a suiside there no cemetery or
nothing one of the near neghbors had to make a wooden box
and they had to make his grave in the corner of our farm but
my brother had him moved and him and my mother and
brothers are sleeping in Red Cloud cemetery and they have a
tumbstone I hope they are restting sweetly. most all is true that
you read in the Book thoug most of the names are changed.[29]

Pavelka's insecurity with American spelling, and the movement of her remembering voice over pauses and punctua-
tion, makes a vivid late link back to the women Cather
would listen to as a child, whose stories, 'even when they
spoke very little English', made her feel, as she would as a
novelist, that 'she had got inside another person's skin'.
Those story-telling voices, which Cather would faithfully use
and utterly transform (Annie Pavelka is both like and quite
unlike the Ántonia of 'the Book') would set the tone for a

great deal of her writing. What took her imagination from the first in Nebraska was not the action-packed success stories of cow-punchers and buffalo-hunters – the West did not have to be written about with jovial brutality, she said in 1919.[30] In remote history, it was not (as yet) the indigenous Indian folklore which interested her but the legend of the first European pioneer, the sixteenth-century Spanish adventurer Coronado, said to have passed by the Republican River in his search for the Seven Golden Cities (a local farmer did find a Spanish sword) and – as Jim Burden remembers from his schoolbooks – 'to have died in the wilderness from a broken heart'. [MA, p.244] From Coronado to Annie Pavelka's father, the stories Cather appropriated had the same theme: the painful, heroic, often defeated attempt of the immigrants to adapt their habits and culture to the unforgiving landscape, and the marks they left on it.

Charles Cather, though, was no pioneer, and Virginia Cather no Ántonia. In 1884 the family moved into a small white frame house in Red Cloud, where Cather opened a loans, insurance and mortgage office. It was never a very thriving business (Niel Herbert, whose father has the same job in A Lost Lady, 'felt there was an air of failure and defeat about his family' [ALL, p.25]); the comfortable but cluttered house was rented, not bought, and it filled up with three more children: James (born in 1886), Elsie (born in 1890) and John, known as Jack (born in 1892). Cather was extremely fond of her brothers (less so of her sisters, whom she seems not to have liked very much), particularly of her 'three boys', as she called them in a homesick letter from Pittsburgh.[31] The older brothers, Roscoe and Douglass, would become travelling companions: her trips in the 1910s to Arizona with Douglass, who worked on the railroads in Winslow, and to the 'wild west' (Colorado, Wyoming) with Roscoe, were tough pioneering experiences she was proud of. (Both brothers later went to California to work in oil and banking; she took their deaths, Douglass' in 1938 and Roscoe's in 1945, very hard.)[32] Her little brothers she would read to and look after (these family affections are indulgently

invoked in 'The Best Years', written out of her last visit to
Roscoe in 1941). When Jack was a raw twenty-year-old she
helped him start at technical college in Pittsburgh, and
introduced him to the great opera singer Fremstad, whom,
like Claude Wheeler in *One of Ours*, he charmed.[33]

But like the small town after the prairie, the small house
full of family was constricting, and in adolescence Willa
Cather increasingly found her interests outside it. At school
she had good teachers, and in the town she was drawn to all
the exceptional figures – anyone who could offer her something: a French-German couple next door, the Wieners, with
a house full of European books and paintings; an erudite
store-clerk, Will Ducker, with a passion for the classics, who
dropped dead one hot summer day with a copy of the *Iliad*
beside him; the daughter of a Norwegian oboe player, Mrs
Miner, with a household of lively girls (Carrie, Irene and
Mary), all to be lifelong friends and correspondents; the old
pioneering Governor Garber and his romantic wife; the
impressive local doctors. Through the winter, travelling stock
companies got off the train and played for a week at the
Opera House: 'The Corsican Brothers' or 'The Count of
Monte Cristo', 'The Mikado' or 'The Bohemian Girl'. Cather
and her friends put on recitations and parades and home
theatricals, and even a full-scale production of 'Beauty and
the Beast' at the Opera House, with Cather as the merchant
father. And all this time, sitting in her father's office at night
or hidden away upstairs in the attic, she was reading,
reading, reading: *Huckleberry Finn* and *Swiss Family Robinson*,
The Pilgrim's Progress, Dumas and Stevenson, mixed up with
Paradise Lost and the *Iliad*, *Sartor Resartus* and *Anna Karenina*.

Cather's writing would always arbitrate between realism
and romance; and her move from early childhood experiences (vivid encounters, strongly-felt landscapes, first-hand
narratives) to adolescent fantasy, escapism and play-acting,
looks forward to that negotiation. The teenage Willa Cather,
at this distance a sympathetic misfit full of potential, but who
cannot have been easy to live with, was awkward, restless,
passionate, arrogant, unconfident: an odd fish in what

seemed to her an increasingly narrow pond. Her juvenile gestures of bravado – equipping herself for a surgeon's career by dissecting frogs, signing herself 'William Cather, M.D.', cropping her hair and wearing a boy's suit and cap, delivering an outstanding high school graduation speech on the conflict between 'superstition' and 'investigation' ('the most sacred right of man') – were the symptoms of a furious resistance to parochial narrowness and the genteel conventions dictated by her mother.

Had she known it, she was not alone: all the American writers growing up in the mid-West in the '80s and '90s – Sinclair Lewis in Sauk Center, Minnesota, Theodore Dreiser in Terre Haute, Indiana, Sherwood Anderson in Clyde, Ohio – went through the same sort of thing. Jim Burden, pacing the streets of Black Hawk after dark with nothing to do, 'scowling at the little, sleeping houses' 'made up of evasions and negations' [MA, p.219], is just like George Willard, Anderson's *alter ego*, roaming around 'Winesburg', Ohio at night full of 'ambitions and regrets', feeling 'set apart', knowing he has to leave. The difference for Cather was that she was thwarted by her sex as much as by her surroundings.[34] She had not only to get away, to find a vantage point in the 'world' from which to look back at the 'parish', but to transform her raw gestures of resentment into writing.

Cather would not become a novelist for another twenty years, a long apprenticeship, of which the first stage was her five years as a student at Lincoln University. Like the girl in 'Old Mrs Harris', a late version of these events, she was ferociously determined to get there, and her parents recognized this and borrowed the money for her education. In 1890, when she arrived, the University, like the town, was only twenty years old, with about 400 students (by the time she left it was three times the size) in 'a city of about 30,000 laid out on the open prairie in a straggling north and south rectangle a couple of miles long and a mile wide.'[35] This 'raw' prairie town, however, had an extremely civilized 'transplanted culture' of East Coast and European settlers, an outstanding generation of students who would become 'distinguished novelists, poets, editors, professors, jurists, governors', five thriving newspapers, and two theatres, touring centres for all the big stars and companies of the day. Far from being a 'wild west' frontier town, Lincoln already had a reputation as a complacent, pious, conservative place, known as the 'holy city' for its surplus of churches, and, as the guidebook puts it, for being 'avoided by criminals'. 'Lincoln is strong in the belief that its destiny has always been a special concern of providence,' an irritated Lincoln professor wrote in 1934. 'Its God is, to be sure, of the republican faith and the Methodist persuasion. But it has served this God long and zealously, with the result, so it feels, that it has been the recipient of many divine favors.'[36] Willa Cather was to make her mark in this rather smug cultural centre with great force and at high speed.

Students from rural high schools had to take two extra preparatory years; Cather was let off the first, and went in as 'second prep' to the 'Latin School'. Here, there was a sudden, crucial change of direction. She went to university still intending to be a scientist, but she changed her mind when her class teacher, without warning her, published a remarkable paper she gave on Thomas Carlyle in the *Nebraska State Journal*. It wasn't the last time she would switch direction under a benevolent, managerial male influence. For the next four years her courses were all in classics and literature. Here, Cather was lucky to have a talented Harvard graduate, Herbert Bates, teaching her, whose modesty and sensitivity she always admired (and who couldn't wait to get out of Nebraska). Unfortunately, her other literature professor was a rigid 'analyst' whose mechanical counting exercises and pedestrian exam questions (as, on Browning, 'Why did Porphyria's lover use her hair to strangle her with? What was the purpose of the last ride together?') could not have been more at odds with Cather's passionate, greedy appetite for great writing. Professor Sherman and his *Analytics* must be partly responsible for Cather's lifelong distrust of critics, writing courses, lectures, anthologies, and bibliographies.

'She had no understanding whatever of what literary scholarship implies', wrote one exasperated academic, who had tried
to persuade her to publish her early work and been
'threatened with the law'.[37]

But Cather was learning to be a writer, not a scholar. In her
second year (when she had already made her mark on the
campus for eccentric dressing and dramatic talents), she started to edit the university newspaper, the *Hesperian*, and to
publish her poetry and articles and stories in it. 'The truth is
the *Hesperian* was Willa practically', said a sophomore colleague. 'The rest of us looked wise and did nothing.' The next
year she took a journalism course with Will Owen Jones, the
young managing editor of the *Nebraska State Journal*, who
hired her straight away to write a regular column (later to be
called 'The Passing Show'), at a dollar a time. The column
covered the 'local scene' and contemporary writing, but it was
mostly theatre reviewing, and Cather sank her teeth into this
avidly. Bursting with high ideals and strong feelings, enormously well-read, very fresh to the work, furiously impatient
with anything that looked parochial or second-rate, she very
quickly acquired a reputation for zest, intelligence and ferocity. 'She wrote dramatic criticisms of such biting frankness',
Jones recalled in 1921, 'that she became famous among actors
from coast to coast. . . . Many an actor of national reputation
wondered on coming to Lincoln what would appear the next
morning from the pen of that meatax young girl of whom all
of them had heard.'[38]

Cather reacted disdainfully to accusations that she 'roasted
every show that came to town'. 'There is only one standard of
criticism, and that is justice; to pay respectful tribute to what is
great, to gladly acknowledge what is good . . . to be gentle to
what is mediocre, to be absolutely uncompromising towards
what is bad.'[39] The tone ranged from the heartfelt and inspired
(on great actresses like Duse and Bernhardt) to the derisory:

And how was it with the rural, robust queen, the royal Kleo-
pawtra? Miss Lewis walks like a milkmaid and moves like a
housemaid, not a movement or gesture was dignified, much less
regal. She draped and heaved her ample form about over chairs

and couches to imitate oriental luxury. She slapped her messenger upon the back, she tickled Mark Antony under the chin.
She fainted slouchily upon every possible pretext and upon
every part of the stage. And it was no ordinary faint either, it
was a regular landslide. When the messenger brings the tidings
of Antony's marriage she treats him exactly as an irate housewife might treat a servant who has broken her best pickle dish.
When she lavishes her affection upon Antony, she is only large
and soft and spoony. . . . And the queer little motions she made
when she put that imaginary snake in her bosom, it was so
suggestive of fleas. And her resounding faint when she saw a
vision of Mark Antony in his cunning little pink wedding tunic
being married to Octavia.[40]

By 1895, when she graduated, she was known as the
Journal's outstanding critic, and was also writing regularly
for the Lincoln *Courier*. The job as assistant editor of a new
Pittsburgh magazine, the *Home Monthly*, which she took up in
the spring of '96, was offered to a twenty-three-year-old
with an exceptional, and growing, reputation; it was quite
clear to everyone who knew and read her that, as one local
(male) journalist put it, 'she is unquestionably destined to be
among the foremost of American literary women'.[41]

If Cather drove through her Lincoln years with extraordinary professional energy and confidence, personally she was
much more confused and insecure. Living alone in a rather
spartan boarding-house, she gravitated, as at Red Cloud, to
'second homes' which would educate and excite her. Mrs
Westermann, a cultured German mother of six sons (one a
promising classicist), with a remarkable brother, Julius Tyndale, who was a doctor and a drama critic, took up the
seventeen-year-old Cather very much as Claude Wheeler is
made at home by the Erlichs in *One of Ours*. She made
another important friendship with the daughter of James
Canfield, the University Chancellor, and his artist wife. In
Vermont, where she went after her marriage, Dorothy
Canfield Fisher would be known for some good novels, some
notable war work, and for her advocacy of Montessori
educational methods. At Lincoln she collaborated with, and

looked up to, Cather, who was six years older, and who found her appealingly lovely. Cather quarrelled with her a few years later, but the breach was temporary, and they were to be lifelong correspondents. The best friend of the time, Mariel Gere (whom Cather was also still writing to forty years later) was a daughter of the editor of the *Journal*, whose whole family Cather fell in love with. Mrs Gere, one of her surrogate mothers, coaxed her out of her boy's suit and haircut, residue of the teenage revolt against Red Cloud, which for a time made Cather a dramatically conspicuous figure among the other students.

Cather's 1890s letters to Mariel Gere are self-obsessed and self-accusing, full of deadly serious rhetorical flourishes about her own impossible idiocies and deepest desires. These centre on Louise Pound, the girlfriend on whom she developed a passionate crush. Louise was clearly exceptional, a delicate-looking tennis, golfing and bicycling champion, brilliant daughter of a notable family, who would become a distinguished scholar of American linguistics and folklore at the University. 'William's' letters to and about her, like most people's school or undergraduate diaries and love letters, are, as O'Brien says, 'infatuated, insecure, and melodramatic'. There is a great deal of self-conscious 'Bohemian' boasting about swopping copies of Daudet's risqué decadent novel *Sapho* (the story of a young man from the country hopelessly infatuated with a beguiling, corrupt, artist's mistress) and about how 'blue' she is for Louise, and how Louise won't call her 'love' in public, and how she's been driving her about the country with only one hand on the reins. Even if the whole Louise episode makes rather silly reading (it ended in a mess when Cather published – in revenge for neglect? – a snide satire on Louise's brother in the *Hesperian*) it reveals to us, for the only time, a touching mixture of bravado and anxiety about her sexuality.

One of the last Red Cloud letters to Mariel, written soon before Willa Cather left for Pittsburgh, is ruefully headed 'Siberia'; and all her holiday correspondence to the Geres is scattered with references to life in bitter exile. She takes a condescending tone now about local pastimes: a rough-and-ready New Year's Eve dance with planks for seats and ham sandwiches passed round in potato baskets and men grabbing her by the elbow; a week looking after the accident-prone little brothers; a 'literary' evening up at 'Catherton', the Virginian colony headed by her Uncle George and Aunt Franc (a clever, ugly, educated woman who spent her life, Cather said, distributing cultural manna in the wilderness), where a young lady who couldn't sing was urged on by her doting mama, and the farmers discussed Emerson, rather well. The feeling for the landscape is as strong as ever (she tried out on the patient Mariel a 'writerly' description of a storm seen with Roscoe from a fifty-foot windmill tower), but she badly wants to be away. With no immediate prospects except more Lincoln journalism, feeling that her family had high, and critical, expectations of her, she was terrified that she would never get out of the cornfields.[42]

The Cather family had their own problems, like most other Nebraskan country households in the mid '90s. In 1890 an almost continuous ten-year drought began in the state. Crops failed, hundreds of families left, the heavily mortgaged farmers went broke; banks closed (including Silas Garber's, as in *A Lost Lady*). 'I have very little news to tell except *dry, dust* and no rain', Mrs Cather wrote to relatives back in Virginia in May 1895. 'Every one is so low spirited it looks as if the good Lord has forgotten us entirely. The poor country people do look so blue. Indeed what will become of us all if it does not rain soon.'[43]

In her 1923 essay on Nebraska, Cather sees these hard times as having 'a salutary effect': 'The strongest stock survived, and within ten years those who had weathered the storm came into their reward.' Cather had no party political allegiance, and was certainly not a radical. But her celebration of the hardworking farmers who took hold echoes the voice of agrarian Populism, the mid-West politics of the 1890s. William Jennings Bryan emerged as its leader as a young radical lawyer in conservative Lincoln in the 1880s. The rural depression gave him his cause: usually conservative immigrant farmers moved towards radicalism, and Bryan campaigned as a Democrat (taking the Populists with him) on the nationalization of railroads, telephones and telegraphs, on the ending of monopolies, and with an attack on the gold standard. In 1896, he was the unsuccesful Democratic candidate for President. Though he failed, his famous 'cross of gold' speech at the Democratic Convention, for free coinage of silver as a remedy for the depression, used a rhetoric on behalf of 'the laboring interests and the toilers everywhere' which would ring on, after his defeat, as the voice of opposition to urban, industrial America. Cather didn't hear the Chicago speech, but she pretended she did in a stirring article on Bryan and his wife for a Pittsburgh magazine in 1900. She would use him again, equivocally, as a key figure in 'Two Friends', a late story about Nebraska in the 1890s. In the article she describes him as the embodiment of the Middle West:

> all its newness and vigor, its magnitude and monotony, its richness and lack of variety, its inflammability and volubility, its strength and its crudeness, its high seriousness and self-confidence, its egotism and its nobility.[44]

Her mixed feelings about Bryan – like all her most inspiring figures, at once a hero and a failure – were also her feelings about the West. Her re-vision of Nebraska was to be a struggle between sentiment and revulsion. Her returns home would fill her each time with the old fear of never escaping, and a recognition that this was the place which would always 'get' her.

3

WORKING HER WAY OUT

I know what I want to do, and I'll work my way out yet, if
only you'll give me time.

My Mortal Enemy, 1926

I know what I want – it stares one in the face, as big and
round and bright as the full moon.

Henry James, letter to his mother, 1879

THE MOVE east was to a city with a hundred times the
population of Lincoln, to the steel manufacturing centre of
Western Pennsylvania, where big business and Christianity
made lucrative, respectable bedfellows. Lincoln's conservative piety was mild in comparison with the sombre Presby-
terianism of 1890s Pittsburgh, 'dirty prosaic Pittsburgh that
doesn't care for anything but coal and iron mills and big
houses on Fifth Avenue and Holy St Andrew Carnegie'.[1]
Cather was to spend ten years there as a journalist and a
teacher, and the stories which used it as a setting ('Paul's
Case', 1905; 'A Gold Slipper', 1917; 'Uncle Valentine',
1925; 'Double Birthday', 1929) would all emphasize the
'harsh Calvinism' and the 'merciless business greed' of 'the
grim, raw, dark gray old city'. [UV, p.16] But the 'iron
kings' whose wealth dominated the city – Henry Frick,
Andrew Mellon, George Westinghouse, H.J. Heinz, 'St'
Andrew Carnegie – also gave Pittsburgh its cultural energy
and distinction: the Carnegie Arts Institute and Opera

House, the Pittsburgh Symphony Orchestra, the theatres and newspapers.

Cather saw the paradoxes: she was caustic about the city's striking class divisions, its stuffy hostility to the very artists it was paying for, its pompous unrelaxed approach to pleasure, its smug belief in purchasing power. She wrote sharp pieces on 'St' Andrew's attempt to 'manufacture himself' a writer ('Andrew Carnegie may control the iron market of the world, but he and all his millions can't make a novelist')[2] and on the absurdity of his providing a French Renaissance library, with concert hall, for immigrants working twelve hour shifts in the Homestead mines.[3] All her Pittsburgh stories are about the opposition between artistic aspirations and individualism, and the crushing, unimaginative orthodoxy of the bourgeois business world. Cather was no Upton Sinclair or Dos Passos, however; her move to the industrial city didn't inspire a political writing. And like the boy in 'Paul's Case', dreamily relishing the legends of the self-made magnates, she was drawn to the idea of tycoons. She met one called Magee,[4] the political boss of the city and multimillionaire owner of the Street Car Company, in one of his newspaper offices, and was impressed by the shabbily dressed, nervy looking man's attentiveness to all his supplicants. As always, it was energy she admired, whether it took the form of the iron foundries blazing away on the high hills by the city's rivers, or the people pouring in year by year to see the American paintings in the Art Institute. Cather threw her own energy to meet it, racing the electric cars on her bicycle on her way to work, raring to go.

She had landed in the pious heart of the Puritan city. Charles Axtell, who had heard of her through contacts in Lincoln, and offered her the job on the *Home Monthly*, also gave her temporary room in his home. So Cather began her Pittsburgh career in a chilly, formal household, where she pretended to an interest in church work and Sunday schools, and joined in with the singing of 'Onward Christian Soldiers'. She found the magazine as 'namby-pamby'[5] as the Axtells, all home and fireside stuff about babies and mince pies. The Lincoln papers had been cheerfully middle-brow; Cather's first published essay on Carlyle in the *Nebraska State Journal* of 1891[6] rubbed shoulders with pieces on 'A Glass-Eating Dog in Western Alabama', 'How an Indian Stands Cold' and 'Gossip for the Fair Ones: Fashion's Favorites in Pastures Green'. The *Home Monthly*, modelled on the enormously popular *Ladies' Home Journal*, was primmer (romances, floriculture, nursing, Christian endeavour) and pandered even more than most American magazines of the time to the sacred innocence of the 'young person'. Like other turn-of-the-century writers, from Henry James to Frank Norris, Cather resented the tyranny of genteel censorship: 'All we demand of a national literature is that it shall not injure our "sweet young girls"', she wrote in 1895,[7] sounding just like Norris a couple of years later:

> The great merit of the stories of the 'magazinists' – the one quality which endears them to the editors, is that they are what in editorial slang is called 'safe'. . . . They adorn the center table. They do not 'call a blush to the cheek of the young'. . . .
>   It is the 'young girl' and the family center table that determine the standard of the American short story.[8]

Cather subverted the 'center table' standard mildly: her first story for the *Home Monthly*, 'Tommy, the Unsentimental', a Kiplingesque tale of a boyish Nebraskan girl who could play whist, mix cocktails and run her father's business, is clearly written not just as an experiment in self-projection but as a reaction to the Axtell's code of girlhood. Still, her tone for the magazine is much blander and more conventional than for the Lincoln papers ('The habit of reading formed in childhood will follow the girls and boys all through this trying life, and will give them comfort and pleasure that nothing else can').[9] She was prepared to adapt for the sake of the job, and she was proud of the new responsibility, writing and putting out most of the first issue herself. Fortunately, she was still contributing regularly to the Lincoln papers, and in between theatre and book reviews she could say what she liked there about Pittsburgh culture. After the first year, when the *Home Monthly* closed, she went on to work as assistant telegraph editor for the *Leader*, Pennsylvania's biggest evening paper, at $75 a month. All she needed for this, she said in a friendly letter to Louise Pound,[10] was some general knowledge of foreign affairs and history, the ability to write headlines for twelve different suicides on the same day, and discretion enough to decide whether to fit a lady who had shot herself in Paris next to an Ohio convention. The excitement of this mechanical work soon wore off; by 1900 she was pulling out, increasingly wanting to find time for writing stories, and limited her journalism to freelance pieces for a periodical called the *Library*, which ran for 26 issues, until the money donated by its rich founder ran out – by which time Cather had turned to teaching.

But in those four years she turned out an extraordinary amount of work: the number of her bylines (Helen Delay,[11] John Esten, Charles Douglass, George Overing, Clara Wood Shipman, Gilberta S. Whittle, W. Bert Foster, Henry Nicklemann) shows how much. These pseudonyms were common practice in American journalism (Samuel Clemens had lots of comic alternatives before he settled for Mark Twain): they allowed her to fill up the *Home Monthly* with her contributions, and to get away with hack work she didn't value. But she had always liked re-naming herself: Willa Love Cather after the doctor who delivered her, Willa Sibert Cather after her Confederate uncle. ('Willa' itself was a family shortening from 'Wilella'.) The dressing up as William Cather Jr was developed now into a professional disguise – some of the *Leader* pieces were just signed 'Sibert' – which could allow a chap like 'Henry Nicklemann' ('I was just off the range; I knew a little Greek and something about cattle and a good horse when I saw one, and beyond horses and cattle I considered nothing of vital importance except good stories and the people who wrote them')[12] to sing the praises of an actress or to hero-worship Stephen Crane, without embarrassment.

Cather's appetite for work and experience moved her on fast from the Axtells' Sunday School parochialism. For all her

disparaging remarks about the feminine culture of literary
societies, her introduction to the Pittsburgh women's club
circuit was a great success: she stood up and recited her old
essay on Carlyle and was mobbed by admiring ladies, who
thereafter never stopped calling on her. She got to know
people at the Carnegie Library, and spent a lot of time
reading French literature with a cultured German-American
family, the Seibels. And she very soon became involved with
Pittsburgh's marvellously active musical and theatrical life,
meeting the musicians through Ethel Litchfield, an ex-
professional pianist, and the actors through the Stock Company's leading lady, Lizzie Hudson Collier, who had been in
Lincoln and was kind and sociable to the young journalist.

Cather was enjoying herself in a new social field, with her
Lincoln *gaucheries* behind her; her letters boast excitedly of
picnics and boat rides and excursions 'and things'. But she
bitterly resented being teased by Mariel for her 'Bohemianism'. She was there to work, and to surprise her Lincoln
critics, and her family, by her dedication and success. The
word 'bohemian', to which she kept returning, was a red rag:
she felt all the dangers (as 'Paul's Case' would eloquently
show) of being attracted to the world of art for the wrong
reasons, of hanging about stage doors without the price of a
ticket or the commitment of a craft. 'Bohemian' artiness,
taken up simply as an antidote to the philistine American
materialism she saw all around her in Pittsburgh, would be a
useless attitude, and she had grown out of attitudinizing –
would come very much to dislike it, in fact. 'Bohemia is
pre-eminently the kingdom of failure' she wrote in 1896.[13]
Her whole programme, in these hard-working years as a
journalist, was to build a solid, technical, pragmatic base for
her romantic worship of the creed of Art – a creed she would
follow, if she had to, she said to Mariel, to a hotter place than
Pittsburgh.[14] Paul's escapist adoration of the artist's world
has something of Cather in it. But Paul has no skills and no
dedication, and destroys himself; Cather yoked her fantasies
to routine work.

All the same, Paul's naive wonderment at the glamour of

stage life was part of Cather's attraction to the performing
arts. She wrote enthusiastically in 1896 about Henry James's
theatrical novel, *The Tragic Muse*, for its brilliant evocation of
'the real spirit of the stage . . . the enthusiasm, the devotion,
the exaltation and the sordid, the frivolous and the vulgar
which are so strangely and inextricably blended in that life of
the greenroom'.[15] Like James, she found that life enormously alluring: one of her best theatre pieces enviously
describes two exhausted, grubby stars, Ada Rehan and her
manager Augustus Daly, eating soup and talking shop obli-
viously in a New York restaurant: 'There were two people
who lived all their real life in a theatre. The world outside
was only a sort of big hotel to them.'[16] She was particularly
fascinated by the complicated relationship between technical
prowess and the force of personality. Fine performances
seduced her; she loved to be moved, and to be aware at the
same time of how the effect was being produced. The
transformation of a hard-working professional actress or
singer, with all her idiosyncrasies and tricks of the trade, into
the impersonal figure of the great performer, would always
engross her. As, in different ways, James used the theatre
and Whitman the opera, Cather would turn her passion for
performers and performance not only into her subject-
matter but into her fictional methods: dramatic, scenic
narratives with figures framed, vigorously in action, as on a
stage. In the Pittsburgh years, the preferences that would
shape the writing – for simplicity, heroism, restraint – were
being worked out through the reviewing of drama and
music.

Her veneration for personality comes through particularly
strongly in her music criticism, where she had strong feelings
but no technical expertise; George Seibel remembered that
'she was not interested in the music for itself, but for the
personalities connected with it'.[17] But it was the *transformation* of personality which excited her (as it would in *The Song
of the Lark*). Her heroes – usually female – were the artists
who seemed able, through power, intensity and concentration, to transcend their egotisms: the dramatic Venezuelan

pianist Teresa Carreno, an Amazon or a 'Valkyr come back
to earth', playing with 'seriousness, consecration, triumph'
as though she had buried everything in life that could come
between her and the keyboard;[18] or the great French
soprano Emma Calvé, able to switch in a moment from the
exotic and coquettish to 'the artist controlled, carried
beyond herself, serene as the polar star'.[19] Her interpretations of music were similarly emotional and programmatic
(Julius Tyndale in Lincoln had accused her of 'too great a
tendency to interpret musical compositions into literal pictures').[20] She liked to be stirred by Brahms, Wagner (especially *Lohengrin* and *Tannhäuser*), Verdi (especially *Falstaff*),
Chopin, Massenet, Dvořák: here, for example, she appropriates the 'New World' Symphony to her own landscape of
feeling:

> [In] the second movement, the largo . . . before you stretch
> the empty, hungry plains of the Middle West. Limitless
> prairies, full of the peasantry of all the nations of Europe;
> Germans, Swedes, Norwegians, Danes, Huns, Bohemians,
> Romanians, Bulgarians, Russians and Poles, and it seems as
> though from each of those far scattered lights that at night
> mark the dwellings of these people on the plains, there comes
> the song of a homesick heart.[21]

She wanted music to be 'of the people',[22] to express its
primitive, popular origins: 'It first came to us many a
century ago . . . as a religious chant and a love song', and it
should still speak to those 'two cardinal needs of human-
ity'.[23] Her ideal was the music of her Pittsburgh hero,
Ethelbert Nevin.

Nevin – a household name then, though not now – was a
young composer of American songs and piano pieces, an
infant prodigy who had grown up near Pittsburgh and lived
in Italy. Cather knew his songs, met him in '98 when he
came back to his childhood home at Vineacre, and half fell
in love with him. His music – little evocative folksongs like
'On the Allegheny' or 'O, That We Two Were Maying!' –
evoked a native scene with just the kind of affecting
naturalness she liked, and she used all her most valuable

words for it: 'idealism', 'sentiment', 'tenderness', 'simplicity'.
Personally, he was young-looking, frail, charming, girlish
(though married with two children), at odds with the gritty,
moneymaking Pittsburgh environment he had grown up in.
He bought Cather violets, and dedicated a song to her. Even
before his death at thirty-eight, her writing about him had
the tone of pastoral elegy: she imagined him as a shepherd
piping in the Vale of Tempe or as Virgil's musical Menalcas,
and read in his face, as in his music, 'the poetic melancholy
of the immortally young'. A good thing for her, perhaps, that
he did die young, so that this idealized Lycidas could safely be
used as the model for all her isolated, tragically short-lived
aesthetes.

Cather would always be attracted partly to that Attic style,
and partly to the daemonic, the barbarous, the earthy. In
either case, what most allured her was the isolation and
distinction of the great artist.[24] In her theatre reviewing, she
wrote with passion about the great stage personalities of her
time: Sarah Bernhardt's 'stone age' savagery and 'primeval
fires', especially as Cleopatra;[25] Eleonora Duse's 'delicacy
and power'[26] ('The great art of other women is disclosure.
Hers is concealment'), Helena Modjeska's pathos, dignity
and restraint in Schiller's Mary Stuart.[27] She was fascinated,
as with opera singers, by the constraints and disciplines that
made the great expressive actress: the suppression of personality (especially in Duse), the years of rigorous hard
labour, the sacrifice of an 'ordinary' life. 'Yes', the actress
Minnie Maddern Fiske told her, 'I think we feed our art with
everything in our lives.'[28] Through the power of these
sanctified votaries, giving their perfect performances – Bernhardt as Camille, Ellen Terry as Portia, Julia Marlowe as
Rosalind – the theatre became a holy place:

> We go to change our atmosphere, to get for a moment into the
> atmosphere of great emotions that are forbidden in our
> lives. . . . The dress circle, the parquet, the orchestra chairs –
> that is all the dead world of fact; but right beyond that line of
> lights are the tropics, the kingdom of the unattainable, where
> the grand passions die not and the great forces still work; a land

of Juliets, Othellos, Theodoras and Marguerite Gautiers. It's the
only place on earth they have left now, those great and
unhappy ones. They are like Heine's 'Gods in Exile'.[29]

At the heart of this feeling is the half-admitted sense that the
theatre was a safe place for her to fall in love with great and
beautiful women. 'The beauty of a love of the theatre' thinks
the aficionado Peter Sherringham in *The Tragic Muse*, 'was
precisely that it was a passion exercised on the easiest terms.
This was not the region of responsibility.'[30] But, at the same
time, it satisfied her desire for a sacred ground enhanced by
heroic presences.

What Cather saw at the theatre between 1895 and 1900
was very mixed indeed: Shakespeare, Ibsen, Shaw, but more
often popular hits like *Cyrano de Bergerac* or *The Second Mrs
Tanqueray*, adaptations of classic novels, native farces, vaude-
ville, music hall, and old war horses like *Camille*, which never
failed to stir her.[31] The American stage was not always, by
any means, the home of 'the gods in exile':

> There are some stage questions which have never been solved
> yet. Among them are why the maids always wear red dresses
> and always dust the same piece of furniture through the whole
> play; why the villains always wear silk hats and smoke
> cigarettes; why the leading lady always wears black in the
> fourth act and faints in the fifth.[32]

On the whole, the American stage of the late nineteenth
century had to rely on imports for first-rate plays and
players. Cather, working out her aspirations and standards
for a native culture, was scathingly critical about the country's lack of 'great national schools of acting'[33] and the
national belief, reminiscent of the Roman empire, that
anything good could be 'bought in' and 'made over'.[34] After
a particularly dismal production of *Romeo and Juliet* in 1900,
she imagined the American company writing to Shakespeare
and suggesting he'd have better success with it if he laid the
scene in Chicago, 'exiling Romeo to Milwaukee. The Spanish
war might be touched upon to give the flag a chance'.[35]

Cather was not, for all that, a snobbish theatregoer. It was the vulgar, commercial 'Americanizing' of other cultures she objected to, not popular entertainment. Though she insisted on the special status of the artist, she also wanted the theatre, like music, to be 'the art of the people'.[36] In the programme she was evolving, through her journalism, for a native art, she struggled (like Whitman before her) to reconcile a belief in the special, separating privilege of the artist with the ideal of a democratic culture.

Her ideas on music and drama were part of an aesthetic programme which she had been working out since the early days of reading and reviewing. By her mid twenties she knew a wide range of Classical, French, English and American literature (also some German, and Russian in translation), and had developed a vigorous, eloquent set of values built around a pantheon of heroes. That 'second prep' essay on Carlyle, such a hit with the Pittsburgh ladies, and a later piece on Ruskin from 1896, typify her position. Carlyle is venerated as a kind of prehistoric woolly beast, 'a great Titan', 'the last of the Mammoths', drawing his strength from wild landscapes, formidably out-of-place in London drawing-rooms, and wrestling with his 'great ideas' in solitude.[37] Ruskin, by contrast, is praised for his harmonious poetic 'glory' and his priest-like dedication to the worship of Beauty.[38] The opposition there between the barbaric and the civilized, the virile and the delicate, the native and the cosmopolitan, would go all through her writing.

Cather's championing of Frank Norris's programme for a robust native literature, in the 1890s debate on 'Romance' and 'Realism', derived in part from her enthusiasm for 'boys' books', 'books of action'.[39] So, in *Treasure Island, The Three Musketeers, The Count of Monte Cristo, The Hunchback of Notre Dame*, Stanley Weyman's romances, Anthony Hope's *The Prisoner of Zenda*, she found 'an atmosphere of adventure and romance that gratifies the eternal boy in us'.[40] The attraction to 'boys' books' was part of a theory of primitivism or neopaganism which belonged to a quite common mood of retreat from *fin-de-siècle* 'decadence' and self-consciousness.

'The world is tired; this century has lived too much and too fast. . . . Jaded, exhausted, satiated we have come back to nature acknowledging that she is best, amid the wrecks of an old life we are beginning anew.'[41] The return to nature could be pursued in Whitman, whom she praised for his 'primitive elemental force', his 'exultation in the red blood in his body and the strength in his arms',[42] or in Burns with his 'purity and beauty',[43] or in Kipling (whom she interviewed in Pittsburgh) with his passion for energy and force.[44] When she praised Whitman or Kipling she used much the same terms as in her reporting on the Norwegian Arctic explorer Fridtjof Nansen, who seemed to her a reincarnated Viking, possessed of that 'old unrest', the call 'to a larger liberty, of meeting Nature once more breast to breast'.[45] The best new writing, by this argument, needed to evoke the best past. Cather's romantic primitivism was, from the first, reactionary and nostalgic. The myths she chose to support her predilections – the Arthurian Grail quest, Heine's story of the gods in exile, Kingsley's end-of-empire fable of the children in the forest tempted into the kingdom of the trolls,[46] were myths of loss: the twilight of the gods, the passing of the golden age.

But she also wanted a proletarian writing rooted in home-feeling and 'ordinary' experience. In a 1901 piece on the Carnegie Art Institute,[47] she applied the word 'Philistine', not, as she usually did, to the unimaginative commercialism of America, but to the enjoyment of commonplace subjects (an old lady sewing, a view of the Pittsburgh mills) by an everyday American audience. Her admiration for the nineteenth-century Russian novelists and for certain French writers – Hugo, Anatole France, Maupassant – who seemed to her to have a deep understanding of people; her fondness for George Eliot's The Mill on the Floss,[48] and later, for Sarah Orne Jewett's stories, or Frost's poetry, or Thomas Mann's Joseph and his Brothers[49]: all these different literary passions, like her opinions on painting, music and theatre, pointed to the heroic spiritualizing of 'common' effort and survival in her own work.

Cather's veneration for natural energies, pure 'life-force', meant a hostility to parlour decadence; she disliked the *Yellow Book* ambience, and she was squeamish about 'squalid' realism in Zola's *Germinal* or Hardy's *Jude the Obscure*. But there were contradictions here. She was allured by exotic writing like Gautier's or Daudet's, and she was drawn to the suffering lonely artist out of place in the bourgeois world. So the enthusiast for Kipling, Weyman and Dumas was also to be found praising Housman or de Musset, or defending Verlaine against Max Nordau's charge of 'degeneration'.[50]

The contradiction is a sexual one, evidently. O'Brien accounts for the paradoxes in Cather's literary taste as a vacillation between sexual models. She initially wants to escape 'femininity' by identifying with virile 'writers-as-heroes', but moves towards a more androgynous version of the writer-as-votary. The vacillation, though, is as much between opposing ideas of the American artist's status, as between alternative sexual identifications. Can the artist be the singer of democracy, the speaker of the real world, if he, or she, also feels himself to be the prisoner of Philistia, a god in exile?

Cather's fiction would show up, again and again, the results of this early debate between romance and realism. But for the moment she felt herself to be, more than anything else, a prisoner of 'Philistia'. She had to earn her living; journalism allowed her to develop her critical ideas, but not to apply them. By 1900 she had published enough short stories in magazines to believe in herself as a writer; she was writing poetry as well, and she wanted to start a novel. So, after a few months' stint in Washington in the winter of 1900, doing government translation work (from French into English) and sending a column of news from the capital to Lincoln and Pittsburgh, she took a job at the Pittsburgh Central High School for two years and at an Allegheny school, over the river, for the next three. In the first year, she had to teach 'Latin, composition and algebra'; the first two subjects were enjoyable, but she lost twenty pounds over the third. This was a short apprenticeship, though; after that she taught only literature.

Cather the schoolteacher is not as vivid a figure as Cather the ambitious, busy journalist. She seems to have liked it, and to have been liked by the brighter students, those she could be bothered with; she was clear, hardworking, and severe on her students' prose style. But apart from the restrictive school in 'Paul's Case', and a 1902 story of a retired teacher who has spent his life trying to inculcate literary taste into his 'practical, provident, unimaginative and mercenary' students [CSF, p.287] the five-year job did not make a mark on her fiction. And, looking back, she remembered these as hard years,[51] of working all day and writing at night. She was working her way out: the teaching was not at the centre of her life.

The centre was now taken up by Isabelle McClung, whom Cather met in Lizzie Hudson Collier's dressing-room in 1899, and whose family house she moved into when she started teaching. It is hard to get close to Isabelle, since her letters to Cather were all burned, with the exception of three that came to light after Cather's death, dating probably from between 1926 and 1930, affectionate and solicitous, and in O'Brien's words, 'attesting to an enduring love'.[52] Cather's earliest biographers are reticent about Isabelle, Edith Lewis possibly out of jealousy, and E.K. Brown, just as possibly, through a fear of offending Edith Lewis. Evidently, she was beautiful, wealthy, and determined. She struck observers with her strength of character: she was a person who got her own way. She shared Cather's literary interests, but was not a writer herself.

When Cather put something of Isabelle into a story, 'Double Birthday', about a widowed Pittsburgh lady and her father, she is described, rather chillingly, as 'tall, handsome, with a fine, easy carriage, and her face . . . both hard and sympathetic, like her father's'. [UV, p.43] He, Judge Hammersley, is a stern old traditionalist, dedicated to a life of order. In the story the rapport between father and daughter is excellent. In life, Isabelle was reacting – as Cather had not had to – against a formidable father figure. Judge McClung was a fierce Presbyterian and pillar of the establishment, who had given the harshest possible sentence to an anarchist friend of Emma Goldman's, Alexander Berkman, for trying to shoot Henry Frick after Frick had broken the '92 Homestead steel mills strike. Frick had survived unscathed, but Cather noted wryly in her column (a couple of years before she met the McClungs) that Berkman was doing time nonetheless.[53]

Isabelle was challenging the Judge's orthodoxies by hobnobbing with 'Bohemians' when she met Cather; and there may have been a family struggle when she insisted that Cather move into the large, grand house on Murray Hill Avenue. Whether or not Isabelle threatened to leave home unless Cather moved in, or her sister Edith decided to go because of Cather's presence in the house, or the two women shared a bedroom (they certainly seem to have led an intimate life, reading and working at the top of the house with a sewing room converted to a study for Cather, as in *The Professor's House*), this was clearly a different matter from Cather's usual attraction to large, warm families who took her in. She had fallen in love (or, to put it more precisely, in the beautiful phrase used by William Godwin of Mary Wollstonecraft's relationship with Frances Blood: 'She contracted a friendship so fervent, as for years to have constituted the ruling passion of her mind.').[54] A letter of 1899 to Dorothy Canfield describes Isabelle looking like part of the Parthenon frieze, and says that she is so good to her she is making her feel 'kiddish'.[55] The dedication to Isabelle in the first edition of *The Song of the Lark* comes with a romantic verse (later removed). They had a long, intimate and emotional friendship – whether or not they were actually lovers, which is unprovable – which lasted until Isabelle's marriage in 1916. The marriage came very soon after the death of Isabelle's father and the sale of the house on Murray Hill Avenue which had been Cather's second home. Isabelle was thirty-eight; she and Cather had been friends and companions for seventeen years. The man she married was a few years her junior, a violinist, one of three musician brothers from a highly-cultured émigré Russian-Jewish family who had lived in London and Toronto. Enough of Cather's letters have survived for us to know that she felt the marriage painfully: it was one of the catastrophes of her life. But she did find a way of continuing the relationship with the couple (though she was never very fond of Jan), and was still close to Isabelle when she died in 1938. In the first years, though, the importance of the relationship with Isabelle was the support it provided at the time when Cather was turning herself into a writer. Isabelle seems to have given her not only a luxurious space to write in but the more valuable luxury of strong emotional encouragement.

In the summer of 1902 Cather made her first journey to Europe with Isabelle (and with Dorothy Canfield, whom they met up with in Paris). She covered the trip in letters back to the *Nebraska State Journal*, so her excitement and pleasure are recorded. As for so many American writers, from Emerson to Henry James, the European experience felt as much like a homecoming as a discovery: the landscape and architecture and society were a confirmation of well-loved, long-known books and paintings. The literary American's response to these wonders could be extremely equivocal: the old political hostility with England, a resentment of Europe's cultural dominance, a distaste for the vestiges of medieval feudalism, and a failing of the spirits before the ruins of ancient empires, affected writers as different as Hawthorne, Twain, and Henry Adams. Cather, however, a 'passionate pilgrim' like Henry James, was unadulteratedly enthusiastic.

To an extent she followed the usual literary tourist's itinerary, exclaiming like Hawthorne over the Liverpool poor, relishing by contrast (as James's Strether would the following year) Chester's medieval charm, recognizing Hogarth and Dickens and Kipling in 'the London shoddy', seeking out painters' studios and the theatre, and, once in

France, tracking down the graves of the famous in Père Lachaise, paying homage to Flaubert in Rouen, and admiring the great French churches and the countryside. The particular interests which distinguished her pilgrimage from that of countless others were a passion for Housman, and a particular liking for the old Provençal cities. The Housman quest took her to Ludlow and Shrewsbury in search of Shropshire Lad settings, and, rather unfortunately, to the poet's home (she got his address out of his publishers), which turned out to be a dreary little boarding house in Highgate. An embarrassed Housman, faced with three strange American girls, one of them enthusing about his poems, took refuge in a long scholarly conversation with Dorothy Canfield about her thesis on French literature. Cather was mortified by the encounter, which deflated her ideal of Housman and of her own romantic quest for him. (It would come back to plague her: Ford Madox Ford made up an embellished version of it, and Housman scholars got on her trail.)

There were no such embarrassments in France. Looking back, in later letters to Dorothy, Cather would say that she felt like a raw, stupid savage in the face of the old world, especially by comparison with Dorothy's well-travelled sophistication (an emotion which gets into the French scenes in *One of Ours*). But the rawness only opened her up the more to the experience.[56] Cather wrote passionately back to Lincoln about the beauty of St Ouen in Rouen (to be saved up for *One of Ours*), the Millet-like pastoral scenes at Barbizon near the forest of Fontainebleau, where the wheat fields and poplars reminded her of home, the little Mediterranean fishing village of Le Lavandou, Avignon, the great city of the Popes, and, best of all, the eloquent old town of Arles, rich with associations of her hero, Alphonse Daudet, where 'besides being shepherds and farmers, almost every Provençal is a poet'.

France would be used over and over again in her writing. But, though she would go back often, she never wanted, like James or Edith Wharton, to move to Europe or centre her writing there. Her subject matter would not be the Europeanizing of Americans, but the transference of European cultures to the American landscape: the survival and reshaping of old orders in pioneer form.

The immediate result of the European rite of passage was a 'slim volume'[57] of poetry, which she paid a vanity press to publish. For its time it was an unexceptionable, and unexceptional, collection. Cather was no lyric poet; she needed bigger scope. *April Twilights*, as its title suggests, was a sentimental collection of parlour pastorals, a *pot pourri* of French and English late-Victorian and *fin-de-siècle* influences, touchingly exhibiting its affection for Housman:

> Lads and their sweethearts lying
> In the cleft of the windy hill;
> Hearts that are hushed of their sighing,
> Lips that are tender and still.
> Stars in the purple gloaming,
> Flowers that suffuse and fall,
> Twitter of bird-mates homing,
> And the dead, under all! ['In Media Vita']

A tone of decorous neopagan wistfulness prevails (inspired as much by Ethelbert Nevin's death as by the European experience) in laments for Marsyas and Eurydice, for a lost Arcady and a vanished Apollo. There was little use of native materials, apart from the Burnsian address to her 'grandmither' and an elegy for her confederate uncle Seibert, 'The Namesake'. The language had just the sort of soft-edged, bookish 'slither' (purple gloaming, dust-begotten doubt, pulses a-sleeping, lissome maiden willows, roundelays, wasted cheeks, and so on) that Ezra Pound would deride ten years later in his 1913 manifesto for Imagism: Don't use such an expression as 'dim lands *of peace*', don't use 'book words' or 'straddled adjectives' like 'addled mosses dank' (Cather has 'windy hillside gray'), don't put into poetry anything 'you couldn't, in some circumstance, in the stress of some emotion, actually say'.[58]

In later years, Cather found *April Twilights* something of an embarrassment. Though she had a few good reviews at the time (George Seibel was kind), she knew it was not going to

make her name. More to the point, in 1903, the stories she
was publishing in magazines attracted the attention of a
brilliant and extraordinary New York editor and publisher,
whose interest in her was to transform her life. It begins as a
fine story of professional good luck and advancement.

S.S. McClure – this *deus ex machina* – sent his cousin
talent-scouting in the provinces for the McClure Syndicate,
and the cousin had Cather's name put to him in Lincoln by
Will Owen Jones. McClure then wrote asking to see her
stories (some of them, unknown to him, had already been
turned down by his staff, a mix-up typical of his office). A
week after they arrived, he summoned her to New York by
telegram. Cather was overwhelmed by the meeting. McClure
extracted her life story, praised her work, ticked off his
readers for turning her down, took her home to Westchester
to meet his family, and promised to bring out a book of her
stories and to publish everything she wrote thereafter. It
meant, she felt,[59] the end of long years of waiting, persever-
ance, and discouragement. She was so encouraged and
strengthened that it made her want to do well as much for
McClure as for herself. He had a genius for proselytizing, she
told Will Jones,[60] a boyish enthusiasm which took hold of
you. After some delay, McClure published her first collection
of seven stories, *The Troll Garden*, in 1905: the real beginning
of Cather's writing career. (I will come back to these stories.)
The following year, after a disastrous walk-out by most of his
staff, McClure rushed over to Pittsburgh, spent a persuasive
evening at the McClungs, and offered Cather a job on his
magazine. By the summer of 1906 she was living in Washington Square and working for one of the most famous
publications in the country.

4

BURIED ALIVE

I feel as if a second man had been grafted into me . . . He is
strong and sullen, and he is fighting for his life at the cost of
mine. That is his one activity: to grow strong. No creature
ever wanted so much to live.

Alexander's Bridge, 1912

SAM McCLURE,[1] an indigent Irish immigrant brought up
in Illinois, who had forged a publishing career with ferocious
energy and gusto, was the kind of vigorous pioneering hero
Cather admired, an antitype to the Nevin/Housman ideal of
delicate grace. When she ghosted his autobiography[2] in 1913
she enjoyed it for its honesty; when she caricatured him as
the editor O'Mally in her 1918 satire on McClure's 'Ardessa',
she showed him as impatient, volatile, but likeable. Cather
would always be loyal to McClure, and, as he must have
guessed she would when he captured her from Pittsburgh,
she worked all out for him, for six years.

Not all his staff found him as congenial. McClure had a
genius for talent-spotting and big ideas, but he was an
extremely erratic magazine publisher. He would commission
articles or appoint staff and then lose interest, and other
people would have to pick up the pieces. Half the time he
was rushing about the country making contacts, spending
money and speculating recklessly; the other half he was in
the office interfering with everybody's work. Staff trying to
meet deadlines would have to be hidden from him in hotel

rooms. 'He could raise a rumpus', said his star reporter
Lincoln Steffens; Edith Lewis compared it to working in a
high wind.

McClure was the pioneer of a journalistic phenomenon to
which President Roosevelt (in the year Cather went to New
York) gave a name that stuck: muckraking. It was part of a
general movement of reform which had been building up at
the turn of the century, in reaction, principally, to the power
of the huge privately-funded monopolies and the dismaying
conditions in American cities: immigrants pouring in to live
in indescribable squalor, pervasive corruption in city government. 'Progressivism' was mainly an urban movement, but
there was a link, all the same, between William Jennings
Bryan back in Nebraska, and S.S. McClure in New York. Like
the 1890s Populists, the reformists of the 1900s wanted social
legislation – whether for tax reform, 'efficiency' in business,
labour laws, or immigrant welfare – to curb the untrammel-
led power of individual wealth. The new realism overlapped
with the reform movement. Shocking novels of urban depri-
vation, like Norris's 1899 *McTeague* (much admired by
Cather), set in San Francisco, or Stephen Crane's 1893 novel
set in New York, *Maggie: A Girl of the Streets*, dealt with the
same conditions as non-fiction 'exposés' like Jacob Riis's
1890s book on city slums, *How the Other Half Lives*. Reportage
and fiction came together most notoriously in Upton Sinclair's stomach-turning account of conditions in Chicago's
Packingtown, *The Jungle* (1906).

McClure was interested in fiction as well as fact: he had
been running a fiction distribution syndicate, and when he
founded his magazine in 1893 he published English writers
such as Stevenson, Conrad, Kipling, Anthony Hope and
Arnold Bennett, as well as the big Americans, Twain, Crane,
and Jack London. He also published some very good poetry.
From the start, he was running 'human interest' stories (Ida
Tarbell, his star woman journalist, wrote gripping lives of
Napoleon and Lincoln), but it wasn't until 1903, when
McClure sent Lincoln Steffens out to investigate municipal
corruption, that the magazine made its name. The January

1903 issue of *McClure's* had Steffens on 'The Shame of Minneapolis', Ida Tarbell on Rockefeller's vicious control of the Standard Oil Company, and Ray Stannard Baker's defence of the non-striking miners in the Pennsylvania coalfields. By the next year, *McClure's*, at ten cents a copy, had a circulation of 750,000, and muckraking had become a national industry. In the office, however, the staff celebrities McClure had created were getting tired of his managerial methods and increasingly wild expansionist schemes – not to mention his complicated private life. When Tarbell, Steffens and Baker took most of the staff with them to found a new magazine, leaving McClure with only the impressive Viola Roseboro (liked by Cather for her energy and independence), he had to hire a whole new team. Cather, it seems, was meant as a replacement for Ida Tarbell.

But her interests were not political or reformist, and *McClure's* was in some ways an alien environment for her. There is a revealing letter of 1911[3] describing a meeting with a woman colleague of Jane Addams, the great social work pioneer who founded Hull House, welfare centre for immigrants in Chicago. Cather compared this woman (whose 'cause' was the white slave trade) to Electra, driven mad by living so long with a single horrible idea. She couldn't talk comfortably, she said, with people who were obsessed with the destruction of social evils. And she is caustic, in 'Ardessa', about the solemnity of the muckrakers, 'the great men of the staff . . . as contemplative as Buddhas in their private offices, each meditating upon the particular trust or form of vice confided to his care'. [UV, p.102] Her own social concerns, inexplicit and indirect, were embedded in her feeling for human survival and heroism. When she wrote in 1910[4] to a new young contributor, Elizabeth Shepley Sergeant (who was to become a great friend) suggesting that while in Berlin she look into an exhibition of inventions for the protection of working men, it's clear that her interest is in the details that would bring those hard lives home to her, not in policies for reforming labour conditions.

Most of Cather's work for *McClure's* was editorial: subbing badly written pieces, soothing the authors[5] whose manu-scripts McClure had picked up and then mislaid or forgotten about, advising young contributors[6] – who reminded her of herself in Lincoln ten years earlier – to condense and simplify, to provide information first and foremost and to restrain their emotions: feelings crushed into the background would be all the more potent, she told one of them,[7] for being scarcely noticeable. By 1909 she was managing editor, successfully keeping up the circulation and being sent off to England to make contacts and issue commissions.

Photographs of Cather in her thirties show a firm, compe-tent, rather formidable looking woman, no longer a young hopeful, but someone in control of a working life. New York felt, from the start, much more like home to her than Pittsburgh. Following the footsteps of famous male writers making their way in the city (Stephen Crane, Theodore Dreiser, O. Henry) she moved into a 'bohemian' studio apartment on the south side of Washington Square, facing the dignified brownstones which still retained the atmos-phere of the old, genteel, parochial New York evoked by James and Edith Wharton. The story 'Coming, Aphrodite!' eloquently remembers all that – the oyster houses, the little shops in the Italian quarter, the French hotel with a restaurant-garden on Ninth Street, the violet gaslights and the horses and carriages of Fifth Avenue seen through the Arch into the Square, the pigeons circling over the fountain and the Garibaldi statue. She would come to feel intense nostalgia for this early New York scenery, as the city filled up – to her disgust – with cars and subways and new buildings. Still, for all her regrets, and frequent quests for remote unspoilt places, New York would from now on always be her base.

The dignified past she caught a vanishing glimpse of in Washington Square was much more pervasive in staid, old-fashioned, Puritan Boston. Cather went to the New England city in 1908 when she was doing her one large-scale piece of investigative journalism for *McClure's*. This was the

rewriting and researching of Georgine Milmine's scrappy but
sensational biography of Mary Baker Eddy,[8] sainted founder
of the Church of Christian Science. Cather produced a
splendidly caustic debunking of Eddy as a neurotic egotist:
'She had developed a habit of falling into trances' . . . 'This
literary tendency was a valuable asset, which [she] made the
most of. It gave her a certain prestige in the community, and
she was not loth to pose as an "authoress".' The robust
ironies learned in Cather's 'meatax' reviewing years are
recognizable; but her name appeared nowhere in the serialization, and Milmine took all the credit – and the outrage.

     What was more important to her than Mary Baker Eddy
was her experience in Boston. It made the last stage in a
formative journey which was a kind of counter-pioneering,
back from the raw Nebraska childhood to the East; back to
Europe; back, now, through a century of literary history. A
new and very civilized Boston friend, the wife of an eminent
lawyer, Louis Brandeis, introduced her to what Henry James
would call a 'waterside museum',[9] the house at 148 Charles
Street, overlooking the river, where the publisher's widow
Mrs Annie Fields and the writer Sarah Orne Jewett kept their
'Boston marriage', preserved their memories, and dispensed
a gracious, archaic hospitality.

> Ah, did you once see Shelley plain,
> And did he stop and speak to you,
> And did you speak to him again?
> How strange it seems and new!

When Cather came to write her 'memorabilia' of Charles
Street in 1922 (and to expand them in 1936), Browning's
poem came aptly to mind, since the charm of this house,
where Mrs Fields had lived for fifty years, was the window it
gave onto 'the richness of a rich past . . . a long, unbroken
chain of splendid contacts, beautiful friendships'.[10] James
Fields, who had died a quarter of a century before, had
published most of the great English and American writers of
his time in his magazine the *Atlantic Monthly*, and his
publishing house, Ticknor and Fields, gave generous terms to

English writers in the days before international copyright laws. Dickens and Thackeray and Arnold had all stayed in the house. Mrs Fields had talked to Leigh Hunt about Shelley and to Joseph Severn about Keats; there was a lock of Keats's hair, as well as Tennyson's copy of his poems, among the relics.

Henry James, who had also been a habitué of this literary salon, and wrote his own memoir of it in 1915, describes the attraction of such a scene perfectly in his preface to *The Aspern Papers*, a more sinister version of a pilgrimage into a literary past:

> I delight in a palpable imaginable *visitable* past – in the nearer distances and the clearer mysteries, the marks and signs of a world we may reach over to as by making a long arm we grasp an object at the other end of our own table. . . . That, to my imagination, is the past fragrant of all, or of almost all, the poetry of the thing outlived and lost and gone, and yet in which the precious element of closeness, telling so of connexions but tasting so of differences, remains appreciable. . . . We are divided of course between liking to feel the past strange and liking to feel it familiar . . .[11]

For James, with his cosmopolitan, part-European upbringing, the visitable past of New England felt somewhat thin and jejune: whenever he describes it (in *The Bostonians*, or *The Europeans*, or the essays on Hawthorne and Emerson) he paints it in cold, pale, raw, wintry colours. For Cather it was quite the opposite: when she 'does' Boston (in *Alexander's Bridge*, or the story 'A Wagner Matinée') it seems to shimmer in 'silvery light'; its inhabitants dress up for the evening in 'all the colours that an impressionist finds in a sunlit landscape'. [TG, p.98][12] By contrast with the naked West, Boston and its literary past made a picturesque, reassuring enclosure.

Cather was a frequent pilgrim to the 'visitable past' of Charles Street and, after Sarah Orne Jewett's death, to Mrs Fields' New England summer retreat in Manchester-by-the-Sea. Her memoir of Charles Street has a hushed, even pious tone: she insists on the house as a 'sanctuary', a safe retreat

from 'everything ugly', where the 'tawdry and cheap' have
been 'eliminated'.[13] 'Eliminated' is ominous, and O'Brien is
probably right to detect something constrictive and artificial
in the relationship with Mrs Fields. Certainly the memoir
brings out Cather's most censorious tone about contemporary life. But it is of course a retrospective, nostalgic piece:
as so often, she is doubly memorializing, the recollection of
her own lost past evoking another. At the time, though
Boston was clearly a welcome antidote to *McClure's* office ,
she could be quite caustic about Mrs Fields' genteel repudiation of the modern world: in a letter of 1913 to Elizabeth
Sergeant[14] she makes a joke of Mrs Fields' horror at the
'naked lady' on the cover of *McClure's*: 'Can't you just hear
her saying "undes*irable*?" ', she asks.

The more enfranchising relationship was with Sarah Orne
Jewett. Cather had already admired her stories before she
met her; now, in the last year of Jewett's life (she died in
1909, aged sixty), they made a brief, profound, vital friendship, one of those fortuitous and invaluable encounters
between a writer who has finished and a writer who is
beginning. Jewett's delicate, responsive, humorous personality, her long accepted 'marriage' to Annie Fields, her carefully treasured and potently used rural background, her
discriminating interest in other writers, and her very precise,
technical encouragement, pointed Cather the way she would
go. Charles Street provided the combination her imagination
most responded to: a sanctified past, and an inspiration to
enterprise.

In Boston Cather played the ingénue for the last time; in
New York her new friendships were with younger women
who would look up to *her* for advice and encouragement.
One of these was Zoë Akins, a young actress from St Louis,
who sent some poems to *McClure's* which Cather rejected,
telling her she should try her hand at plays. And Akins did
become a successful and well-known playwright. Cather's
lifelong letters to her in California, where she went to live,
are full of enthusiasm for her work and thanks for the exotic
presents – hothouse plants, a crucifix from the Southwest

– which Zoë regularly sent her. Another protégée was Elizabeth Shepley Sergeant, a young, socially committed journalist from Boston, who came to the office with a piece on New York tenement workers, expecting Cather to share her muckraking interests, but found a literary mentor instead. Cather's early letters to 'Elsie' are fondly intimate, and for about ten years – her crucial period of transition from *McClure's* to full-time writing – they were very close. Cather wrote her long, witty, eloquent descriptions of her trips back West, confided in her about her writing and her life, criticized her work and took her – a special privilege – to the 'sanctuary' in Boston. Sergeant was an attentive and helpful reader of the early fiction, especially of *O Pioneers!* Her 1953 memoir of Cather gives a vivid picture of her in the *McClure's* era: brusque, dressed in striking colours, enthusiastic, domineering.[15] But it's clear from the memoir that problems developed between them, as Elsie Sergeant became less of a 'learner and tyro' and more of an independent, confident journalist. In the war years they drew further apart: Elsie reported for the liberal *New Republic* (and was injured inspecting a French battlefield); Cather's war novel seemed to her out of touch and romanticized. For all this, Cather was still writing to Elsie at the end of her life as one of her dearest, oldest friends.

The least distinctive of these young admirers was the most important – Edith Lewis, the daughter of a conventional banking family in Lincoln, whom Cather had met there in 1903, and introduced onto the staff of *McClure's* in 1906. If Isabelle McClung cuts an impenetrable figure as the beautiful romantic 'lost lady' of Cather's life, Edith, the devoted wifely companion, is a mere shadow. Her hagiographical memoir, published in the same year as Elsie's, *Willa Cather Living*, is such a self-effacing tribute that it's difficult to get much sense from it of the faithful Boswell. She says next to nothing about their relationship, nothing about her own interests (and nothing, either, about Cather's feelings for Isabelle or Elsie). Occasional details[16] reveal her acceptance of a supportive role: for instance, it was 'perhaps by a fortunate accident' that she came down with a severe attack of influenza when they visited Quebec in 1928, since this enabled Cather to go 'roaming about' the town for ten days, collecting material for *Shadows on the Rock*. Cather's increasing reserve and privacy in later years, the discreetly eulogizing memoir, the censorship and defensiveness exercised by Lewis when she became the literary 'widow' and executor, make this lifelong companionship as hard to examine as they would both have wished. Cather wrote feelingly about Isabelle to friends like Dorothy Canfield or Elsie Sergeant, but she hardly ever mentioned Edith, except to say that she'd been seasick again on a transatlantic journey, or that Cather needed to have her on a trip to help her, because she had a hand injury and couldn't manage packing or dressing alone. She never dedicated a book to her, as she did to Isabelle. The only letter to Edith that survives, from 1936,[17] is a description of Jupiter and Venus seen from one of their favourite places, the Shattuck Inn in Jaffrey, New Hampshire (where they would both be buried). But this romantic passage concludes with praise for Edith's packing of Cather's clothes: not a wrinkle!

Recently, some letters came to light that Edith Lewis[18] wrote in the late '40s and the '50s after Cather's death, to their friend Stephen Tennant, the eccentric, talented English aristocrat, painter, art-lover and collector, who was for a time Siegfried Sassoon's lover, and who was one of Cather's great admirers. Speaking much more intimately than in her careful memoir, Lewis is revealed in the letters as an affectionate, emotional, anxious, rather fussy person, a keen music lover and reader (she has missed *Bohème* at the Met because di Stefano was replaced as Rodolfo, she enthuses over Rilke and Pater, Shelley and Swinburne), and a lonely 'widow' ('I don't think of her as in the past . . . to me she seems more in the present than ever before'), completely devoted to Cather's memory:

> [She was so] sensitive to everything – the tone of a voice, the look on anyone's face. Her spirit was so firm and valiant. She guarded the things she cared for, and nothing could shake her or intimidate her.

When we used to go to concerts I was always so proud of her. She seemed so fine, so above all that crowd of people. She would never admit that she was at all musical − but she used to say wonderful things about music − it was as if she had a direct communication with the spirit of the composer − with that of any great artist − regardless of the medium they worked in. She seemed to know his intention at once.

Her nervousness over who should write the biography − E.K. Brown had to pass all kinds of tests of his sensitivity and suitability before she gave him permission − echoes Cather's obsession with privacy:

You know how she absolutely refused to let the world in on her personal life. She often said in her letters to people that every-thing the world was entitled to know was in her books. She had to have that feeling of security − had to know that her friends would protect her in that way. It was necessary for her very life as an artist. I keep telling myself that this *Life will be* a protection from the world − written as I hope it will be written − I don't believe the cheap and vulgar and the merely curious will get any foothold there.

At times the letters sink under the responsibility of making sure that Cather is remembered exactly as she would have wished; it was like being 'the ancient mariner, with the albatross, around his neck − it is all so difficult!' But if her heroine came also to be her albatross, in happier mood the letters with their reminiscences about their travels and their musical experiences, show how much they shared the same tastes, and how well they got on together. Edith was Nebraskan, she understood Cather's background. As well as enjoying music and foreign countries (even if she did get seasick), she enjoyed making places pleasant to live in, and she was an attentive critic: she proofread all the books and attentively watched over the work in progress.

At first she was just a helpful friend. Cather was going back regularly to Pittsburgh to see Isabelle (she may have been hoping that Isabelle would move to New York) and in 1908 they went to Europe again (this time to Italy as well as France, where Cather saw scenes from the Georgics re-enacted on the slopes of the Apennines). Immediately after this Virgilian interlude with Isabelle, she took an apartment with Edith at 82 Washington Place, just off the square. But she didn't take Edith with her when she went back to Red Cloud in 1909 (she never did take her home), nor on her business trip to London that year (rich with new contacts – William Archer, Galsworthy, Lady Gregory, Katherine Tynan); and she had holidays with Isabelle in 1911, and with Douglass in Arizona, in 1912. All through these years she was still very close to Isabelle. But in 1913 it seems she and Edith had become more interdependent; they moved into 5 Bank Street, in Greenwich Village, which would be their home until it was knocked down in 1927. This large, old-fashioned, solid building was the centre of Cather's life after she left *McClure's*: she and Edith furnished it simply and traditionally (mahogany chests and oriental rugs), kept it full of flowers, had regular Friday 'at homes', and brought in a French cook and housekeeper, Josephine Bourda. (Good cooking, as the novels make plain, was one of Cather's passions.) But even after Bank Street was set up, Cather was still planning a holiday with Isabelle in 1915, and only after Judge McClung dissuaded them from going to Europe did she go with Edith instead to the Mesa Verde in Colorado: a dramatic adventure, as it turned out. Then the old Judge died and Isabelle almost immediately married. Hereafter, all Cather's pioneering journeys were made with Edith Lewis, who, in the end, would be buried at her feet: not – at a guess – a position that Isabelle McClung would have wanted to assume for eternity.

Cather had gone to New York with high hopes for her career as a writer, and her first book of stories was certainly a much more promising start than *April Twilights*. *The Troll Garden* is an awkward book which hasn't yet found its way to the control of the mature novels. But it dramatically displays all Cather's preoccupations about becoming an artist, all her sense of frustration, ambition, and fracture. The best stories, which are the most emotional and angry, give off painful feelings. Cather – as usual dismissive of all her work before *O*

Pioneers! – would look back on them, within ten years, as 'warped' expressions of the 'raging bad temper' of a young person kept from the things she wanted, howling for 'music-dramas' in the cornfields.[19] Part of the awkwardness of the stories, as David Daiches notices, is that they make 'an almost feverish attempt' to 'demonstrate that she was at home' in the world of art.[20] But at the same time the volume comes armed with warnings as to the dangers of that world, ominous quotations from 'Goblin Market' and from Charles Kingsley's *The Roman and the Teuton*, which lends the book its title.

Christina Rossetti's poem, as we've seen,[21] spoke to Cather of the dangers of art for the woman writer. In Kingsley's fable of the children of the forest tempted into the fairy palace of the trolls, the makers of 'things rich and strange', the primitive forest children are driven mad by the spell of the palace. They destroy its treasures and wander back disconsolate to the forest, in need of a redeemer. Kingsley is making a Christian, political parable (like the Nibelungen saga, he says) of the overthrow of the Roman Empire by the barbaric Teutonic tribes, a painful lesson of a people 'who have to be educated by suffering'.[22] For Cather, the story is more about art than empire, a fable of mutual destructiveness. Primitive barbarianism wants to tear down art and illusion; but civilization may also destroy a barbarian innocence.

The weakest of the *Troll Garden* stories are those that show off the most. Cather would always say that as a beginner she 'laboriously' strove to imitate Henry James.[23] The influence had some benign after-effects, but it certainly made for artificiality early on. In 'Flavia and Her Artists', a domineering businessman's wife, locked in 'the icy fastnesses of her self-esteem' [TG, p.23], neglects her children for a salon of lions. She is observed by a young, serious philology student, an Alice-in-Wonderland who is losing her illusions. The story stiffly replicates the atmosphere of one of James's literary house-parties (in 'The Death of the Lion', for instance). 'The Marriage of Phaedra', about the life and legacy of a medievalist English painter like Burne-Jones, with a philistine aristocratic wife, a loyal Cockney servant (very embarrassing) and an expatriate American admirer, borrows the plot of the artist's wife who dislikes and distrusts his work from James's 'The Author of "Beltraffio"', and looks back to a story such as 'The Figure in the Carpet' in the decisions which have to be made about the dead man's work. The other 'Eastern' story, 'The Garden Lodge', is less artificial, and, as would *Alexander's Bridge*, sets a controlled adult life against a secret romantic feeling. Caroline Noble has stifled her artistic impulses in order to salvage, and escape from, her shabby Bohemian family. She married a wealthy man and keeps a good house. But the visit of a glamorous Wagnerian tenor called, in chivalrous mode, 'd'Esquerré' (one of several versions of Ethelbert Nevin in these stories) unlocks her secret self. Romantic sexual feeling and the desire for artistic fulfilment coalesce in her sense that 'a happy, useful, well-ordered life was not enough . . . the other things, the shadows – they were the realities'. [TG, p.55] She longs, for one night, for a Wagnerian garden of art, spring and passion; but in the morning she pulls herself together.

The best stories are set in the West, and in Pittsburgh. In all of them a solitary figure with artistic talents or inclinations is destroyed by the 'desert', the philistine wilderness. In three of them, a male observer with artistic sympathies, half in and half out of the destructive scene, acts as an intermediary between us and the drama. (This figure is a beneficial legacy of her apprenticeship to James, and would grow up to become the crucial observing characters in *My Ántonia, A Lost Lady*, and *My Mortal Enemy*.) And in all of them, the dangerous attractions of cosmopolitan culture and the deadening weight of rural provincialism are completed unreconciled.

In 'The Sculptor's Funeral', a ferocious, unforgiving satire on mid-Western philistinism (and an angry elegy for Nevin, unappreciated by his townsfolk), the body of Harvey Merrick, who has made his name as a maker of beautiful things and died young, is returned to 'Sand City, Kansas', 'a bitter, dead little Western town', almost entirely inhabited by spiteful, ugly, mean-minded moneygrubbers. (The winter night-time arrival of the train carrying the body, the shuffling men on the platform, is very fine.) Merrick's last pupil, a young Bostonian, looks on in horror at the ghastly family scene – hideous house, violent mother, decrepit father, sad mulatto servant – and at the censorious, resentful townspeople. The story culminates in an enraged attack on the town's values by a red-headed lawyer, a drinker who has failed to get away, but who understands Merrick's vision. Only one touch suggests a possible reconciliation between this 'parish' and the 'world' of art, the 'singularly feeling and suggestive bas-relief' Merrick once made of 'a thin, faded old woman, sitting and sewing something pinned to her knee', with a little boy trying to attract her attention. It is a domestic American interior, of the kind Cather would come to celebrate; but not yet.

Where 'The Sculptor's Funeral' is enraged, 'A Wagner Matinée' is pathetic. The narrator, a Western farm-boy escaped to Boston, is playing host to his Aunt Georgiana.[24] He owes her his first education in music, Shakespeare and the classics, and though at first he sees her as 'a pathetic and grotesque' figure, by the end he has entered more deeply into her feelings. He takes her to hear the Boston Symphony Orchestra play pieces from *Tannhäuser*, *Tristan* and the *Dutchman*, with Siegfried's funeral march as the climax. The music breaks 'a silence of thirty years; the inconceivable silence of the plains' [TG, p.98] and rouses his aunt to a painful sense of everything she has missed, and a deep reluctance to go home again.

In 'A Death in the Desert', a once-successful singer, Katharine Gaylord ('Gayheart' is anticipated) is dying ('lungs') in her brother's house near Cheyenne, Wyoming. She was a pupil of, and in love with, the gifted composer Adriance Hilgarde (the courtly name, as usual, suggests the Nevin type) whose brother, coincidentally, turns up in Cheyenne. Everett is always being mistaken for his famous brother, who has everything he has not: an artistic career, the love of this woman. But, as in a fairy-tale, what the (offstage) successful brother does not have is human kindness, and it's with this that Everett solaced Katharine's last days. The opposition between the two brothers is interesting, but the strongest emotion in the book is the dying singer's yearning for a world elsewhere: '"She got to Chicago, and then to New York, and then to Europe, where she went up like lightning, and got a taste for it all; and now she's dying here like a rat in a hole, out of her own world, and she can't fall back into ours. We've grown apart, some way – miles and miles apart – and I'm afraid she's fearfully unhappy."' [TG, p.61] The devoted brother's words speak loudly of Cather's fears for herself.

The sculptor, the singer, the composer, are real artists. In the subtlest and most impressive story of the collection, 'Paul's Case', which transfers 'Philistia' from the mid-West to bourgeois puritanical Pittsburgh, the aesthetic type has no talents or capacity for the discipline required by 'the madness of art' (James's phrase, applied to Katharine Gaylord), only a fantasy of escape into the glittering sources of 'world-shine' and Romance. He doesn't read books, he doesn't want to be an actor or a musician, he just wants to 'float' in the atmosphere of 'an exotic, a tropical world of shiny, glistening surfaces and basking ease'. [TG, p.106] (An eloquent language of watery, tropical escapism – 'blue leagues' and yellow sands – runs throughout: 'Here drifted/An hedonist'.[25]) Paul is a 'case', all right: Cather's horror of feckless, self-destructive Bohemianism is strongly felt in the story. But she makes a case for him, too, so that we are absorbed into his dream-world, and follow with pleasure his release into the world of music and theatre, his escape to New York, and his brief 'performance' as an habitué of the Waldorf (on the firm's stolen money), before the real world catches up, and he goes out into the snow to throw himself, like Anna Karenina, under a train. Against Paul are ranged all the conventional authorities – family, teachers, employers – set in the world of 'respectable beds' and 'kitchen odours', crowned by 'his father, at the top of the stairs, his hairy legs sticking out from his night-shirt, his feet thrust into carpet slippers'. [TG, p.107]

The opposition is sexual as much as cultural, the hairy patriarch forbidding the white-skinned, blue-veined aesthete. And in all the stories conventional sexuality is avoided or anathematized: marriage damages the artist, passion is always absent or thwarted, the sympathetic figures are androgynous artists or neutral male narrators. O'Brien reads the stories as Cather's 'struggle to define herself as a woman writer in the context of a male-dominated literary tradition'.[26] But Cather is also trying to find ways for writing to be in control, impersonal, free of the conflicts it describes, whether these are fractures between private feelings and sexual stereotyping, or between an unyielding native environment and a world culture.

The Troll Garden, as yet, is a negative performance, written out of a deep rage at the obstruction of the artist.[27] Its most powerful images are of a landscape which crushes and resists attempts to shape or transform it. Listening to Wagner, Aunt Georgiana's nephew has a vision of:

> the tall, naked house on the prairie, black and grim as a wooden fortress; the black pond where I had learned to swim, its margin pitted with sun-dried cattle tracks; the rain gullied clay banks about the naked house, the four dwarf ash seedlings where the dishcloths were always hung to dry before the kitchen door. The world there was the flat world of the ancients; to the east, a cornfield that stretched to daybreak; to the west a corral that reached to sunset; between, the conquests of peace, dearer bought than those of war. [TG, pp.98–9]

This landscape need not be brutally opposed to art. It could (as the narrator glimpses here without acknowledging it) be the source of its own kind of epic writing, in which barbarian Teutonic strength and rich, fine emotions could be reconciled. Heroism, redemption, magic – the Wagnerian themes – might be drawn from what is, as yet, a repudiated landscape.

The sense of arrival and release Cather had when *The Troll Garden* was published in 1905 soon began to slip away. The reviews were not effusive,[28] and she was criticized by her old patron Will Jones for denigrating her home state, especially in 'A Wagner Matinée'. (Cather replied defensively that she had intended a tribute to the courage of the pioneer women.)[29] Then the hard stress of six years' managerial and editorial work closed in on her writing. McClure, as promised, went on publishing her stories. But she produced only seven between 1904 and 1911, and apart from 'The Enchanted Bluff',[30] and a touching tribute to her Civil War uncle, 'The Namesake', they were mechanical, 'sophisticated' performances, with Jamesian house-parties, ocean liners, and expatriate studios for settings. (The New York job was later used for a few brisk, harsh, French-realist style stories of office life, 'Ardessa', 'Her Boss', and 'The Bookkeeper's Wife'). Something was going wrong. Sarah Orne Jewett, in her marvellous letter of advice and encouragement at the end of 1908, could see exactly what it was:

> I cannot help saying what I think about your writing and its being hindered by such incessant, important, responsible work as you have in your hands now. I do think that it is impossible for you to work so hard and yet have your gifts mature as they should – when one's first working power has spent itself nothing ever brings it back just the same, and I do wish in my heart that the force of this very year could have gone into three or four stories. . . . If you don't keep and guard and mature your force, and above all, have time and quiet to perfect your work, you will be writing things not much better than you did five years ago. This you will be anxiously saying to yourself! but I am wondering how to get at the right conditions.[31]

And she goes on to give those words of advice which meant so much to Cather: go from the 'parish' to the 'world', find a quiet centre of life: 'We must be ourselves, but we must be our best selves'. The letter (which Edith Lewis said 'became a permanent inhabitant of her thoughts') provoked a long, despondent, revealing reply from Cather [32] about her present state of mind. The work at *McClure's*, she said, made her feel like a trapeze artist who had to keep catching the right bar or fall into the net; she was using up so much energy on the magazine's concerns – what McClure called 'men and measures' – that she was too exhausted to write in the evenings. The images she used for her editorial work were all of entrapment and undernourishment: she couldn't breathe, she felt as if she were living in a tepid bath, she was getting as much food as she would from artithmetic, she was turning into a card catalogue. Though she was loyal to Sam McClure, he was beginning to have a stultifying effect on her. He wanted her to write nothing but clear-cut journalism, like Ida Tarbell, and was now telling her that she was a good magazine executive but would never be a very good writer. And perhaps he was right: she knew that her writing had not improved since *The Troll Garden*, and that it should have done, but she didn't know how to make it better. Every time she started a story she felt like a newborn baby, naked, shivering, with everything still to learn. Perhaps she shouldn't set out to do the one thing at which she felt inept? But meanwhile she was worn out. She might be called an 'executive', but inside, she was more like a hunted animal. The psychologists had a new word for it, she believed: split personality.

In *Alexander's Bridge*, the novel she would begin two years later, the hero's public success as a builder of bridges creates just this sort of constraint and frustration: '"You work like the devil and think you're getting on, and suddenly you discover that you've only been getting yourself tied up. A million details drink you dry,"' he says. The narrator reiterates, with feeling: 'It was like being buried alive. . . . There was still something unconquered in him, something besides the strong work-horse that his profession had made of him'. [AB, p.33] It is an early and revealing example of an impassioned autobiographical statement transposed into a male voice. But though Cather characteristically masculinizes her dilemma in the figure of her tormented bridge-builder (a man with a double life whose bridge cracks under the strain and 'buries him alive'), and though she had built herself an independent and unconventional life for a woman, her professional predicament was very much a female one. William Godwin, in 1798, made an excellent analysis of the danger to any writer of being trapped by hack work:

> It perhaps deserves to be remarked that this sort of miscellaneous literary employment, seems, for the time at least, rather to damp and contract, than to enlarge and invigorate, the genius. The writer is accustomed to see his performances answer the mere mercantile purpose of the day, and confounded with those of persons to whom he is secretly conscious of a superiority. . . . He is touched with the torpedo of mediocrity.[33]

The point is general, but the passage refers to Mary Wollstonecraft, one of many outstanding literary women who spent years working their way out – through translation, journalism, reviewing, editing, or anonymous 'ghosting' – before they came into their own. Wollstonecraft's translations in the years before she published the *Vindication of the Rights of Woman*, George Eliot's anonymous unpaid editorial labours for Chapman's *Westminster Review*, Virginia Woolf's long years of anonymous reviewing for the *Times Literary Supplement* while trying to write her first novel, are only the most famous examples of women writers' slow starts. What prevented them? Lack of time, lack of independence, lack of confidence, lack of money: or a combination of them all.

Certainly Cather worried about the last: the family's hard times in the 1890s and the tough Pittsburgh days had left their mark. She saved her income carefully, still sending some home, and was nervous of leaving a safe job at the age of thirty-nine. Her lack of confidence shows up, as O'Brien points out,[34] in one peculiar detail: she accepted McClure's suggestion at about this time that she advance her date of birth by a few years for *Who's Who*; a deception which, thanks to Edith Lewis's complicity, would persist on her tombstone (it reads 1876) and which suggests considerable anxiety about her progress.

By 1912 she was nearly there. She began *Alexander's Bridge* in the summer of 1910, and in 1911 she finished it and wrote a long Nebraskan story, 'The Bohemian Girl', to be followed by two sketches, 'Alexandra' and 'The White Mulberry Tree', which would turn into *O Pioneers!* Both *Alexander's Bridge* and 'The Bohemian Girl' were published in 1912, and the appearance of her first novel (which was received kindly, as 'promising'), quickly followed by a long, exciting, liberating journey to the Southwest, finally sprang the trap. Even then the impetus came as much from circumstances as from within: McClure's erratic financial ventures had finally got out of hand; he had to sign over his empire to his son-in-law, and in 1913 (by which time his staff had seen it coming, and left) he was pushed out. As a parting gesture of loyalty, to help him financially, Cather agreed (even after the success of *O Pioneers!* in 1913) to 'ghost' his autobiography (anonymously and without payment), concentrating not on his fall, but on the man's energetic, enterprising rise from Western poverty to international success. It was a story Cather naturally found sympathetic, and some of its dynamic energy leaks into the novel she started immediately afterwards, *The Song of the Lark.* But that was her last piece of subservient hack work.

Once these 'miscellaneous literary employments' can be seen as apprenticeship, and not as a life's work, their value is apparent. Like George Eliot in her thirties, Cather had been finding out for the past twenty years how to write, and what she thought: 'seeking constantly and urgently for explanations of her own desires . . . and for keys which [would] unlock the mysteries.'[35] Jewett saw that, too: 'You have been growing I feel sure in the very days when you felt most hindered, and this will be counted to you.'[36] Editing factual pieces taught her, as well as her contributors, to 'crush feelings into the background', and to subdue the lavish rhetoric of her theatre-reviewing days. Ghosting McClure's autobiography trained her to appropriate the colours of a man's voice and personality: making herself speak his plain abrupt language, she said (at once revealingly and disingenuously) in a letter of 1919,[37] was the inspiration for Jim's narration in *My Ántonia.* She rescued herself from the numbing effects of the 'torpedo of mediocrity' just in time. All the same, she would not have become the writer she was, without those years of training; and she knew it.

Looking back, Cather was always dismissive[38] about her first novel: only a year after its publication she was talking about its moral flimsiness, and she would come to see it as a mistaken attempt to imitate James and Wharton. The Boston and London settings were the material she felt at the time an American novelist *ought* to use. It's true that *Alexander's Bridge* is awkward and immature, and that, as with many of the early stories, her imitation of civilized East Coast writers went against the grain. But it is more revealing of strong personal feeling than she would ever acknowledge.

The story is framed (in a contrast she would use again between one of life's observers and a man of action), by the point of view of an old professor of philosophy, wise Aristotle to a heroic Alexander. Bartley Alexander, the professor's pupil when he was growing up in the West, has gone East, made an empire for himself as a bridge-builder, married a distinguished civilized woman (met when he was on his first assignment in Canada), and settled down in Boston. At the height of his success, he meets again an Irish actress called Hilda Burgoyne, now a great hit in London in a play called 'Bog Lights', whom he had been in love with in the days of 'the youth who had worked his way across the ocean on a cattleship and gone to study in Paris without a dollar in his pocket'.[AB, p.33] Their affair resumes, and Bartley, already frustrated by administrative burdens, is tugged transatlantically between the two women, guilt-struck but unable to resolve the strain. Then, the 'engineered' crisis: the bridge he has been designing shows signs of a fatal flaw; he goes up to Canada – scene of his first triumph – to inspect it, and it snaps in two when he is on it. He is drowned with a letter of confession to his wife in his pocket, rendered forever illegible. The two women's lives are left without meaning, and the old professor sums up: 'He belonged to the people who make the play, and most of us are only onlookers at the best.'[AB, p.111]

The first title was *Alexander's Masquerade*,[39] and the novel, like a great deal of her work, is about performance: Bartley is an elevated figure on a heroic stage, and he is also a dissimulator, a bad actor trapped in conflicting roles. (He also owes a good deal to Ibsen's Master Builder, for whom youth and troll-like power are embodied in 'Hilda' Wangel.)[40] Hilda's enchanting performance in her Irish play (a wonderfully silly concoction, complete with potheen smugglers, cabins, fairy rings, primrose wreaths and a donkey) provides a fairy-tale illusion to satisfy Bartley's romantic escapism. And the whole theatrical conception allows Cather to project Bartley's fatally strained split self into the dramatic breaking of the bridge.

It's a crude device, but it is Cather's first extensive treatment of her deep and lifelong obsession with doubling. The obsession belongs not just to her interior life, but to a powerful tradition in American writing. The split self, symbolically projected, goes from Hawthorne's guilty Reverend Dimmesdale, nursing his hidden scarlet letter, and Poe's doomed, fissured House of Usher, to James's failed hero Roderick Hudson, caught between art and love and crashing appositely to his death off a Swiss mountain, or the revenant encountering his terrifying doppelgänger – the man he might have been – in 'The Jolly Corner'. William Carlos Williams and D.H. Lawrence, writing about American literature in the 1920s, discerned a fatal, morbid split throughout it, and put it down to the Puritan repression of the 'terrific energy' of aboriginal instincts: a history of making walls instead of 'bursting into flower'.[41]

There is something of that morbid 'fissure' in Bartley's feeling that 'a second man has been grafted into him'. [AB, p.84] His split self is, as we've seen, partly Cather's: he is the Westerner gone East, creative energies trapped by desk work, the pioneer feeling his age. Fictionalizing this personal sense of strain, she calls on the archetypal opposites which have always fascinated her, the rugged Carlylean hero and the delicate artist, the pagan and the Christian, the barbaric and the civilized. Like a god in exile, Bartley is a tamed natural force whose primitive energy strains against its confines. His wife Winifred (beautiful and dignified in the Isabelle McClung mode) stands for the civilizing con-strictions: their central scene together takes place in their home, elegantly decorated with wreaths and azaleas for Christmas. She nourishes his finer feelings, but not his energy. Hilda, by contrast, is identified with Bartley's pioneering youth, with romance, freedom, sexual fulfilment, and love of life. The power of the book, though, is not in the relationships, but in the sinister qualities of Bartley's 'second man', ominously described as 'restive', 'strong', 'sullen and powerful', like an underground troll, or the waters that will bury him.

In a strange lyrical passage near the end, Bartley crosses his first bridge by train, on the way to his last, and remembers how he used to walk it by moonlight, when he was first in love:

> And always there was the sound of the rushing water under-neath, the sound which, more than anything else, meant death; the wearing away of things under the impact of physical forces which men could direct but never circumvent or dimi-nish. Then, in the exaltation of love, more than ever it seemed to him to mean death, the only other thing as strong as love. Under the moon, under the cold, splendid stars, there were only those two things awake and sleepless; death and love, the rushing river and his burning heart. [AB, p.95]

I think Cather is momentarily echoing Whitman — one of her admired 'barbarian' writers — in his poem about the making of a writer. In 'Out of the Cradle Endlessly Rocking', the antiphonal voices of the bird and the sea both speak to the emerging poet. The bird sings of night, the moon, the water, lost love, all blurred together; the sea, as if in answer to the listener's questions

> Whisper'd to me through the night, and very plainly before
> daybreak
> Lisp'd to me the low and delicious word Death:
> And again Death — even Death, Death, Death

and the poet, walking in the moonlight on the grey beach, has to 'fuse' these two songs of Death and Love. Death, of course, is much more Bartley's desired lover than any Hilda or Winifred, and the strength of this first novel is in its impulse towards what destroys and obliterates. This time the flawed hero is sucked under; but in the future, the battle between the actor and the dark indifferent 'physical forces' would be renewed. As yet she hadn't found the right landscape for the struggle, but Bartley has a glimpse of it out of his train window, when he sees a group of boys sitting around a little fire on the edge of a marsh, and it reminds him of 'a campfire on a sandbar in a Western river'. [AB, p.94] In her next story, 'The Bohemian Girl', the lovers are not destroyed, they escape, as Cather was about to escape into the freedom of writing. The paradox of her life and work is that the place they escape from is the place she had to get back to for her true subject.

5

A WIDE, UNTRIED DOMAIN

Come, Muse, migrate from Greece and Ionia;
Cross out, please, those immensely overpaid accounts,
That matter of Troy, and Achilles' wrath, and Eneas',
Odysseus' wanderings;
Place *'Removed'* and *'To Let'* on the rocks of your snowy
Parnassus . . .
For know a better, fresher, busier sphere – a wide, untried
domain awaits, demands you.
Walt Whitman, 'Song of the Exposition', 1871

IN THE SPRING of 1912 Cather took one of the most important journeys of her life, her first visit to the South-west. She went to visit her brother Douglass, working on the railroad in Winslow, a small town in Arizona, and travelled with him on horseback into the wild country around, to the Grand Canyon, and down into New Mexico, before going back to Red Cloud for the summer. At first she resisted the 'untried domain'. In one of the first of her vivid, affectionate letters to Elsie Sergeant about the trip, she wrote that she still has her fears of the *bigness* of the West; when she gets back to it she feels, as she did in her childhood, that it will put her to sleep. She will die there, never get out. She can't let herself 'go with the current'.[1] And at first Winslow seemed ugly and dusty; Douglass's cockney cook was always drunk, and his brakeman, Mr Tooker, was a terrible bore, the kind of self-educated Westerner who read his bound copy of

Emerson *all the time*, never used words of one syllable (when the wind blows it 'retards' his freight train), and said things like 'You have me buffaloed'.[2]

But very soon she gave herself up to this dramatic, vivifying journey. The landscape of the Southwest, 'big and bright and consuming',[3] inspired her. She felt it should be the setting for 'a new tragedy or a new religion', perhaps a new Crusade. Out in the hills, even Mr Tooker improved,[4] shed his 'magazine' culture (it sounds like Leonard Bast describing the dawn in *Howard's End*) and became a decent sort. Her postcards to Elsie give a glimpse of what she was seeing: a seventeenth-century Spanish mission church at Acoma; adobe huts; Hopi Indian pueblos discovered by Coronado's army in 1540; and an Indian village on the Rio Grande, thirteen miles south of Albuquerque, with a mission church where the priest, Cather noted, had a wonderful garden with parrots and snow-white doves. These sights – the Spanish mission churches with their gardens, the native Indian villages, the glamorous high-coloured landscape, and above all the ancient cliff-dwellings of the vanished Indian tribes, relics of an extraordinary and beautiful civilization, which she saw at Walnut Canyon, Arizona, would haunt her for ever. This was far older history than that of the mid-Western pioneers (though it provided a more ancient version of the interweaving of cultures which so interested her at home), one that had fascinated her since childhood. Seeing it, at last, had a very powerful effect on her.

The emotions of the journey were centred on their native guide to New Mexico, the romantic Julio.[5] Unlike Tooker, Julio's speech was not a waste product of modern American culture, but a 'new language', restrained, unliterary, direct. He told her an old Aztec story of love and death (which she inserted into 'Coming, Aphrodite!') with 'sharply cut figures' in it; he took her to a Mexican dance, and sang her a Spanish serenade in the desert, against a background of stars and the dead Indian city on the mesa. But he could not understand her interest in the Cliff-dwellers. The dead should be left alone; 'We are the living'.

Julio seems to have been, for Cather, a primitive version of Ethelbert Nevin, a delicate, youthful male artist, a source of 'real' folklore, but unlike Nevin a figure perfectly in tune with his landscape. O'Brien describes it as 'a love affair',[6] which seems excessive. Cather's romantic holiday feeling about Julio was part of a new, welcome, liberating sense that she was coming back to life in an inspiring American landscape.

The 1912 journey plays as vital a part in her writing as the transition from Virginia to Nebraska. How much of it she saved up! The whole experience would be given to Thea in *The Song of the Lark*, and Tooker would return as Thea's faithful railroad man, Ray Kennedy and, in a later version, as Roddy Blake in *The Professor's House*. Douglass's tough colleagues would be remembered for Captain Forrester, old hero of the railroads, in *A Lost Lady*. The priest in his garden would come back as the central subject of *Death Comes For the Archbishop*. And the cliff-dwellings, silent lessons in the creation of communal, functioning, domestic art forms, would be at the heart of *The Song of the Lark* and *The Professor's House*. She had found, just at the point when her new life as a writer was about to begin, a landscape which needed a new writing. Interestingly, though, the effect was not direct. At the end of the summer, indeed, she felt she had to retreat:[7] the desert was intoxicating, but she was afraid of being consumed by it. Though traces of the journey do come into *O Pioneers!*, the immediate result was not a story of the Southwest, but a sudden sense of how to deal with her Nebraskan materials, as though she had at last found the necessary perspective on them.

By the time she was back in Pittsburgh in the autumn, staying with Isabelle on her way back East, she was combining the stories she had been writing, 'Alexandra' and 'The White Mulberry Tree', into what she revealingly calls 'a two-part pastoral'.[8] It was now, she suddenly realized, not a collection of stories, but a novel in which she lets the country 'be' the hero – or the heroine.[9] She has done what Dvořák did in the Largo of the New World Symphony, she says, remembering her early music criticism, taken the little themes that were hiding in the long grass and worked them out. It is an image of disclosure and enfranchisement which reflects her own 'working out' of what she wants to do. And by calling the writing a pastoral she makes it clear that it belonged as much to a historical tradition as to her own autobiography.

O Pioneers! was published in 1913 with a title page which pays homage to a careful selection of forerunners. The title quotes Whitman, the male bard appropriating the classical epic to celebrate the American victory over the wilderness. The dedication is to Sarah Orne Jewett for the 'perfection that endures' of her 'beautiful and delicate work', terms suggesting a combination of courageous stoicism and fine, detailed perceptions. There are two epigraphs, Cather's own poem 'Prairie Spring', written that summer in Red Cloud, which sets the heavy, silent, sullen earth against the rapturous desires of 'youth', and a quotation from the great exiled Polish poet Adam Mickiewicz's nationalistic epic of his lost land, *Pan Tadeusz*, an exclamation on 'the fields colored by various grains'. Not for the last time (*The Song of the Lark* would lift its title from Jules Breton's sentimental French rural painting, *My Ántonia*'s epigraph would be a regretful line from Virgil's *Georgics*) Cather deliberately frames an apparently simple, unsophisticated narrative inside the paradoxical tradition of pastoral.

The doubleness of pastoral is as old as the form. Like Cather, the classical writers who influenced her, Theocritus and Virgil, were neither of them actually down on the farm when they were writing about crops and shepherds (though Virgil, like Cather, carried the rural memories of his childhood with him). Pastoral has always been liable to accusations of absenteeism, artificiality and insincerity. Johnson's attack on the conventions of Milton's *Lycidas* – what did all these river gods and shepherdesses have to do with real grief? – would resurface in nineteenth-century America as an anxiety about truthfulness and relevance: what could the pastoral dreams of the New World have to do with the machine age? The debate over pastoral is extraordinarily persistent and recognizable. Boileau, in the poem *L'Art Poétique* of 1674, could as well be describing Cather's Nebraskan novels: 'The artlessness of the pastoral is a matter of artistry; its humble simplicity is not the effect of negligence but the product of an elaborate and deliberate craftsmanship.'[10]

The relationship between 'humble simplicity' and 'deliberate craftsmanship' is necessarily a duplicitous one. Pastoral has never been written by shepherds. William Empson distinguishes it succinctly from other folk literature in its relation to 'the people': 'Most fairy stories and ballads, though "by" or "for", are not "about"; whereas pastoral though "about" is not "by" or "for".'[11] And if it is not written by shepherds, more often than not its characters don't talk much like shepherds, either. 'Humble' folk speaking in beautifully polished hexameters led to fierce arguments over decorum versus realism, classicism versus naturalism, an argument all pastoral writers have to resolve one way or another. Cather deliberately plays down the representation of dialect or immigrant speech: on the whole she doesn't want a grotesque, potentially satirical literalism. But the relation of the 'deliberate' craftsman to the 'humble' material is a political, not just a technical matter. Empson points out that in one modern re-enactment of pastoral, the proletarian novel, there is always a doubleness in 'the attitude of the artist to the worker, of the complex man to the simple one ("I am in one way better, in another not so good")'.[12] Jim Burden's feeling for Ántonia expresses this ambiguity.

The doubleness is partly a tension between belonging and not belonging. From the start, the writer of the pastoral, half identifying with the rural scene he evokes, half looking away from it to the world outside, has been an equivocal figure, a temporary resident, like Virgil saying farewell at the end of his *Eclogues*, self-consciously detaching himself from Arcadia.[13]

The sadness of leave-taking links classical and modern pastoral. Once the gods went into exile and the pagan pastoral became Christian, Arcadia was identified with Eden, the lost garden; and increasingly, the pastoral place was the place you had to leave. The apple was eaten, the golden bowl was broken, and the nymphs were departed. That famous phrase of seventeenth-century pastoral painting, 'Et in Arcadia Ego'[14] gradually changed its sense, in later interpretations, from the stern warning of the death's head ('Even I, Death, am in Arcady') to the wistful rememberings of the exiled humans ('I too was once in Arcady'). No modern writer of pastoral could possibly avoid these contradictions and anxieties. Post-romantic American pastorals are full of temporary residents – Thoreau in *Walden*, Hawthorne in *The Blithedale Romance*, Cather's revenants (Carl in *O Pioneers!*, Jim in *My Ántonia*) in her Nebraskan pastorals – re-enacting Virgilian mixed feelings.

Those mixed feelings were not just to do with the writer's equivocal position on the edge of his landscape. They bore on the pastoral scene itself. What was that landscape: primitive or idyllic, wintry or summery, hard or soft? If Arcadia was an image of the 'golden age' – a garden, a bower, an oasis where you could live outdoors in perfect sympathy with nature, playing your flute while apples dropped into your lap, your sheep grazed safely and the ox lay down with the lion – then pastoral writing was bound to be a lament for 'the great good place and the good old days'.[15] Arcadia as a fixed unchanging idyll would then be the opposite of the 'real' world, subject to time and decay. The theme of contrast is persistent, from Tasso's lament in *Aminta*:

> Il mondo invecchia,
> E invecchiando intristisce

('The world grows old, and, growing old, grows sad'), to the more ambivalent comparisons between the 'cold pastoral' and the mortal world in Keats's *Ode on a Grecian Urn* and Wallace Stevens's *Sunday Morning*. In this version, pastoral writing has to be about an imagined or a vanished place: Poland's lamented national past in *Pan Tadeusz*, a changing English rural society in *Silas Marner* and *The Mill on the Floss*.

By an easy leap, the idea of the lost youth of the world could be turned into a lament for the writer's own lost youth: 'So sad, so sweet, the days that are no more'. Jim Burden, contemplating the scenes of his own childhood once he has left them, places himself carefully in this tradition of 'golden age' pastoral by invoking Virgil's 'Optima dies . . . prima fugit': 'In the lives of mortals, the best days are the first to flee'. [MA, pp.261–2]

The dangers of pastoral as nostalgia are obvious.[16] A preference for past days combined with the idealization of rural life can be perniciously used, as Leo Marx points out, tracing the pastoral idea through American thought, 'in the service of a reactionary or false ideology'.[17] Cather is not exempt from this criticism, especially in her later years. But in the Nebraskan novels she sustains the complexity by not settling, merely, for the nostalgic model of pastoral.

In any case, nostalgic, 'golden age' pastoralism is bound to be problematic. How could there have been suffering in the 'best days'? Yet our main associations with pastoral poetry are the funeral elegy (the brother poet as dead shepherd) and the lament for a lost love. The initial, true meaning of 'Et in Arcadia Ego' is an ominous one: Arcadia has always encompassed human suffering and death. The very first of Virgil's *Eclogues* is about a shepherd who is being driven off his land into exile. And the 'real' Arcadia, a barren district of central Greece, described by Polybius as 'a poor, bare, rocky, chilly country, devoid of all the amenities of life and scarcely affording food for a few meagre goats',[18] was no more idyllic or easy to farm than Nebraska in the 1870s.

There have always been two kinds of pastoral. Sometimes they overlap, sometimes they split apart into what is often called 'soft' and 'hard' pastoral.[19] 'Soft' pastoral is a romance, a dream of celebration, carnival, song and love: guiltless, prelapsarian gratification, innocent hedonism, to which tender feelings of nostalgia are attached. But soft pastoral has the death's head within it. It can be elegiac as well as idyllic, a pastoral of melancholy or solitude as well as love. In *As You Like It*, Jacques and Orlando co-exist in the Forest of Arden.

The other kind of pastoral admits that rural life is 'hard'; it is a realist narrative of labour and endurance. In the *Georgics* we don't hear of singing competitions or fond lovers, we learn how to rotate crops and keep bees. The golden age is recalled as an idyllic, vanished period of harmony between man and nature. That was all very well; but the iron age, in which this 'realistic' pastoral is set, has taught people how to work, 'to make boats, to hunt, to fish and to build'. 'Labor omnia vicit', 'Toil conquered the world'. Gardens have had to be made, they don't spring up naturally. The dignity of labour is embodied in an old man tending his garden – an 'obscure destiny' who could easily make a character in a Cather novel – at the end of the *Georgics*:

> I saw an old man, a Corycian, who owned a few poor acres
> Of land once derelict, useless for arable,
> No good for grazing, unfit for the cultivation of vines.
> But he laid out a kitchen garden in rows amid the brushwood,
> Bordering it with white lilies, verbena, small-seeded poppy.
> He was happy there as a king. He could go indoors at night
> To a table heaped with dainties he never had to buy.
> His the first rose of spring, the earliest apples in autumn:
> And when grim winter still was splitting the rocks with cold
> And holding the watercourses with curb of ice, already
> That man would be cutting his soft-haired hyacinths, complaining
> Of summer's backwardness and the west winds slow to come . . .
> He had a gift, too, for transplanting in rows the far-grown elm,
> The hardwood pear, the blackthorn bearing its weight of sloes,
> And the plane that already offered a pleasant shade for drinking.[20]

There is a quiet, contemplative tenderness in this[21] which makes the old man's busy-ness feel heroic and dignified, and manages to blend the idyllic with the realistic, to reconcile the soft and the hard pastoral. Like his later epic writing, Virgil's pastoral is weighted with the sense of 'the tears there are in things': 'sunt lacrimae rerum'. It was that tone which attracted Cather[22] to Virgil and to the pastoral writers –

Robert Burns, Turgenev, Sarah Orne Jewett, George Eliot, Housman, Robert Frost – who found, in their quite different contexts, Virgilian ways of reconciling rural hardship and suffering with a tender retrospect on lost youth, with a celebration of dignified human endeavour, or with what Hazlitt, writing on Burns and the old Scottish ballads, calls 'the sentiment of deep-rooted, patient affection' triumphing over all.[23]

This tone of reconciliation was not usual in twentieth-century American fiction, and it is one of Cather's extraordinary qualities that she was able to use it so unembarrassedly. The myth of pastoral, as Leo Marx points out, was deeply involved with the American dream of a new golden age in the New World; politically, it provided a blueprint for expansionism and development, and hence it was a peculiarly persistent ideal: 'Down to the twentieth century the imagination of Americans was dominated by the idea of transforming the wild heartland into . . . a new "Garden of the World".'[24] Long after the ideal had been violently distorted and invaded by the 'counterforce' of technology and mechanization, the pastoral myth of hopefulness and amelioration lingered on as a sentimental rhetorical formula, 'enabling the nation to continue defining its purpose as the pursuit of rural happiness while devoting itself to productivity, wealth, and power'.[25] So from the early nineteenth century, pastoral in American writing was fraught with irony. The pastoral retreat in Hawthorne's *The Blithedale Romance* is mere childish escapism; Thoreau's communion with nature in *Walden* has a train rushing through it ('So is your pastoral life whirled past and away'),[26] and his neighbouring 'husbandmen' are mean, capitalist Yankees. By Cather's time the good green place was either an absurd unreality (as for Nathaniel West's *Miss Lonelyhearts*), a bitter realist environment of brute force and struggle, or an excuse for self-destructive fantasy, like Gatsby's dream of going back to innocence and happiness. Cather was almost the only and the last American writer to make wholehearted use of pastoral, and to find a way of negotiating the fundamental opposition between myth and fiction:

Myths are the agents of stability, fictions the agents of change. Myths call for absolute, fictions for conditional assent. Myths make sense in terms of a lost order of time . . . fictions, if successful, make sense of the here and now.[27]

Book Two of the *Georgics* contains instructions on the grafting and transplanting of wild trees,[28] a fine example of the improvability of the wilderness through man's labour. It is a perfect image for Cather's annexation of the pastoral tradition. Like Whitman in the 'Song of the Exposition', urging the Muse to 'migrate from Greece and Ionia' for the 'wide, untried domain' that awaits and demands her, like Thoreau making a symbolic location out of his New England pond – 'another embodiment of the American moral geography' – she grafts the classical model onto the national material, and makes out of it 'a native blend of myth and reality'.[29] And in doing so, she appropriates a male tradition – Hesiod, Virgil's Greek model, had no women in his description of the Golden Age, and the loves of classical pastoral are predominantly male friendships[30] – and transforms it, as no American pastoral writer had ever done before her, into celebrations of female heroism.

The process of grafting provides an image, too, of her narrative methods. The original meaning of 'eclogue' was 'extract' or 'selection', and classical narratives and their imitators have always been filled with 'extracts' and episodes grafted onto larger growths: the wonderful 'inset' of the story of Orpheus, a miniature epic sprouting from the bee-keeping passage at the end of the *Georgics*; the pastoral oases[31] in the *Aenead*, in Dante and in Tasso; the interpolations of 'bucolic episodes'[32] in Cervantes. The whole of Renaissance pastoral was a process of intercutting apparently contradictory traditions: 'satirical allegory and idyllic romance, realism and high poetry'.[33] Empson's comprehensive definition of all pastoral is of 'putting the complex into the simple'.[34] Cather follows the tradition of inserting anecdotes, episodes, 'extracts', into her narrative. By a process of grafting – or of quilting, if you prefer the indoor female image of artful labour to the one drawn from male husbandry

— she interworks eclogue and georgic, soft and hard pastoral, heroism and realism, apparently without strain. It was typical of the process that her first pastoral novel should have been patched together from two stories, and that she would set versions of her very early Nebraskan sketches inside the longer narratives.

Those early stories hadn't yet acquired the Virgilian tone of reconciliation; they were written in the 1890s, when Cather was still heading her letters from Nebraska 'Siberia', and most of them are done with a vigorous, gleefully savage realism. They have barbaric male heroes and grim descriptive language. Far from being in sympathy with 'mother' nature, the isolated primitives of these early stories feel her as an oppressive force: 'Nature did not comfort him any, he knew nothing about nature, he had never seen her; he had only stared into a black plow furrow all his life.' [CSF, p.537] Their religion is apocalyptic and prohibitive; their pleasures are rough explosions of desperate drinking and dancing, their loves are brooding and obsessional. Those who stay go mad, kill themselves, or sink into bestial indifference.

When the early stories (the death of a Bohemian violinist, the religious fanatic living wild in the woods) are reworked and inset into the Nebraskan novels, they shed this harsh cynical tone and become part of a more humane, complex treatment of the pioneer's landscape. In the '90s, though, Cather wanted strong brutal lines. It was not until after the *Troll Garden* stories that Cather found the right way of writing pastoral. The change came with a marvellous story of 1909, 'The Enchanted Bluff'.

Six boys are making camp, as they have done year after year, on one of the sandbar islands thrown up by the changing course of a Nebraskan river. The narrator, who is about to leave the others behind him to go 'up to the Divide' and teach school, is feeling homesick in anticipation. Nothing much happens. They swim, eat their supper, make a fire, watch the stars come out and talk about them, hear the different, heavier noise the river makes after dark, and see the moon rising over the bluffs 'like a galleon in full sail, an enormous, barbaric thing, red as an angry heathen god'. Under the eye of this fierce male deity they talk desultorily about heroes and legends of conquest and exploration: Columbus, Napoleon, Aztec sacrifices, the Mound-Builders, Coronado's quest for gold along this very river. The talk turns to places they want to see. Tip Smith, the grocer's son, excitedly tells the 'dolorous legend' that his wandering Uncle Bill has told him, of a cliff-dwelling down in New Mexico, where a peaceable Indian tribe was said to have made its home 'away up there in the air' before some of them were massacred at the foot of the cliff and the rest left to starve. No one has ever been up there since, but Tip has a plan to climb it. After his story, a crane screams, flying past, and the boys fall gradually asleep. The narrator dreams he is racing the others to get to the Bluff, and wakes up in 'a kind of fear' of losing his chance. The fire is out, the sky is turning pale. The dawn comes up suddenly, and the boys go in for another swim. At Christmas they meet again to skate to their island, and 'renew their resolution' to find the Bluff. Then, a coda describes their destinies twenty years on. The narrator has gone away. The German tailor's sons, one of them injured on the railroad, have inherited their father's business. Stupid Percy Pound is a Kansas City stockbroker, the older boy Arthur, charming, clever and feckless, has stayed drinking in the town's saloons and died young; and Tip Smith is a storekeeper with a 'slatternly' wife. But he has told his son Bert the legend, and he in his turn 'thinks of nothing but the Enchanted Bluff'.

The story anticipates much that is to come (childhood riverside idylls in *My Ántonia* and *A Lost Lady*, dreams of heroic endeavour inspired by the cliff-dwellers in *The Song of the Lark* and *The Professor's House*). And it is the first time Cather finds her true tone. The atmosphere, slow and resonant, goes back to Virgil's shepherds talking under the evening star. But there are powerful modern pastoral models too: the night-time river feeling is very like *Huckleberry Finn*

('The sky looks ever so deep when you lay down on your back in the moonshine: I never knowed it before. And how far a body can hear on the water such nights!'),[35] and as Eudora Welty points out in her eloquent tribute to Cather, the sense of mystery and space is like Turgenev's 'magical' story 'Behzin Meadow'.[36] Turgenev's huntsman loses his way and spends the night by a campfire with a group of boys who are minding the village horses and talking of ghosts and old superstitions. Their voices carry on the summer night like Cather's boys; and there is the same sense of a scene opening out and out into time and space:

I sat up in my damp clothes and looked at the other boys, who lay tumbled in uneasy attitudes about the dead fire. It was still dark, but the sky was blue with the last wonderful azure of night. The stars glistened like crystal globes, and trembled as if they shone through a depth of clear water. Even as I watched, they began to pale and the sky brightened. Day came suddenly, almost instantaneously. I turned for another look at the blue night, and it was gone. [CSF, p.76]

All around absolute quiet descended, as usually happens only just before morning: everything slept the deep, still sleep of the pre-dawn hours. The air was not so strongly scented, and once again it seemed to be permeated with a raw dampness. O brief summer nights! The boys' talk died away along with the dying of the fires . . . A sweet oblivion descended on me and I fell into a doze . . .
    I opened my eyes to see that morning was beginning. . . . The pale-grey sky shone bright and cold and tinged with blue; stars either winked their faint light or faded; the ground was damp and leaves were covered with the sweat of dew. . . . I got briskly to my feet and walked over to the boys. They slept the sleep of the dead about the embers of the fire . . .[37]

Virgil, Turgenev, and Twain, all write pastorals of male companionship. 'The Enchanted Bluff' shows that the male disguise releases Cather into a particular tradition of writing.

She takes from Turgenev, too, an emotional ambivalence which wasn't there in the earlier stories, crudely split between romance and realism. It is very hard to say whether

'The Enchanted Bluff' is a story of sorrowful regret or tender hopefulness. Ostensibly it is a story of failure. The heroes and civilizations the boys talk of have been defeated: Napoleon's star went out, they say, when he began to lose battles; the peaceable cliff-dwellers are destroyed. Coronado's fate is not mentioned here, but we will learn in *My Ántonia* that 'he died in the wilderness of a broken heart'. [MA, p.244] None of the boys succeeds; they grow up into so many Babbitts, 'losing their chance' under the pressures of small town life. Their 'magic island', like the legendary Enchanted Bluff, can never be refound. But the bitterness of the early stories is not there; instead, a sense of continuity prevails, as the narrator's memory goes back through his own childhood into the distant past, and on into the still undisillusioned boyhood of the next generation.

The narration makes an order and continuity out of time; and the story is layered with orderings and shape-makings, of which the human imagination is only one. The evening light makes the unpromising rough materials of the scene into scenery, 'flickering' and 'quivering'. The river, gouging out its banks, makes new islands, and the islands at once make their own landmarks: 'a little new bit of world, beautifully ridged with ripple marks, and strewn with the tiny skeletons of turtles and fish'. [CSF, p.70] The boys in their 'new world' contemplate astral orderings ('"Queer how the stars are all in sort of diagrams. . . . You could do most any proposition in geometry with 'em"'), the source and direction of their river, the formation of the Bluff from glaciers. They are all historians, in love with the idea of connections. Tip carries 'some little pill bottles' (bought from a Baptist missionary) 'that purported to contain grains of wheat from the Holy Land, water from the Jordan and the Dead Sea, and earth from the Mount of Olives', and seems to 'derive great satisfaction from their remote origin'. They laugh at stupid Percy, trying to work out whether the Spanish explorers came through before the Mormons. A sense of inevitability is suggested – their destinies seem to have been inescapable, written in the stars – but at the same time we keep being told of the human need – a natural tendency – to order, persist, and make 'new worlds'.

The revenant of 'The Enchanted Bluff' is a Virgilian observer, back from a life elsewhere to pick up on the old story (Cather often said that going home again was like catching up with characters in a play or a novel) and keeping quiet about his own destiny. In 'The Bohemian Girl', the revenant is the prodigal son, an actor in the drama, and the effect is much more passionate and active. 'The Enchanted Bluff' was a tone-poem, an exercise in understatement. Now, in her first extended pastoral, she risks incorporating the early melodramas of love and conflict into a detailed evocation of the life of the immigrant communities 'on the Divide'. The grafting of romance and realism is a bit shaky as yet, but it opens the way for *O Pioneers!*[38]

Nils Ericson has been away from his mother's 'grim square house' for twelve years (making a living on a shipping line back in Norway, though his family thinks he's a wastrel). He is the misfit, more lively and imaginative than his dour, stingy Norwegian relatives, not cut out for a life wringing money from the land ('The Ericsons', says a tenant, 'they've spread something wonderful – run over this country like bindweed!'). His inheritance is his dead father's 'roving blood' and warm feelings. By contrast, the mother's forceful, self-serving qualities are seen again in the older brother Olaf: 'The one thing he always felt in Olaf was a heavy stubbornness, like the unyielding stickiness of wet loam against the plow.' [CSF, p.20] Olaf has political ambitions (in Cather's view this makes him a crook) and to get the Bohemian vote of the district he has married the daughter of the innkeeper Joe Vavrika. One of Cather's impetuous, romantic heroines, Clara Vavrika is as resentful of the Norwegian family as her childhood playmate, Nils – who of course has come back for her – and spends most of her time lying in bed (eight o'clock is late for the Ericsons), dressing, visiting her jolly father, and stirring up her gipsy blood galloping her temperamental horse over the prairie. Olaf is placated by the housekeeping of Clara's devoted aunt (a good early sketch for Cather's self-denying domestic helpers), who 'keeps the bear sweet' with poppy-seed bread and prunes spiced in honey.

With Nils's eyes, we look through a series of frames at a selection of contrasting pastoral views: the screen door to Mrs Ericson's well-ordered lamp-lit kitchen, Olaf's big barn doors opening onto a Dutch painting of the heroic old women at the feast, Joe Vavrika's garden inside its wooden fence, with Clara reading the Bohemian papers to him under the cherry tree. These pastoral scenes seem static, but they are changing as we look at them: Mrs Ericson, after all, has a car and a telephone, and Joe is running out of Hungarian Tokai. 'The second generation' of Bohemians, says Clara, 'are a tame lot'. Looking back, Cather is catching the moment of transition which perpetually fascinates her. Not yet homogenized into Americanness, each of the distinct immigrant groups has survived in the alien landscape by persisting in their cultural identities. But soon there will only be two directions to go in: an assimilation into an undifferentiated national culture, or a retreat back to the old world.

Because the contrast between the Norwegians and the Bohemians is still distinct, it allows for a vivid opposition between the two kinds of pastoral – hard and soft – which will come back as the double plot of O Pioneers! The old women and their pies in the barn, set against the Bohemian swigging Tokai under his cherry tree, make a 'georgic' of labour and endurance against an 'eclogue' of sensual hedonism. Cather makes it easy enough to prefer the Vavrikas to the Ericsons: she takes a Shavian line on hypocritical, cheerless Puritanism, so often the enemy in the early work. (Nils's conflict with Mrs Ericson has something in it of Dick Dudgeon's resentment of his Calvinist mother in The Devil's Disciple.)[39] Emotionally, though, it is not so simple. Clara seems to embody a free, pagan, erotic force, but Nils is in love with her because she reminds him of his childhood. (Cather very often evasively subdues adult sexuality in this way, by making it the legacy of sanctified memories.) Clara points out to Nils that he really prefers women like his mother, and though the plot seems to disprove her, the narrative is ambivalent. The story ends, not with the escaped lovers, but with the return of Nils's younger brother Eric, who was being lured to Bergen by Clara and Nils, but who finds he can't leave his mother and the land, and comes back from his abortive running-away to find her sitting in the dark outside her house, 'as only the Ericsons and the mountains can sit'.

The mother is associated with the land, and the land is hard to leave. Though 'The Bohemian Girl' is good at Dutch paintings of homely interiors, its virtuoso writing is reserved for the outdoor scenes. Cather's double feeling about the power of the West is acted out in Clara's struggle between the earth and her lover. The language is that of mastery and subjugation:

> The great, silent country seemed to lay a spell upon her. The ground seemed to hold her as if by roots. Her knees were soft under her. [CSF, p.37]

You can almost see Clara turning into a tree. This is a country which will metamorphose its inhabitants into passive parts of itself, unless they assert their separateness, or run away. Marks, traces, shapes, have to be made, or the landscape will unmake all human life and turn it back to void and formlessness, like a genesis in reverse.

6

WOMEN HEROES

A personality that carried across big spaces and expanded
among big things.

The Song of the Lark, 1915

O PIONEERS! begins with a primal scene made up of
negatives. The human marks on the landscape are barely
evident.

> One January day, thirty years ago, the little town of Hanover,
> anchored on a windy Nebraska tableland, was trying not to be
> blown away. A mist of fine snowflakes was curling and
> eddying about the cluster of low drab buildings huddled on the
> gray prairie, under a gray sky. The dwelling-houses were set
> about haphazard on the tough prairie sod; some of them
> looked as if they had been moved in overnight, and others as if
> they were straying off by themselves, headed straight for the
> open plain. None of them had any appearance of permanence,
> and the howling wind blew under them as well as over them.
> [OP, p.3]

There are shops in the 'two uneven rows of wooden buildings', but no shopkeepers to be seen – they are 'keeping well
behind their frosty windows'. There are children, but they
are invisible, in school. There is 'nobody about' but a few
countrymen; their wives can be glimpsed – momentary,
minimal human detail – by the flashes of their red shawls
going from the shelter of one shop to another. The station is
empty – there will be no train until night. In this landscape of

negations, the only human action is helpless and infantile: a small Swedish country boy is crying because his kitten has run up a telegraph pole and got stuck. The first definite, ordering mark is made on the scene by his sister Alexandra, 'walking rapidly and resolutely' up the street, wearing a man's cape 'like a young soldier', her eyes 'fixed intently on the distance'. She takes off the brown veil round her head to warm her brother's neck; as her shining hair is revealed, light and colour enter the scene. With a 'glance of Amazonian fierceness' she repudiates a passerby's admiring glance; taking control, she fetches her friend Carl Linstrum, who is indoors looking at the chemist's 'portfolio of chromo "studies"'. (These lithographs are sold to the townswomen, who copy them for their china painting. It is the first thin detail of the local culture, and tells us at once about Carl's interests.) When he has rescued the kitten, at some risk to himself, Alexandra finishes her shopping and fetches Emil from play with a beautiful little Bohemian girl, Marie Tovesky, the centre of attention for her Uncle Joe and his friends. The children – Alexandra anxious about her dying father, Carl depressed and 'bitter' – drive back out into the 'stern frozen country', which at once obliterates the town 'as if it had never been'. 'The great fact was the land itself, which seemed to overwhelm the little beginnings of human society that struggled in its sombre wastes.' [OP, p.15]

The whole book is latent in this wonderfully evocative, controlled, impersonal scene, with its slight incident and powerful sense of the relation of the people to the 'great fact' of the land, and (less importantly) to each other. Like Alexandra's entrance into the book, the novelist's entrance, this time, has the calm purposeful air of someone who knows what she is doing, has her eyes fixed on the distance, on the whole shape of the thing, but who is, all the same, tenderly attentive to detail.

The clear, spare, two-part plot is immediately established. Almost all its main ingredients are in that first scene: Alexandra's control, Carl's exile, Emil's feeling for Marie, the sexual contrast between the two women and their two stories. Marie is conventionally wilful and seductive, like the kitten; Alexandra (who like all Cather's main characters first appears being admiringly watched, like the heroine of a play) is at once androgynized. She is a young soldier *and* a fierce Amazon, a striding hero *and* a kind sister, wearing a man's coat *and* a woman's veil, with a severe look *and* a shining head of hair. (And though she is bold she is not 'boyish': she doesn't shin up the telegraph pole herself, but gets Carl to help her.) The attributes of the strong pioneer figure who *combines* masculine and female qualities is firmly introduced. Alexandra is about to take over the land from her father, John Bergson, the first-generation immigrant from Stockholm, who failed to conquer it and dies exhausted, in debt and despair. She controls the family: the father, though sympathetically presented, is a broken man, the two older brothers Lou and Oscar are grudging and unadventurous, and the mother is a comfortable Swedish housekeeper, dedicated to gardening and 'preserving', not just jams but a whole way of life.[1] They are all given subdued, ineffectual parts so that Alexandra can be mother, father, sister and wife. But as well as transcending and mixing roles, she also fits realistically into a family pattern. The novel is partly about inheritance, and Cather is always interested in the division of family characteristics. John Bergson's father was a Stockholm shipbuilder, a self-made man, who later in life married an unscrupulous woman and speculated dishonestly. Reminders of him recur: we see that Alexandra has his strength, Lou and Oscar his tendency to dubious dealings, and Emil his emotional susceptibility. The family displays, too, all the possible responses to the 'great fact' of the land: being obliterated by it, being repelled by it, or putting one's mark on it.

Sixteen years later (the time is jumped over, as if a spell has been cast) the 'Divide' has been conquered and given up its fertile riches, and Alexandra, who had the prophetic faith and the shrewd business acumen to hang onto and invest in the high land, is the manager of a great farm. Her home incorporates and maintains the old Scandinavian pioneer

culture, with its giggly Swedish housegirls waiting to be
married to sombre Swedish farmhands, visits from Lou's
unregenerately 'old country' mother-in-law Mrs Lee, and
the presence of saintly-simple old Norwegian Ivar, kept as a
blessing on the house, in spite of the grumblings of the
ever-conventional, rapidly Americanizing brothers Lou and
Oscar, who now have separate farms. The counter-
movement of repulsion from the land is given to the two
sympathetic male characters, Carl and Emil. Artistic, unsatisfied Carl goes to the city; he is not good enough to be a
painter, and gets work as an engraver, but the cheap modern
techniques 'sicken' him. Like the chemist's 'chromos' he was
seen looking at as a child, his art work seems to him false
imitation, in contrast to the 'true' work of Alexandra's life.
He sets out gold-prospecting on the Klondike (another kind
of male pioneering story, which Cather could only do
offstage). His visit, en route to Alaska, to see Alexandra, is cut
short by the brothers' mean suspicions about their relationship, and they do not find each other again until the very end
of the novel, in an ambivalent and subdued reunion.

Carl is a pale, melancholic character; the other 'returning'
figure, Emil, embodies all the eroticism and excitability so
carefully omitted from Carl and Alexandra's friendship. He
has been brought up by Alexandra to have interests other
than the land, has gone to university, and is meant for a
lawyer. Emil has something of Carl's impatience with the
hard Nebraskan pastoral ('"I get tired of seeing men and
horses going up and down, up and down"' [OP, p.156]) but
he is driven away – to Mexico and back – more by his passion
for Marie, who ran away from her convent at eighteen and
married a handsome Bohemian 'buck', Frank Shabata, now
a difficult and resentful husband. The inevitable romantic
tragedy is simply told, like an old tale of passion and revenge.
After Emil and Marie's deaths, and Frank Shabata's impri-
sonment, the book is given back to Alexandra and her
destiny. But the closing celebration of her relationship to the
land now has a muted, elegiac tone.

Like the land, Cather said in a letter to Elsie,[2] the work had no skeleton, it was all soft form with no hard lines or bold modelling. This telling remark is partly deceptive: there is in fact a strong, clear, two-part form to the novel, and it is concerned with the making and inheriting of forms. But it is true, and crucial, that there are no hard lines. A male narrative of driving action, struggle and climax is refused. Instead the form is gradual, surveying, circular, full of pauses and retrospects. It builds up not through a suspenseful linear progression, but through careful associations and juxtapositions, and so it is like Alexandra: in a sense, she *is* the book. Cather makes this explicit in a passage about memory which is also a passage about writing. It follows a remembered scene of happiness between Alexandra and Emil, watching a solitary wild duck playing under some willow trees:

> Most of Alexandra's happy memories were as impersonal as this one; yet to her they were very personal. Her mind was a white book, with clear writing about weather and beasts and growing things. Not many people would have cared to read it; only a happy few. She had never been in love, she had never indulged in sentimental reveries. Even as a girl she had looked upon men as work-fellows. She had grown up in serious times. [OP, p.205]

Like the beginning of the novel, the passage makes a shape out of negatives. Alexandra's white book, the *tabula rasa* inscribed by her destiny, is analogous to the white space of the land, which takes shape as we read the book, and to the white pages on which Cather is writing a hitherto unwritten woman's pioneer novel. The description applies equally to her heroine, to the countryside she is identified with, and to the kind of text she requires, which will select its own readers by virtue of its special qualities. (Pastoral, it is implied, has become an élite genre, only acceptable to the few.) This negative description of Alexandra's personality suggests to us what her text omits: no psychological complexity, no sexual passion (the white book implies virginity), no preoccupation with relationships, no business interests that are not rendered spiritual by her commitment to the land (Cather carefully keeps Alexandra clean of the kind of sharp dealing carried on offstage by Charlie Fuller the real estate man, the first of her hard-headed successful crooks), no politics (Lou is given these, disparagingly), no modern self-consciousness or ennui (Carl has that, and is kept on the edges of the book), 'not the least spark of cleverness'. Instead, her personality is 'impersonal', built out of its relation to nature and its preservation of memory: it is a white book of associations and contemplation.

This passage is at the centre of a careful accumulation of images that make us feel Alexandra as a life-force as much as an individual. Just before the 'white book' passage, her 'personality', 'her own realization of herself', is described as 'submerged', like 'an underground river'. Just after, there is a strange, powerful passage about Alexandra's mystic lover. In bed as a child, and later when she is very tired, she has the sensation of being carried by a strong male figure across the fields, a fantasy which, in youth, she always reacted against by fiercely washing 'the gleaming white body which no man on the Divide could have carried very far'. [OP, p.206] It is an extraordinarily bold idea (in what is also a realist novel) of the heroine as a chaste Diana, an Amazon, her body consecrated to the 'genius' of the land. When she has decided to put her faith in the high land, Emil sees her looking at it with 'love and yearning', as if raising her face to her spirit-lover.[3] 'The history of every country begins in the heart of a man or a woman', [OP, p.65] the narrator comments famously, getting away with this pious generalization because she makes Alexandra embody it with such calm confidence. When Carl comes to see her before going away he finds her in her garden, 'not working', but like Keats's Autumn, supervising the riches of the land, surrounded by pumpkins and drying vines, 'lost in thought, leaning upon her pitchfork'. [OP, p.48] At the end of the novel's first section, before the land has been conquered, Alexandra's faith in it is described, like an author's, as both attentive to detail – she identifies with the insects and the 'small wild things' hidden in the grass – and transcendent, in touch with cosmic order: she likes to think of the 'ordered march' of the stars, 'it fortified her to reflect upon the great operations of nature'. [OP, p.70]

'Fortified', 'reflect', 'operations': the language is purposely formal and impersonal. When Carl comes back after sixteen years and finds a fruitful land, Alexandra describes the change as having happened in spite of her; she did it 'just by sitting still'. She seems to have the magical efficacy of a nature-god:[4] Carl says to her, comparing their art work: '"I've been away engraving other men's pictures, and you've stayed at home and made your own."' [OP, p.116] The 'white book' – obscure destiny, wild land, pioneering text – has been shaped and coloured; Alexandra is felt to be creator and writer as well as pioneer. Paradoxically, she makes the picture by sitting still and looking beyond the immediate scene, as though the true artist is always going beyond the close-up picture to the 'great operations'.

But the 'white book' passage is also practical and realistic. Alexandra has to be read both as mythical super-being and as a Swedish farm-manager in late nineteenth-century Nebraska. When she describes herself as part of nature, it is in practical terms: '"If you take even a vine and cut it back again and again, it grows hard, like a tree."' [OP, p.171] Her eyes may be fixed with a dreaming look on the moon over the pasture, but eventually they go back 'to the sorghum patch south of the barn, where she was planning to make her new pig corral'. Her mystic faith in the land is also (as she points out firmly to her brothers) a shrewd conviction of the potential value of alfalfa.

The fusion of the contemplative and the functional in Alexandra's pastoral life is eloquently, and oddly, illustrated through her affinity to 'Crazy Ivar'. This Norwegian Thoreau, learning his Bible in his sod house by the pool where migrating birds converge, banning all guns from his terrain, his hair uncut and his feet bare, is a figure who combines classical and biblical pastoral:[5]

He best expressed his preference for his wild homestead by saying that his Bible seemed truer to him there. If one stood in

the doorway of his cave, and looked off at the rough land, the
smiling sky, the curly grass white in the hot sunlight; if one
listened to the rapturous song of the lark, the drumming of the
quail, the burr of the locust against that vast silence, one
understood what Ivar meant. [OP, p.38]

Alexandra's bond with Ivar is part of her magical affinity
with the land – he understands the birds, he tells old
animistic legends of a boy possessed by a snake. When she
takes this troll-like figure under her protection she is staying
in touch with the primitive relation of the pioneer to nature.
(Hence her patronage of Ivar is greatly disliked by the
Americanized brothers, who want to tidy him away into an
asylum.) But it is also a practical bond: when she first goes to
see him it is to ask him how she should keep her hogs; he
knows how to make hammocks and cure sick animals; and
though he can't read or speak American, like Alexandra he
can read and interpret the orderly text of nature's 'great
operations', such as the migrations of birds: '"They have
their roads up there, as we have down here. . . . Never any
confusion; just like soldiers who have been drilled."' [OP,
p.43] He embodies the 'georgic' pastoral of works and days –
labour, sympathy, reiteration – as expressed by Alexandra to
Carl: '"Our lives are like the years, all made up of weather
and crops and cows"' [OP, p.131] and by Carl to Alexandra:
'"There are only two or three human stories, and they go on
repeating themselves as if they had never happened before;
like the larks in this country, that have been singing the same
five notes over for thousands of years."' [OP, p.119]

This carefully simplified text of repetition sanctified by
association doesn't allow for personal involvement. Alexandra's story is ascetic and impersonal. The georgic pastoral
tradition allows Cather to project her own sexuality into a
female figure who is at once nurturing, heroic and indifferent to sexual passion. But this creates a narrative difficulty
which will always be acute: how to attach a heterosexual
emotional life to a character whose strength comes from her
transcendence of usual sexual roles? Our own resistance to
the idea of Alexandra in love is articulated by characters in

the novel. '"Alexandra's never been in love"' Emil says. "She wouldn't know how to go about it. The idea!"' [OP, p.154] For Emil and Marie, love is intensely present and momentary. For Alexandra (as for many of Cather's central figures) love is memory. When Carl decides to go away, they rehearse their affinities by way of leave-taking: '"We've liked the same things and we've liked them together."' [OP, p.52] While he is away he dwells on his memories of her as a girl, and when he returns he goes over his memory of those memories. In them she appears as sunshiny, vigorous and youthful ('She looked as if she had walked straight out of the morning' [OP, p.126]), but these sexual qualities are muted through the double retrospect. When Carl and Alexandra finally kiss, it is 'softly'; she leans 'heavily' against him and says she is very tired. It's as if she is being put, not into a lover's bed, but into a peaceful grave.

Alexandra's elegiac asceticism puts her out of touch with passionate young love. It's one of the subtlest things in the book that she fails to observe Emil's feelings for Marie until it's too late, and that her tranquil fatalism even irritates Marie. The difference between Alexandra's 'georgic' pastoral and Emil and Marie's eclogue – a brilliant and apparently simple achievement – can be felt by comparing Alexandra's 'white book' passage with Emil's last ride to Marie:

Everywhere the grain stood ripe and the hot afternoon was full of the smell of the ripe wheat, like the smell of bread baking in an oven. The breath of the wheat and the sweet clover passed him like pleasant things in a dream. He could feel nothing but the sense of diminishing distance. It seemed to him that his mare was flying, or running on wheels, like a railway train. The sunlight, flashing on the window-glass of the big red barns, drove him wild with joy. He was like an arrow shot from the bow. His life poured itself out along the road before him as he rode to the Shabata farm. [OP, pp.257–8]

Alexandra's 'marking' of her life is nourishing and accumulative; as it is for her narrator, everything is 'clear' and everything is saved up. Emil's perception, by contrast, is evanescent, blurred, spendthrift. Bypassing 'sweet' images of

domestic husbandry (not for him) he is transfigured into
water, light, joy, speed, elements at once sexual and mortal:
what is poured out could be life's blood as much as semen or
love song. All this rushes past as 'in a dream', and when he
finds Marie lying in the orchard under the mulberry tree, she
is already dreaming of him.[6]

The narrative gives the lovers' dream-romance no chance
in the real world; no surprise attaches to the tragedy. From
the first, the writing for Emil and Marie links death and love
in naturalistic images of helpless creatures. This is made
more poignant because the vantage point is often Carl's or
Alexandra's, with their melancholy sense of mortality and
recurrence. The young friends, undeclared lovers who hardly
understand their own feelings, are first seen by Carl shooting
ducks together. The contrast with Alexandra is obvious:
Marie is first excited, then distressed, as she sees the blood
dripping from 'the live color that still burned on its plumage.'
[OP, p.128] She is always associated in this way with tender,
vulnerable animal life. Alexandra compares her to 'a little
brown rabbit'. [OP, p.133] '"Am I flighty?"' Marie asks Emil
in the orchard. '"I suppose that's the wet season, too, then.
It's exciting to see everything growing so fast."' [OP, p.150]
When they at last acknowledge their love it is in the dark
surrounded by fireflies; when Marie is longing for Emil she
creeps out of the house like 'a white night-moth out of the
fields', feeling the weight of the years to come, 'like the land',
not – as Alexandra does – as an inspiring prospect, but as a
burden, chaining her 'instinct to live'. [OP, p.248]

The lovers are kept picturesque and simple. The story of
Marie's marriage is potentially more complex, but it is not
allowed to take over. We see Frank Shabata, the glamorous
newcomer from Bohemia, charming all the girls with his
curls and his yellow cane, turning into a resentful, self-
pitying, angry farmer, unsuited to the life, who quarrels with
all his neighbours and bullies his once-adoring wife. His slide
into annihilation – the muddled, panic-stricken killing of the
lovers, his dehumanization in jail ('"You know, I   most
forgot dat woman's name"' [OP, p.295]) – is very strong.

Cather gives Frank and Marie only a few scenes together, but enough to show their difficulties. Like Browning's Duke with his 'last Duchess', Frank is jealous of Marie for being universally agreeable. He wants to crush her spirit: 'The spark of her life went somewhere else, and he was always watching to surprise it.'[OP, p.222] Marie, who is much more adult and acute about Frank than about Emil, understands this: '"The trouble is"' (she says to Alexandra) '"you almost have to marry a man before you can find out the sort of wife he needs; and usually it's exactly the sort you are not. Then what are you going to do about it?"' [OP, p.197]

There is a feminist argument here, as strong as anything Cather would write. Just as the older brothers ineffectually try to contain Alexandra in a traditional, subordinate role ('"The property of a family really belongs to the men of the family"' [OP, p.169]), so Frank wants to bend 'dat woman' to his will. Alexandra survives by transcending all 'roles', and by taking over the land which had been, up to then, male property.[7] Marie, by contrast, is destroyed by her traditional femaleness. This is strongly felt. But the Shabata marriage has also to be played into the pastoral. Frank, as well as being a self-destructive male chauvinist, is also part of the mythical, legendary texture, a Polyphemus to the lovers' Acis and Galatea, who comes upon them in their Arcadian Eden,[8] the lush, wild orchard, where Marie can become a Dryad: '"I'm a good Catholic, but I think I could get along with caring for trees, if I hadn't anything else."' [OP, p.153] It is characteristic of the novel's mixing of myth and reality that Marie can be, in one breath, a Dryad and a 'good Catholic' girl.

The lovers' natural, secret desires are attractively set against the public, communal life of their friends in the French Catholic district. In part this is a contrast between the sanctioned and the illicit: Emil bitterly compares his own hopeless longing with his friend Amédée's 'sunny, natural, happy love', and the stages of Amédée's and Angélique's story – young marriage, first child, Amédée's sudden death, the grief of his friends – are marked by scenes of church festivity and ritual which the narrator finds (as she always

will) gracious and consolatory, though Emil feels cut off from
them. One of the novel's most spectacular scenes, the climax
of its public moments, done in strong colours and bold
strokes, is the joint preparation at the French church for the
great confirmation service and for Amédée's funeral. The
troups of boys – 'the Church's cavalry' – riding across the
fields to greet and escort the visiting Bishop, averting their
eyes from the new grave to the gold cross on the church's
steeple; the church half filled with mourners in black, half
with white communicants; the rapturous singing of a Rossini
Mass and of Gounod's 'Ave Maria', are all in dramatic
contrast to the lovers' secret sanctuary of natural desires, or
to Alexandra's and old Ivar's transcendental, simplified,
mystic union with nature. Cather worried later about having
forced these different immigrant cultures too much together
in the novel.[9] But she should not have: it is one of the book's
great charms that they are so smoothly reconciled by the
controlling narrator. And in fact she makes the Catholic
community part of the classical scene: the 'Church's cavalry',
those eager groups of boys of whom Amédée is the boldest
and the best, are always seen outdoors, 'jumping and wrestling and throwing the discus'. [OP, p.159] Cather can even
turn a Nebraskan baseball game into an Olympiad.

O Pioneers! is a deceptive book. It is an 'early' novel, her
first full-length treatment of her true subject, which is also
impressively mature and achieved, its plain style and concealed organization giving off a very strong sense of control.
It is at once celebratory and elegiac; about pioneering, but
also about the lost past. Its sustained effect is of simplicity, a
'white book' with few clear marks. And yet it contains a
complex interweaving of cultural detail and historical perspective, and makes a sophisticated grafting of an American
subject onto a classical form.

In one reading, O Pioneers! is a history book, an absorbing
documentation of the mid-West immigrant pioneers between
about 1880 and 1910, from the first determination never to
'lose the land', through the terrible years of the depression,
to the mixed blessings of prosperity and Americanization.

Sometimes Cather allows herself to moralize on 'progress', as when Marie's ear-pieces – bits of straw from a broom, worn until her ears are ready for gold rings – are described as happy features of 'those germless days', [OP, p.216] or Emil reflects that 'Lou and Oscar would be better off if they were poor'. [OP, p.238] But mostly she lets the rich, attentive presentation of detail speak for itself. All the variegated forms these cultures make to sustain and identify themselves, in the face of the great undifferentiated land, are sympathetically marked, from the hunting scene old Mrs Lee cross-stitches on her apron, to the devoted practice Raoul Marcel puts in on the 'Gloria' while he is polishing the mirrors in his father's saloon. At the same time, like Alexandra, the narrator keeps moving out and away, giving a sense of worlds elsewhere: the plains of Lombardy, compared to the Divide; a French landscape conjured up in Marie's fortune-telling for the young exiled French priest; 'the old Mexican capital' in the days of Porfino Diaz, evoked in Emil's letters home. These are pointers to later novels, signs that the narrator will need more than her Nebraskan material, and wants her novel to be read as something larger than a local history.

Yet for all its tone of assured, impersonal control, the interchange between the historical and the legendary creates difficulties for Cather, very acutely felt at the end of the novel. Alexandra reclaims the book – the last section has her name – and tries to anneal the tragedy through gestures of forgiveness. So she is moved out of her pastoral context for the first time, and we see her, 'ill at ease', registering in a Lincoln hotel, carrying her handbag down to supper, walking round the campus, brushing her hair by 'the electric light', taking the elevator. It has an extraordinary effect, as though she has suddenly been put into another kind of novel. And when she gets to the State Penitentiary for her desolating conversation with Shabata, she begins to meet characters from that novel: a genial warder, a convict-clerk with a high collar, fine white hands, 'his sharp shoulders shaken every few seconds by the loose cough which he tried to smother'. [OP, p.291] Historically, this is the realistic end for the pastoral novel, which ought to, or could, move into a dislocated, Kafkaesque urban scene. In this landscape, Alexandra loses all her magic powers – she can do nothing for Shabata. Cather shows, as usual very economically, that she can see this as a possibility, but chooses to deny it: she lets Alexandra go home and re-find Carl. And she also invokes another possible conclusion, that of the 'new start', the next pioneering departure: Carl and Alexandra will go away, marry, travel. But their wedding seems more like a burial, and their journey will end up as a returning.

And 'returning' is Cather's final solution to the dilemma of concluding her pastoral without relinquishing a celebratory note, and without admitting that there might have to be a closure: no more pioneering, no more pastoral. Alexandra, crouched over Emil's grave in the rain and dark like a propitiatory spirit, comforts herself by thinking of death as a returning: '"If they feel anything at all, it's the old things, before they were born, that comfort people like the feeling of their own bed does when they are little."' [OP, p.281] And her own childhood feeling, in bed when she was little, of being carried by strong arms, returns now as a vision of Death, a classical figure, 'mightiest of all lovers', for whom like a Stoic hero she now feels prepared. So, feeling and memory, the two qualities that give energy to Cather's narratives, are turned at the end into aspects of death. The text itself, in the reminiscing reunion between Carl and Alexandra, becomes a kind of return, going over its own story like the dead in their graves: '"You remember what you once said"' (Alexandra reiterates or 'returns' to Carl) '"about the graveyard, and the old story writing itself over? Only it is we who write it, with the best we have."' [OP, p.307]

The concept of death (like writing) as a form of 'returning', refuses the concept of mere stoppage. So the novel closes with an opening out:

They went into the house together, leaving the Divide behind them, under the evening star. Fortunate country, that is one day to receive hearts like Alexandra's into its bosom, to give them out again in the yellow wheat, in the rustling corn, in the shining eyes of youth! [OP, p.309]

Specific marks are smoothed away and generalized, and what Panofsky calls Virgil's 'vespertinal' tone (found at the end of great pastorals such as the *Eclogues* or Milton's *Lycidas*) is beautifully imitated. All the same, it is a strange and evasive ending. 'Youth', after all, has had its shining eyes brutally closed in this novel, and it seems an ambivalent apotheosis for Alexandra to be metamorphosed, not into a white butterfly like Emil or Marie, but into a kind of spiritual manure. Cather charms us into acceptance with her marvellous simple-seeming lyricism. But she has given an air of strength to something fragile and contradictory: a woman's writing made impersonal, a pioneering story made into an elegy. These tensions are very serenely handled in *O Pioneers!*. *My Ántonia* is a more exciting and complicated pastoral because this time they are less smoothly resolved.

But Cather did not pass directly from one great pastoral novel to another. *O Pioneers!* was enthusiastically received by friends and reviewers. But it would be some time before Cather returned to its pastoral mode. Though *O Pioneers!* and *My Ántonia* belong so closely together, they are divided by five years. That space is filled by a very different kind of book, in which everything Cather had been accumulating in the forty years of her life – her history, her apprenticeship, her idea of the artist, her feeling of having arrived – was acted out. *The Song of the Lark* is a commentary on her own achievement, and could not have been written 'if she were not already sure of her own creative abilities'.[10] Though it stands between the two great early novels, drawing its confidence from one and pouring its discoveries into the next, it feels quite unlike them. *The Song of the Lark* is the kind of thick, heavy, straggling, detailed narrative she would only allow herself once again, in *One of Ours* (which also had a subject that required special treatment). It is the fullest expression of one side of her aesthetic sympathies, always in negotiation between the barbarian and the civilized. As with *O Pioneers!*, the novel's shape and feeling fits its heroine. This is the book of a heroic female artist, a great Wagnerian singer from the American West who, unlike all Cather's other artists, is born to victory, not defeat. It is much less ambivalent and melancholy, therefore, than most of her celebrations, and meets the need for a large voice, deep breaths, and big gestures.

Cather came to feel, I think rightly, that these were not her best methods. It was always her way to start with too much material and then to cut down, and when she first published *The Song of the Lark* she shortened it from a mighty 200,000 words to 163,000 (and lost a whole section about Thea's musical education in Germany).[11] Even so, she agreed retrospectively with her English publisher Heinemann, who turned it down because 'the full-blooded method, which told everything about everybody, was not natural to me'.[12] She criticized herself in the preface to a 1932 reissue for not having 'disregarded conventional design and stopped where my first conception [of Thea's 'awakening and struggle'] stopped, telling the latter part of the story by suggestion merely'.[13] For the Autograph Edition of her books in 1937, she cut it by about a tenth, particularly the last part describing Thea's triumphs. Even so, the 1937 version still feels large and lax. A.S. Byatt is right to say that the hard labour by which Thea prepares for her career needs the 'amplitude and detail'[14] that Cather came to dislike. But there is too much self-pity early on over the family's hostility to their exceptional child and, later, too much wallowing in what 'Paul's Case' calls 'world-shine': fur coats and New York dinners and knowing chat about opera stars.

So there were sound technical reasons for Cather's feeling that she had diverged onto the wrong road with *The Song of the Lark*, and picked up the right one again with *My Ántonia*.[15] All the same, her later queasiness about a novel with which at the time she felt passionately involved ('Thea pulled at me', she wrote to Elsie in 1915, 'until I was hers more than she was mine')[16] was more than a technical matter. *The Song of the Lark* is by far her most personal and revealing novel; it is a splendid source book for biographers, because so many of the details of Thea's early life are Cather's. She would never be so explicit again about her struggle to become an artist, and with her increasing dislike of exposure, she may have regretted its heartfelt directness.

Thea Kronborg is a singer, not a writer. *The Song of the Lark* is an autobiography, but it is also a dramatization of Cather's credo. The novel's most interesting operation is the transposing it does between two keys, for two different instruments: the writerly and the dramatic, the personal and the objective. There are some revealing technical remarks on this in Cather's letters to Dorothy Canfield. After publication, she told her that the whole book was in indirect discourse, and that she had begun by having two sets of quotation marks, single and double, all the way through.[17] The book had two manners, she said, the intimate (for Thea's secret growth) and the remote (for her public profession). Many years later, when she was thinking back on the novel, she told Dorothy that most people wrote in the third person as if it were the first – that is, too intimately.[18] Thea is Cather's 'second self'. [SL, p.273] But to tell her own story, Cather had to find an 'objective correlative' which would enable her to be remote as well as intimate.

She had already thought of writing a novel about a singer when she met the great Wagnerian soprano Olive Fremstad. Cather's passion for opera had survived her Lincoln days, and once settled in Bank Street she and Edith went to the Metropolitan as much as they could; Edith's retrospective letters are full of opera-going memories. The meeting with Fremstad was professional. Cather had been asked to write a piece for the December 1913 edition of *McClure's* on three American woman singers. When she went to interview Fremstad the singer was too exhausted and hoarse to talk. But that same night at the Met, to Cather's amazement, she came on as a replacement for the soprano in *Tales of Hoffmann*, and sang magnificently. On a later occasion she saw Fremstad just after she had given a tremendous performance as the evil Kundry in *Parsifal*, completely used up, her eyes like empty glass.[19] She would use these startling disjunctions for Thea, and they are keys to Cather's fascination with the transformation processes which Fremstad revealed to her.

Of course she had written often about performance before, but now she was given a powerful close-up view of it, in a singer whose main gift was to project herself into the *idea* in the music: 'With Madame Fremstad', Cather wrote in her piece, 'one feels that . . . the idea is so intensely experienced that it becomes the emotion.' Personally, Fremstad attracted her because of her familiarity. She had grown up in a small town in Minnesota, in a poor, religious family of Swedish immigrants, and had to battle her way out of a hard childhood in a 'new crude country where there was neither artistic stimulus or discriminating taste'.[20] She seemed to Cather exactly like the pioneer women on the Divide,[21] Alexandra Bergson transformed into Brünnhilde. Her own relationship with Fremstad replicated that transformation: she wanted to turn herself into the singer, in order to find out how the singer could turn herself into, say, Isolde.

Familiarity with this Nordic superwoman fell into the category of Cather's troll friendships (and thereby set the tone for the novel): it was more like being swept up by Sam McClure than visiting the shrine of Sarah Orne Jewett. Rough, bossy, temperamental, Fremstad was also enthusiastic and honest. When Cather was ill (early in 1914 she had to go to hospital for an unpleasant infected scratch on her neck, which involved having her head shaved, and made her feel disgusted and miserable),[22] Fremstad burst in, a bracing mother-nurse figure bearing gifts and rousing her from despondency.[23] She invited Cather up to her 'camp' in Maine; a terrifyingly savage prospect.[24] But as the audience for her heroine's inexhaustible energies – chopping wood, swimming, tramping, gardening, cooking – Cather found it a grand show of human vigour and grace.[25] Those two words, mixing the virile and the feminine, sum up the language she uses for this woman-hero. Fremstad had a Teutonic, boisterous, even comic energy which Cather did not have, and which comes out in the letters to Elsie about Fremstad, and in Thea's jovial, 'rough-house' quality. Above all, Fremstad is a performance – a grand show, a bright show – with Cather as audience.

The 'piece-picture' of Napoleon's retreat from Moscow which the young Thea admires in the Moonstone home of her friends the Kohlers, the musical German tailor and his wife, [SL, p.35], is an image for the way Cather pieces her own childhood together with Fremstad's. Thea's parents, for instance – the fine, plain, calm, disciplined mother, and the unsympathetic Norwegian methodist minister, happy to make money out of his daughter's piano lessons – are more Fremstad's than Cather's. Thea's painful progress from Moonstone to Chicago, and her drudgery as an accompanist, is the story of the singer's early years. But all the feelings are Cather's. Thea has Willa's childhood double life, divided between her attic room, a secret space for reading and thinking, and the annihilating, boisterous tyranny of family life. She feels Cather's fierce adolescent hostility to the pious philistinism of her 'natural enemies' in the small town. Thea's humiliation at the Sunday School Christmas concert, when her difficult piano solo bores the audience, and her talents are eclipsed by the popular charms of Lily Fisher, the Baptists' blonde 'angel-child', singing 'Rock of Ages', is done with the personal ferocity of a long-held grudge. 'She would rather be hated than be stupid, any day'. [SL, p.81] And Cather draws strongly on her own memories for Thea's friendships with all the people in the town who have something more to offer than 'common' Moonstone values, like the Kohlers with their garden, where Mrs Kohler 'had tried to reproduce a bit of her own village in the Rhine valley'; [SL, p.28] or the Mexican 'Spanish Johnny' with his bouts of uncontrollable wanderlust.

Thea also has Cather's passionate attachment to the landscape of the West. Red Cloud, as Moonstone, is cunningly transposed from Nebraska to Colorado, so that Thea can be put in a brilliant, dramatic desert setting and compared to 'the yellow prickly-pear blossoms that open there in the desert', thorny and sturdy. [SL, p.122] The Southwestern setting, derived from her recent travels, allows into Thea's story heroic figures of the railroad, exotic Mexican scenes, and, above all, a spectacular, glorious rush of desert colours, lovingly and repeatedly described. But though Cather gives her heroine a more dramatic childhood landscape than her own, they have the same feeling for the pioneering West. In a stirring early scene, Thea and Mrs Kronborg are taken by Thea's devoted railroad man, Ray Kennedy, to the 'Turquoise Hills', sand dunes ten miles out of town, where he tells them 'tales of adventure, of the Grand Canyon and Death Valley', and Thea thinks of an earlier trip with her father to Laramie, Wyoming. (Mother and father thus equally oversee her vision of pioneer history.) There an old rancher takes them to a high plain still marked by 'the wagon-trails of the Forty-niners and the Mormons':

> There was not one trail, as Thea had expected; there were a score; deep furrows, cut in the earth by heavy wagon-wheels, and now grown over with dry, whitish grass. The furrows ran side by side; when one trail had been worn too deep, the next party had abandoned it and made a new trail to the right or left. They were, indeed, only old wagon ruts, running east and west, and grown over with grass. But as Thea ran among the white stones, her skirts blowing this way and that, the wind brought to her eyes tears that might have come, anyway. . . . The wind never slept on this plain, the old man said. Every little while eagles flew over. [SL, pp.68–9]

The old man tells the tale (that Cather loved so much) of the first telegraph message across the Missouri – 'Westward the course of Empire takes its way' – and Thea is given Cather's sentiments for the heroic pioneer past ('the spirit of human courage seemed to live up there with the eagles'). They have the same desire: to make a mark in high places, superimposed on, but drawing strength from, the trails of male endeavour and endurance.

Cather speaks of herself through all of Thea's early life. Her knowledge that she is 'different', which comes over her like the visits of a friendly spirit; [SL, p.100] her ferocious desire to 'get something big' out of life; her terror, when she comes back after her first stint in Chicago, of never getting away from the desert again; her despair, out in the world, at being a cultural savage with everything to learn, are all intensely personal. And her life in Chicago is full of revealing analogies with Cather's years as a journalist and teacher. Like Cather in Pittsburgh, Thea starts off in a pious environment, singing in the choir of a Swedish Reform Church to earn her keep, and lodging with devout German ladies. Her difficult, strenuous piano lessons with the sympathetic Hungarian musician Harsanyi, where she struggles for professional excellence against the grain of her natural gifts, allows Cather to re-work her own feelings of frustration and distortion. Like Cather, Thea is rescued – Harsanyi discovers her voice and sends her to the brilliant, cynical Madison Bowers for lessons – but, as for Cather at *McClure's*, that promising new direction is submerged by the drudgery of playing as accompanist for Bowers's lady singers. This section, scornfully called 'Stupid Faces', is fraught with unresolved painful feelings. Thea is liberated at last into a clear sense of her vocation through her journey to the Southwest and her discovery of the 'ancient peoples'' cliff-dwellings. There she learns from the Indian relics, as Cather did, that all art is 'an effort to make a sheath, a mould in which to imprison for a moment the shining, elusive element which is life itself'. [SL, p.378] By analogy, Thea is Cather's 'mould': she pours herself into her.

Cather's projection via Fremstad into Thea is a mixture of self-exposure, wish-fulfilment and hero worship, and is thus an extremely revealing description of her idea of the woman as artist. When Thea refuses the 'Lily Fisher' style of feminin-ity, or distances herself from Bowers's facile lady *artistes*, or tells her lover that she needs to be '"waking up every morning with the feeling that your life is your own, and your strength is your own, and your talent is your own; that you're all there, and there's no sag in you"', [SL, p.394] she is speaking as Cather. But the narrative is a love song as well as an autobiography; Thea is both 'intimate' and 'remote'. What is carefully avoided is an erotic presentation of Thea as an object of desire. She is the cynosure of all eyes who never-theless transcends personal sexuality.

Almost all Thea's watchers are male, but they are all carefully disqualified from being sexual partners. Instead, they prepare the way for the voice that is going to outsoar them like an eagle. In Moonstone, she is started on her journey by the derelict old German piano teacher, Fritz Wunsch, who teaches her *Lieder* and Gluck's *Orpheus* and gives her her first whiff of the great musical world: by the sensitive, unhappily married Dr Archie, her friend and lifelong admirer (rather a pale character, in spite of his later jump from small-town doctoring to wealthy, politically influential mining interests) and by Ray Kennedy, the self-educated railroad man, touchingly manly and simple, who has a dream of Thea's growing up to be his wife, but knows at heart that 'she was bound for the big terminals of the world; no way stations for her'. [SL, p.187] Ray is given a tragic death on the line, so that he can leave Thea his savings instead of becoming an obstruction. A native philosopher, he recognizes his role as part of an ordained pattern: '"There are a lot of halfway people in this world who help the winners win and the failers fail. . . . It's a natural law, like what keeps the big clock up there going, little wheels and big, and no mix-up."' [SL, p.156] In Chicago, Harsanyi is stirred – 'her eagerness aroused all the young Hungarian's chivalry' [SL, p.220] – but he is usually made to seem, not young, but exhausted by her. Cather even gives him one eye, so that he can be like Wotan in *The Valkyrie*, paternal adviser to Sieglinde.

Finally there is Thea's 'sweetheart', Fred Ottenburg, a wondrously cultured, rich, generous, affable, music-loving brewer's son, whose only disqualification is his secret marri-age to an 'insufferable' woman he can't divorce. So he too becomes one of the chivalric spectators, like Dr Archie 'watching her contemplatively, as if she were a beaker full of chemicals working'. [SL, p.305]

In their love scenes in Panther Canyon, Fred and Thea are seen as 'two boys' playing together, throwing stones and making camp in a cave and climbing perilously down the rocks in a thunderstorm. (Similarly, the only offstage detail of her later romance with the Teutonic singer Nordquist is an adventure story of their rowing for their lives through a storm on an icy lake.) Close up, Fred treats Thea like a savage young Amazon: '"I'd like to have you come at me with foils; you'd look so fierce!" he chuckled.' [SL, p.386] But she gets away from him, climbing to the horizon:

> Even at this distance one got the impression of muscular energy and audacity – a kind of brilliancy of motion – of a personality that carried across big spaces and expanded among big things. [SL, p.397]

The erotic element in his admiration is displaced onto his recollection of the elderly Jewish music lover who played host to Thea's first concert: '"Old Nathanmeyer," [Fred] mused, "would like a peep at her now. Knowing old fellow. Always buying those Zorn etchings of peasant girls bathing. No sag in them either. Must be the cold climate."' This brief touch of voyeurism is hastily brushed away by Fred's next thoughts, which reinstate Thea as tomboy-goddess: '"She'll begin to pitch rocks on me if I don't move."'

Changes in the later edition suggest that Cather had some difficulties with this relationship. Fred's parting with Thea after she has learned about his marriage is toned down (he no longer caresses her hands or lifts her up or kisses her) and, in the much-curtailed epilogue, their offstage marriage is wisely omitted. At the same time, she moderated Thea's masculine qualities: Fred's description of her voice as 'virile' [SL, 1915, p.420] is changed to 'warm', and in her account to him of her debt to the cliff-dwelling civilization, the words 'heroic' and 'muscular' are cut out. [SL, 1915, p.463, SL, p.554]

As these changes show, a delicate balance is being maintained. Thea is deliberately associated with images of domineering male heroes: the Napoleon of the piece-picture, or Julius Caesar, a photograph of whose bust hangs in her room, or the statues of the Dying Gladiator and an 'evil, cruel-looking general' she admires in the Chicago Art Institute. (These images are in contrast to Breton's painting of the barefoot peasant girl with reaping-hook, listening to 'the song of the lark', which associates Thea with pastoral virtues, not with art and conquest.) She is, also, intensely physical and female, but it is her mother, not a lover, who perceives this most closely:

> Mrs Kronborg noticed how white her arms and shoulders were, as if they had been dipped in new milk. . . . Her body had the elasticity that comes of being highly charged with the desire to live. [SL, p.282]

The most sensual scene in the novel is the moonlit Mexican ball at Moonstone, where Thea is surrounded by Julio-like indolent, admiring youths, sexy Mexican love songs float on the summer night, and she feels 'as if all these warm-blooded people débouched into her'. [SL, p.292] Cather said she wanted the scene to mark the flowering of whatever was feminine in Thea. Nevertheless, eroticism is transcended: to her Mexican admirers she is untouchable ('Silvo dropped on his back and lay looking at the moon, under the impression that he was still looking at Thea' [SL, p.292]), and the sexuality is all poured into her voice, with the male spectators providing, not an active challenge, but a ground-bass:

> . . . the guitar sounded fiercely, and several male voices began the sextette from 'Lucia'. . . . Then . . . the soprano voice, like a fountain jet, shot up into the light. . . . How it leaped from among those dusky male voices! [SL, p.296]

Thea as a leaping voice, intensely and sensuously female, but escaping from sexual confinements into the impersonal power of the artist, has her destiny confirmed, after long drudgery, by her vision of an 'ancient' native artistry in the cliff-dwellings of 'Panther Canyon', Arizona. Cather would return to the cliff-dwellings in her life and in her writing; they would play a rather different, more complex part in *The Professor's House*. Here, in a short section of wonderfully bold and passionate writing that leaps up, like Thea's voice, from

this big heavily-furnished novel, they provide an extraordinary but convincing context for the making of an androgynous American artist.

The landscape itself – the pine forests of Northern Arizona
with their lonely trees, places of 'inexorable reserve'; the
deep fissures of the canyons cutting down through the flat
table-land; the blue air of the gulfs between the two sides of
the canyons, full of swallows; the trees and streams right
down in the gorge between the cliffs – all this strikes Thea
with a sense of alien 'resistance' to human beings. All
Cather's characters have this emotion – Jim Burden arriving
in Nebraska, the Bishop riding through the mesa country,
the seventeenth-century French apothecary 'on a gray rock
in the Canadian wilderness' – to great undomesticated
landscapes. In the cold early morning the canyon wakes 'like
an old man . . . with a dull, malignant mind'. [SL, p.389]

> The sullenness of the place seemed to say that the world could
> get on very well without people, red or white, that under the
> human world there was a geological world, conducting its
> silent, immense operations which were indifferent to man. [SL,
> p.388]

That people have succeeded in domesticating such a place
by building their homes into the shape of the cliffs, is felt
(like the more recent struggles of the pioneers) as an almost
incredible human victory over inimical matter. So the Indian
relics give off a sense of tribulation and melancholy: 'From
the ancient dwelling there came always a dignified, unobtru-
sive sadness'. [SL, p.375] The 'simple, insistent and monoto-
nous' feelings Thea recognizes in the place are all to do with
survival. These feelings 'translate themselves' to Thea not as
words, but as bodily sensations. Cather, in turn translating
into words which will be as close as possible to these
sensations, uses a language which negotiates very deliberately between male and female struggles and effort.

Ellen Moers and Sharon O'Brien call Panther Canyon 'the
most thoroughly elaborated female landscape in literature',[26]
with its fissures, its womblike nest/cave where Thea spends

her days, and its concealed 'cleft in the heart of the world' from which she watches the flight of the eagle. The relics of the ancient peoples' culture to which she responds, the fragments of decorated pots once used by the women for water-carrying, are, as O'Brien says, the work of women artists 'whose art was profoundly female, integrating pro-creative and creative powers'. Thea identifies physically with these creators, and finds herself trying to walk as they must have walked. She understands that their water vessels, functional 'moulds' for catching the stream of life, essential shapes made for survival but decorated for pleasure, can be symbols for her of what her own voice can do. Like them, she can make shapes in which to catch life. By implication the process is a negation of and a triumph over that grudging, malevolent spirit of the forbidding landscape, which Thea imagined as a sullen patriarch.

But Thea's response to the female elements of the cliff-dwellings is only half the story. She is as much in touch with the 'muscular tension' and 'naked strength' of the young men she imagines snaring the eagles in their nets, and with the eagles themselves in their 'strong, tawny flight'. [SL, p.399] The language of the whole section is as valiant and heroic as it is maternal and creative. Thea's time in the cliff-dwellings fills her with 'driving power' and 'vitality', as she moves rapidly through a process of 'persistent affirma-tion – or denial'[27] to the concluding epiphany that brings together the flight of the eagle and the relics of the Indians, in a celebration of 'Endeavour, achievement, desire, glorious striving of human art!' [SL, p.399] Bounding up from her 'cleft' in the rock, 'as if she had been thrown up . . . by volcanic action', to strain her eyes after the eagle, she is poised to take flight as a heroic artist who fuses together 'gendered' characteristics – female nurturing, male strenu-ousness – so as to transcend them.

She also looks as if she is in training to play one of the Valkyrie, those fierce daughters of Wotan who ride about the mountains making their unforgettable yodelling noises as they collect up the dead heroes and carry them off to

Valhalla. This is how Gertrude Hall describes the Ride of the Valkyrie in her book on *The Wagnerian Romances*, much admired by Cather for its ability 'to reproduce the emotional effect of one art through the medium of another art'.[28]

> The eight are at last arrived; their war-cries, their hard laughter, and the shrill neighing of the battle-steeds mingle in harsh harmony. The shrieks of an autumn gale, exulting in its freedom to drive the waves mountain-high and scatter all the leaves of the forest, have the same quality of wildness and force and glee.[29]

Thea's Nordic vigour will serve her well. But Cather also gives her the transcendent, spiritual parts in Wagner. For the rest of the novel, which describes Thea's success through a succession of Wagner performances, Cather uses the operas – 'these noble, mysterious, significant dramas in roughly made verse'[30] – to raise Thea to mythic status and to express her own feelings about art.

Thea's Wagner performances are the culmination, the re-enactment, of her American life. When she plays Elizabeth (the saintly Princess who saves Tannhäuser's soul by dying for him) she puts her grief for her mother's death into the part. Fred reports: '"It's as homely as a country prayer-meeting: might be any lonely woman getting ready to die"'. [SL, p.540] As Wotan's 'nagging' wife, usually played unsympathetically, she does her hair like her mother's and makes Fricka 'clear and sunny'. [SL, p.539] As Elsa, the unjustly accused maiden who is rescued by Lohengrin on condition she doesn't ask his name, she is 'supernatural' and visionary. But as Sieglinde in *The Valkyrie*, in the love scene with her brother Siegmund, the climax of Thea's career in the novel, she is fervent, blossoming, impassioned, and full of 'pride in hero-strength and hero-blood'.[31] [SL, p.568] It seems as if the whole book is building up towards a performance of Brünnhilde, Wotan's passionate and heroic 'wish-maiden', the Valkyrie who defies her father, is released from the circle of fire by the hero Siegfried, and, after his betrayal, immolates herself on his pyre. In the earlier edition Fred

anticipates this performance: '"It takes a great many people
to make one – Brünnhilde."' [SL, 1915, p.465] But this is cut,
and Thea never does play Wagner's greatest soprano part,
perhaps because Cather wanted us to feel that Thea *is*
Brünnhilde, so doesn't need to play her.

Otherwise, Cather's appropriation of Wagner is very explicit. It may even be that the shape of the novel, with its
detailed, prolonged, scenic story of aspiration erupting into
triumph, was meant to replicate Wagner's methods, which
Cather later described as 'trying out to the uttermost' 'the
value of scenic literalness'.[32] (She compares this to Balzac,
who, in the novel, is Dr Archie's favourite writer.) All the
discussions of music[33] apply directly to Cather's own work.
Fremstad and Wagner brought together the two great questions of Cather's life: how was the artist made, and what
should art be for? Fred comments: '"She simplifies a character down to the musical idea it's built on, and makes everything conform to that."' [SL, p.511] That apparent simplicity
requires dedicated training. The artist needs a 'big personality' to start with. [SL, 1915, p.448] But 'every artist makes
himself born', as Harsanyi, sounding rather Conradian, tells
Thea. [SL, p.221] And this can't be done without the kind of
'desire' that took Columbus to the New World [SL, p.95] or
the Flying Dutchman across the wild seas. [SL, p.338] That
'fierce, stubborn self-assertion' [SL, p.274] may take ruthless
form: Thea doesn't go to her mother's death-bed when it
means she would lose the chance of singing Elizabeth;
instead she puts her grief into the performance.[34] The great
artist turns something secret and concealed, into something
public and impersonal.

All this exactly describes Cather's own career and practice
as a writer. Furthermore, she felt a strong sympathy for the
Wagnerian programme, as her earlier reviews demonstrate
(for instance on *Lohengrin* as an affirmation of faith over the
destructive power of analysis).[35] She warmed to the battle
between the pagan and the Christian in Wagner. She learned
from his use of the Nibelungen story for the Ring cycle; like
him she wanted to connect human characters to ancient

mythologies, so as to give heroic stature and a long perspective to their quests for their particular Grail or dragon. Like Wagner she believed that 'art is only a way of remembering youth'. [SL, 1915, p.460] And her fundamental theme is the one described by Shaw in *The Perfect Wagnerite* (which Cather had reviewed as, in parts, 'interesting and brilliant'):

> The only faith which any reasonable disciple can gain from
> The Ring is not in love, but in life itself as a tireless power
> which is continually driving onward and upward . . . growing
> from within, by its own inexplicable energy.[36]

Shaw's Wagner is a revolutionary socialist and a great popular writer. Cather said that she made Thea a singer so that she could be intelligible to Moonstone, the point of the novel being what she took from Moonstone and what she gave back to it.[37] In the last part of the novel, Thea often refers to her childhood as the source of her art, and the epilogue returns us, as so many of the novels return, to Aunt Tillie in Moonstone, fondly dwelling on her memories and her news of Thea, now singing Isolde in London for the King. It is an awkward coda (much reworked later) which exposes an old, unsolved problem. If to be a Wagnerian singer was to be a great *democratic* artist, what of the scornful emphasis on the 'stupid faces' and 'natural enemies' inimical to an 'uncommon' figure in 'a common, common world'?[38] [SL, p.268] Loathing of 'Philistia' sits uneasily with the artist's duty to '"get it across to the people who aren't judges"'. [SL, p.482] *The Song of the Lark* is Cather's most revealing and explanatory book about her own writing, a kind of commentary on everything else she would do. Yet it quite fails to resolve this very American contradiction. But though the failure makes for some awkwardness here, it is the reverse of disabling. In the rest of her work, it persists as the difficult and enriching tension between escape and return.

7

THE ROAD OF DESTINY

And the end of all our exploring
Will be to arrive where we started
And know the place for the first time.
T.S. Eliot, 'Little Gidding', 1942

AT THE end of *My Ántonia*, the story-teller Jim Burden says
that he has retraced his 'road of Destiny' and come back full
circle to take possession of his past (in the 'figure' of
Ántonia), recognizing as he does so that this circular journey
has been a predetermined one. Back at the beginning of the
book, there is a double entrance to this 'road of Destiny'. The
novel begins, not with Jim's story, but with an Introduction,
a conversation on a train journey. The speaker of this
Introduction, a neutral and asexual voice standing for
Cather, travelling either towards or away from Nebraska (it's
not clear which), with Jim, an old childhood friend, says:
'During that burning day when we were crossing Iowa, our
talk kept returning to a central figure, a Bohemian girl whom
we had both known long ago'. Jim's subsequent narrative
reduplicates this entrance: it too begins on a train journey,
with Jim arriving as a child in Nebraska. 'I first heard of
Ántonia', he starts, 'on what seemed to me an interminable
journey across the great midland plain of North America'.

Because the frame journey of the Introduction covers the
same ground as the novel's first journey, the book straight
away establishes the feeling it will end with, of circular

infinity, renewable time. In its end is its beginning. Jim's wry introductory word for the journey, 'interminable', is tied by affinity and by opposition to the solemn, concluding word 'predetermined', like the sun and the moon Jim sees on one of his return journeys, confronting each other 'across the level land, resting on opposite edges of the world'. [MA, p.322] The journey – ours, Cather's, Jim's – doesn't close, it 'keeps returning' (Jim and Ántonia, we are made to feel, are still living as we read it). But it has a point, which is to understand what the journey has been for. These concepts of renewal and purpose are consolatory: *My Ántonia* is an exceptionally heartening and affirmative book. But to be on an interminable and predetermined journey is also a source of anxiety; and the novel is 'burdened' too with the difficulty and strangeness of returning, and the shadowy presence of what the circle might exclude.

That the way back into the past is not as easy a journey as the novel makes it seem is suggested by the difficulties Cather had with her Introduction, which is itself a duplicated text. The version she wrote for publication in 1918 was rewritten in 1926.[1] In both versions, the narrator describes her shared childhood with Jim, and characterizes him as a romantic, whose love of the West has inspired his work as 'legal counsel for one of the great Western railways'. (The 1918 version has more detail about his disappointing marriage and his 'big Western dreams'.) In the earlier version of the Introduction, Jim and the narrator agree that they will both write down their memories of Ántonia. Jim says: '"I should have to do it in a direct way, and say a great deal about myself. It's through myself that I knew and felt her . . ."' When Jim turns up some time later with his notes, the narrator has written hardly anything. Jim says, 'Now, what about yours?', warning her not to be influenced by his narrative. But she reproduces it as it stands, without attempting to write her own. In the later, rewritten Introduction, Cather simplifies, abandoning the idea of rival narratives, and thereby making her disguise as Jim seem inevitable and necessary. Jim says on the train that he has 'from time to time' been writing down his memories of Ántonia; some months later he comes to the narrator's apartment and produces what he calls 'the thing about Ántonia'. In both versions of the Introduction, the emphasis is on the spontaneous, natural shape of Jim's recollections:

> 'I didn't take time to arrange it; I simply wrote down pretty much all that her name recalls to me. I suppose it hasn't any form. It hasn't any title, either.'

Only at the very last does Jim give 'the thing' the name 'Ántonia', prefixing this after a moment with the word 'my', just as the Introduction prefixes the story.

An introductory frame in which the author returns to the scene of his past, or listens to someone talking on a journey, or comes into possession of a manuscript, is a familiar device. Cather borrowed it, as she freely admitted,[2] from French and Russian novels, and in doing so lent her 'raw' Western American novel a deep, rich, melancholy, Old World flavour. *The Kreutzer Sonata* was one model, with its tragic marital story told on a long night's train journey across Russia – one of the short Tolstoi novels which Cather read so often in her youth that they seemed to Russianize her American landscape.[3] So the Introduction gives the novel its shape[4] and tone. And it looks ahead to the book's last words, Jim's reclaiming of the *incommunicable* past: as though all its language has been as close as possible to a kind of feeling silence. Cather's comments on *My Ántonia* insist on its simple and faithful memorializing, its truth to the past.[5] But this simplicity is the product of enormous prowess and control. Remote though she makes herself look from the flamboyant modernist texts of her contemporaries, which weave back through time to investigate an ambivalent relationship between narrator and subject – 'Heart of Darkness', *The Good Soldier, The Great Gatsby* – the journey back in *My Ántonia* is quite as deliberate and complex.

The writing came out of a literal, and a literary, returning. In 1914, after her unpleasant neck infection, she went to

Fremstad's camp to recuperate, and then to Red Cloud for the summer. She was still working on *The Song of the Lark*, but the groundwork for *My Ántonia* was being done now, as she caught up with the lives of all the local families – including her models for Ántonia (Annie Pavelka, née Sadilek) and for the Harlings (the Miners). It was like revisiting characters in a book, as various, she said, as in *War and Peace*.[6] In 1915 she went to the Southwest on an adventurous trip with Edith. That winter, Judge McClung died, and the Pittsburgh house which had been her second home since 1901 was closed up. It was her second loss that year: Annie Fields had died in February. Then, very soon after the death of her father, Isabelle married. Cather was devastated.[7] Using Edith, her family, and the West, for consolation, she spent 1916 in Taos, in Wyoming with Roscoe and his wife and children, and in Red Cloud, keeping house all summer for her sick mother. By the time she went back to New York in the autumn, she had written several chapters of *My Ántonia*. So, though it drew so deeply on the material of her childhood, it was strongly coloured too by these recent feelings: her desolation at Isabelle's betrayal, her rediscovery of the old Western stories, and her temporary assumption of a domestic, quasi-maternal role in Red Cloud. Underlying these personal feelings was a horror at what was happening in the world. *My Ántonia* is very strikingly *not* her *War and Peace*: the war (which she would need more time to write about) makes the loudest silence in the book, the most noticeable 'presence of the thing not named'.[8] But it powerfully motivates the need to reclaim and find lasting value in the past.

The novel is a return, too, to her best methods, after the Wagnerian literalness of *The Song of the Lark*. 'Quite of itself and with no direction from me', Cather said in 1931, insisting on the novel's naturalness, *My Ántonia* 'took the road of *O Pioneers!* – not the road of *The Song of the Lark*'.[9] Elsie Sergeant famously recalled her, early in 1916, placing an old Sicilian jar filled with scented stock in the middle of a bare, round, antique table, moving the lamp to fall on its glazed colours, and saying (her voice faltering and her eyes filling with tears): '"I want my new heroine to be like this – like a rare object in the middle of a table, which one may examine from all sides."'[10]

The lamp falling on the pot, as an image for narration, recalls her use of Virgil in the novel. Jim Burden sits in his room at the University of Nebraska, preparing to read the *Georgics*, while a Virgilian evening star hangs outside 'like the lamp engraved upon the title page of old Latin texts'. [MA, p.263] By its light, like the lamp Cather angles onto the pot, Jim sees the 'figures' of his past standing out 'strengthened and simplified'. Illuminating sentences from Virgil are 'engraved' in the text, one of them, indeed, on the title page of the book: '*Optima dies . . . prima fugit*': 'the best days are the first to flee'. Another sentence consoles us for that thought: '*Primus ego in patriam mecum . . . deducam Musas*': 'I shall be the first, if I live, to bring the Muse into my country'. The equation seems simple and heartening. By the light of the Virgilian example, Cather as Jim consoles herself for her lost youth (and for the lost golden age of American pioneering history) by turning the figures of her local past into an American pastoral, in an utterance as perfectly appropriate to its subject as the *Georgics*, 'where the pen was fitted to the matter as the plough is to the furrow'. [MA, p.264]

But there is tension, too, between the tranquil, luminous Virgilian example, and the 'places and people of my own infinitesimal past'. When Jim shuts the window against the evening star and regretfully lights his own lamp, 'the dim objects in the room emerged from the shadows and took their place about me with the helpfulness which custom breeds'. [MA, p.263] We have just been told that when he set himself up in this room, he pushed a lot of the furnishings out of the way and 'considered them non-existent, as children eliminate incongruous objects when they are playing house'. [MA, p.259] But customary, incongruous objects reassert themselves. Jim's contemplation of Virgil is about to be broken in on by the reappearance of Lena Lingard, one of his 'figures' from the past, not at all shadowy or distant, but firmly flesh and blood. Later, Jim will realize that poetry like Virgil's depends for its existence on girls like Lena, and her female figure will be superimposed, like a floating picture, over the mournful words of the classical text, *'Optima dies . . . prima fugit'*. [MA, p.271] The analogy between the classical pastoral and Jim's narrative, apparently so secure and consolatory, is in fact equivocal and unsettling. Not all his 'figures' will stay in place, safely 'simplified and strengthened' as part of the lost best days. They go on living and changing, refusing to be 'eliminated'. The lamp can only 'affix its beam'[11] if the subject is dead – a stone pot, or the lost past. But Jim's pastoral figures are not static, they are not like the frieze on Keats's Grecian Urn, 'cold pastoral'. They talk, dance, grow up, improvise, change, disappear, return, go in and out of his reach. One of the pleasures of *My Ántonia* is its dynamic between mournful, selective Virgilian retrospect, and the incongruous energies of living reality. This is, also, a negotiation between traditions of male writing (pastoral elegy, classical epic, romance) and the real shapes, the 'true stories' of women's lives, with Jim as a mediator between the two.

In the first part of *My Ántonia*, 'The Shimerdas', Jim, secure in his well-run Protestant grandparents' home, grows up alongside Ántonia, who is doing her best in her struggling, poor, ill-adapted Bohemian family. Together, they make sense of the 'materials' to hand: he teaches her language, she tells him stories. Their mutual discoveries keep pace until after the suicide of Mr Shimerda, the central event of the first section. Then they begin to move apart. In the second section, 'The Hired Girls', Jim's family moves into the town, Black Hawk, and Ántonia soon follows, to work for his neighbours, the attractive Harlings. As Jim becomes increasingly restless, the narrative opens out into the life of the town, in particular of Jim's friends, the immigrant 'hired girls' – Ántonia, Lena, Tiny, and the others. In the third section, 'Lena Lingard', he is at university. A visit from Lena, now a smart Lincoln dressmaker, starts a subdued flirtation (coloured by their emotional response to a performance of *Camille*) which they renounce in the interests of his future. The fourth section, ambiguously named 'The Pioneer Woman's Story', is set two years after Jim, now in training as a lawyer, has gone East. He comes back to hear from the Widow Steavens (his grandparents' tenant on their old farm) the story of what has been happening to Ántonia: deserted by a selfish, unscrupulous railroad man, she has come back home with an illegitimate baby. She and Jim meet again, 'like the people in the old song, in silence, if not in tears', and speak of their old friendship. In 'Cuzak's Boys', twenty years on, much-travelled Jim comes back once more (after seeing Lena and Tiny, prospering in San Francisco) to find Ántonia married to a Bohemian, on a thriving farm, with ten or eleven children. He is given an emotional welcome, spends the night there, and promises himself a renewal of the friendship. Black Hawk disappoints him, but he retraces his steps over the country where Mr Shimerda was buried, recognizing his 'predetermined' road.

This apparently bare, inconsequential narrative, which notably fails to fulfil the title's promise of a love affair or a heroine's life story, gives up its meaning through the shape it takes. And the shape of the book is the making of Jim's memory. Its 'formless' structure — two long and three short sections spread over about forty years — is, in fact, very carefully formed to represent the process of memory-making. In the first two sections the material accumulates for retrospection. 'I can remember exactly how the country looked to me' Jim says. [MA, p.16] or: 'All the years that have passed have not dimmed my memory.' [MA, p.28])[12] In the last three the past is gone away from, returned to, and made sense of. So the book's shape enacts the relation between Cather's early life and her writing. But by using Jim as an equivocal, limited, reserved surrogate, she avoids the unmediated autobiographical literalness of *The Song of the Lark*. Jim is and is not 'her', just as Ántonia is and is not 'his'.

Jim, unlike Cather, is an orphan, when he makes his journey (like Cather) from safe Virginia into the 'utter darkness' and undifferentiatedness of Nebraska, where there seem at first to be no whereabouts: 'There seemed to be nothing to see'; 'not a country at all, but the materials out of which countries are made'. [MA, p.7] We recognize this dark negative space, like chaos before the Word, from the beginning of *O Pioneers!* As in the earlier pastoral, this blank stuff is going to be created and ordered through speech, love, endurance, and the making of shapes.

From the moment Jim emerges from the train, and sees Ántonia and her huddled, 'encumbered' family also emerging, the shape of his narrative replicates the process of growth from infancy to adulthood. Like a child's book, the first section has simple, coloured, apprehensible things standing out on every page – food, clothes, animals, plants – in a primary environment of smells, warmth, light, space, snow, sky. Useful objects have their uses explained; Grandfather's silver-rimmed spectacles for reading prayers, grandmother's hickory cane tipped with copper for killing rattlesnakes, Mrs Shimerda's feather quilt for keeping her food warm. (Sometimes the usefulness is untranslatable, like Mrs Shimerda's *cèpes* from the Bohemian forests, thrown on the fire by Jim's suspicious grandmother.) The child's perspective sees things either very close or very far. This, as Eudora Welty says, is Cather's usual perception of the world:

> There is the foreground, with the living present, its human figures in action; and there is the horizon of infinite distance . . . but there is no intervening ground . . . There is no recent past. There is no middle distance.[13]

So Jim, taking possession of his Nebraska, is at once investigative child and retrospective author. On his first day, Jim comes out of his grandmother's warm basement kitchen and moves up through the farmyard, the sea of red prairie grass his own height, the cattle corral, the garden set away from the house, towards 'the edge of the world'. His impulse is towards 'the horizon of infinite distance': 'I had almost forgotten that I had a grandmother'. But there she is, very real and close, digging potatoes and warning him against rattlesnakes. She leaves him in a sheltered spot in the garden:

The earth was warm under me, and warm as I crumbled it through my fingers. Queer little red bugs came out and moved in slow squadrons around me. Their backs were polished vermilion, with black spots. I kept as still as I could. Nothing happened. I did not expect anything to happen. I was something that lay under the sun and felt it, like the pumpkins, and I did not want to be anything more. I was entirely happy. Perhaps we feel like that when we die and become a part of something entire, whether it is sun or air, or goodness and knowledge. At any rate, that is happiness; to be dissolved into something complete and great. When it comes to one, it comes as naturally as sleep. [MA, p.18]

Jim could be another Thoreau or Emerson ('I am nothing, I see all')[14] or Whitman loafing at his ease, 'observing a spear of summer grass',[15] as the narrator contemplates his 'intimations of immortality' in the language of American transcendentalism. But at the same time he seems tiny and animal, a vivid microscopic part of the natural scene.

This pull between earth and space, near and far, solidity and dissolution, is the constant factor in Jim and Ántonia's childhood. They are always coming out from underground (Jim from his secure kitchen, Ántonia from her dark constricting cave) into infinite space.

Jim's response to the death of Mr Shimerda is at the heart of this movement. Jim imagines the old man's spirit resting in his grandparents' kitchen before his long journey home: 'Outside I could hear the wind singing over hundreds of miles of snow'. Through his intense re-imaginings of everything Ántonia has told him about her father's life, Jim encloses him inside a protected space, before his memory 'fades out from the air', and dissolves. His crossroads burial on 'a very little spot in that snow-covered waste', which will be preserved as 'a little island' in the changing landscape, sums up the movement between enclosure and dissolution which makes the whole shape of the book.

As Jim and Ántonia grow up, this shape is cross-cut with

other patterns, as in the confusing, complicating growth from childhood into adolescence and adulthood. In the town scenes, there is still an attraction towards safe enclosures, like the grandparents' Black Hawk house, a 'landmark' for country people coming into town, or the Harlings' convivial kitchen, or the town laundryman's pleasant prospect, like a framed Degas:

> On summer afternoons he used to sit for hours on the sidewalk in front of his laundry, his newspaper lying on his knee, watching his girls through the big open window while they ironed and talked in Danish. [MA, p.221]

But the town's spaces – the hotel with its partition between parlour and dining-room, the temporary dance-pavilion on the vacant lot, the school, the Fireman's Hall, the depot, the Opera House – are more ambiguous enclosures, where social and sexual partitions take complex shape. And Jim's relation to these enclosures is less accepting: he climbs out of his bedroom window at night, resenting, now, his grandparents' security; he paces the streets feeling that 'the little sleeping houses' are places of 'evasions and negations', producing nothing but waste. [MA, p.219] (In a parallel but subordinated movement, Ántonia is also breaking out from the enclosures of her home and the Harlings' protection, into more dangerous spaces.)

Once, towards the end of the section, they rediscover the essential, childhood relationship between the close and the infinite, in an extended Arcadian idyll by the river. It begins with Jim swimming alone and naked in the river, then dressing in a 'green enclosure' under a growth of grapevines. As he leaves, he repeats his possessive childhood gesture of crumbling the earth in his fingers: 'I kept picking off little pieces of scaly chalk from the dried water gullies, and breaking them up in my hands'. [MA, p.234] He finds Ántonia under the side of the river bank, grieving over the memories aroused by the smell of the elderflowers. Consolingly, crouched under the bank and looking at the sky, they retrace the story of Mr Shimerda. Then, with the other girls, they move up to the chalk bluffs, with a view of the town and the prairie, and lie about in the sun, their talk opening out through their personal history and desires (it is a feminine version of 'The Enchanted Bluff') to the history of the first pioneers. The long, imperceptibly shaped scene concludes with their momentary sighting of the plough on the horizon, magnified in the frame of the setting sun. Though the whole passage is adult, socialized, sensual, historically conscious, it re-enacts the shape of the childhood scenes.

Jim's adult life is made up of dislocation and absence. He inhabits or looks in on makeshift, improvised spaces, like his awkwardly furnished college room. After he moves East, he seems an absentee in his own narrative, coming back in from long disappearances to catch up on the old stories. His first return to Ántonia, in her troubles, goes back over the familiar routes, to his childhood bedroom, to Mr Shimerda's grave, to the 'old pull of the earth' at nightfall, to Ántonia's face 'at the very bottom of my memory'. But these items seem recapitulated as a prelude to leave-taking. It's not until the very end of the book (which is balanced against the whole weight of the long first part) that Jim refinds the shape of childhood so as to keep it. Ántonia's innumerable children re-enact (but with more energy and vigour than Jim and Ántonia) the original processes. They too keep rushing up and out from underground hidden places to the outside:

> We were standing outside talking, when they all came running up the steps together, big and little, tow heads and gold heads and brown, and flashing little naked legs; a veritable explosion of life out of the dark cave into the sunlight. It made me dizzy for a moment. [MA, pp.338–9]

With Ántonia in her orchard, Jim feels himself back in a protected place, the town and America and the world kept out:

> There was the deepest peace in that orchard. It was surrounded by a triple enclosure; the wire fence, then the hedge of thorny locusts, then the mulberry hedge which kept out the hot winds

of summer and held fast to the protecting snows of winter. The
hedges were so tall that we could see nothing but the blue sky
above them . . . [MA, p.341]

But appeasing and consolatory though this is, this is not
Jim's place, or his childhood; it's as though he is trying to rein-
sert himself into the womb. Trying to get back inside is what
memory does. Memory grafts together the close and the far,
making scenes of the past 'so near that I could reach out and
touch them with my hand' – like the earth he crumbled
through his fingers – and so distant as to be 'incommunicable'.

Jim's last sentence implies that his past is 'incommunicable' to
anyone who has not shared it. But that is precisely what the
book has been doing: communicating his past to us, or that
part of his past, at least, which 'fires his imagination' (as he
says of Ántonia [MA, p.353]). So this book, which makes itself
look so natural and unwritten, is all to do with language and
reading. If the incommunicable past is to be read, it must be
decodable. When Jim, as a child, is baffled by the hieroglyphic
cuff-buttons of the train conductor, who is covered in buttons
and badges and 'more inscribed than an Egyptian obelisk',
[MA, p.4] or has the decorations on the cowboy boots of his
grandfather's hired help, Otto Fuchs, interpreted for him ('the
undraped female figures . . . he solemnly explained, were
angels' [MA, p.13]), or when Lena makes up for the dullness
of the Nebraska prairie by reading her glum Norwegian lover
Ole Benson's tattoos ('"We used to sit and look at them for
hours; there wasn't much to look at out there. He was like a
picture book"' [MA, p.282]), their naive decipherings mimic
the whole operation of the novel. Hieroglyphs need keys;
landscapes and people have to be read.

> All about us the snow was crusted in shallow terraces, with trac-
> ings like ripple-marks at the edges, curly waves that were the
> actual impression of the stinging lash in the wind. [MA, p.64]

Such 'tracings', 'marks', 'impressions' (the book is full of syn-
onyms for signs) may be purely phenomenological, but the
tendency of the human mind is to supply human meanings.

The rows of Nebraskan sunflowers may have been, according to the botanists, a native growth, but Jim prefers the legend that the persecuted Mormons, on their first pioneering, left a trail of sunflower seeds to mark 'the roads to freedom'. [MA, pp.28–9]

When, like Thea looking at the waggon trails or the cliff-dwellers' relics, Jim is 'stirred' by the faint marking on the grass of 'a great circle where the Indians used to ride', or goes back to the cross and the island of grass which mark the grave of Mr Shimerda, or refinds, at the end of the book, the traces of the old pioneer roads, now as faint as that Indian circle, his reading of these 'old figures' connects remote and immediate history. The tone of these readings is almost always elegiac. There *are* more cheery, forward-looking interpretations of landscape, like Jim's grandfather foreseeing, with his 'clear, meditative eye' that the Nebraskan cornfields would one day be a great economic force in the world. [MA, p.137] But this strikes an uncharacteristically celebratory, even chauvinistic note. More often the readings of landscape are revaluations of what has been lost or destroyed or is passing away.

The climax of these readings is the famous sighting of the plough against the sun, which, though often extracted as Cather's most characteristic piece of heroic pastoral, is deeply embedded in the context of readings and signs. The moment takes its force from the long scene that precedes it, in which the girls have given a history of the sufferings of the women pioneers – the stories of their mothers – and Jim has countered with the male story of Coronado's heroic defeat, which recalls to Ántonia her father's desolate death. Remote and immediate history have been linked together in their apparently idle talk. When the light changes (always a signal in Cather for a moment of transcendent revelation), and the plough stands out for them like 'a picture-writing' on the sun, it seems a heroic consolation for the painful 'destinies' they have been contemplating. But this figure is as much part of the past, for the narrator, as Coronado's sword; and even as they look at it, the vision disappears, the light goes, and 'that forgotten plough had sunk back to its own littleness somewhere on the prairie'. [MA, p.245]

These 'old figures' have their value restored through imaginative sympathy: without it, they are meaningless hieroglyphics. History is incommunicable unless the necessary connections are made between the past and the present. *My Ántonia* is full of appropriations and recognitions. Some of these take comical, childish form. When Jim hears the terrifying story of Peter and Pavel throwing a young bride and groom from their sledge to the pursuing wolves, he transposes the story from the Russian steppes to 'a country that looked something like Nebraska and something like Virginia'. [MA, p.61] Little Nina Harling, under the spell of Ántonia's stories of Christmas in the old country, 'cherishes a belief that Christ was born in Bohemia a short time before the Shimerdas left that country'. [MA, p.176] But this is just what the adult Jim does when he superimposes the figures of his past onto Virgil's poetry. It's only by such appropriations that 'dead' languages can be brought back to life. And the same applies to people: Ántonia, refound after almost a quarter of a century, would be merely a stranger, a 'stalwart, brown woman, flat-chested', with grizzled hair and bad teeth, [MA, p.331] if her essential 'identity', underlying those marks, could not be recognized by her attentive re-reader.

Early in the novel there is a wonderful example of this attentive, sympathetic recognition, which is for Cather, (rather than sexual passion or self-involvement) life's most valuable emotion. Mr Shimerda has come to visit the Burden household at Christmas:

> As it grew dark, I asked whether I might light the Christmas trees before the lamp was brought. When the candle-ends sent up their conical yellow flames, all the coloured figures from Austria stood out clear and full of meaning against the green boughs. Mr Shimerda rose, crossed himself, and quietly knelt down before the tree, his head sunk forward. His long body formed a letter 'S'. I saw grandmother look apprehensively at grandfather. He was rather narrow in religious matters, and

sometimes spoke out and hurt people's feelings. There had been
nothing strange about the tree before, but now, with someone
kneeling before it – images, candles. . . . . Grandfather merely put
his finger-tips to his brow and bowed his venerable head, thus
Protestantizing the atmosphere. We persuaded our guest to stay for supper with us. He needed
little urging. As we sat down to the table, it occurred to me that
he liked to look at us, and that our faces were open books to him.
When his deep-seeing eyes rested on me, I felt as if he were
looking far ahead into the future for me, down the road I would
have to travel. At nine o'clock Mr Shimerda lighted one of our lanterns and
put on his overcoat and fur collar[. . . .] He made the sign of the
cross over me, put on his cap and went off in the dark. As we
turned back to the sitting-room, grandfather looked at me
searchingly. 'The prayers of all good people are good', he said
quietly. [MA, pp.87–8]

Mr Shimerda injects his own associations – Catholic, feudal,
Eastern European – into the room: the shape of his body in
prayer spelling the first letter of his own name. Grandfather,
sensitive to his response, nevertheless by a figurative gesture
translates what Christmas means to him back into his own
language. The reciprocal sympathy of the two old men –
almost, but not quite, comical – is turned more solemnly
towards the child (both of them are reading *him* as he now, as
a remembering adult, is reading them) and the scene becomes
his education, like a text in a Christmas sermon for him to
contemplate.

My Ántonia is full of such sympathetic readings. The admirable Widow Steavens tells the story of 'her' Ántonia, carefully
and painstakingly, with an attention to female details – the
wedding clothes Ántonia brings back with her, the soap she
has ready for her baby – which speak to us of Ántonia's life
more directly and intimately than Jim's version ever does.
Ántonia's children read her photograph album with a 'pleased
recognition' [MA, p.349] which revitalizes what would otherwise just be stiff, faded, absurd snapshots of Jim's past: 'two
men, uncomfortably seated, with an awkward-looking boy in
baggy clothes standing between them'. [MA, p.350]

These readings are forms of translation: a metaphor which, obviously, suits a novel about immigrants in America. The emphasis on language is very often historical and sociological: even more than *O Pioneers!*, *My Ántonia* gives a full, detailed picture of a particular culture at a transitional moment. Early on, small struggles with language, touching or comical – Otto labouring over his Christmas letter to his mother in German, after so long away, or greedy Mrs Shimerda grabbing the words she needs: '"Pay no more, keep cow?"' – point to the immigrants' painful difficulties. It is a history of assimilation obstructed by native hostility (foreigners give you diseases, Jake the Virginian hired man tells Jim) and mutual suspicion: the Austrians hate the Czechs, the Norwegians won't have Mr Shimerda in their graveyard.

What Jim learns from the Christmas scene with his grandfather and Mr Shimerda is racial tolerance, and 'The Hired Girls' is, in part, a ferocious satire on small-town xenophobia. Jim's preference for the bold, sensual, immigrant girls, with their strong values of family loyalty, self-improvement and their energetic pleasure-seeking, over the timid, snobbish Black Hawk natives, is often expressed as a comparison between languages. The 'beautiful talk' Ántonia remembers from the old country comes through in the 'impulsive and foreign' quality of her speech, in her 'deep vibrating voice': 'Everything she said seemed to come right out of her heart'. [MA, p.176] Lena, more smoothly assimilated, has learnt the small town 'flat commonplaces', but speaks them with a 'caressing intonation' which seems to translate them back into her own language. Native American, by contrast, seems to Jim a 'furtive and repressed' speech. [MA, p.219] To find that, at the end of the novel, the Cuzak family have reverted to the 'rich old language' of Bohemia seems a judgement on the world outside.

But 'the language problem' goes deeper than cultural adaptation. If there is no communication, no true 'reading' of signs, then we are left with no sympathy or memory or value in life, just the impenetrable runes of extinct civilizations.

The precariousness with which meaning is sustained is always being touched on – for instance in a subtle comment on Jim's university teacher Gaston Cleric's extraordinary aptitude for bringing the classics to life in his talk, which may have been 'fatal to his poetic gift': 'He squandered too much in the heat of personal communication'. [MA, p.260] Valuable language must be saved up as well as given out. Two strange, deprived minor characters in the novel bring home to us the perilous fragility of communication. One of them cannot speak, the other cannot see. Ántonia's 'crazy' brother Marek, web-fingered and retarded, can only make 'his queer noises' for food and attention. Jim translates even these – he knows Marek wants 'to bark like a dog or whinny like a horse' for him [MA, p.77] – but the boy won't always have such sympathetic interpreters, and stands no more chance in America than Benjy in *The Sound and the Fury*: we hear later that he has 'got violent and been sent away to an institution', [MA, p.314] (just as Alexandra's brothers wanted to send away old Ivar), his incommunicable meanings silenced for ever. The other misfit has been luckier. He is a famous blind black pianist[16] (who comes through Black Hawk on his travels) who, as the blind child of a slave in the post-Bellum South – the most deprived of the deprived – found his way, by instinct, to his employer's piano. His story, which is only superficially a diversion from the main narrative, describes his salvation by the only language – music – which could 'piece him out and make a whole creature of him'. [MA, p.188]

Blind d'Arnault survives by improvising, and improvisation is one of the novel's most insistent expressions of energy. Under duress, people make something out of whatever comes to hand, whether it's Jim's homemade Christmas, or the Harlings' charades and costume balls, or Cuzak pulling from his pockets, like an amateur conjuror, an endless succession of toys ('penny dolls, a wooden clown, a balloon pig that was inflated by a whistle' [MA, p.359]) for his children. The book's leading improviser is Ántonia, a story-teller, inventor, translator, namer of names and recapitulator of memories. The energy that pours out of her in the childhood section is primarily verbal. In her scenes with Jim she is learning as many words as quickly as possible, or interpreting to him the story of Peter and Pavel, or turning his killing of a snake into a tall tale, 'with a great deal of colour'. [MA, p.49] When she is in trouble or unhappy – after her father's death or her desertion – she loses her capacity for improvisation, and can only talk about the crops and the weather. But at the end, she is still making a shape of life out of language, telling her childhood to her own children, so that her story-making seems to hold off old age.

Jim's summing-up of the Ántonia who 'fires his imagination', in another of Cather's much-quoted, transcendent passages, is like his vision of the plough. 'His' Ántonia – mother of sons, rich mine of life – is a 'figure' which he now, definitively, reads for us: one who leaves 'images in the mind that did not fade', who stays in the mind in 'a succession of pictures, fixed there like the old woodcuts of one's first primer', who 'lent herself to immemorial human attitudes which we recognize by instinct as universal and true'. [MA, p.353] Just so, the lamp falls on the pot in the centre of the table, or the plough stands out against the sun, or the 'figures' of the naked land are superimposed on the classical pastoral. It is a moving conclusion to the narrative's process of reading and remembering. All the same, Ántonia is a woman, not a plough. She is not as 'fixed' as Jim would have her.

Jim's elegiac pastoral expresses Cather's deepest feelings: it would be perverse to argue that his reading of Ántonia is meant to be distrusted.[17] But his imagination is only 'fired' within limits. Figures which do not speak to his sense of what is 'immemorial' or 'universal' or 'true' (Lena Lingard, or Tiny Soderball) are relegated to the edges of his circle of memory, like the awkward items of furniture pushed out of the way in his college room. And what might have been powerful emotions in Ántonia's story – the aftermath of sexual betrayal, for instance – are muted in the interests of Jim's memorializing.

But the presence of alternative possibilities make themselves felt inside Jim's narrative from the first. As in Twain's *Huckleberry Finn*, where the made-up bookish adventures of Tom Sawyer look dubious against Huck's real emergencies, Jim's childhood reading of *Robinson Crusoe* or *Swiss Family Robinson* is always being outdone by realities. When he gets up after the blizzard, eager for new excitements – 'Perhaps a barn had burned; perhaps the cattle had frozen to death; perhaps a neighbour was lost in the storm' [MA, p.94] – what he gets is the suicide of Mr Shimerda. A deflation of romance goes on throughout. Jim weeps his heart out over *Camille*, but he has 'prudently' remembered to bring his umbrella with him for going home.

Cather's version of American pastoral may not be as brutal or jovial as Mark Twain's or Bret Harte's, but she can go in for a tough Western humour which brings us down with a bump from Jim's heroic sunsets. '"I don't see how he could do it!"' the grandmother laments over Mr Shimerda, to which Otto replies: '"Why, ma'am, it was simple enough; he pulled the trigger with his big toe."' [MA, pp.96–7] The reunion with the Cuzaks is full of benign memories, but the high point of the dinner is the horrible story of the money-lender Wick Cutter's murder of his wife. '"Hurrah! The murder!" the children murmured, looking pleased and interested.' [MA, p.361]

It's the ogre-like Wick Cutter (the ugly name sounding both brutal and sexual) who makes the two most startling irruptions into Jim's Arcadia. 'The Hired Girls' does not end, as might have been expected, with the transcendent vision of the plough on the horizon, but with the grotesque story of the money-lender's attempt to rape Ántonia. Cutter is a vividly horrid small-town character, a gambler and lecher masquerading as a good clean-living American (he is always quoting 'Poor Richard's Almanack' and talking about the 'good old times'). His vicious treatment of his wife, whom he loves to make jealous, and whose frenzied reactions excite him more than the sex itself, is horrifyingly convincing. Ántonia goes to work for the Cutters in rebellion against Mr

Harling's strictures on her dance-hall evenings, but comes back in a fright when Cutter tells her he is off on a journey, hides all his valuables under her bed, puts a heavy Yale lock on the door, and orders her to stay alone in the house. Jim takes her place for the night, and Cutter, having tricked his wife onto the wrong train, creeps back, thinking to find Ántonia, and assaults him. The scene makes an extremely disconcerting conclusion to Jim's childhood memories; why has Cather placed it there?

It is partly that Wick Cutter, like his Yale lock, is the future (he will come back as Ivy Peters in *A Lost Lady*). He stands for the debased American currency which Cather saw buying out the pioneers' values. Benjamin Franklin's 'Poor Richard's Almanack' is all about thrift; Cutter's attempted assault on Ántonia is like a miser's theft. He tries to make her as debased as the usurer's notes under the bed. The golden figure of the plough against the sun was like a glorious stamp on a coin; Cutter's licentious hoarding, by immediate contrast, introduces another system of valuation. (His wife is just as 'base': 'I have found Mrs Cutters all over the world; sometimes founding new religions, sometimes being forcibly fed.' [MA, p.214] This is one of Cather's most disagreeable moments, but there's no avoiding it as part of her feeling about changing values.) When Cutter finally murders his wife so that she won't get his property, and then kills himself, the 'spiteful' suicide is set, at the end of the book, against Mr Shimerda's at the beginning, who had nothing, and died of a broken heart.

But Wick Cutter is also a priapic monster who fills Jim with revulsion. His fantasies of protecting Ántonia like a chivalric knight, are obliterated by the 'disgustingness' and ignominy of the event, and, very revealingly, Cather has Jim blame Ántonia: 'I felt that I never wanted to see her again. I hated her almost as much as I hated Cutter. She had let me in for all this disgustingness'. [MA, p.250] It feels like Adam blaming Eve after the fall. And the next thing we know Jim has left his Arcadia, and never *does* see Ántonia again until she has really lost her sexual innocence and become, not the child of Mr Shimerda he always wants to remember, but an adult woman, capable of being lover, wife and mother.

Jim's squeamishness is an interesting element in his ambivalent sexuality. Cather was somewhat defensive about her first extensive use of a male narrator. She may still have been thinking of Sarah Orne Jewett's criticism of an earlier story, that a male 'masquerade' was not necessary for expressing emotions towards a female character.[18] She tended to explain Jim away by saying that he came out of her experience of ghosting McClure's autobiography, or seemed appropriate because most of her original stories about 'Ántonia' were told her by men.[19] What she does not say is that he allows her free entry into male literary traditions of pastoral and epic, and enables her to speak from her own sexual identity and express her own emotions for women.

To read Jim Burden, however, simply as a mask for lesbian feelings, is a narrowing exercise.[20] He is more complicated than that, an androgynous narrator who mediates between male and female worlds like those Shakespearean pastoral hero/ines, boys dressed as girls dressed as boys. In childhood, he is attracted to the male outdoor pioneering of Otto and Jake – their Wild West exploits, their tackling of bulls and blizzards. No tough pioneer himself, as a young adult he finds male companionship in scholarship; his friendship with Gaston Cleric is like the pastoral brotherhood of male poets and singers. But he also participates in the female world, sitting indoors with his grandmother, or with the motherly and sisterly Harlings, or the hired girls, a privileged pet and a listener. (This is like a contemporary androgynous narrator, also engaged in refinding his past, Proust's Marcel, *A l'Ombre des jeunes filles en fleurs*.)[21] He is privy to the women's stories, those matriarchal narratives which so inspired Cather in her childhood: stories of women giving birth on the immigrant ships, or of the Swedish and Norwegian and Bohemian mothers, or Widow Steavens' female account of Ántonia's disasters. Adolescent Jim, reading his Latin for university, spending his evenings with the telegrapher and the cigar-maker, and making a May-basket for Nina Harling, is both boyish and girlish.

Being androgynous makes Jim an empathetic narrator, but he is not allowed a love affair, either with Ántonia or Lena, and his marriage is an offstage failure. (There is a definite prejudice here: all the marriages in the book give ammunition to Jim's exclamation: 'I wondered whether the life that was right for one was ever right for two!' [MA, p.367]) Yet, in its way, *My Ántonia* is a very sexy book. Those alluring foreign girls who cluster around Jim, are written up in pleasurably erotic language, whether they are dancing, dressing, lying around, or ironing:

> their white arms and throats bare, their cheeks bright as the brightest wild roses, their gold hair moist with steam or the heat and curling in little damp spirals about their ears. [MA, p.222]

At the centre of this pagan bacchanal (over which Blind d'Arnault at one point presides 'like some glistening African god of pleasure, full of strong, savage blood' [MA, p.191]) is seductive Lena, who seems sensual to Jim in a passive, cat-like way quite unlike the energetic, 'outdoor' Ántonia. Dancing with Lena is like sinking into 'a soft, waking dream' on a 'soft, sultry summer day'. [MA, p.222] On their hot day out by the river she is 'panting' and 'supine'; she is always touching and tempting him. Her flirtation with Jim in Lincoln is subtle and uncommitted; she leads him on and holds him off at once, even in her farewells, made from a typically 'supine' position on her couch: 'At last she sent me away with her soft, slow, renunciatory kiss'. [MA, p.293] It is no accident that *Camille*, which makes them both cry so much, and for which Cather allows so much space (she wanted their naive wallowing in it to be comical, but couldn't resist a wallow herself)[22] is a play about renunciation as much as about seduction.

Lena's later history as a plump successful businesswoman in partnership with Tiny Soderball in San Francisco is pointedly placed at the margin of the last three parts of the novel, as though her independence from the past and her assimilation into America disconnects her from Jim's imagination. This marginalizing is even more noticeable in the narrative treatment of Tiny, whose amazing life story is briefly fitted into the section called 'The Pioneer Woman's Story'. The title refers to Widow Steavens' account of Ántonia (both are pioneer women) but it would suit Tiny even better. This neat, slender Norwegian girl makes a dramatic journey (like Carl Linstrum, and again offstage) to the Klondike in the gold rush, sets up a hotel for the gold miners, inherits a claim romantically from a dying Swede, makes a fortune in the wilds, is lamed in the arctic weather, and comes back a rich, 'hard-faced', grimly ironic woman. Jim catches up with her in Salt Lake City 'in 1908'. That '1908' is the only date in the book, and shows how Jim associates her, and Lena, with contemporary American life. 'This is what actually happened to Tiny', [MA, p.299] her story begins: it may sound like a tall tale, but it is 'actually' a slice of life, like a story in a newspaper. Tiny and Lena are modern; they have cut off the past. Their relationship, asexual, dry, companionable, fails to inspire him. Jim describes Tiny as someone 'in whom the faculty of becoming interested is worn out', [MA, p.302] but he also means, of becoming interesting.

Ántonia's peculiar place in his imagination is contrasted with Lena throughout. Whenever Lena tries to seduce him, Ántonia is censorious; she wants to keep Jim's innocence as much as he wants to keep hers. His revealing erotic dreams of the two girls spell this out:[23]

> I used to have pleasant dreams: sometimes Tony and I were out in the country, sliding down straw-stacks as we used to do; climbing up the yellow mountains over and over, and slipping down the smooth sides into soft piles of chaff.
> One dream I dreamed a great many times, and it was always the same. I was in a harvest-field full of shocks, and I was lying against one of them. Lena Lingard came across the stubble barefoot, in a short skirt, with a curved reaping-hook in

her hand, and she was flushed like the dawn, with a kind of luminous rosiness all about her. She sat down beside me, turned to me with a soft sigh and said, 'Now they are all gone, and I can kiss you as much as I like'.

I used to wish I could have this flattering dream about Ántonia, but I never did. [MA, pp.225–6]

'Tony' and he are like boys together; but they also keep slipping back down into a soft, protected womb-like place. Lena appears as threateningly erotic, a reminder of his (unused) potency, but also a figure of mortality. Sex is death: the only way he can preserve Ántonia from simply growing old is to censor his sexual feeling for her. He must never have *that* dream about her. His love scenes with Ántonia are carefully controlled. When, as an adolescent, he tries to kiss her like a grown-up, she insists on treating him 'like a kid', and he welcomes it. It means that 'she was, oh, she was still my Ántonia!' [MA, p.225] Their most passionate scene is a valedictory renunciation:

'I'd have liked to have you for a sweetheart, or a wife, or my mother or my sister – anything that a woman can be to a man. The idea of you is a part of my mind; you influence my likes and dislikes, all my tastes, hundreds of times when I don't realize it. You really are a part of me.'

To which she replies:

'Ain't it wonderful, Jim, how much people can mean to each other? I'm so glad we had each other when we were little. I can't wait till my little girl's old enough to tell her about all the things we used to do. You'll always remember me when you think about old times, won't you?' [MA, p.321]

Jim renounces the possibility of an active relationship with her ('I'd have liked to have you') so that she can take her place in his mind as a generalized female inspiration for his memory. Following his lead, she promises to inspire it ('You'll always remember me'). The point of motherhood seems, here, to be the opportunity it gives her of recalling their past.

Another kind of story could have been written about

Ántonia: a bright immigrant girl, shattered by her father's suicide, living in abject poverty with her mean, grim mother and brother, working in the fields like a man, her attempt to upgrade herself in service wrecked by her seduction and abandonment, shamed (like Hardy's Tess) by having to return home pregnant, surviving the terrible times of the Nebraska depression, finding satisfaction, in the end, only in interminable childbearing and domestic work. That this harsh realist pastoral does make itself felt inside the novel is one of its strengths. In its light, Cather's conclusion for Ántonia may look sentimental. The lavish associations with breeding, nourishment, milk, preserves, harvest, life itself, might seem uncomfortably like an idealization of maternity. But the associations do work as metaphors for 'home'. Ántonia's destiny, in the end, is to fire Jim's – and Cather's – imagination, to be the 'home' to which they return from their exile in time and space.

My Ántonia, like all Cather's great novels, powerfully gives the sense that 'the thing not named', in her famous phrase, is the myth underlying the fiction. My Ántonia is not a religious book, but it has religious feelings. It would be quite plausible, if your mind worked along those lines, to make Mr Shimerda into the Fisher King of the Waste Land, Jim into the Questing Knight of the Grail, and the Cuzak home into the place of redemption. This pilgrimage points us towards death. Jim's 'predestined road' takes him, finally, back to Mr Shimerda's grave. Though the last paragraph tries to suggest that there will be a future for him and Ántonia ('the road was to bring us together again') – a future rather feebly gestured to in the Introduction – it feels much more as if Jim's return home is his preparation for oblivion. As in O Pioneers!, the reunion at the end of My Ántonia is coloured by a deeply melancholy determinism. Jim recognizes 'what a little circle man's experience is'; that 'all we can ever be' (not much, perhaps) is predetermined, that the past makes up for 'whatever we had missed'. It sounds more like a lament than a celebration; a heavy burden is being placed on the past to make it console us for, even replace, the present. The present – and the future – are kept out of the circle of return, by a very strong process of elimination which gives this beautiful novel its aura of simplicity and containment. But what is eliminated presses on it. Now it would have to come in.

8

THE LOST AMERICAN

'All my beautiful lovely safe world blew itself up here with a
great gust of high explosive love,' Dick mourned persistently.
'. . . the silver cord is cut and the golden bowl is broken . . .'
                    Scott Fitzgerald, *Tender is the Night*,
                    1934, revised 1951

He had been to touch the great death, and found that, after
all, it was but the great death. He was a man.
                    Stephen Crane, *The Red Badge of Courage*, 1895

CATHER WROTE to Dorothy Canfield in March 1916 that
the state of the nations was like souring milk.[1] She could
have found stronger words. As with many Americans, it
would take some time for her to respond more fully to what
was happening. She spent the Great War writing *My Ántonia*;
after it came out in 1918 it would be a long four years before
the publication of *One of Ours*, the novel which tried to come
to terms with the world's having – as she put it later – broken
in two.

During these years she found herself new refuges from
what seemed to her the increasingly inimical modern times.
Two East Coast rural retreats replaced her lost Nebraskan
pastoral, and provided intermittent escapes from New York.
One was a small village in New Hampshire, Jaffrey. She went
there first for a reunion with Isabelle and her husband, fell in
love with the place, and returned to it with Edith for many

summers and autumns. She stayed in two attic rooms in the Shattuck Inn, looking out over a hilly, wooded New England landscape dominated by Mount Monadnock. In the summer of 1917, when she was working on *My Ántonia*, she put a tent in a field half a mile from the Inn, on a farm belonging to friends, and wrote in it every day, surrounded by peaceful, solitary woods. She chose this as her burial place, 'just at the corner of the old burial ground' (Edith Lewis described it to Stephen Tennant) 'where you look off over fields and woods to the mountains beyond'.[2] In the summer of 1921 she found an even more remote haven, on Grand Manan, a Canadian island seven miles off the coast of Maine, at the mouth of the Bay of Fundy. It was an extremely wild and beautiful place, with steep wooded cliffs rising sheer out of the sea, waterfalls, masses of wild flowers in summer, fogs blowing down from Greenland, and nothing to interrupt except the steamer coming in from the Canadian shore and the fishing boats below.[3] She corrected the proofs of *One of Ours* there, and later (in 1926) she and Edith had a small house built for them, Whale Cove Cottage, looking straight out over the sea.

Professionally, too, she found a safe haven in the post-war years which would last her for the rest of her life. She had been dissatisfied with Houghton Mifflin's proofreading of *The Song of the Lark* and their jacket for *My Ántonia*; the book was mostly well received, but sold badly (she made $1300 in the first year but only $400 in the second). Though this was partly due to the coincidence of its publication in wartime, she felt she was not being well promoted. She admired the young publisher Alfred Knopf for his Borzoi Books; early in 1920 she walked into his office, they had a long conversation, and she asked him then and there to be her publisher. For the next twenty-seven years they were good friends. Cather admired his 'fiery temperament' and 'severe taste', and liked the loving care he took with his books. He understood her, and treated her well from the first, giving her good advances and as much control as she wanted over blurbs and book jackets.[4]

Knopf wanted a novel, of course, but agreed to start with a book of short stories. *Youth and the Bright Medusa*, published in 1920, reprinted the best four stories from *The Troll Garden* ('Paul's Case', 'The Sculptor's Funeral', 'A Death in the Desert', 'A Wagner Matinée'), with its quotation from 'Goblin Market' ('We must not look at Goblin men/We must not buy their fruits'), which, like the new title, suggested her old theme of the dangerous seductions of art. (The 'Bright Medusa', who turns her youthful admirers to stone, stands for the love of artistic success; but also, in some of the stories, for other kinds of dangerous desires.) The four new stories, written between 1916 and 1920, were left-overs from *The Song of the Lark*: they were all about American opera singers struggling against their 'natural enemies' in a philistine, envious, interfering world. It's a mark of Cather's mood that these are not, like Thea's, stories of triumphant escapes, but of compromises and spoilings. In her future returns to the theme of *The Song of the Lark* – 'Uncle Valentine', her touching 1925 memorial to Ethelbert Nevin, and the late novel *Lucy Gayheart* – it would be the death, not the victory of the artist which preoccupied her.

There are three not very distinguished new stories. In 'A Diamond Mine', the singer Cressida Garnet is preyed on by her envious family, her Svengali-like Greek coach, and two parasitic husbands in succession – a hedonistic Czech composer, a Wall Street gambler. She goes down historically in the *Titanic*, but was already being eaten alive by sharks. In 'A Gold Slipper' and 'Scandal', Kitty Ayrshire, yet another beautiful American soprano, does battle with the censorious disapproval of a philistine Pittsburgh businessman, and the vicious gossip of a New York Austrian-Jewish 'patron of the arts'. (It's an unpleasant feature of these stories that they display a streak of anti-semitism, which may have had something to do with Cather's feelings about Isabelle's husband Jan Hambourg.)

One long story, though, stands out. 'Coming, Aphrodite!' is the story of a bohemian (with a small 'b'!) love affair in the Washington Square of old New York, between a young singer fresh from the West, and a painter, Don Hedger, a foundling brought up by a Catholic priest, who has been living in solitude with his bulldog, Caesar, until the arrival next door of the enticing, and enticingly-named, Eden Bower. (She has changed her name from 'Edna', so as to take on the role of the self-made artist-heroine of the New World: a role which Cather, here, treats more cynically than usual.) The story (which beautifully evokes the city of Cather's early *McClure's* days)[5] makes a fierce moral comparison between the American artist who stays put, refuses the lure of commercial fame and goes on making original experiments which earn a small but high reputation, and the travelling showbiz star with a huge following and a hardened soul, who finds that 'a "big" career takes its toll, even with the best of luck.' [YBM, p.63] It is also one of the most erotic love stories Cather ever allowed herself to write.

Hedger with his surly dog in his dusky room is dark, underground, intent. Through a crack in his closet, he watches the girl next door, naked, doing her callisthenics: 'the soft flush of exercise and the gold of afternoon sun' enveloping her in a 'luminous mist'. This extraordinary voyeuristic episode (a more sexualized version of Fred's sighting of Thea on her clifftop) is sublimated into myth: Hedger is a troll-like, goblin force of darkness and earthiness, and Eden is another of Cather's uncapturable, semi-divine female figures, associated throughout with air, dream, light, stars and freedom. For Hedger – and later, for her public – she is Aphrodite, goddess of love. But for herself she is Diana, goddess of the moon, the hunt, and chastity. Standing on the roof of the house on a hot night, their figures in shadow against the sky, they become archetypes: 'nothing whatever distinguishable about them but that they were male and female'. [YBM, p.49] Hedger's sexual force pulls her earthward ('they moved, at last, along the roof and down into the dark hole; he first, drawing her gently after him' [YBM, p.49]), but she escapes him. The fearsome risk of sexual passion is inscribed in a 'brutal' Mexican story Hedger tells her – it is his courtship – called 'The Forty Lovers of the

Queen'. (Cather took it, years before, from the wonderful Julio,[6] though there is more than a touch of Flaubert's *Salammbô* in it, and like the Mexican scenes in *The Song of the Lark*, it injects an exotic, erotic flavour.) A chaste princess with magical rain-making powers is assaulted by a savage captive chief, who is castrated and has his tongue cut out as punishment, and is kept as her servant when she marries an Aztec King. She uses him as a go-between when she wants to summon her lovers; but when she gets too fond of one of them, the Captive betrays her to the King, the Princess and the Captive are burnt to death together, and the rains fail.

The Medusa-like dangerousness of desire (which will be a very strong subject in the post-war novels) conflicts with the rival risks of a chaste dedication to art. Our sympathies are equivocally directed: Cather expresses herself both through the solitary, male 'troll' figure, his thwarted passions transferred into his powerful work, and the escaping, aspiring, woman artist.

The relations between them are acted out in an enchanting scene, a day out at Coney Island, where they go to see one of Hedger's models, an Irish-American girl who makes an extra living by going up in a balloon. Eden, having seen her, takes a fancy to the stunt.

'Yes, go along,' said Eden. 'Wait for me outside the door. I'll stay and help her dress.'

Hedger waited and waited, while women of every build bumped into him and begged his pardon, and the red pages ran about holding out their caps for coins, and the people ate and perspired and shifted parasols against the sun. When the band began to play a two-step, all the bathers ran up out of the surf to watch the ascent. The second balloon bumped and rose, and the crowd began shouting to the girl in a black evening dress who stood leaning against the ropes and smiling. 'It's a new girl,' they called. 'It ain't the Countess this time. You're a peach, girlie!'

The balloonist acknowledged these compliments, bowing and looking down over the sea of upturned faces, – but Hedger was determined she should not see him, and he darted behind the tent-fly. He was suddenly dripping with cold sweat, his mouth was full of the bitter taste of anger and his tongue felt stiff behind his teeth. Molly Welch, in a shirt-waist and a white tam-o'-shanter cap, slipped out from the tent under his arm and laughed up in his face. 'She's a crazy one you brought along. She'll get what she wants!'

'Oh, I'll settle with you, all right!' Hedger brought out with difficulty.

'It's not my fault, Donnie. I couldn't do anything with her. She bought me off. What's the matter with you? Are you soft on her? She's safe enough. It's as easy as rolling off a log, if you keep cool.' Molly Welch was rather excited herself, and she was chewing gum at high speed as she stood beside him, looking up at the floating silver cone. 'Now watch,' she exclaimed suddenly. 'She's coming down on the bar. I advised her to cut that out, but you see she does it first-rate. And she got rid of the skirt, too. Those black tights show off her legs very well. She keeps her feet together like I told her, and makes a good line along the back. See the light on those silver slippers, – that was a good idea I had. Come along to meet her. Don't be a grouch; she's done it fine!'

Molly tweaked his elbow, and then left him standing like a stump, while she ran down the beach with the crowd.

Though Hedger was sulking, his eye could not help seeing the low blue welter of the sea, the arrested bathers, standing in the surf, their arms and legs stained red by the dropping sun, all shading their eyes and gazing upward at the slowly falling silver star. [YBM, pp.37–9]

It is not quite like anything else in Cather, with its Boudin lighting, its cheery American holiday crowd, its modern girl (like the 'New Women' music-hall *artistes* Cather used to admire), and its coolly ballooning heroine, quite happy to be the cynosure of all eyes, in a pantomime version of Thea's eagle-like climb on the cliffs, who must at last come 'slowly falling' down from her flight.

'Coming, Aphrodite!' gave Cather time off – an indulgent flight, like Eden's – from the novel she had been writing since 1918.[7] It was slow work: even after she had thought of the story, she did not start it for six months; she spent a long time gathering material, and the writing took three years of very intense feeling.[8] Cather always saved things up (sometimes for much longer than four years), and the slow process this time matched the slowly accumulating impact on her of the war. She differed with her friend Elsie Sergeant over this, who had immediately become involved as a war correspondent for the *New Republic* and felt that, to Cather, the war was just a 'story'.[9] Elsie was injured inspecting a battlefield a few weeks before the armistice; Cather, in her shocked letter of condolence, compared Elsie's injury with her own fuss about her shaved head in 1914.[10] Elsie seemed fated to let the war get under her skin, she said; perhaps an unfortunate phrase to use to someone whose leg had just been filled with bits of steel. She went on to tell her how modest, alive, and picturesque she found 'our' American boys in New York, just off the *Mauretania*.

The letter suggests differences in their vantage point which have a crucial bearing on *One of Ours*. Cather was not there; and though the war did 'get under her skin' in a particular and personal way, there was much of it she failed to understand.

The point of ignition for the novel was the news of two particular deaths in 1918. The first was that of a cousin, Grosvenor ('G.P.') Cather (son of the clever, ugly Aunt Franc who had been a partial model for 'A Wagner Matinée') who was killed at Cantigny on May 27, 1918. G.P. had always seemed to her a depressed, dull Nebraskan farmboy without much future. But when the war broke out she had been staying on his father's farm, and she and G.P. had long conversations sitting on top of the haywagons.[11] After he went over in July 1917 he seemed, from his letters home to his mother, to find a new meaning in life; his death, she thought, was a 'glorious' thing to have happened to someone whose life had seemed so pointless.

The other boy's death which affected her strongly was that of a young violinist, David Hochstein, a talented civilized person, a nephew of Emma Goldman, with deep reservations about the war, who had signed up because he was 'too proud not to fight'. She first met him at a musical evening in New

York when he was playing second violin in the Trout Quintet, and then a few weeks after his military training started. At that point he seemed 'frozen in a kind of bitter resignation', but three months later she found that 'something keen and penetrating and confident' had come back into his face; he could only account for it by his friendship with the other men. In his letters home from the Front, he spoke of having found a faith 'that for all these heroic souls gone to the beyond there is some future'.[12]

These two very different soldiers would find their way into the characters of Claude Wheeler, the Nebraskan farmboy brought to life by the war in France, and his violinist friend David Gerhardt. But, as usual, her fictional figures were composites: G.P. and Hochstein were mixed up in her mind with a general feeling about young America in the war, and personal memories of her own raw shock at being confronted with an old civilization on her journey to Europe twenty years before. And she gathered information from many other witnesses. In the winter of 1918 she visited wounded soldiers in a New York hospital and heard their stories.[13] When she was ill with 'flu in Jaffrey, in the autumn of 1919, the doctor who treated her had a diary from his time as a medical officer on a troopship during a 'flu epidemic: she used it for Claude's crossing to Europe, 'The Voyage of the Anchises'.[14] She read newspaper accounts avidly, and other stirring first-hand sources such as the *Letters from France* of Victor Chapman, the first American aviator to be killed in the war (his father said: 'It was the cause that made a man of him'), and the poems of Alan Seeger, who wrote before he was killed of having been given 'that rare privilege of dying well'.[15] After she had begun to write the French parts of the book, she felt that she needed to be there, and in the summer of 1920 she and Edith spent six weeks living in the Hôtel du Quai Voltaire, visiting the battlefields and seeing G.P.'s grave with Isabelle and Jan (now, it would seem, safely become good friends) and appreciating all over again the intense beauty of Paris. The young crippled soldiers in the Luxembourg Gardens, being wheeled about by old veterans of the

1870 Franco–Prussian war, brought home to her the cost of preserving that beauty.[16] Edith Lewis, however, remembered her avoiding all the marks of modern life in Paris and saying that 'she wanted to live in the Middle Ages'.[17] The visit to France was more an escape from modern America than an investigation into the aftermath of the war.

The sources and the attitudes that went into the making of *One of Ours* lent themselves to an idealized version of war which is likely to make us extremely uneasy now, and which was, at the time, ferociously castigated by the big male American writers. This was partly a territorial defence. If the pioneering West had had to be taken back from a male language, the battlefields were even harder material to appropriate. It is ironical that although *One of Ours* was the book that made Cather, at fifty, famous and well-off (it sold 30,000 copies in two months, and the royalties for 1923 were $19,000),[18] and won her the Pulitzer Prize, it was also the book for which she received the most savage criticism. Ernest Hemingway wrote, in a letter to Edmund Wilson in 1923:

> E.E. Cummings' *Enormous Room* was the best book published last year that I read. Somebody told me it was a flop. Then look at *One of Ours*. Prize, big sale, people taking it seriously. You were in the war weren't you? Wasn't that last scene in the lines wonderful? Do you know where it came from? The battle scene in *Birth of a Nation*. I identified episode after episode. Catherized. Poor woman she had to get her war experience somewhere.[19]

H.L. Mencken, who had praised *The Song of the Lark* and *My Ántonia* very highly, and who was a well-disposed acquaintance, reviewed *One of Ours* severely:

> What spoils the story is simply that a year or so ago a young soldier named John Dos Passos printed a novel called *Three Soldiers*. . . . At one blast it disposed of oceans of romance and blather. It changed the whole tone of American opinion about the war . . .
> Unluckily for Miss Cather she seems to have read *Three Soldiers* inattentively, if at all. The war she depicts has its thrills and even its touches of plausibility, but at bottom it is fought

out not in France but on a Hollywood movie-lot. Its American soldiers are idealists engaged upon a crusade to put down sin; its Germans are imbeciles who charge machine-guns six-deep, in the manner of the war dispatches of the New York *Tribune*. There is a lyrical nonsensicality in it that often glows half pathetic; it is precious near the war of the standard model of lady novelist. . . . It is a picture of the war, both as idea and spectacle, that belongs to Coningsby Dawson and 1915, not to John Dos Passos and 1922.[20]

The comparison with Coningsby Dawson (also made in a scathing review by Sinclair Lewis) put her into sentimental, patriotic company. Dawson's war writings (*The Test of Scarlet, Out to Win*) turns average men into heroes through the ordeal of the trenches, and presents the American soldier as God's gift to Europe:

> . . . the American in khaki has astonished the men of the other armies. . . . The soldier from the USA seems to stand always restless, alert, alone, listening, waiting for the call to come. . . .'Let me get into the trenches,' that was the cry of the American soldier that I heard on every hand. Having witnessed his eagerness, cleanness, and intensity, I ask no more questions as to how he will acquit himself.
>
> I have presented him as an extremely practical person, but no American that I met was solely practical. If you watch him closely you will always find that he is doing practical things for an idealistic end.[21]

'One of Ours', indeed. This is at the opposite extreme from the war writings of e.e. cummings (*the enormous room*, 1922) or of Dos Passos in *One Man's Initiation: 1917* (1920) and *Three Soldiers* (1921), in which an anti-American passion for France and the French is matched by a profound disgust at the war as the 'fullest and most ultimate expression' of a sham, futile, crumbling civilization, 'an old bitch gone in the teeth', as Ezra Pound had it in 'Hugh Selwyn Mauberley'. In Dos Passos and cummings (as, later, in Hemingway's *A Farewell to Arms* of 1929 and Edmund Wilson's *Patriotic Gore* of 1962), American war rhetoric – 'We're going to see the damn show through', 'making the world safe for democracy'

– is disgusting, camouflage for 'organized piracy', part of 'the ocean of lies through all the ages that must have been necessary to make this possible'. The kind of language that inspired Cather – 'that rare privilege of dying well', 'it was the cause that made a man of him' – was precisely the language that these writers found obscene and dangerous. Once, they felt, America had offered the immigrant Europeans 'freedom from the past, that gangrened ghost of the past that is killing Europe today with its infection of hate and greed of murder'.[22] The American entry into the war was seen as a tragic betrayal of that possibility of freedom.

Cather deliberately set herself to write a 'truer' picture of American boys in the war than *Three Soldiers*,[23] and some of the hundreds of letters that poured in after *One of Ours* was published congratulated her for answering the 'sourness and pessimism' of Dos Passos.[24] She was extremely defensive about her novel (which she always, emotionally, thought of as *Claude*, though Knopf wisely made her change the title),[25] and cited her fan letters as proof (as they certainly were) that though the 'highbrows' and the 'pacifists' might be scornful, ordinary American readers loved it.[26] But she resented the fuss (in a letter to Dorothy[27] she wondered whether perhaps she should have written it anonymously) and felt that the book was being misunderstood. It was a fiction, not a piece of propaganda, and Claude was not intended as a glorification of war, but as the portrait of a dim young farmboy (like Henry Fleming in Crane's *The Red Badge of Courage*), confronting his destiny.[28]

Cather's defence against her critics is only partly convincing. *One of Ours* stands, awkwardly, midway between the flag-waving heroics of Dawson and the lacerating disillusion of the 'lost generation'. In some ways, her story of an unhappy mid-Westerner, bitterly at odds with the American way of life, finding his first and last happiness at war in France, is not so remote from Dos Passos as Mencken made out. Martin Howe, in *One Man's Initiation*, is set free from his past on the journey to Europe in a very similar way to Claude Wheeler:

'He had never been so happy in his life. . . . At last things have come to pass.'[29] And Martin is as enthusiastic as Claude in his response to French Gothic architecture and the 'old romances of chivalry'[30] it evokes. The difference, though, between *One Man's Initiation* and *One of Ours*, is that Martin sees his Gothic abbey being shelled to fragments, and understands, as Claude seems not to, that the war he is fighting means the destruction of the very civilization he has fallen in love with.

Mencken's and Hemingway's condescension about her feminine 'Catherization' of the war scenes is something of an injustice. It is Claude, not Cather, who is the naive idealist, and the narrator is careful to give an unsettling context for his idealism, just as Crane does for Henry Fleming. The influence is acknowledged:

> These were the first wounded men Claude had seen. To shed bright blood, to wear the red badge of courage, – that was one thing; but to be reduced to this was quite another. Surely, the sooner these boys died, the better. [OOO, p.335]

And the sooner the better for Claude, the novel makes us feel. There is a gap between the idealistic hero and the deflating, realist narrative. Here, Claude, on the march at last, wears 'a stoical countenance, afraid of betraying his satisfaction in the men, the weather, the country' as he sees 'the reassuring signs of the nearing front':

> long lines of gaunt, dead trees, charred and torn; big holes gashed out in fields and hillsides, already half concealed by new undergrowth; winding depressions in the earth, bodies of wrecked motor-trucks and automobiles lying along the road, and everywhere endless straggling lines of rusty barbed-wire, that seemed to have been put there by chance, – with no purpose at all. [OOO, p.358]

Not only the landscape of war – just a 'great dump-heap' – but all the characters surrounding Claude on his way there, undermine his aspiration of 'dying for an idea'. All his potential role-models refuse for themselves any language of heroism. Dr 'Trueman', courageously treating the appalling epidemic on the 'Anchises', speaks only matter-of-fact realities ('There's not castor oil enough on this boat to keep the men clean inside' [OOO, p.296]) in order to deal with the conditions. Claude may be 'enjoying himself' on board, [OOO, p.311] filled with a new sense of purpose, but all round him 'the air was fetid with sickness and sweat and vomit' and men are dying in agony, being chucked overboard like 'rotten ropes'. Victor Morse, the Anglicized aviator, seems to Claude a glamorous figure, with his scorn for his small-town Iowa background, his worldly knowledge of sex and European society, and his desperado recklessness, but in reality his London mistress is old enough to be his mother, he has a dose of the clap (indirectly but clearly hinted at in Dr Trueman's refusal to treat him) and his bravery is suicidal: '"In the air service", said Victor carelessly, "we don't concern ourselves about the future. It's not worth while."' [OOO, p.306] David Gerhardt consoles himself with a half-formed idea that 'the young men of our time had to die to bring a new idea into the world'. [OOO, p.409] But what he feels far more acutely is the destruction of beautiful and historical things (his Stradivarius is symbolically 'smashed into a thousand pieces', [OOO, p.409]) the waste of his talents and the futility of what they are doing: '"Oh, one violinist more or less doesn't matter! But who is ever going back to anything? That's what I want to know!"' [OOO, p.409] What there is to go back to is seen by Claude's mother, his most intimate and dedicated supporter, who, for all her grief at his death, is bitterly relieved that he has not had to come back to post-war America and wake up from his 'beautiful beliefs'.[OOO, p.458]

All the same, it is sometimes difficult to separate Claude's beautiful beliefs from the narrator's. *One of Ours*, like *The Song of the Lark*, was an intensely personal book: she felt as close to Claude in the years she was writing it as she had to Thea.[31] The title doesn't only denote a patriotic sentiment; it also suggests an intimate sympathy with the hero. When Claude, as a student, chooses to write a thesis on Joan of Arc, he 'flattered himself that he had kept all personal feeling out of the paper'. [OOO, p.61] But the personal feeling comes through; and so it does in this novel. There can be no doubt that we are meant to take Claude to our hearts as Cather did those fine, brave, modest American boys she saw in New York, fresh off the *Mauretania*, in 1918. When Claude enlisted, 'he believed that he was going abroad with an expeditionary force that would make war without rage, with uncompromising generosity and chivalry'. [OOO, p.248] And though he learns the realities of war from those he meets and what he sees, he does not unlearn his faith in 'our' American boys. At the start of 'The Voyage of the Anchises', the troops pull out of New York harbour cheering the Statue of Liberty and singing 'Over There', while a passing clergyman on a Staten Island ferry-boat takes off his hat and recites Longfellow's 'Sail on, O Ship of State'. No irony is intended: 'The scene was ageless; youths were sailing away to die for an idea, a sentiment, for the mere sound of a phrase . . . and on their departure they were making vows to a bronze image in the sea.' [OOO, p.274] When Claude and his men encounter a distressing refugee family (Claude recoils in distaste from the raped mother's German baby), the girl who talks to him knows that Americans are safe: 'She only listened to hear whether the voice was kind, and with men in this uniform it usually was kind.' [OOO, p.361] There is no getting round this as the dominant tone of *One of Ours*. Cather completely fails to take on the disillusioning process of the war itself (as Dos Passos and Hemingway so passionately do) or the less than ideal behaviour of the American army in France (brilliantly satirized in cummings's *the enormous room*). If all that the novel were doing was presenting a heroic picture of 'our' noble American boys sacrificing themselves at the front for an ideal, then Mencken's and Hemingway's attacks on the novel would have to be the last word.

But, though *One of Ours* is usually described as her 'war novel', the war is not, in fact, its central subject. Like *The Song of the Lark*, with its long detailed account of Thea's childhood and apprenticeship, the novel gives three slow first sections to the unhappy story of Claude's Nebraskan childhood, education and marriage. It is the last time Cather would use these long-winded methods ('The Novel Démeublé' came out in the same year as *One of Ours*) but, as in *The Song of the Lark*, they have a point here. The Nebraskan chapters of *One of Ours* are as burdened with detail as Claude feels himself to be burdened, buried alive, under the weight of his life. This weight has all to be balanced by the last two sections on the ship and in France. David Daiches calls the novel 'structurally broken-backed'.[32] But she wanted[33] to give the feeling of a broken world, and to point up the crucial irony of the novel, that this young American hero comes out of a civilization which is rapidly doing away with the possibilities of heroism.

One of Ours makes a heartfelt lament for the end of the old American pioneering west:

> The statue of Kit Carson on horseback, down in the Square, pointed Westward; but there was no West, in that sense, any more. There was still South America; perhaps he could find something below the isthmus. Here the sky was like a lid shut down over the world; his mother could see saints and martyrs behind it. [OOO, p.118]

Claude in Denver, bitterly feeling his own 'wasted power' as he looks at the statue of the famous Wild Westerner (and anticipating Cather's own fictional moves, in work to come, from the West to the Southwest) embodies all her own national nostalgia for a lost American heroism. And this entails a loss of faith: Claude can't feel, as Alexandra Bergson or even Jim Burden could, a spiritual relation to the land. It's interesting to compare Cather's wartime disillusion with her contemporary and admirer, Scott Fitzgerald. According to Dick Diver in *Tender is the Night*, the silver cord is cut and the golden bowl is broken. Cather thinks so too. But Dick is grieving over the end of *European* traditions, the long nineteenth-century 'love story' of empire, middle-class life, and settled hierarchies. The difference between Fitzgerald's treatment of the war, as an American writer abroad, and

Cather's, as an American at home, is that her sense of an ending is directed at the closed pioneering frontier, not at the blowing up of the European world.

There are still some traces of the old America in *One of Ours*, like the old flour mill owned by Claude's father-in-law, kept on out of sentiment 'for there was not much money in it now'. [OOO, p.121] Claude's childhood Bohemian friend Ernest Havel speaks a muted version of Alexandra's contemplative stoicism:

> 'In old countries, where not very much can happen to us . . . we learn to make the most of little things. . . . Nothing is going to reach down from the sky and pick a man up, I guess.' [OOO, p.53]

Cather's tender feelings for Margie Anderson, the servant girl who came with the family from Virginia, are evoked in 'simple', illiterate, adoring Mahailey, with her scraps of stories of the Civil War, her star-embroidered quilt, her old memories of Jesse James ballads, her superstitions, and her own ways of ordering things:

> She could count, and tell the time of day by the clock, and she was very proud of knowing the alphabet and of being able to spell out letters on the flour sacks and coffee packages. 'That's a big A,' she would murmur, 'and that there's a little a.' [OOO, p.22]

But the landscape is more brutal and bleak than in *O Pioneers!* and *My Ántonia*. Claude identifies, in retreat from it, with moonlight, which he associates with distant countries, other civilizations, and challenging adventures. It seems to him that idealists like himself, 'children of the moon, with their unappeased longings and futile dreams' are 'a finer race than the children of the sun.' [OOO, p.208]

The 'children of the moon' are misfits in a country which has been pasted over with a layer of philistinism and materialism. Most of the Nebraskan characters are fitted relentlessly into this cultural analysis. Claude's aggressive, callous father, and his older brother Bayliss, censoriously hostile to anything other than commerce, are the obvious

inheritors of Wick Cutter's values. Claude's younger brother
Ralph, though slightly more engaging, is interested in nothing but machinery: the cellar of the Wheeler house is not,
like Ántonia's cellar, full of Bohemian preserves, but cast-off
bits of American junk:

> Mysterious objects stood about him in the grey twilight;
> electric batteries, old bicycles and typewriters, a machine for
> making cement fence-posts, a vulcanizer, a stereopticon with a
> broken lens. [OOO, p.20]

There is just a hint there that junk, once it starts ageing into
antiques, might be seductive (an American writer with more
entropic tendencies, like Nathaniel West or Thomas Pyn-
chon, would have loved that cellar) but, more often, junk is
just pitiful, like the debris of Claude's marital house: 'How
inherently mournful and ugly such objects were, when the
feeling that had made them precious no longer existed!'
[OOO, p.223] When Claude comes to the 'dump-heap' of the
French battlefields, he has already been living in a civilization (Cather suggests) which has not needed a war to turn
itself into rubbish. Claude, himself, feels like a run-down
machine.

Philistine commercial values are sanctified by the kind of
hypocritical, repressed domestic life that Jim Burden was
already resenting in My Ántonia. The Wheeler family life is
one of poisonous reticence: 'It wasn't American to explain
yourself; you didn't have to!' [OOO, p.44] Victor Morse
comes from the same kind of background.

> 'My God, it's death in life! What's left of men if you take all the
> fire out of them? They're afraid of everything. I know them:
> Sunday-school sneaks, prowling around those little towns after
> dark!' [OOO, p.308]

The loss of manhood which the sexually adventurous Victor
hints at there is spelt out in Claude's dreary, frustrating
marriage to Enid Royce. Vegetarian, pious, prohibitionist,
sexually frigid, Enid is a dismal embodiment of sanctimoni-
ous mid-Western nonconformism.

Above all, Cather resented the loss of commitment to the land in the children of the pioneers.

> With prosperity came a kind of callousness; everybody wanted to destroy the old things they used to take pride in. The orchards, which had been nursed and tended so carefully twenty years ago, were now left to die of neglect. It was less trouble to run into town in an automobile and buy fruit than it was to raise it. [OOO, pp.101–2]

In this pastoral turned to junk, property becomes a dubious good. Cather had no political anxieties about the history of the white pioneers. When the nineteenth-century settlers staked their claims and homesteaded, mastering and domesticating the terrain, they did it, she felt, with some kind of moral or spiritual relationship to the land. In her version of American history (a common one, that goes from Jefferson to Robert Frost) the force of the ideal gave them inalienable rights of property. But with the replacement of ideal by commercial values in the next generation, property rights became questionable. In that context it might be better to give up the land and the whole historical idea of inheritance. Claude (who has been trapped into working his father's land instead of studying history) is given these reflections after a conversation in the wheatfields with the hired man Dan, who explains his lukewarm harvesting techniques to him:

> 'It's all right for you to jump at that corn like you was a-beating carpets, Claude; it's your corn, or anyways it's your Paw's. Them fields will always lay betwixt you and trouble. But a hired man's got no property but his back, and he has to save it. I figure that I've only got about so many jumps left in me, and I ain't a-going to jump too hard at no man's corn.' [OOO, p.79]

When self-employed shepherds become hirelings, having to sell their labour in the market-place, it is always a sign that the golden age has passed away. No political solution is offered except renunciation. 'He often felt that he would rather go out into the world and earn his bread among strangers.' [OOO, p.80] The choice is a trap: either a spoilt pastoral domicile, or dispossessed orphan wanderings.

Cather was not alone in her bitterness about the crushing materialism of small-town life in the mid-West. It is found in other fictions of the time, such as Sinclair Lewis's *Main Street* (1920) and Sherwood Anderson's *Winesburg, Ohio* (1919). But Cather's satire on contemporary life was especially hostile because of her powerful feeling for what had gone before.[34] Claude's quest is, thus, also the novelist's: as *The Song of the Lark* acted out her struggle to fulfil her sense of a vocation, *One of Ours* acts out her search for a new mythology to replace the loss of the old.

The site of the new mythology is France, and Cather pours into the novel all the feelings about the country she had had since her student days of reading French literature (with Dorothy Canfield, the memory of whose friendship is a powerful influence on the book)[35] and her first sightings of Paris and Provence. Claude is not the kind of character who has a 'picture-making'[36] facility, so Cather restrains herself from long descriptions of the French country, character and architecture. But she does give Claude many of her own perceptions: the pleased recognition of the cottonwood trees in the French landscape, the delight in the 'energy and fire' [OOO, p.356] of the French language, the spiritual satisfaction in French Gothic cathedrals. After this book she would return repeatedly to France, always using the country as a focus for her feelings about the dignity of old values, and increasingly associating those feelings with Catholicism. Though Claude does not become a Catholic in France, in his pilgrimage there he finds what he needs: idealism to replace materialism, a living for a dead language, a carefully tended pastoral existing in the very centre of the destruction. Even the cherry tree which his father brutally hacked down in his childhood orchard metamorphoses into a cherry tree in a French garden, as though giving Claude back his spoilt youth.

Claude's new faith is expressed by David Gerhardt's dim, vaguely pagan hopes of immortality, and by the girl Claude meets in the carefully tended garden of the convent, outside a shelled Red Cross barrack. The convent setting pays a characteristic tribute to order and tradition preserved against heavy obstacles. Values can be made to last, even if objects cannot. '"This war has taught us all how little the made things matter,"' the girl says. '"Only the feeling matters."' [OOO, p.386] Claude responds with a hazy but consolatory sense that it is possible to transcend the 'dump-heap' of rubbish and destruction and win through to some other intangible world of value:

> Ruin and new birth; the shudder of ugly things in the past, the trembling image of beautiful ones on the horizon; finding and losing; that was life, he saw. [OOO, p.391]

The knight questing for redemption through renunciation in the waste land, and seeing beautiful visionary possibilities trembling on the horizon, derives all too manifestly from Wagner.[37] Like *The Song of the Lark, One of Ours* yokes literal Wagnerian narrative methods to a Wagnerian *leitmotif*.[38] Claude is meant to be like Parsifal, 'the blameless fool by pity enlightened' of Wagner's last opera, who is brought up as an innocent by his mother, Herzeleide ('Heart's Sorrow') and who, after discovering his identity and resisting the temptation of the seductive Kundry, at last after years of wandering heals the wound of the old King and inherits the Holy Grail. Cather had planned to call the last section 'The Blameless Fool by Pity Enlightened', but decided that this was too explicitly Wagnerian, and changed it to 'Bidding the Eagles of the West Fly On', from Vachel Lindsay's chauvinist poem to William Jennings Bryan,[39] thus fleetingly identifying Claude with a lost hero of the agrarian movement. But the mythological status of her hero is still explicit. The ship he goes to France on is named after the father of Aeneas, founder of the Italian empire. Claude's friendship with Gerhardt is sealed in a wood with trees curving like 'the pictures of old Grecian lyres'. They might be Achilles and Patroclus – or Orpheus and Eurydice.

The possibility of reading modern destinies in terms of ancient history is underlined, half comically, by an officer in Claude's battalion who has excavated, in Spain, the ruins of

'one of Julius Caesar's fortified camps', and can talk of
nothing but the Roman Emperor's campaigns: 'Everything
was in the foreground with him; centuries made no difference.' [OOO, p.314] When a soldier reads an item from the
Kansas City *Star* which says that a group of British Tommies
in Mesopotamia have come across what they think is the site
of the Garden of Eden, a religious Swedish boy, Oscar
Peterson, is outraged.

> 'That's a lie!'
> Dell looked up at him, annoyed by the interruption. 'How do
> you know it is?'
> 'Because; the Lord put four cherubims with swords to guard
> the Garden, and there ain't no man going to find it. It ain't
> intended they should. The Bible says so.'
> Hicks began to laugh. 'Why, that was about six thousand years
> ago, you cheese! Do you suppose your cherubims are still
> there?'
> 'Course they are. What's a thousand years to a cherubim?
> Nothin'!' [OOO, p.368]

The loss of Eden, we are meant to feel, is taking place now;
Claude's mother used to read to him from *Paradise Lost*.[40]
These scattered, hybrid references to myth, legend and
ancient history try to give this modern war, and this 'simple'
Nebraskan soldier, the dignified status of epic history. By
going back to the old world, Claude has become part of a
long line of heroic deeds: 'centuries made no difference'.

But, after all, Claude is not one of the cherubim guarding
Eden, or a mythical knight: the Wagnerian resonances seem
uncomfortably grandiloquent. He is a miserable, repressed
Nebraskan boy who gets killed in a horrible war.[41] For all its
mythologizing, intended to move and console, *One of Ours* is
a painful and unsatisfactory book. Faced on the one hand
with an unprecedentedly futile, large-scale slaughter, and on
the other with a civilization which seemed increasingly
resistant to restorative, sympathetic readings, Cather's characteristic attempt at consolatory myth-making fiction broke
down. We are left with a conscientious but not always
convincing attempt to dignify the war into historical epic

while 'telling it like it was' (but how many American soldiers, one wonders, called each other 'you cheese'?) and a hero so thwarted that the only solution for him is a violent early death.

One reading[42] of *One of Ours* suggests that it is only in war and killing that the frigid, mother-dominated Claude can find erotic satisfaction. Though I don't think Cather was writing about perverted blood-lust, certainly *One of Ours* gives off strong signals of sexual distress. Until he gets to France, Claude's mixed sexuality is only a source of confusion and pain.

As a boy he dislikes the 'shyness and weakness' of his face, [OOO, p.17] and his 'chump' name, 'another source of humiliation'. [OOO, p.17] His casebook identification with his sensitive mother and resentment of his bullying father are illustrated by the father's chopping down of the cherry tree to spite the mother and unman the son. Claude's physical self-mortifications, his social diffidence, his hysterical tempers giving way to passive fatalism ('He had come to believe that the things and people he most disliked were the ones that were to shape his destiny' [OOO, p.31]) are symptoms of the shaming sense that Cather herself had in her youth of being the wrong sex, or wrong for her sex. Enid's rejection of Claude on their honeymoon – a lethally quiet, banal scene of humiliation – compounds his violent feelings of inadequacy, and sends him back to the pre-sexual protection of his mother and Mahailey.

Growing out of this feminine, mothered, unhappy virgin, however, is a tall, muscular, red-headed pioneering soldier, protector of defenceless women and children, faithful companion, and brave warrior. Does war, then, 'make a man' of Claude, as it did of one of his models, Victor Chapman? Cather partly wants us to think so, but it is not as simple as that. She is careful to put her knight under the protection, not of a legendary male leader like Richard Coeur de Lion, but of a female hero, St Joan, whom he associates with his mother, and whose martyr-knight-saint status (which at once transcends and incorporates her sexuality)[43] is mirrored through the book by other female heroes: the Statue of Liberty, a German aviatrix shot down by Victor Morse, the girl in the convent whose brother has been killed, and a girl Claude hears about who falls in love with a German and kills herself, martyr to the conflict betwen love and patriotism. Susceptible to these women heroes, Claude's male heroism is feminized. His friendship-at-arms with Gerhardt is given all the tenderness that was lacking in his marriage. That this love is meant to transcend erotic homosexual feelings is suggested when Gerhardt and Claude and their men kill a decadent German officer who has white hands, gorgeous clothes, and a portrait round his neck of 'a young man, pale as snow, with blurred forget-me-not eyes'. [OOO, p.431] Claude (though not Gerhardt) is innocent of the German's nature: '"Probably a kid brother"', he says of the portrait. The strange scene marks a denial – even, perhaps, a fear – of explicit homosexuality. For androgynousness to be a source of strength it must be spiritualized. Cather makes Claude censor out the homoerotic possibilities in his love for Gerhardt, so that that relationship can be one of untroubled nobility.[44]

Censorship remains, though, strongly felt as an ingredient in the novel, giving it a muted, frustrated feeling to the end. Censoriousness – social, sexual, imaginative – is the main quality of American life: '"I thought this was a country where a man could speak his mind"', a German farmer on trial for disloyalty in Nebraska says bitterly. [OOO, p.241] There is censorship, to an extent, of the realities of war in the text. Claude's death is itself a form of censorship: his mother, the last guardian of his virginity (with Mahailey as faithful acolyte) rejoices that he has been kept pure to the last, 'safe, safe' from post-war disillusion. [OOO, p.459]

A very disturbing episode in *One of Ours* describes amnesia as a form of censorship. Claude has been following a pair of lovers – a boy with an injured neck and his distressed girlfriend – through the French streets. Later, he finds out that the boy is an American soldier whose neck injury has made him a psychopathic 'case'. He has censored out his

previous sexual and social identity in America and has been
reborn as a son of France. Claude envies him:

> 'The fellow has forgotten almost everything about his life
> before he came to France. The queer thing is, it's his recollec-
> tion of women that is most affected. He can remember his
> father, but not his mother; doesn't know if he has sisters or
> not. . . . His photographs and belongings were lost when he
> was hurt, all except a bunch of letters he had in his pocket.
> They are from a girl he's engaged to, and he declares he can't
> remember her at all; doesn't know what she looks like or
> anything about her, and can't remember getting engaged. . . .
> He was found on a farm out in the country here, where the
> sons had been killed and the people sort of adopted him. He'd
> quit his uniform and was wearing the clothes of one of the
> dead sons. . . . They call him "the lost American" here.'
>   . . .Claude . . . wished he could do something to help that
> boy; help him get away from the doctor who was writing a
> book about him, and the girl who wanted him to make the
> most of himself; get away and be lost altogether in what he had
> been lucky enough to find. [OOO, pp.337–8]

In all her novels up to now, the consolation for mortality has
been memory, and the value of the novelist has been as
memorializer. Now, in a broken world, the only consolation
is forgetting. The function of the novelist is thus put at risk,
and may become more difficult, alienated and obscured.

9

THE THING NOT NAMED

Whatever is felt upon the page without being specifically
named there – that, one might say, is created.
                                  'The Novel Démeublé', 1922

WE KNEW one world and knew what we felt about it, now
we find ourselves in quite another;[1] so Cather wrote to
Dorothy Canfield in 1922, just before *One of Ours* came out.
She was nearly fifty; for the rest of her long life, this theme of
the world's having broken apart in about 1922, leaving her a
stranger on the wrong side of the time divide, would settle
into a permanent grudge. Her nostalgic mid-1920s essays,
looking back on the New England dignities and graces of '148
Charles Street' and Sarah Orne Jewett, are full of sour
references to the 'tawdry' cheapness of the present, to the
'ugliness of the world', and to the 'new American' cut off
from 'the old moral harmonies'.

The early to mid-1920s – the period, paradoxically, of
three of her very best novels, *A Lost Lady* (1923), *The
Professor's House* (1925), and *My Mortal Enemy* (1926) – seem
to have been a time of personal discomfiture and depression,
not altogether accounted for by the facts.[2] From 1922 to
1925, she was ill a good deal, and moving from place to
place. In the summer of 1922, while the proofs of *One of Ours*
were coming in, she was suffering from mastoiditis, and had
her tonsils out. The operation proved difficult and exhaust-
ing, and she spent some time recuperating in a sanatorium in

Pennsylvania.[3] She also had several bad attacks of 'flu that year. After the sanatorium, she spent part of the summer writing *A Lost Lady* at Grand Manan, and took it with her to Breadloaf College in Vermont on a three-week teaching assignment (a rare occasion, not repeated, in spite of repeated requests from the course director). She spent that winter in Red Cloud with her parents; it was their fiftieth wedding anniversary. The following year she went to France for six months; at first staying with Isabelle and Jan in their new house in Ville d'Avray, near Paris. She had already made a long stay with them two years earlier when they were in Toronto (it was that first trip to Canada which had led to the discovery of Grand Manan). But, though we have no information except for Edith's memoir and a few inexplicit letters, it is clear that this 1923 visit was a tense and difficult one – even if not, as O'Brien surmises, 'disastrous'.[4] The Hambourgs had set up a study for her, but, Edith wrote, 'she felt . . . that she would never be able to do any work there',[5] and left for Paris and Aix.[6] All this time she was suffering from neuritis in her right arm and shoulder, for which she took mineral-bath treatments in Aix. O'Brien's conjectural claim that 'this was a physical sign of her creative paralysis', or, even, the 'punishment' she half expected for venturing into 'masculine territory' in *One of Ours*, seems over-interpretative.[7] But the arm-ache does sound like a psychosomatic complaint, whether a demonstration of pain to Isabelle, or a symptom of writer's anxiety. When she went back to New York in the autumn of 1923 and started to write *The Professor's House*, a sense of unease filled the novel, and spilled over into the writing of *My Mortal Enemy* early in 1925. It was not until her long journey to the Southwest and her stay in Santa Fé in the summer of 1925 – a visit that prepared the ground for *Death Comes for the Archbishop* – that this mood of anxiety seems to have lifted.

She had mixed feelings in these years, too, about her public reputation. The Pulitzer Prize and the fan letters for *One of Ours* were pleasing, of course, but she was distressed by its savage reviews. She was by now a famous American

writer, exposed, as she had not been before, to the extremes
of praise and blame that go with this position. There had
been a pleasure, she told Dorothy, in the 'unsuccess' of her
early books: it meant she could write as she chose, without
pressures. Now everyone was demanding something of her,
and trying to spoil her fun.[8] She wanted to confuse people,
not to give them what they expected from her; she wanted to
get away from her readers, like an old wild turkey flying off
on its own.[9] Her letters are ambivalent about her success.
She was busy enough to have a secretary; she resented the
huge piles of mail. She was famous enough to have her
portrait painted (by Leon Bakst, during her stay in Paris); she
disliked the gloomy results. She was increasingly in demand
for interviews, honorary degrees, and visiting lectures; she
was pleased at the honours, but hated the sacrifice of time
and privacy. (She would have loathed being interviewed on
television.) She was certainly not a recluse: she kept in touch
with her family and a large number of friends, entertained
with Edith (rather like Gertrude Stein with Alice Toklas) on
Friday afternoons at Bank Street, had a New York circle
centring on Blanche and Alfred Knopf and their musical
friends (Cather got to know Myra Hess very well, for
instance, through the Knopfs) and made contacts in her
Jaffrey and Grand Manan hideouts. But she maintained her
privacy, and was increasingly resentful of intrusions. Perhaps
the most telling indication of her need, in these years, for an
area of retreat, was her confirmation in the Episcopal Church
at Red Cloud in the winter of 1922.

The letter to Dorothy of 1922, with which I began this
chapter, instances Futurist painting, wide open art forms,
and the disappearance from the world of a conception of sin,
as reasons for her alienation. This disapproval of all things
modern, with its stifling suggestion that the 'new' equals the
'a-moral', is a hard thing for us, her present admirers – who
belong to the future she so hated the thought of – to deal
with. Yet her conservatism was a kind of pioneering: she
needed to blaze her own trail (like the wild turkey) and not
be co-opted under the 'isms' of the New. Her repudiation of

the modern world may have made her, personally, inflexible. But in her work it enabled her to make her own way. As a writer she was now at her most confident: her personal malaise seems, obscurely, to have nourished the work.

In her literary statements of the 1920s there is the same powerful sense of assurance as there is in the novels of the period. Cather was not a theorist of fiction[10] on the scale of James or Woolf or Lawrence, and once she started reserving her energies for writing novels, her views have to be gleaned from letters and interviews and a few important essays. But through these remarks a philosophy of writing emerges which illuminates the 'middle period' novels very clearly, and which puts her into a closer, more vital relationship with modernism than might have been expected. Indeed the anti-modernist polemic was something of a smoke-screen: she could see that (as Virginia Woolf put it in the twenties) new art forms were needed for the new conditions.[11]

There is a difference in tone, of course, between the critical outpourings of the 1890s, when Cather was eagerly working out her feelings about all the books, music, theatre and art that she could lay hands on, and the experienced, judicial statements of the 1920s. But her passion is still for authenticity of feeling and naturalness of effect, and she is, as ever, suspicious of analysis. She likes to give the impression that her writing is unconscious and spontaneous, and her replies to analytical enquiries are evasive. She can only write a story if she is possessed by it, she says in 1922, and if she analyses it, she kills it.[12] She never stops to think if a story is good or not, she just plays out the play and has fun – though perhaps not as much fun (she writes in a letter of 1925 from Santa Fé) as a pack trip over desert and mountain country.[13] There is something disingenuous in this no-nonsense position, firmly rooted though it is in the American tradition of the writer as outdoor philosopher. Like the wild turkey, Cather is asking to be let alone.

When she is writing more openly to closer friends, she reveals herself as much less of a primitive; this ostensibly natural writer in fact has a sophisticated strategy of elision and suggestion. Her admissions often come in the form of advice to her women friends – Dorothy Canfield, Elsie Sergeant, Zoë Akins, Viola Roseboro – who would send her their books, and to whom she would always reply with truthful and tough responses. These show her at her most sympathetic, generously passing on the example of Sarah Orne Jewett. Like Jewett's letters to her, Cather's letters to her friends express her own literary principles. Years before, in 1913, she had criticized Elsie for a novel written in letter form, because its heroine had to keep calling attention to herself. Since the character talked and wrote too well and too much, there was no chance to view her through an atmosphere, to see her distanced or idealized.[14] In 1922 she warned Dorothy against telling too much about a character; it blurred the effect. She believed in *withholding* character.[15] She was still arguing along the same lines in 1929. A story of Elsie's began with an introduction by a writer, and Cather preferred to forget that a book was 'written'. That was why she didn't like Proust's *La Prisonnière* (1923), in which 'Marcel' begins to turn into the author.[16] What she liked, she wrote in a long letter to Viola praising her novel of American provincial life, was vividness and vigour: the sound of a hammer striking an anvil.[17]

That masculine, functional image is echoed in an interview of 1925, where she says that the point of view must be built into a novel like 'an engineer's deciding on the strain of a bridge'.[18] So in her critical language, as in her fiction, there is a fertile crossing between sexual characteristics. She insists on force, workman-like efficacy; but in the same breath she speaks of the virtues of elusiveness and impressionism. Her essay 'On the Art of Fiction' of 1920 uses Millet's painting as an analogy for the kind of writing she admires. He is the 'good workman' who makes draft after draft of his peasant figures and at last condenses them all into one picture, 'The Sower', where 'the composition is so simple that it seems inevitable'. This is like the writer who eliminates detail after detail to 'preserve the spirit of the whole', 'so that all that one has suppressed and cut away is there to the reader's consciousness as much as if it were in type on the page'. Virile simplicity and female suggestiveness are here fused, to create a special and probably indefinable quality which is the mark of 'true' art. This is set, very emphatically, against cheap or commercial art, the inferior product of 'standardized values'.[19] So, Stephen Crane, described in an essay of 1925 as 'the first of the post-impressionists', knew how to select the details he needed. But his realist successors applied 'thoroughly good business methods' to art, '"doing" landscapes and interiors like house decorators, putting up the curtains and tacking down the carpets'.[20] It is the familiar attack on the twentieth-century American substitution of materialism for idealism, transferred to a manifesto for contemporary writing.

'Manifesto', a word so closely connected with the bold, revolutionary projects of modernism (Imagism, Vorticism, Futurism) usually suggests positive determinations and sharp shocks. Cather's manifesto, inasmuch as the word can be applied to her, speaks of negatives, omissions, and tradition. Certainly her two most famous essays, 'The Novel Démeublé' (1922) and 'Katherine Mansfield' (1925) do not look like modernist manifestos. The very use of 'démeublé' suggests an undemocratic, Francophile, Jamesian aestheticism, and sure enough the essay begins with a scathing distinction between great art and cheap mass-produced entertainment like Woolworth's Kewpie dolls. There is the same haughty denunciation of materialism as in the piece on Crane; the essay's attack on over-furnished realism instances a story about a banker which tells us too much about the Stock Exchange: 'Have such things any proper place in imaginative art?' She attacks D.H. Lawrence, in *The Rainbow*, for literalness, for reducing characters to 'mere animal pulp'. The models for great *suggestive* writing are Tolstoi and Hawthorne; the desire is for a return to the bare stage of the classic theatre or the bare room 'into which the glory of Pentecost descended'.[21]

All the same, her description in these essays of 'true' writing – which is also a description of her own writing – is not, as the tone might lead one to suppose, conventional or

conservative. She wants material details to work as 'the
emotional penumbra' of characters (so Tolstoi is preferred to
Balzac); she wants 'suggestion rather than enumeration';
she wants to feel a mood encircling the actual words on the
page, like the 'twilight melancholy' of Hawthorne's *The
Scarlet Letter*.[22] Katherine Mansfield is praised for ap-
proaching major subjects through trivial incidents, choosing
'a small reflector to throw a luminous streak out into the
shadowy realm of personal relationships'.[23] It is by those
means – concentration on the 'slight', evocation of atmosphere – that Mansfield creates her 'emotional penumbra',
'the hazy sort of thing that . . . lies behind and directs
interesting or beautiful design'. There can only be a 'hazy
sort of' language for this 'thing', as in the much-quoted
passage in 'The Novel Démeublé':

> Whatever is felt upon the page without being specifically
> named there – that, one might say, is created. It is the
> inexplicable presence of the thing not named, of the overtone
> divined by the ear but not heard by it, the verbal mood, the
> emotional aura of the fact or the thing or the deed, that gives
> high quality to the novel or the drama, as well as to poetry
> itself.[24]

'Penumbra', 'luminous', 'hazy', 'overtone', 'aura': these
figurative terms for suggestiveness and impressionism, set
against 'literalness' and 'materialism', are remarkably close
to Virginia Woolf's more well-known contemporaneous
arguments for the representation of life as a 'luminous halo,
a semi-transparent envelope',[25] as opposed to the photographic representation of 'every detail' in the Edwardian
fiction of Bennett, Wells, and Galsworthy. (Cather's equivalent American materialists would, I suppose, be Theodore
Dreiser and Sinclair Lewis.)

Cather's repudiation or ignoring of modernism (which
excepted, however, interested even if not sympathetic readings of Mansfield, Lawrence, Proust, Conrad and Mann) and
the apparent refusal in her fiction of experimentalism and
fragmentation, have led (male) authorities on the movement
to leave her out altogether.[26] O'Brien, leaning the other way,

too blithely calls 'The Novel Démeublé' the work of 'the modernist writer endorsing allusive, suggestive art and inviting the reader's participation in the creation of literary meaning'. This, given Cather's refusals and prejudices, takes some justifying. The connection is more subtly made in a fine essay by Phyllis Rose, which describes Cather's affinity with modernism as 'an urge to simplify and to suggest the eternal through the particular'.[27] And certainly her alliance to modernism is felt in the marked similarity of Cather's 'manifesto' and Virginia Woolf's, and the surprising affinities between Cather's preoccupations – the fractures with the past, the need for order, memory and its gaps, heroism, myth – and those of great modernist works such as *Ulysses, To the Lighthouse, The Waste Land,* and *A la Recherche du temps perdu.* The modernism of this reactionary writer is as much of a paradox as the craftiness underlying her apparent simplicity. In the writing of the 1920s – the essays, the two novellas of 'lost ladies', and above all in her great, complex novel *The Professor's House* – Cather places herself in the company of Proust, Lawrence, Eliot, and Virginia Woolf.

The essay on Katherine Mansfield begins with a shipboard encounter on a sea journey in 1920 (when Cather was coming back from her post-war stay in France). Cather talked to a crotchety, Jamesian New England bachelor who recalled a long-ago meeting, also on a ship, with Katherine Mansfield as a child. It is one of Cather's favourite strategies. As in *My Ántonia,* the 'real' encounter in the prefatory journey opens the way into a recollected journey, which takes us closer to the female figure we are trying to apprehend. As in the later essay, 'A Chance Meeting', where Cather tells of her lucky encounter in a hotel in Aix-les-Bains with Flaubert's niece, now an old lady, the way into a writer is through the narrative of someone who knew or met them: 'And did you once see Shelley plain?' Madame Grout, Flaubert's niece Caroline, has the same effect on Cather as Annie Fields and Sarah Orne Jewett once did (her recollections of them are published in the same volume as 'A Chance Meeting' and 'Katherine Mansfield'). These grand old ladies (like, also, the 'old beauty' of a late story) open the door onto 'a long, unbroken chain of splendid contacts'[28] with the 'great shades' of the past.

In all these approaches to the past, by way of the magnetic, beckoning figure of a woman, there is a tension between enchantment and disillusion, romance and reality. Annie Fields, Sarah Orne Jewett, Madame Grout and 'the old beauty' are revered at the expense of the 'ugly' present, which presses in on the enchantment of the special encounter. If the charmed, separate figure allows herself to be incorporated into the values of the present, a sense of sacrilege and disillusion is felt. So, the old man on the ship is 'bitterly' disappointed when he reads one of Mansfield's modern stories of sexual betrayal ('Je Ne Parle Pas Français'), finding it 'artificial, and unpleasantly hysterical, full of affectations'. He wants to remember her as the lively, charming, idiosyncratic child he met, and when he catches sight of her years later in a theatre, 'looking ill and unhappy', he wishes 'he had never seen or heard of her' again.[29] She is a 'lost lady' for him, as Marian Forrester is for Niel in the novel of that title.

But Cather's essay on Mansfield rescues her from that repudiating judgement by showing how the sources of her best writing came from the life of the very child who was thought to be 'lost'. Her pursuit of Mansfield's writing about children (involving a brilliant and heartfelt analysis of the tensions of family life)[30] is a pursuit of the 'true', the 'best' Katherine Mansfield. She is hard to analyse and pin down. Mansfield was herself a writer interested in elusiveness and suggestion. Cather quotes her comparing her methods of creating character to the early morning mists of childhood: 'I try to lift that mist from my people, and let them be seen and then to hide them again'.[31] In her portrait of Mansfield, Cather in turn tries to lift the veil from the quality that 'escapes analysis' in her work, the 'thing not named' on her pages:

> One goes back and runs through the pages to find the text which made one know certain things about Linda or Burnell or Beryl, and the text is not there – but something was there, all the same; is there, though no typesetter will ever set it.[32]

To pursue this unwritten 'overtone' needs more sympathy than the old bachelor on the ship could muster. Cather seems to be on the brink of saying that a woman reader is needed, who can reinscribe, through her own knowledge of domestic life and female experience, the 'white book' of gaps and silences and spaces under the printed text. But she doesn't quite say this, and the disillusioned male version of Mansfield remains in our minds, coexisting with the sympathetic female reading.

An intimate and crucial link is being made, at this central point of Cather's writing life, between her subjects and her methods. Her fictional pursuit, into past time, of her 'lost ladies', is bound up with her desire for a writing that can evoke the unspoken. Of course we want to know what 'the thing not named' is, just as we will want to know what the indefinable 'something' is that makes Marian Forrester and Myra Henshawe so special. What, for instance, are the 'certain things' about the characters in Mansfield's 'Prelude' which are 'there' under the text? Does Cather mean that Mansfield implies Linda's frigidity and Burnell's sexual clumsiness, without naming them? Any approach to Cather's work which sees her lesbianism as its central inspiration will want to read 'the presence of the thing not named' as sexual, 'the unnameable emotional source of her fiction' that she is forced to disguise or conceal.[33] Since Cather's theory of suggestion and omission is so closely linked in her mind with her portraits of magnetic, enchanting women, the extrapolation seems plausible. All the same, there is something reductive in trying to identify 'the thing not named' in Cather's texts as, specifically, a sexual secret, or a personal trauma (Isabelle's departure, the reaction to post-war America, her feelings about her mother, a 'midlife crisis'). Certainly, these elements in her life make themselves felt in the fiction. But 'the thing not named' *remains* unnameable – that is its point. It is not a buried bone to be dug up, but the 'luminous halo, the semi-transparent envelope' of atmosphere and feeling evoked by the writing.

10

LOST LADIES

A compelling, passionate, overmastering something for
which I had no name.

My Mortal Enemy, 1926

THE MOST complex and ambitious of the 'middle period'
novels is *The Professor's House.* On either side of it, chronologi-
cally, are two short novels, perfectly embodying Cather's
philosophy of suggestion, two 'portraits of a lady' which
mirror and counterpoint each other. Both *A Lost Lady* and *My
Mortal Enemy,* as their ominous titles imply (a long way from
the celebratory confidence of titles like *O Pioneers!, The Song of
the Lark* or *One of Ours*) involve a sense of betrayal felt by, and
about, the central figure. Though Marian Forrester and Myra
Henshawe are very unlike, they share certain dangerous
characteristics. They are both alluring, sexual, magnetic
women caught inside a marriage which began as a romance.
(These novels of the twenties are, uniquely, apart from
Sapphira and the Slave Girl, deeply intrigued by marriages.
Isabelle's new marriage, and the Cather parents' 50-year-old
one, may have been behind this.) There is a crucial change,
now, from the earlier pioneering novels. The focus has
shifted from the immigrants to the American 'aristocracy',
and from female heroism to femininity. These heroines are
'ladies', socially adept, self-conscious, sophisticated, decorative. They have no children, they are separated from their
family roots, they have no independent occupations, and

they define themselves in terms of their relation to men. They are confined and thwarted, not expansive and self-fulfilling. Their energies are poured, not into something impersonal and bigger than themselves – the shaping of the land, the making of an art – but into personal feelings and self-expression. They are much more elusive and less reliable than the pioneering women-heroes.

Cather's lifelong admiration of and attraction to rare, beautiful women – from stage actresses and singers to Isabelle McClung – is mixed in these portraits with her distrust and rejection of the image of the 'lady' – genteel, pleasing, feminine – in part associated with her mother. These women are not in a stable, conformist relation to the role of 'lady'. They are manipulative but susceptible; capable of cruelty, but also self-punishing. Their jewels – which in both novels brilliantly evoke their rare value and the dangerous possibility of cold artifice – are ambiguous symbols. The glittering images advertise a fixed value which their wearers resist and evade. Though Myra Henshawe is a much colder, fiercer, older and more embittered 'lady' than Marian Forrester, both subvert an idealized valuation of them by their admirers. So both portraits depend for their meanings on their vantage points, and here too there are interesting similarities.

Both 'portraits' were drawn 'from life'. An interview of 1925 described Marian Forrester as a 'beautiful ghost', the portrait of 'a woman I loved very much in my childhood'.[1] The woman was Lydia Garber, the glamorous Californian wife of the old pioneer Silas Garber, who, exactly like Captain Forrester in the novel, staked his claim to Red Cloud in the 1870s, named the town, built his fine house on the outskirts and settled there (when not entertaining in Lincoln and Colorado) with his young second wife Lydia, the adornment to his property. Silas Garber was governor of Nebraska, the most important local figure in Cather's childhood. He seemed to her the embodiment of the grand pioneer dream. As in the novel, Garber's dream and his fortunes collapsed when his bank failed in the 1890s depression. Lydia Garber stood by him in his decline and nursed him after he had an accident; but when he died she left Red Cloud for the West coast and remarried. She was an object of romance to Cather in her childhood, and went on interesting her: letters of the early 1900s refer to the charming Mrs Garber being much aged and saddened,[2] and to her seclusion after the governor's death.[3] But it was not till Cather heard the news of her death in the summer of 1921, when she was staying in Toronto with Isabelle, that she thought of writing about her. In a late letter to Irene Miner,[4] she describes how, having heard the news, she went and lay on the bed, on a hot day, and suddenly thought of the story as though she had read it somewhere. The source of Myra Henshawe in My Mortal Enemy is more obscure, but evidently as personal: Cather said in a letter of 1940 that she 'knew her very well'.[5] She had been dead for fifteen years when Cather wrote the story, but many of her friends and relatives recognized her.

The point of these identifications is not to try and ascertain the closeness of the novels to life.[6] But the sources of the novels do have a bearing on the way they are told. In both books Cather projects her younger feelings through an observer who can also incorporate a later sense of loss and disillusion. She was at pains, in her remarks about A Lost Lady,[7] to play Niel down: he was just a point of view, she said, a 'peephole' into that world, not a character. In fact he gave her some trouble: though the story came to her in a flash, she had difficulty finding the right approach. First she tried setting it in Colorado (without Niel, presumably) but had to take it back to the scene of her childhood impressions. For a time she tried to use a first person narrative, as in My Ántonia. But then, perhaps wanting Niel's memorializing to be less sympathetic than Jim Burden's, she went back to the third person. In My Mortal Enemy, though 'Nellie Birdseye' tells the story, her pared-down first-person narrative is full of gaps and omissions about her own life. So, in both novels, the observers are not entirely our familiars. Niel/Nellie resemble each other in other ways too. Both are younger than the women they admire, and are profoundly affected by them. For both, a chivalric desire to idealize is cruelly subverted by their objects of admiration. Nellie accepts this, Niel does not. And, with both observers, there is a sense that they are trying to pin down something which finally escapes them. Their 'bird's eye' 'peepholes' try to spy out and see round their 'lost ladies', but the ladies remain, in the end, uncaught.

A Lost Lady has three parallel plots, grafted imperceptibly together. One is the grave, slow story of Captain Forrester's decline: his (offstage) visionary pioneering youth; his substantial prime, enjoying the rewards of his 'dream'; his accident, his financial landslide (made worse by his honorable insistence on paying in full all the depositors who trusted him), his stroke, and his collapse into a 'wounded elephant', or fallen mountain. This plot is mournfully and weightily told, like an old tragic legend of a deposed king or a god in exile. Alongside it is the quite different story of Marian Forrester, agitated, impassioned, contradictory: her (offstage) romantic youth in California (a scandalous match broken off, a rescue from death in the mountains by the Captain); her (offstage) brilliance as a Colorado hostess, her unwilling retreat to Sweet Water, and the double life she lives there (as a devoted nurse to her dying husband and a gracious figure in the community, and as a restless discontented adulteress); finally, her (offstage) departure and lucrative re-marriage to a rich old English ranch-owner. Quite other narrative models – Madame Bovary, or Anna Karenina – are invoked and relinquished in this plot. The third story, which is also the frame for the first two, is Niel Herbert's: his distaste for his own home (unsuccessful widowed father, sloppy housekeeper, proud dead Southern mother who hated the West), his attachment to his old-fashioned uncle Judge Pommeroy and to the Judges' friends, the Forresters; his romantic admiration of Marian and his processes of disillusion with her; his sacrifice of a year's study at Harvard to help her nurse the Captain; his change in profession from law to architecture; and his embittered departure from the town. Niel has a touch of Henry James's attentive, deprived observers; but there is something in his story too of the painfully sweet infatuation and bitter enlightenment in Turgenev's *First Love*.

These three personal plots make part of Cather's now-familiar historical story. The values which 'dreamed' the settlement of the old West into being are on the way out, due to the inability of romantics like Captain Forrester to make a profit out of the land they laid claim to. The small town is losing its pioneering character, after the end of the railroad boom (like the relapsing into obscurity of Mark Twain's Mississippi river villages when the river changes its course and by-passes them). Sharp commercial interests, as in *One of Ours*, are rapidly profiting from the shake-up of the depression, and cutting up the 'princely carelessness of the pioneer' into 'profitable bits, as the match factory splinters the primeval forest'. [ALL, p.104] The change is here described in class terms, as a decline from an aristocracy ('princely carelessness', 'lost lady', 'great landholders') into a standardized democracy. Ivy Peters, the Bayliss Wheeler/ Wick Cutter type, and like them a grotesquely ana-thematized character with no redeeming features, has to stand for the new world. The symbol of the decline is his profitable draining of the Captain's marsh – which precedes his equally cynical take-over of the Captain's wife. But the book insists throughout, and not just in Niel's voice, on contrasts between the 'rare' and the 'common': between the distinguished dinner party given early on by the Captain and his wife, and the dinner she gives to the town boys at the end of the book; or between the feudal attitude of the German tailor's sons to the Forresters ('They realized . . . that such a fortunate and privileged class was an axiomatic fact in the social order') [ALL, p.15] and the revengeful pleasure of the townswomen when they at last get into the house (in a wonderful Hardyesque scene)[8] and find 'they have been fooled all these years'; it is full of undusted rooms and tarnished silver.

Much of the material I have been summarizing is buried,

peripheral, or withheld. Some of the crucial events (the
Captain's accident, the failure of the bank, Marian's departure and re-marriage) are reported, not seen. Some important pieces of behaviour (Niel's treatment of Marian after he
has discovered her affair with Frank Ellinger, for instance)
are passed over. And some vital ingredients in the story,
like the Forresters' first meeting, are held back for a long
time. Cather commented tellingly on her elisions for this
book.

> You can't get a delicate face laughing at you out of a minia-
> ture . . . and also have a lot of Western atmosphere and a
> dramatic bank failure. I like a book where you do one thing.[9]

The effect of A Lost Lady is of a loosely connected series of
pastoral scenes with the mobile, elusive figure of a woman at
their centre. The woman is approached by way of the
cottonwood grove 'that threw sheltering arms to right and
left' of Captain Forrester's house, the two creeks and the
Lombardy poplars which lead to it, and the marshland
anyone else would have drained for profit, but which the
Captain has kept because 'he liked the way the creek wound
through his pasture, with mint and joint-grass and twinkling
willows along its banks.' [ALL, p.6]

Like Marian's bright eyes and dangling earrings, these
landscape pictures seem to glitter and shimmer as we look at
them. The seductive words used for scenery are also the
words associated with her – twinkling, glittering, crystalline,
limpid, fragrant, tender. Sometimes she appears in these
glimmering landscapes as a white ghost out of the past. In the
book's first anecdote ('but we will begin this story with a
summer morning long ago') Niel and the town boys are
playing in the Forresters' 'silvery marsh', like Tom Sawyer
and his gang, or like the boys in 'The Enchanted Bluff', when
they see 'a white figure coming rapidly down through the
grove, under the flickering leaf shadows'. [ALL, p.13] After
she has materialized into the provider of hot cookies and
friendly chat, she metamorphoses back into a woodland
spirit, haunting this now 'long ago' vanished greenwood:

'they watched her white figure drifting along the edge of the grove'. She will return as a 'white figure'. When Niel comes back after his absence at college, he finds her lying in her hammock in the grove, feigning sleep and watching him under her white hat. He gathers up her 'suspended figure' 'like a bird caught in a net'. [ALL, p.109] When he goes out that summer into the 'sleeping garden' of the hot night, he finds her 'white figure' 'motionless in the clear moonlight' on the bridge over the creek, staring into the water and dreaming of escape. [ALL, p.121] But if she haunts Niel's memory as a vanished ghost, she is alive in the text. These white, ghostly, pastorals are counterpointed with sensual, coloured scenes, palpitating with energy: like the sharp winter day when Niel drives her home in her cutter, tucked in under her buffalo robes, while 'the late afternoon sun burned on the snow-crusted pastures' [ALL, p.33] and she looks up at him, characteristically, 'holding her muff up to break the wind'; or the freezing dusk after the blizzard when she insists on getting out of the house in her rubber boots, and looks at the 'clear arc of blue and rose colour' in the bare sky, taking deep breaths of cold, fear, and impatience.

The novel's beautiful artifice of a feeling landscape culminates in the two most sensual scenes, Marian's escapade with Frank, and Niel's discovery of her adultery. The winter sleigh ride with Frank is, crucially, not observed by Niel (instead, Marian, who never escapes observation, is spied on, mutely and uncritically, by one of the German boys) and so has none of his idealizing emotive language. There is no description. Instead, natural things are seen and felt only as they occur in the sexual adventure: the bits of snow flying up from the ponies' hooves, the deep ravine in the dark cedar woods the lovers disappear into, the blue still air in which the Blum boy can 'almost hear her breathe', the strokes of Frank's hatchet, felling the cedars, which send 'soft shivers' through her body. It is in contrast to the lush summer dawn of Niel's disillusionment, reeling with significant colour and fragrance:

> There was an almost religious purity about the fresh morning
> air, the tender sky, the grass and flowers with the sheen of
> early dew upon them. There was in all living things something
> limpid and joyous, – like the wet, morning call of the birds,
> flying up through the unstained atmosphere. Out of the saffron
> east a thin, yellow, wine-like sunshine began to gild the
> fragrant meadows and the glistening tops of the grove. [ALL,
> p.82]

As if this insistent 'new world' imagery weren't enough,
before we reach the fallen Eve we take a further lesson in the
danger of passion and the transience of beauty from a handy
thicket of wild roses:

> Where they had opened, their petals were stained with that
> burning rose-colour which is always gone by noon, – a dye
> made of sunlight and morning and moisture, so intense that it
> cannot possibly last . . . must fade, like ecstasy. [ALL, p.82]

Everything prepares us for Niel's rejection of his lady in
terms of this allegorical pastoral iconography – plucking a
moral flower from Shakespeare ('Lilies that fester smell far
worse than weeds'),[10] transforming his 'bouquet for a lovely
lady' into a 'prickly bunch of wild roses' to be thrown in the
mud.

But this pastoral writing is double, evoking, inside Niel's
judgemental aesthetics, the feeling of Marian's sexual pleasure, itself, like the dawn and the roses, 'tender', 'joyous',
'stained', 'ecstatic'. The very shape of that sentence describing the rosebuds, with its withholding and yielding punctua-
tion, imitates a sexual climax and aftermath. The climax of
the scene – the overheard sound of the two laughs behind
the closed shutters, the woman's 'impatient, indulgent,
teasing, eager', the man's 'fat and lazy – ending in something
like a yawn' – writes in the erotic joy that Niel would like to
censor out.

A Lost Lady, as its title forewarns us, is full of forewarnings,
portents of disaster, grave reminders of time. But danger is
also an ingredient in the sensuality and excitement that
makes the novel seem to tingle and shimmer so. In the first

story the Captain tells about Marian, she is running away from a bull, laughing and 'stubbornly clinging to the crimson parasol that had made all the trouble'. [ALL, p.7] Her pleasure in danger recurs when she tells the boys, laughing and shivering, about the 'water snakes and blood-suckers' in the Sweet Water creek. Immediately afterwards, Ivy Peters ('poison ivy') appears, and, in an extraordinarily sudden, horrifying little scene, catches a woodpecker ('Miss Female', he calls it) and slits its eyes, sending it into 'wild and desperate' circular paroxysms. The blinding of the bird, and Niel's fall from the tree trying (and failing) to reach it is the most startling of the novel's pastoral accidents and cruelties: the winter blizzard that imprisons the Forresters, the floods through which Marian struggles to contact Frank.

Marian is dangerous, but she is a victim of danger too: the blinded woodpecker is one of several metaphors – butterfly wings, a bird in a net, a dying rose – which tell us so. The taxidermy kit Ivy Peters gets out to use on the bird ('tiny sharp knife blades, hooks, curved needles, a saw, a blow-pipe, and scissors' [ALL, p.19]) anticipates Frank's cedar-chopping axe-strokes, which seem to penetrate her, and the shears which Niel snatches up to cut the telephone wire before her outburst at Frank can be overheard by anyone except himself. Whether the attitude to her is predatory or protective, this bird/nymph/flower-lady is likely to be crushed, cut, or pierced. Even the benign, immovable figure of the Captain, with his dark heavy furniture and his set phrases repeated like 'inscriptions cut in stone', seems to enclose and weigh her down. Leaning on his canes like 'an old tree walking' [ALL, p.114], as if he has metamorphosed into the willow tree that he planted long before, as his stake to the land; sitting stiller and stiller, with a view of his forced hyacinths and his sundial carved of stone from 'the Garden of the Gods' [ALL, p.108], he seems by his end to be Time himself, the warning figure in the pastoral idyll.

The minatory pastoral of *A Lost Lady* has two explicit sources, which suggest a great change in associations from *O Pioneers!* or *My Ántonia*. Niel, the pious custodian of past values, provides us with a classical analogue. Sitting in his uncle's office in the long Nebraskan winter, he reads Ovid's *Heroides* 'over and over', feeling as if he is 'living a double life, with all its guilty enjoyments'. To him, Ovid's heroines are:

> living creatures, caught in the very behaviour of living, – surprised behind their misleading severity of form and phrase. [ALL, p.79]

Obviously this is very like Jim's reading of Virgil in *My Ántonia*. But the Ovidian model introduces into the text quite different elements – seduction, danger, betrayal, sexuality – from Virgil's serene memorializing. Niel's 'peephole' onto the past ('double life', 'guilty enjoyments', 'eavesdropping') seems sexual and furtive, appropriate, perhaps, to Ovid's eavesdropping onto the letters of lamentation written by various legendary women to their unfaithful or absent lovers. Ovid listens in on those heroines just as Niel listens in on Marian's epistle-by-telephone to Frank: Ovid catches the 'living creatures' just as Niel, when he takes hold of Marian in her hammock like a bird in a net, would like to 'catch' her and take her out of the sad world. The first word Niel speaks in the book is 'Hush'; the most decisive action he takes is to cut off her voice. Ovid takes over the voices of his lost ladies and speaks for them: Niel too would like to silence and speak for his lost lady, to be, like Ovid, a ghost-writer. But she, as various and contradictory and 'breathing' as all of Ovid's ladies – Penelope and Dido, Ariadne and Helen of Troy, Medusa and Hermione – speaks for herself in spite of his custodial authoring of her story.

The other pastoral model is more innocent and artless than the Ovid, but just as much of a frame to fix the lady in. This model is old English, not classical, suitable for the feudal associations Cather wanted for the Forresters' 'princely' regime. From 'Alexander' to 'Lucy Gayheart', Cather loved meaningful names. When she calls the Captain 'Forrester', (and turns him into an old tree), the upstart parasite 'Ivy', the town 'Sweet Water', and the heroine 'Marian', addressed by her husband as 'Maidy', she is letting us know that the cottonwood grove is meant for the greenwood, a Nebraskan Sherwood Forest.[11] From the Elizabethans to the Romantics (and on into Tennyson's pseudo-Shakespearean late play 'The Forresters', where Maid Marian appears as a moon-goddess and makes Sherwood 'Eden o'er again'),[12] the greenwood was always linked to the lost golden age, with Robin Hood and Maid Marian as its rulers, sometimes in the guise of the King and Queen of the May. (Hawthorne, very much admired by Cather, transposed the 'Golden Age' to the 'fresh woods of the West' in his story 'The Maypole of Merry Mount', where the King and Queen of the May, re-enacting the Arcadian rites of 'ancient fable', transported from 'Merry England', have to leave the greenwood and become Puritan American citizens.) The Duke in the Forest of Arden is said to live 'like the old Robin Hood of England'; he and his 'merry men' 'fleet the time carelessly as they did in the golden world'.[13]

Keats, Cather's favourite English poet,[14] in a mood of regret for Elizabethan poetry, equated its generous splendours with the lost days of Robin Hood: 'All are gone away and past!' The forest where 'men knew not rents nor leases' (the greenwood is always pre-capitalist) has been spoilt and despoiled: if Robin and Marian came back they would find the trees cut down and turned into rotting ships, and honey unobtainable 'without hard money'.[15] This lament is precisely Niel's for the golden age of the West ('It was already gone, that age; nothing could ever bring it back'). [ALL, p.172] (By an intriguing coincidence, Keats put 'Robin Hood' in a letter to his friend Reynolds, of whose decision to give up poetry for law Keats disapproved. Niel's feeling that the 'law' of the greenwood – honour, fidelity – is lost, goes with his distaste for the law as a profession. And Ivy Peters is a lawyer, dealing with 'rents and leases'.) The Captain's fidelity to his working-class creditors ('railroad employés, mechanics, and day labourers') while all about him are cutting their losses, makes him a kind of Robin Hood, robbing himself to give to the poor.

But for the greenwood to be Arcadian, Maid Marian must

be chaste and faithful, the consort of the Lord of the Forest. When the dying Captain keeps calling out 'Maidy, Maidy', she must keep calling back 'Yes, Mr Forrester'. [ALL, p.143] These verbal transactions (eavesdropped on approvingly by our pastoral custodian) have no useful value: 'perhaps, he merely liked to call her name and to hear her answer.' Like all the Captain's fixed repetitions, they merely reiterate the system of values ('the Captain knew his wife and . . . knowing her, he . . . valued her') now closing down with the Captain's death and the despoiling of the greenwood.

It is usual to say of *A Lost Lady* that the 'valuation' of Marian Forrester is restrictive and oppressive; but two quite different readings of the novel emerge from that judgement. One is that Cather entirely endorses Niel's snobbish nostalgia and the Captain's traditionalism and judges Marian harshly for betraying these values. So, she goes 'quite to pieces' after the Captain's death, 'ballooning' off without any ballast. Mary Ellmann puts the case ironically:

> Mrs Forrester *seems* a delightful person as long as she is faithful to her grandfather surrogate, but she immediately rots under the attentions of men who are not only in good health and of her own age, but of a distinctly lower social status than the Captain.[16]

This view finds corroboration in Cather's much earlier attacks on the destructive, emotional self-indulgence of the Bovaryish Edna Pontellier. But a different reading rightly points out that, for all the novel's ominous warnings, Marian is not, after all, much like Emma Bovary, or Anna Karenina, or Edna Pontellier: her passions are *not* fatal to her, she gets away and survives, like the ballooning lady in 'Coming, Aphrodite!'. In this version, 'the reader departs from Niel' in his 'harsh judgement' on Marian,[17] and recognizes that 'there is more life' in the lost lady 'than Niel thinks – or wants to recognize'.[18]

The truth is that the novel has a 'double life', and that both readings coexist, like the two versions of Katherine Mansfield in the essay on her. This double life of the novel holds together, with breathtaking dexterity, what Marian is, and how she seems. At every point there is a delicate negotiation, in the tradition of literary pastoral, between artifice and nature. Niel's first sighting of Marian, a boyhood memory of seeing her arrive at church in her carriage, consists entirely of effects:

> On the back seat was a lady, alone, in a black silk dress all puffs and ruffles, and a black hat, carrying a parasol with a carved ivory handle. As the carriage stopped she lifted her dress to alight; out of a swirl of foamy white petticoats she thrust a black, shiny slipper. She stepped lightly to the ground and with a nod to the driver went into the church. The little boy followed her through the open door, saw her enter a pew and kneel. He was proud now that at the first moment he had recognized her as belonging to a different world from any he had ever known. [ALL, p.38]

And he turns from his memory to look up at 'the hollow, silver winter moon'. Like that protean goddess, Marian appears to Niel as an icon for worship, 'all puffs and ruffles', white petticoats, a shining slipper, an attitude of devotion and an air of distinction. She has no lines to speak. His attitude to this tableau is exactly like Cather's youthful feeling about the theatre as a sacred place, separate from common life. Niel's adult reactions to Marian – his refusal of her sexuality, his disappointment in her for not having 'immolated' herself on her husband's pyre, and his last hope that if 'the right man could save her' [ALL, p.169] she might still be able to 'play her old part' – are all aspects of his wish to preserve an illusory sanctuary for aesthetic admiration.

He *knows* it is an illusion, and likes to know it. That her 'elegantly wild' charm, 'seemingly so artless', is 'really the most finished artifice' [ALL, p.109], gives him pleasure. This puts Niel at odds with his American contemporaries, democratic realists. Ivy Peters, who, when he gets his chance, just treats Marian like any woman he can have, takes pleasure in seeing through and taking possession of the Forrester traditions: 'Good deal of bluff about all those old-timers'. [ALL, p.102] But Niel does not want to cross the footlights or see through the bluff. When Marian starts using rouge or telling the town boys she must go and powder her nose, he dislikes it partly out of sexual squeamishness, partly out of snobbery, but mainly because he doesn't want the artifice to collapse. And so she must only speak the lines of 'her old part':

> 'If you came to see me any oftener than you do, that would make talk. You are still younger than Ivy, – and better-looking! Did that never occur to you?'
> 'I wish you wouldn't talk to me like that,' he said coldly.
> [ALL, p.156]

Still, the words are spoken. Marian's erotic appetancy makes itself felt through, and in spite of, Niel's self-protecting frigidity. And though his first sighting of her as a boy may give her no lines, she speaks through all the words of movement – lifted, alight, swish, thrust, stepped lightly – that describe her in that passage. The scene frames her, but she won't stay put.

Marian's dynamism surges up against Niel's desire to frame her as a beautiful ghost. She is 'live' like an electrical current; she gives off a charge:[19]

> As she turned quickly away, the train of her velvet dress caught the leg of his broadcloth trousers and dragged with a friction that crackled and threw sparks. [ALL, p.56]

> She was using up all her vitality to electrify these heavy lads into speech. [ALL, p.164]

Niel may try to cut off her current, as he does the telephone wire, but it is endlessly renewable, a force for life, which she will have 'on any terms'. Whether we see her shedding her rings in a quick rush, or drinking too much, or wanting to dance, or setting off in a sleigh with her lover, lifting her chin and sniffing the air, or 'eating toast and making humorous comments', [ALL, p.71] she is never inert. And, like electricity, she is infinitely adaptable: her 'contradictions', her mockery, her imitations of other people, are part of her drive for life. She manipulates her own image in order to manipulate others. So to Cyrus Dalzell she is the enchanting Lady

Forrester, to Ivy Peters she is a woman with a bucket and rolled-up sleeves, good for a few laughs. In her domestic life with her husband, glimpsed in a few touchingly matter-of-fact scenes, she is another person again, patient and practical:

> While he was undressing he breathed heavily and sighed, as if he were very tired. He fumbled with his studs, then blew on his fingers and tried again. His wife came to his aid and quickly unbuttoned everything. He did not thank her in words, but submitted gratefully. [ALL, p.54]

But she can go straight from that room into an edgy, sexually charged scene in front of the parlour fire with Frank.

Marian's speech is tough and forthright, and deals in realistic values: '"Money is a very important thing"', she tells Niel. '"Realize that . . ."' [ALL, p.113] '"I'm quite sure she makes it worth his while"', she says of her cook's boyfriend. Her diatribe against Frank is ferociously cynical: '"You've got a safe thing at last, I should think; safe and pasty! How much stock did you get with it? A big block, I hope!"' [ALL, p.134] She herself has no time for an idealized pastoral: the Forrester home is just the place she means to leave as soon as she can sell it: '"I can't stand this house a moment longer"'; [ALL, p.72] '"That's what I'm struggling for, to get out of this hole."' [ALL, p.125] Her will to survive gives her more affinity with the earlier women-heroes, Alexandra, Ántonia and Thea, than might appear: they are all, as A.S. Byatt puts it, products of 'a great novelist's capacity to show human beings almost as forms of energy'.[20]

Still, Niel's vision of an Arcadian ghost lingers on. The deep delight of *A Lost Lady* is its 'magic of contradictions'. [ALL, p.75] It's this which enchants Niel, and the novel casts the same spell as the lady; as usual, Cather's book behaves like its central figure. For all its formality, elegance and traditionalism, it is as teasing and elusive as more ostentatiously modernist narratives. One of the lady's old-fashioned admirers, a friend of the Captain's, has a strange way of looking at Marian because of a cast in his eye:

When Mrs Forrester addressed him, or passed near him, his
good eye twinkled and followed her, – while the eye that
looked askance remained unchanged and committed itself to
nothing. [ALL, p.41]

Mr Ogden's double looking – half-sympathetic, half-cold;
half-admiring, half-dubious – makes an incongruous, unsettling mimicry of the double life of the novel, which while it
frames its lady in a beautiful portrait with its 'good eye', loses
her, as she escapes out of sight, off the edge of the page.

My Mortal Enemy, on the other side of *The Professor's House*, is
a fierce, chilling, severely economical novella. With 'Old Mrs
Harris', it is an outstanding example of the use Cather made
of this beautiful form, which she derived from James,
Turgenev and Maupassant. Yet it has always been a hard
book to 'place' in her work. She herself spoke of it as having
been difficult to write and likely to be overlooked or misunderstood.[21] (She was sure that if she had still been with
Houghton Mifflin and not Knopf, they would never have
had the confidence to publish it as it stood).[22] It has tended to
be described uneasily as 'curious' or 'unsatisfied'.[23] One
interesting comparison, with Edith Wharton's New England
novella *Ethan Frome* (1911) – a terrifying story of a
touching illicit passion turned through a 'mortal' accident
into lifelong incarceration, the object of desire become a
source of punishment – suggests its very disturbing quality.[24]
It is often overshadowed by the two great novels on either
side of it. Taken out of its chronological place and set against
A Lost Lady, its peculiar quality asserts itself.

Like *A Lost Lady*, *My Mortal Enemy* is a story that starts with
a story. But the change of tone is very striking.

Thirty or forty years ago, in one of those grey towns along the
Burlington railroad, which are so much greyer today than they
were then, there was a house well known from Omaha to
Denver for its hospitality and for a certain charm of atmosphere. [ALL, p.3]

I first met Myra Henshawe when I was fifteen, but I had
known about her ever since I could remember anything at all.

She and her runaway marriage were the theme of the most
interesting, indeed the only interesting, stories that were told
in our family, on holidays or at family dinners. [MME, p.9]

The expansive, regretful air of *A Lost Lady*, invoking the
elusive 'penumbra' that is to be its theme, gives way to a
much more pointed tone. Myra Henshawe's runaway marriage is as much a legend of the past as Captain Forrester's
house, but it is sharply and sardonically introduced. The
narrator begins with a name and a fact, not an approximate
time and an unnamed house. The casual phrasing of 'she and
her runaway marriage' is somewhat debunking of romantic
legend, and is itself dryly undercut by the lack of interest at
the family dinner-table: it wouldn't have to be a *very*
interesting story to be more interesting than most. The
feeling is of a realistic observer looking back on something
that used to impress her.

The two ladies come at us differently, too. Marian was first
seen rushing out of the house to greet her husband's friends
in dishabille. Myra Henshawe is first encountered by Nellie,
alone, in her aunt's house, before we find out about her past.

I could see, at the far end of the parlour, a short, plump woman
in a black velvet dress, seated upon the sofa and softly playing
on Cousin Bert's guitar. She must have heard me, and,
glancing up, she saw my reflection in a mirror; she put down
the guitar, rose, and stood to await my approach. She stood
markedly and pointedly still, with her shoulders back and her
head lifted, as if to remind me that it was my business to get to
her as quickly as possible and present myself as best I could.
[MME, p.11]

No 'spontaneous' dishabille here. The moment of introduction (for us as for Nellie) feels perilous. It is very like the first
meeting in James's *The Portrait of a Lady* between Isabel and
Mme Merle (also a friend of her aunt's), who is to be so
dangerous to her:

The drawing-room at Gardencourt was an apartment of great
distances, and, as the piano was placed at the end of it furthest
removed from the door at which she entered, her arrival was
not noticed by the person seated before the instrument. This

person . . . was a lady whom Isabel immediately saw to be a stranger to herself, though her back was presented to the door. This back – an ample and well-dressed one – Isabel viewed for some moments with surprise . . . she became aware that the lady at the piano played remarkably well. . . . When it was finished she felt a strong desire to thank the player, and rose from her seat to do so, while at the same time the stranger turned quickly round, as if but just aware of her presence.[25]

Like another Mme Merle, Myra stage-manages the scene; her artifice is meant to give a sense of power, Marian's to give a sense of freedom. Myra makes people come to her; she wants to attract, but she also wants to command. The difference between them is acutely felt, too, when they speak. Both want people to do things for them, but their means of persuasion are different. Marian 'whispers coaxingly':

'Remember, you are coming over tomorrow, at two? I am planning a drive, and I want you to amuse Constance for me.' [ALL, p.54]

Mrs Henshawe told him he had better leave us. 'Remember, you are to bring her to dine with us tomorrow night. There will be no one else.' [MME, p.21]

The change from one personality to another is marvellously subtle, from the insidiousness of Marian's present participles ('you are coming', 'I am planning'), her coaxing question mark, her sweet 'I want you to', to the peremptory grand command of Myra's 'you are to' and 'there will be'. Their laughter is similarly contrasted. When Niel is tired of everything, he longs for his 'long-lost-lady's' laugh:

Never elsewhere had he heard anything like her inviting, musical laugh, that was like the distant measures of dance music, heard through opening and shutting doors. [ALL, p.38]

Myra's laughter is equally well-remembered by Nellie, but it is 'terrible':

She had an angry laugh . . . that I still shiver to remember. Any stupidity made Myra laugh – I was destined to hear that one very often! [MME, p.17]

A Lost Lady is a tender novel, *My Mortal Enemy* is cold and fierce; one ends with consolatory words spoken out of 'a warm wave of feeling', the other with a dying curse. And the context for these two heroines is different. There is no settled home in *My Mortal Enemy*, and, until the western seashore that consoles Myra at her death, no landscape, only city scenes and rooms in cities. It is Cather's 'Waste Land'. Like Eliot's poem it is highly cultured, poisoned with regret, and broken into pieces. And Myra, like Eliot's narrative voice, is sexually disenchanted, longing for a healing grace in the wilderness, and shoring fragments of language, tradition and ritual against her ruin.

My Mortal Enemy is as dramatic as *The Waste Land*. Of all Cather's novels it is the one which most concentratedly shows the legacy of her theatrical apprenticeship. It is not just that there are scenes at the theatre or with performers, though these are important. In that sense *My Mortal Enemy* is no more theatrical than *The Song of the Lark* or *Lucy Gayheart*, with their emphasis on the craft of performance, or *My Ántonia* and *The Professor's House*, with their 'set piece' visits to *Camille* and *Mignon*. But in its effects and its construction – a prologue and two acts – it follows what Henry James characteristically called (when he too was applying what he had learned from the stage to his novels) 'the divine principle of the Scenario'.[26] Long before Nellie meets Myra, her Aunt Lydia has given her the big scenes from Myra's play. Myra's spoilt childhood as the adopted daughter of her wealthy, 'picturesque' Irish-Catholic great-uncle John Driscoll; her quarrel with him over the penniless, handsome Oswald Henshawe (son of German and Ulster Protestants, and so anathema to the old man); John Driscoll's hard bargain – her love, or his money – reached their climax with Myra's proud exit, walking down the drive from his house and fortune 'with her head held high' to an audience of admiring conspirators: a performance which was 'probably the most exciting night' of Aunt Lydia's life. This offstage romance, and Nellie's own dramatic associations with the Driscolls – the glamorous rituals of John Driscoll's Catholic funeral, the spellbound 'chanting and devotions and disciplines' of the nuns who have taken over the house that might have been Myra's – have been the only scenic elements in her otherwise bleak Protestant childhood in 'Parthia', southern Illinois.

But this is not to be a simple melodrama in which Myra's 'Parthian' shot – the world well lost for love – will suddenly be revealed as a catastrophe, and Nellie's illusions go crashing to the ground. Certainly the story has the tragic shape of fortunes reversed, and as befits tragedy, hubris goes before a fall, the young lovers become each other's punishment, and the old man's parting curse ('"better to be a stray dog in this world than a man without money"' [MME, p.22]) comes home with a vengeance. But the tensions are built in from the start:

> 'But they've been happy, anyhow?' I sometimes asked [Aunt Lydia].
> 'Happy? Oh, yes! As happy as most people.'
> That answer was disheartening; the very point of their story was that they should be much happier than other people.
> [MME, pp.24–5]

By the time Nellie, already wary, first meets 'the real Myra Henshawe', she is 'twenty-five years older than I had always imagined her'. [MME, p.27] A dry voice of experience undermines whatever idealization there may once have been. Myra is still holding her head up high, but she is doing this 'partly, I think, because she was beginning to have a double chin and was sensitive about it.' [MME, p.12] Presumably Nellie 'thinks' this at the time of telling her story, not at the time of meeting. But her irony seeps back into the past.

Myra's first act is to embarrass the awkward, clever fifteen-year-old girl, her next to laugh at her husband. She shames Nellie, who is too shy to look any higher than Myra's amethyst necklace, by offering to take it off if it 'annoys' her. She mocks Oswald, who has lost one of his expensive new shirts, by telling him she has given them all away to the janitor's son, because '"You know I can't bear you in ill-fitting things"'. [MME, p.16] He responds with a look of 'amusement, incredulity and bitterness'. The whole history of their relations is latent in the brief exchange. Like Nellie, the reader feels 'fascinated, but very ill at ease'. With few details, Cather establishes in her prologue the portrait of a woman who creates 'scenes', who is likely to be difficult, whose charm and 'zest' are risky and unreliable, who is both choosy and reckless over material possessions, and who demands a great deal of her admirers. People keep their eye on her out of interest, but also out of fear.

The prologue sets the scene for a first act which brilliantly, and with the utmost economy, pursues the tension between 'fascination' and 'unease'. The set for Act I, 'Old' New York at Christmas time, is civilized and impersonal. Nellie's arrival, by way of Jersey City Station, the ferry-boat ride and the crosstown cab to the Fifth Avenue Hotel at Madison Square, gives us the double satisfactions of new excitement (Nellie strains her eyes for a first sight of the city, as Cather once did) and nostalgic recall. To Nellie, New York is an indoor stage set, with its violet lighting, its 'open-air drawing-room' feeling [MME, p.34], its tamed winter ('like a polar bear led on a leash by a beautiful lady'), and its picturesque walk-on cast – an old man selling violets, an Irish boy with a penny whistle, messengers carrying potted plants and wreaths. Indoors from this indoor-outdoors, the Henshawe's apartment is sketched in with theatrical 'touches': long, heavy velvet curtains the colour of 'ripe purple fruit', a dinner service with 'thick grey plates' and a 'soup tureen painted with birds and big, bright flowers'. [MME, p.37] Oswald is disclosed in this set, propped up against the fireplace drinking a whisky and soda and waiting for the rest of the cast to make their entrances. All the New York settings – the restaurants, the study of a dying poetess whom Myra visits, the theatres themselves – are as if framed by a proscenium arch. At one point, even, Nellie and her aunt look up and see the Henshawes 'standing together in one of their deep front windows, framed by the plum-coloured curtains'. [MME, p.45] Each scene has its crucial prop – a jewel, a key – and each actor has a striking, stagy look: Oswald's 'sorrowful . . . strange, half-moon eyes', [MME, p.47] Myra's dangerous curl to her mouth 'like a little snake'. [MME, p.67] Vividly contrasted tableaux of secrets, asides, conspiracies, subterfuges, and confrontations are played, often actually at the theatre, with Myra always centre-stage, and almost always in charge. These scenes do not last long, but they show off Myra in poses that display to Nellie her generosity, extravagance, love of luxury, talent for friendship, jealousy, superstitions, greed, passion, cruelty, and appetite for control. She advises a young actor on his love affair, warning him against giving unlucky opals; she insists on sending the most expensive holly tree in the shop to her friend, the great Polish actress Helena Modjeska. In a box at the opera, she baits Oswald about his topaz cuff-buttons, a present from a young girl which he has tried to pass off as a gift from the ever-conspiratorial Aunt Lydia. Nellie sees Myra, in turn, scornful of her husband's business friends, consumed with envy of a smart acquaintance in a carriage, magically charming to the dying poetess, and bitterly unforgiving of a treacherous friend seen at a matinée: 'The scene on the stage was obliterated for her; the drama was in her mind'. [MME, p.56]

She is the playwright and star of her own life, with Nellie as the silent, attentive audience/transcriber of her scenes and speeches, and of the histrionic responses she evokes: 'He dropped his hand quickly and frowned so darkly that I thought he would have liked to put the topazes under his heel and grind them up.' [MME, p.48] For Nellie, Myra's talk is, like the language of the stage, 'a highly flavoured special language'. As she turns to each of the supporting characters, her addresses and invocations give them for their moment the stature of heroes and heroines:

> When she liked people she always called them by name a great many times in talking to them, and she enunciated the name, no matter how commonplace, in a penetrating way, without hurrying over it or slurring it; and this, accompanied by her singularly direct glance, had a curious effect. When she

addressed Aunt Lydia, for instance, she seemed to be speaking
to a person deeper down than the blurred, taken-for-granted
image of my aunt that I saw every day, and for a moment my
aunt became more individual, less matter-of-fact to me. [MME,
p.55]

The climax of these dramas is the Henshawes' New Year's
Eve party for their thespian friends ('Most of them are dead
now') which ends with a moonlit tableau of the queenly,
exiled Modjeska, sitting in her long cloak by the window, the
curtains drawn back, 'the moonlight falling across her
knees', listening to her Polish friend singing the aria 'Casta
Diva' from Bellini's *Norma*. Oswald, ever in the stoic supporting role, stands 'like a statue' behind her chair. Myra
crouches beside it, 'her head in both hands, while the song
grew and blossomed like a great emotion'. [MME, p.60] It
would be more usual for a great emotion to blossom like a
song, but in this fiction of expressionist stagings, the 'compelling, passionate, overmastering something' which Nellie
recognizes as the source of Myra's power cannot be defined,
it can only be acted out. The dramatic correlative Cather uses
here for Myra's power is so strong that everything risks getting
out of control. Norma, the Druid high priestess who has
betrayed her vows for love and who is in turn betrayed, who
prays to the chaste moon in the sacred grove for peace, but
who is in thrall to the bellicose power of the Roman empire,
makes an opulent tragic symbol for Myra (with marked
resemblances to Flaubert's luscious, violent *Salammbô*, often
an inspiration for Cather).[27] But the specific parallels are less
important than the powerful atmosphere of beauty and
sadness transferred (by a bold stroke) from the real Modjeska
and the legendary Norma to Myra.

All this passionate grandeur is immediately subverted (as
in *My Ántonia* where the vision of the plough is followed by
the story of Wick Cutter) by a spiteful quarrel between Myra
and Oswald over a key: the key, by implication, to their
sexual life. Their banal exchange, nervously eavesdropped
on by Nellie (How dare you – the hell you did – I might have
known it – well, you needn't) is cheap drama after high art,

the underside of Myra's 'passionate, overmastering something'. After a final encounter with a scornful Myra on the train leaving New York, Aunt Lydia declares she is sick of her old friend's 'dramatics'.

And the line between 'dramatics' and 'drama' is a thin one: Myra is always on the edge of being just an uninterestingly self-centred, trivial, difficult woman. Why should Nellie (or we) be drawn to her? Coldly described, Myra's actions in Act 1 (matchmaking, paying court to Modjeska, baiting Oswald) do not sound worth much attention; they certainly don't compare in scope and grandeur with carving a farm out of hard land or making a career as a great singer. But Myra's sense of herself as a heroine turns her into one. And in Act II her staginess becomes a form of stoicism, and so not as inferior to Alexandra's strength or Thea's energy as it might seem at first. Struck down by real misfortunes, poverty and illness, she plays a deposed monarch, a fallen Caesar, a medieval saint. That nothing is real for her, not even her own death, unless it is dramatized, is very disturbing; but the show she puts on is a gripping one.

Act II begins, as with a stage direction, 'ten years after'; the scene has changed from old New York to a 'sprawling' new West Coast town 'in the throes of rapid development'. All the characters (like so many Americans in the 'throes' of the 1890s) have fallen on hard times: Nellie's family is impoverished and squabbling over their few heirlooms, Nellie is teaching and living in obscure boarding-houses; the Henshawes are rumoured to have failed financially and to have moved west after Myra, as ever too proud for her own good, refused to let Oswald take an inferior position in his old company. By extraordinary coincidence, Nellie comes across them in her seedy apartment-house: Myra is a sick old woman, bitterly resentful of her changed conditions; Oswald has 'a humble position, poorly paid, with the city traction company', and is wearing himself out looking after her.

The rediscovery of the Henshawes is very beautifully done, in a subdued crescendo, from Nellie's hearing, through the thin walls, the man next door moving about quietly, trying

Willa Cather's father Charles, as a
young man
Virginia, Willa Cather's mother

Willa Cather as a child

Dug-out home, Nebraska, 1880s
The attic bedroom in the house at
Red Cloud

Annie Pavelka and family
With Louise Pound, c.1892
At the *Nebraska State Journal*
office, 1890s

Ethelbert Nevin

Riding a handcar along the railroad, Wyoming, 1905

With Isabelle (left), camping in Wyoming, 1905 Sarah Orne Jewett (right) and Annie Fields at 148 Charles Street, Boston

As managing editor of *McClure's*,
1910 or '12
Sam McClure
Olive Fremstad as Salome
Edith Lewis

At Mesa Verde, 1915
Richard Wetherill and his brother in
the Spruce Tree House Ruins, Mesa
Verde, *c*.1869

Cliff Palace, Mesa Verde

Bishop Lamy, Cather's
'Archbishop'

With Isabelle, Ville D'Avray, near Paris, 1923

At Grand Manan, 1931

Charles, Willa,
Virginia and Douglass
Cather, *c*.1925
Quebec in 1699
With Yehudi
Menuhin, Pasadena,
1931

to keep the details of his 'housekeeping' to himself, humming a Schubert song as he switches on the 'gasolene' and cleans his neckties, to her encounter with a much-aged Oswald carrying a supper tray on the stairs, and her climactic reunion with Myra. Oswald prepares for the disclosure with an intensely histrionic speech:

> 'She is ill, my poor Myra. Oh, very ill! But we must not speak of that, nor seem to know it. What it will mean to her to see you again!' [MME, p.74]

And after this build-up she is revealed on her stage, the lighting carefully set ('the electric bulbs in the room were shrouded and muffled with coloured scarfs'), dressed to impress in a bright Chinese dressing-gown, surrounded by props from the past – including, of course, the old velvet curtains – and ready on cue to flash out into an aria of high theatricality about premonitions, fortunes, and her 'temporary eclipse'. 'She looked strong and broken, generous and tyrannical, a witty and rather wicked old woman, who hated life for its defeats, and loved it for its absurdities'. [MME, p.80]

Act II is a series of long soliloquies from this daunting figure (with Nellie upgraded – like a grown-up daughter – from silent watcher to confidante), bitter disquisitions on poverty, age and sickness, culminating in statements of horrifying emotional recklessness: '"We've destroyed each other. . . . It was money I needed. We've thrown our lives away."' [MME, p.91] '"A man and woman draw apart from that long embrace, and see what they have done to each other."' [MME, p.105] To make her effects, she uses all the cultural remnants she can clutch to her. 'Her old poets', like her velvet curtains, are in both senses her 'props'. Nellie hears her murmuring speeches of Shakespeare's deposed or failed kings 'at the very bottom of her rich Irish voice'. [MME, p.99] When she takes her for a drive to a bare headland overlooking the sea, Myra at once appropriates it for her own tragic requirements:

> 'Why, Nellie!' she exclaimed, 'it's like the cliff in *Lear*, Gloucester's cliff, so it is!' [MME, p.87]

After a particularly savage outburst against Oswald, she calls Nellie in and asks her to read her Heine's poem 'about how he found in his eye a tear that was not of the present, an old one, left over from the kind he used to weep'. [MME, p.95] The poet addresses his 'anachronistic tear' in a brief drama of regret which re-enacts the losses of his past. 'Ah, my love itself dissolved like an empty breath! Old, lonely tear, you too must now dissolve!'[28] Nellie, drily narrating, sees Myra turning the poet's drama into her own, reacting and re-enacting all in one.

> My friend lay still, with her eyes closed, and occasionally one of those anachronistic tears gathered on her lashes and fell on the pillow, making a little grey spot. Often she took the verse out of my mouth and finished it herself. [MME, p.96]

The moment sums up the book's emotions: the cold eye registering, and yet moved by, the 'dramatics'; the painful luxury of 'romantic' self-pity; the grand futility of the whole performance. It sums up, too, Myra's combination of helplessness ('My friend lay still') and her persistent desire for control ('Often she took the verse out of my mouth'). Though physically dependent on Oswald and Nellie, she continues to fix, manage and conspire, locking Oswald out or turning Nellie away when the mood takes her, secretly hoarding money to pay for masses for Modjeska, summoning her priest, insisting on candlelight to die by, and finally staging her own death on 'Gloucester's cliff'. 'She can do anything she wills', Oswald says. Like Sapphira and 'the old beauty' in stories to come, this figure of the tyrannical, crippled, manipulative older woman makes an alarming matriarchal contrast to the energetic women-heroes of the earlier books.

Cather projects herself, as always, indirectly. In part, she is the observer in hiding. 'Here is Nellie Birdseye, rapping at the gates.' [MME, p.63] 'Her room is thirty-two; rap gently . . .' [MME, p.74] Nellie, rapping gently, is let into Myra's room, but what she finds there is dangerous to herself. This reads like bitter personal experience. Nellie's alienation from her home town, her youthful stoicism, her grim ambition ('"I know what I want to do, and I'll work my way out yet, if only you'll give me time"' [MME, p.79]) must remind Cather of herself. In Nellie's desire to prove herself to Myra, and in the hard lessons she learns from her, there may be a memory of Cather's relationship with her mother. But Cather is also the bitter old woman, inveighing against ugly new buildings and ugly new poetry. The memory of Modjeska (one of Cather's own early heroines) listening to 'Casta Diva', lingers on, for Myra as for Cather, as an emblem of all that was good in the past.[29] And all that is bad in the present is summed up by another kind of enforced listening, to the people upstairs. The violent neurotic language used for their tramping and shrieking — they are 'animals', 'cattle', the woman is an 'adder' — gives away a personal obsession. Cather was, indeed, extremely touchy about this: Godfrey St Peter in *The Professor's House* also makes sure that there is no one 'tramping over him'. [PH, p.26] The tyranny of uncontrollable, random city noise is made to stand for all the messiness of twentieth-century life.

But Myra's tragic embitterment is not simply a projection of Cather's nostalgia. *My Mortal Enemy* is stranger and more interesting than that. In fact it is Oswald who most cherishes the past, and urges her to remember 'the long time we were happy'. [MME, p.91] Her response to this is brutal:

'He's a sentimentalist, always was; he can look back on the best of those days when we were young and loved each other, and make himself believe it was all like that. It wasn't. I was always a grasping, worldly woman; I was never satisfied.' [MME, p.104]

Cather said of Myra that she was the sort of woman who could never have been at peace. And it is a powerful picture of congenital discontent. Like the pelican tearing at her own breast, Myra Henshawe devours her own memories and refuses the past as consolation: 'We were never really happy.' The novella is as brutal as its heroine about the impossibility of contentment for the kind of woman who

feeds continually off her emotions. Myra tells Nellie that if
she had had money she might have been consoled for the
loss of 'the power to love'; or, if she had had children her
feelings might have gone through 'natural changes'. But we
are made to feel that nothing would ever have been enough.
The role of the 'lady' is a self-destructive performance, since
it is entirely based on the personal. Cather is reiterating her
judgement of heroines like Edna Pontellier, who 'really
expect the power of love to fill and gratify every need of
life'.[30]

If a life lived for the personal self-destructs, then the object
of personal feeling is likely to be destroyed too. '"Perhaps I
can't forgive him for the harm I did him"', Myra says
penetratingly of her ferocious treatment of the ever-chivalric
Oswald. The most desolating aspect of *My Mortal Enemy* is
Myra's punishment of the person she loved. With a very few,
telling details, Oswald's aptitude for victimization is made
apparent, enough to make us understand his part in this
terrible, indissoluble marriage. Those strange, listless, half-
moon eyes belong to someone who is living a life that is
wrong for him: 'He possessed some kind of courage and force
which slept.' [MME, p.65] He is sexually susceptible (young
girls, such as the giver of the topazes, or the Cather-like
bright, awkward journalist in the boarding-house, are
always falling for him) and so makes Myra violently jealous.
But he is also sentimental and uxorious, and so allows her to
tyrannize over him. Though their sexual life is evidently over
by Act II, he refuses to think of her as an old woman:

> 'These last years it's seemed to me that I was nursing the
> mother of the girl who ran away with me. Nothing ever took
> that girl from me. She was a wild, lovely creature, Nellie. I wish
> you could have seen her then.' [MME, p.121]

Touching though this romantic fantasy is, it is also dangerous; he refuses to accept her old age, and thereby makes it
harder for her to resign herself. There is nothing else in
Cather quite like this intense picture of mutual damage.

As she gets iller, Myra is appeased by religion. The solution comes as no surprise at this point in Cather's life and work. From the first, she had been writing about visionaries, idealists, characters motivated by spiritual rather than material ends. The argument of *The Professor's House* is about renunciation: both Godfrey St Peter and Tom Outland see appetancy as self-destruction, and losing as finding. But, until now, orthodox religion had not figured largely. Official believers – all minor characters – had been fanatics or hypocrites or mystic simpletons. Myra's deathbed reversion to her great-uncle's Catholicism gives orthodox religion its first central place in Cather's work. The ground is being prepared for the historical novels of heroic faith; and Cather's increasing preoccupation with resignation is being displayed.

But the religious feeling of *My Mortal Enemy* is disconcerting. For all her speeches about absolution and renunciation, Myra goes on clutching and wanting till the last. There is something extravagant and manipulative in her last-minute Catholicism, as in all her gestures. It is another scene in her 'dramatics'. She is as histrionic over her 'holy rites' – hoarding the secret money for Modjeska's masses, or staging her death, ebony crucifix in hand, overlooking the sea – as she once was over her jewels and matchmaking.

This sensual attraction to ritual (which expresses a very strong feeling of Cather's) is characterized as primitive and reactionary. Myra's Catholicism is like her old great-uncle's: her death is as scenic as his funeral was. And since her memories of him are all of an indomitable ruthlessness, her reversion to his religion recalls all these qualities. She can feel old John Driscoll's 'savagery' strengthening in her. (So her Irishness is rather tiresomely accentuated towards the end.) This belief is alarmingly phrased. '"The nature our strain of blood carries is inside there, waiting, like our skeleton."' [MME, p.99] Our destiny, Myra tells Nellie, is to revert to type. So the return to religion opposes the possibility of individual choice. It operates as a form of determinism, and as an expression of hostility to the contingencies and 'free-thinking' of the modern world. Myra's priest even suggests that she is like a saint of the early Church: '"She's not all modern in her make-up, is she?"' [MME, p.111]

The troll-like power of old beliefs emerges, distorted, in spoilt, civilized Myra, as superstition and vindictiveness. Her religion may be her only comfort against dying, but she also uses it as a means of revenge. The iller and more religious she gets, the more she turns it against the object of her old 'idolatries'. '"It is one of her delusions that I separated her from the Church"' [MME, p.116] Oswald says pitifully. By the end there is nothing to choose between her prayer and her curse: her terrible words to Oswald ('"Why must I die like this, alone with my mortal enemy?"') linger on in Nellie's mind 'like a confession of the soul'. [MME, p.122]

Cather resisted interpretations of the phrase which assumed that Myra was her own worst enemy. Oswald, she insisted, was the 'mortal enemy'.[31] But the misreading of the title, if it is one, is understandable, since Myra turns against herself quite as much as she turns against her lover. And readers of this discomforting novella have continued to reinterpret the cryptic title. Oswald is Myra's 'mortal' enemy, says Rosowski, because he refuses to accept the realities of her old age, and is thus 'the enemy of her mortality'.[32] Her 'mortal enemy' is not Oswald, says Judith Fryer, but time itself.[33] Myra could even be thought of as Nellie's 'mortal enemy'. It is Nellie who speaks, and might therefore (like Jim Burden) have given the narrative its title. And, like the unlucky amethysts which Myra left her, and which cast a 'chill' over her whenever she wears them, Myra's words have been a blight on Nellie's whole life:

> Sometimes, when I have watched the bright beginning of a love story, when I have seen a common feeling exalted into beauty by imagination, generosity, and the flaming courage of youth, I have heard again that strange complaint breathed by a dying woman into the stillness of night, like a confession of the soul: 'Why must I die like this, alone with my mortal enemy!' [MME, p.122]

If Myra has been destined to inherit her ancestral beliefs,

then Nellie seems doomed to have taken on this quasi-maternal legacy of cynicism and despair. It is a chilling conclusion.

Cather's titles are often possessive; but they make us think twice about possessing. *My Ántonia* and *One of Ours* sound reassuring enough; but the books ask the meaning of 'my' and 'ours'. As for *The Professor's House*: does the professor own his house, or does his house possess him? *My Mortal Enemy* is about the fatal – the mortal – flaw in the desire for possession: what we think we own, we must lose; what we clutch at turns to dust. The title seems to give off one of Myra's dark terrible laughs. And she herself escapes possession: the 'my' disappears into 'myra', and no one can have her; all that's left is 'a compelling, passionate, overmastering something for which I had no name'.

11

TAKING POSSESSION

It all came together in my understanding, as a series of
experiments do when you begin to see where they are
leading. Something had happened in me that made it possible
for me to co-ordinate and simplify, and that process, going on
in my mind, brought with it great happiness. It was
possession.

The Professor's House, 1925

GODFREY ST PETER, the professor of *The Professor's
House*, is a historian, and his story is a recalling of the past. He
is the most articulate and reflective memorializer in all
Cather's work. The novel he inhabits is about splits and
disjunctions: between the male and the feminine, language
and silence, materialism and idealism, and above all, the past
and the present. Poised, as the novel begins, between the old
house he is reluctant to leave and the new house that is
being forced upon him, Cather's historian is poised between
the past and the present. The professor's house is, in one
sense, the house of memory.

We already know how Cather saved herself up, and
projected her time past into the fictive time of her novels.
This book, exactly in the middle of her writing life, reaches
back as deep into her own experience as *The Song of the Lark*
or *My Ántonia*, but puts it to more oblique and fragmented
use. She buried herself very deep inside the novel. Cather
projects herself as St Peter in many ways, and one of the

fascinations of this novel is its revelation of intense personal feeling. At the same time, St Peter is one of her most impersonal and realistic characters: substantial, complex, objectified. We feel from the first sentence of the book to the last that this middle-aged scholar with a demanding family, living in a university town near Lake Michigan, is thoroughly imagined, not merely a transparent 'stand-in' for Cather.

The 'house' of his life is built up, piece by piece, in Book One, 'The Family'. His equivocal relation with his wife – forbearing, habituated social contact covering a profound estrangement – is not simply or explicitly discovered. We only gradually come to understand how his 'romance of the heart' has been chilled, over many years, by his distaste for her ambitious worldliness and by her growing – and understandable – incomprehension of what she perceives as an intolerant withdrawal from his family.

That family life thickens around us as St Peter moves, in a subtly organized double direction, through his domestic and professional present, and through his memories. His reluctance to transfer his study to the smart, new, 'all mod. cons.' house, from the inconvenient attic at the top of his old house, which he has shared for years with the family's Catholic German sewing-woman, Augusta (his great work on *Spanish Adventurers in North America* taking shape in the company of her 'forms' and patterns for the girls' dresses) comes to stand for his alienation from the whole of his family's life. Gradually we understand how the unacknowledged separation in the marriage is involved with his relation to his two married daughters, with his work, and above all with the part his dead pupil, Tom Outland, played in his life.

St Peter's long life-story weaves Tom's short one in and out of its narrative. For a long time he withholds the sudden appearance of the twenty-year-old boy from the Southwest in the garden of his old house. These early memories, dating back to about 1906, are simple, gallant and touching. St Peter calls vividly to mind Tom's giving out his Indian relics as gifts, his quiet determination to be educated, his awkward table-manners, his stories of adventure told to the little girls. But after these tender pictures, his story, as it affects St Peter's, becomes more intangible. Tom's success as a student, his attachment to the Professor's family, his years of scientific research under Dr Crane at the university, his invention of a new gas and his willing of the patent to Rosamond, St Peter's older daughter, before his tragic death in the war in 1916, are referred to, but not visualized. Tom's life is concealed underneath the story of St Peter, until we come to the sound of his own voice.

So St Peter's memories of Tom are inseparable from his own retrospect. And much of the book's painful irony lies in Tom's unconsciousness of how he has affected the other man's life. Tom, involuntarily, was responsible for St Peter's estrangement from Lillian, who began, after about two years, to be jealous of their 'romance of the imagination'. Posthumously, Tom has caused a breach between St Peter's two grown-up daughters, which the father observes with grief. The 'new gas', willed to Rosamond, was turned after Tom's death into the 'Outland vacuum engine', now 'revolutionizing aviation' in America.[1] Thanks to the energetic efforts of Rosamond's husband, Louie Marsellus, Tom's inspiration has become a business of 'chemicals and dollars and cents'. This material success, which gives Lillian, Rosamond and Louie great satisfaction, is much resented by St Peter and by his younger daughter Kathleen.

The story of the two sisters and their husbands would, for another American novelist interested in social realism – William Dean Howells, say – have made a marvellously substantial fiction. Cather restrains it. So that Tom can be preserved, in memory, as innocent and asexual, we hear almost nothing about his courtship of Rosamond, and the possibility that Kathleen was secretly in love with him is only hinted at. But the adult family feelings that encompass St Peter are powerfully established. The rivalry between the older, conventionally beautiful Rosamond, hard and determined like her mother, and the more vulnerable Kathleen, closer to her father, and married to a restless young journalist, Scott, who thinks himself too good for his work, is brilliantly touched in. We find out everything we need about the Marselluses' exhibitionist, lavish appropriation of 'Outland' as an inheritance of worldly goods, about Kathleen's resentment at Rosamond's betrayal of Tom's memory, Scott's anti-semitic hostility to Louie, and Lillian's transference of her sexual emotions from her husband to her sons-in-law.

Individually, there are subtle sympathies. Apart from the chilling Rosamond (whose name and behaviour recall George Eliot's Rosamond Vincy), each member of the family makes an appeal to St Peter, and to us. Kathleen and Scott are attractive in their insecurity and their affection for him: they are at their best in their scenes alone with St Peter. Lillian suffers in her own way from the failed marriage, and at moments her interior life is sharply and surprisingly felt. When the husband and wife are watching *Mignon* at the Chicago Opera, it is not only St Peter who sadly remembers their Paris courtship. Lillian's hard surface dissolves to reveal 'something that spoke of an old wound, healed and hardened and hopeless'. [PH, p.94] Her own sense of loss, and her own estrangement from the person she loves, are just glimpsed. Most interesting of all these familial knots is St Peter's reluctant but increasing fondness for the thick-skinned, florid, irrepressible Louie, at first an unwelcome substitute son-in-law, but eventually acknowledged as generous and benign. It is as though, in this peripheral but important relationship, Cather's own tendency to anti-semitism – put off onto Scott – is being argued with and overcome: Jan Hambourg, the dedicatee in the first edition of *The Professor's House*, was probably on her mind.

But although the family members make individual inroads on the Professor's compassion, as a unit they are made to stand, unforgivingly, for the sins of envy and covetousness. (Cather even has St Peter refer to the seven deadly sins in the lecture he gives to his students.) They represent the corrupt, sexualized world, and are seen in little dramas of greed and malice. Lillian and Louie bend over a casket of jewels, Kathleen turns pale green with envy over Rosamond's furs, and

Rosamond drags her father round Chicago on 'an orgy of acquisition'. [PH, p.154]

The family betrayal of Tom Outland is paralleled by the Professor's disillusionment at work. The university where he and Tom once worked together has become a site for 'the new commercialism', a 'trade school', rapidly replacing its courses in 'purely cultural studies' with book-keeping and domestic science. [PH, p.140] The botched execution of a well-designed but cheaply built physics laboratory is one example of the many 'lost causes' [PH, p.143] the Professor has spent his working life trying to defend. Cather is always good at entering into vocations she finds sympathetic: the very title of this novel suggests the emphasis on professionalism. She is extremely interested, as elsewhere, in the relation of character to job, and makes this felt through St Peter's susceptibility to his good students, his arduous negotiations between teaching and research, his long feud with a 'sham' historian who set up against him in the department, his struggles alongside Tom's old teacher Dr Crane, to preserve the integrity of the university, and, now, his dismay at finding that even the scrupulously puritanical Crane is trying to get something from his pupil's posthumous profits.

The strong, autonomous sense of character is one of the novel's great virtues. But Cather also embodies herself, as she has done before and will again, in her objectified male character. Godfrey St Peter is fifty-two, the same age she is when the novel is published. As a child he was taken away from the landscape he loved (the blue inland sea of the lake) to 'the wheat lands of central Kansas', and 'nearly died of it'. [PH, p.30] Like Cather, he has tender memories of his time as a young man in France, and all his associations with that country — youth, spring, sweetness — are Cather's. And his professional history mirrors her own. The lifetime of 'eliminations and combinations' [PH, p.29] which have enabled him to write his great book and be a good teacher remind us specifically of Cather's hard years in Pittsburgh.[2] There is a wider connection, too, with her whole writing life. His early work only reached a small audience: 'Nobody saw that he was trying to do something quite different.' [PH, p.32] That neglect has come to seem to him, retrospectively, like freedom. Now, in middle age, he has acquired 'a certain international reputation' for his eight-volume *Spanish Adventurers in North America*. He is beginning to have 'what were called rewards': an Oxford prize for history, 'with its five thousand pounds' [PH, p.33], which, as the Pulitzer did for Cather, has changed his life in ways he could have done without. There is enough here (without even embarking on the more arguable terrain of Isabelle's loss, the possible resemblance of Louie to Jan Hambourg, and the shadow of a 'midlife crisis') to let us know that a personal feeling underlies the Professor's weariness and alienation, his sense that he is in retreat from 'the human family'.

Another voice, and another authorial self, though, enter into this split text. Set inside the enclosing house of the Professor's editorial memory, Tom Outland's story derives from the raw material of Cather's own past, transformed into a boy's story of pioneering in the Southwest. It begins when he is eighteen. Outland, orphan child of pioneers, is working on the railroads in the raw town of Pardee, New Mexico. He does a good turn to a footloose working man with a rough past, Roddy Blake. The older and younger man befriend each other, and go off in the summer cattle-ranching in the land around the Blue Mesa, a great cliff landmark, said by the 'old settlers' never to have been climbed. They make camp with an old 'castaway Englishman', Henry Atkins, for 'housekeeper', and these three social outsiders make a 'happy family'.

Chasing the runaway cattle which keep getting into the mesa in pursuit of a wild herd, Tom swims the river into the canyon and suddenly, at the novel's quiet, secret, central climax, comes upon the mesa's undiscovered, 'prehistoric' Indian cliff-dwellings. His story is a 'plain' account, as recorded in his diary, of the pioneering that led to his involuntary discovery, of the work of path-building, exploration and cataloguing that he and Roddy then undertake, of old Henry's dramatic death by snake-bite and of the advice of Father Duchene (Tom's Latin teacher, a wise tough Belgian priest with many years' local experience.) All this is coloured by Tom's powerful but unspoken feelings about the mesa and the cliff-dwellings. Then the story changes: Tom goes to Washington to try to arouse interest in the native treasures, and is bitterly disillusioned by the lack of interest among the place-seeking politicians. On his return he finds that Roddy, not understanding Tom's feelings, has sold the relics to a German trader. The mates part in anger – for ever, as it turns out – but once Tom is left alone on the mesa, studying Spanish and reading Virgil's *Aeneid*, he seems to 'take possession' of the place. A year later, he walks into the Professor's garden.

Compounding the sense of the novel as a writer's disguised autobiography, Tom Outland's story itself mimics the act of authoring: it is a record of exploration and disclosure, loss and repossession, which could stand on its own as a metaphor for the writer's process of finding, losing and recreating experience. So the novel provides two different, split models of writing-as-memory. Only at the end, and with difficulty, are the two parts made to cohere.

Like the Professor in his study, and then like Tom in his mesa, Cather excavates the layers of her past to get at Tom's story. It is saved up for a long time inside the novel, just as she had been saving up its sources. 'Raw' and fresh though it reads, it is in fact a reworking of slowly accumulated material. When she began *The Professor's House* in 1923 it was fourteen years since she had found her voice as a writer with 'The Enchanted Bluff'. In that story, the boys' unfulfilled dream of getting down to New Mexico and exploring the legendary, inviolate Indian cliff-dwelling, set sadly against the compromise of their adult lives, anticipated her own lifelong enchantment with the subject. Then her crucial, transforming journey to the Southwest in 1912 had poured itself into *The Song of the Lark*, where the experience of the cliff-dwellings shapes Thea's art as it shaped her author's. And in 1914, the year *The Song of the Lark* was published, Cather went back to the country that she said[3] drove her crazy with delight. She returned in 1915, and this journey (which, like her, I have been saving up until now) would eventually give her Tom Outland's story.

1915 was the year that Judge McClung not unreasonably thought it dangerous for Isabelle and Cather to go to Europe. Instead she went with Edith Lewis back to the Southwest, on a dramatic train journey along the mountainous border of Colorado and New Mexico, to Durango and on to Mancos, at the foot of the La Plata range, the nearest town to the Mesa Verde. This great cliff-plateau, intercut with hundreds of canyons, its slopes covered in sagebrush, pinyon and juniper trees, the site of the biggest and most astonishing collection of Indian cliff-dwellings in America, had begun to be explored In the 1870s, and had been made a National park in 1906. Tourism had only just begun to be developed, and Cather could still identify with the pioneers of the mesa, the more so since, in Mancos, she heard almost at first hand the story of the discovery of the ruins by the rancher, Richard Wetherill. His brother told her how, in pursuit of strayed cattle, Wetherill and a friend forded the Mancos River, struggled up the steep canyon, and suddenly saw, as she would make Tom Outland see alone, 'through a veil of lightly falling snow . . . practically as it stands today and as it had stood for 800 years before, the cliff palace'. 'It stood as if it had been deserted yesterday; undisturbed and undesecrated.'[4] (She would have heard, too, of the controversy over the Wetherill family's sale of their cliff-dweller artefacts to museums, after their initial failures to attract archaeological interest in the remains.)[5]

The climax of Cather's own week-long exploration of the cliff-dwellings was almost as dramatic as Richard Wetherill's. She and Edith visited an unexcavated cliff-village, the Tower House, with a less experienced guide than usual, who got them lost on the way back, and had to leave them at dusk to go for help. They were rescued by men from an archaeologist's camp, who helped them make a rough and difficult climb to safety. Lewis remembered the hours they were left alone 'watching the long summer twilight come on, and the full moon rise up over the rim of the canyon',[6] making a profound impression on Cather. She herself played down the adventure in her report to Elsie Sergeant:[7] it was a rough twenty-four hours, she said, but it taught her more than any other twenty-four hours in her life. (The local newspaper reports were more sensationalist: 'TWO NOTED WOMEN GET LOST ALL NIGHT IN MESA VERDE WILDS: Misses Willa Cather and Edith Lewis, Magazine Editors and Novelists, Have Nerve-Racking Experience', ran the headline.)[8]

Cather's immediate response to the place was to ask herself how it could be rendered. The camera, her letter to Elsie continued, became inarticulate in the face of that light, those heights and depths. What was needed was a big painter, with an egotism commensurate to that of the cliff-dwellers'.[9] In 1916 she published an essay on the Mesa Verde which, though she didn't yet know it, was a first version of Tom Outland's story.[10] Characteristically, the essay grafted her own responses onto the witness of others, Richard Wetherill, and the Swedish explorer Nordenskjold, whose 1893 book on the cliff-dwellings Cather had evidently read. At once personal and historical, the essay vividly recreates the magical first sight of the ruins, and their silent eloquence, messengers of 'custom, ritual, integrity of tradition'.[11] Straight afterwards, she thought of writing a story called 'The Blue Mesa', and abandoned it.[12] It was to be saved up for seven years. When she did start work on *The Professor's House*, it was 'The Blue Mesa' – 'Tom Outland's Story' – she began with.[13] In it, the cliff-city is described as 'preserved in the dry air and the almost perpetual sunlight like a fly in amber'. [PH, p.202] That phrase, like many in the novel, reworks the essay, where Wetherill sees the ruins 'preserved in bright, dry sunshine, like a fly in amber'.[14] Like the cliff-city itself, the narrative of adventure and discovery had been preserved in the amber of Cather's memory, waiting its time.

The insertion of that memory into the house of the Professor's thoughts makes the most startling dislocation in the whole of Cather's work, more daring and unexpected than –

say – the interpolation of the Peter and Pavel story into *My Ántonia*, or the jump from America to France in *One of Ours*, or the sudden shift of fortunes in *My Mortal Enemy*. Cather felt she needed to justify the structure. Her title page quotation from Louie Marsellus, 'a turquoise set in dull silver', refers to Tom's blue stone from the mesa – simple, glowing, ancient – which is made into a bracelet for Rosamond; it also describes the shape of the novel. Later, in an essay on *The Professor's House*,[15] Cather said that its structure resembled the free handling of the sonata form, and that it followed early French and Spanish novels in their interpolation of a 'novella' (a long short story) into a '*roman*'. Above all, she said, the form was like the Dutch paintings she had seen in Paris, where 'a warmly furnished' living room or kitchen would have 'a square window, open' looking out onto 'the masts of ships, or a stretch of gray sea'.

Though they give us important hints for the novel, the analogies from jewellery, music, painting and literature are somewhat misleading. Cather purports to have made a formal experiment for this particular book. But, in fact, its 'massive dislocation' was very much in keeping with her persistent interest in doubleness.[16] Cather's formal explanations of her divided narrative structure cover up the obsessional, personal nature of the split, and do not suggest how much fracture and dislocation there is throughout the novel. The attempt to make a coherent, harmonized shape through memory is constantly straining against processes of separation and substitution.

The first page of the novel, very unlike most of Cather's first pages, shows the signs of strain.

> The moving was over and done. Professor St Peter was alone in the dismantled house where he had lived ever since his marriage, where he had worked out his career and brought up his two daughters. It was almost as ugly as it is possible for a house to be; square, three stories in height, painted the colour of ashes – the front porch just too narrow for comfort, with a slanting floor and sagging steps. As he walked slowly about the empty, echoing rooms on that bright September morning, the

Professor regarded thoughtfully the needless inconveniences he had put up with for so long; the stairs that were too steep, the halls that were too cramped, the awkward oak mantles with thick round posts crowned by bumptious wooden balls, over green-tiled fire-places. Certain wobbly stair treads, certain creaky boards in the upstairs hall, had made him wince many times a day for twenty-odd years – and they still creaked and wobbled. He had a deft hand with tools, he could easily have fixed them, but there were always so many things to fix, and there was not time enough to go round. He went into the kitchen, where he had carpentered under a succession of cooks, went up to the bath-room on the second floor, where there was only a painted tin tub; the taps were so old that no plumber could ever screw them tight enough to stop the drip, the window could only be coaxed up and down by wriggling, and the doors of the linen closet didn't fit. He had sympathized with his daughters' dissatisfaction, though he could never quite agree with them that the bath should be the most attractive room in the house. He had spent the happiest years of his youth in a house at Versailles where it distinctly was not, and he had known many charming people who had no bath at all. However, as his wife said: 'If your country has contributed one thing, at least, to civilization, why not have it?' Many a night, after blowing out his study lamp, he had leaped into that tub, clad in his pyjamas, to give it another coat of some one of the many paints that were advertised to behave like porcelain, and didn't. [PH, pp. 11–12]

Cather's novels usually open with a sense of wide space or historical distance, a prospect or a retrospect: 'One January day, thirty years ago . . .' 'I first heard of Ántonia . . .' 'One summer evening in the year 1848. . . '. Less often, in the big emotional novels of enfranchisement – *The Song of the Lark, One of Ours* – she begins in a place of narrow, materialistic confinement. *The Professor's House* awkwardly, and exceptionally, combines the two modes, setting a character given to retrospection inside a clumsy, constricting frame. The whole account of the disoriented owner inside his 'dismantled' house is made of negatives. Though the novel will find its way to end with the words 'the future', it begins with a sense of elegiac finality, in a phrase of sombre double negation: 'the moving was over and done'. 'Needless inconveniences', insisted on by 'too narrow', 'too steep', 'too cramped'; lack of time to fix things, and their refusal to be fixed; the failure of plumbers, the dissatisfaction of daughters and his never quite agreeing with them, the paint that 'didn't', all compound the negations.

Nothing 'fits' or is 'fixed', the house is all makeshifts (the dripping tap), shams (the fake paint) and pretensions (the wooden balls on the mantelpiece). Physical and mental discomforts and dissatisfactions overlap: the Professor's wincing answers the creaking and wobbling of his stairs, his incongruous activities in the bath reiterate the house's awkwardnesses. The very sentences, long, trailing, as if randomly constructed (especially 'It was almost as ugly . . .' and 'He went into the kitchen . . .') seem not to have been neatly 'fixed'. Everything we learn about this man and his house – his preference for French simplicity over American civilization, his passive, even affectionate contemplation of discomforts and omissions, his satirical association of his wife with good plumbing, the exigencies that have had him carpentering during the cooking, or painting the bath at night after a day's work – set up at once, with brilliant suggestiveness, a general air of dislocation, awkwardness and compromise. There is nothing so simple as an idea that he is having to move from a beautiful house he loved to an ugly house he hates. It is the old house, the house of his past, and through that the whole 'house' of his narrative, which is made of makeshifts, substitutions, shams, betrayals, and regrets. Even the language is ill-at-ease with itself.

It is clear from the first page that disjunctions don't just make the form of the novel – two narratives, two heroes – but are its subject. St Peter's life is one of compound fractures. His childhood was shaped by a Methodist mother and a Catholic father, by an inland sea and an unbounded prairie. His adult emotions have been split between his romance of the heart and of the imagination. Professionally, divided between his writing and his teaching, he has for

years 'managed to live two lives, both of them very intense.'
[PH, p.28] The most profound dislocations are between his
domestic and intellectual life, and between his past and
present selves. The attic sewing room has provided 'insulation from the engaging drama of domestic life'. [PH, p.26]
Sealed off, he has preserved himself from 'the human house'
[PH, p.27] and might say of it, as Flaubert did of a family with
children he once visited (as reported by his niece Caroline,
whom Cather was soon to meet): 'Ils sont dans le vrai'.[17]

But this insulation from 'le vrai' has not been complete:
'All the while he had been working so fiercely at his eight big
volumes, he was not insensible to the domestic drama that
went on beneath him.' [PH, p. 101] Cather uses some
eloquent metaphors of female art-work to describe this
'interpenetration'. The attic has always been Augusta's
sewing-room by day and the Professor's study by night: 'they
did not elbow each other too much', and he has grown
attached to the female 'forms' – 'those terrible women' – on
which Augusta has hung a succession of his daughters'
dresses. At either end of the box-couch, his manuscripts and
her patterns co-exist: 'In the middle of the box, patterns and
manuscripts interpenetrated.'[18] [PH, p.22] Later, the possibility of 'interpenetration' between the life of the mind and
of the family is beautifully and formally compared to a
famous female composition, a comparison which displays
Cather's pleasure in an androgynous art that can interweave
the heroic and the domestic:

> Just as, when Queen Mathilde was doing the long tapestry
> now shown at Bayeux, – working her chronicle of the deeds of
> knights and heroes, – alongside the big pattern of dramatic
> action she and her women carried the little playful pattern of
> birds and beasts that are a story in themselves; so, to him, the
> most important chapters of his history were interwoven with
> personal memories. [PH, p.101]

(That idea of a female 'composition' which can reconcile into
a natural-seeming art form the domestic and public, the
physical and the spiritual, is touchingly demonstrated too by
the pious Augusta, who tells the Professor, to his 'intense

interest', that 'the Blessed Virgin composed the Magnificat'. [PH, p.100])

In the past, then, the splits in his life have been just reconcilable. But not now. The whole world has broken in two, and that split can't be healed. The 'great catastrophe' which has intervened between Tom's youth and the Professor's middle age – in which 'all youth and all palms, and almost Time itself' [PH, p.260] have been swept away (a passage which Cather excised, as being perhaps too emotional, from the novel's later edition) has fractured the Professor's single life, as it has everyone's. (In national politics, too, there is a large-scale fracture, as Scott remarks when he is complaining about Prohibition: '"This country's split in two, socially, and I don't know if it's ever coming together."' [PH, p.108]) The world change is embodied for St Peter in a double loss. He has lost his own delight in life: he would have to learn to live without it, 'just as, in a Prohibition country, he supposed he would have to learn to live without sherry'. [PH, p.282] And he has lost the original Tom Outland, now translated into a 'glittering idea', [PH, p.111] a public legend, a squabble over profits, and the conspicuous expenditure of the Marselluses. 'Was it for this,' asks St Peter, bitterly contemplating 'families and fortunes', [PH, p.90] that 'the light in Outland's laboratory used to burn so far into the night!' [PH, p.91] When Louie and Rosamond call their fake Norwegian house 'Outland' ('"Outlandish!"' murmurs the envious Scott), or when Louie dresses up in Tom's old blanket, a substitution is taking place: the real Tom Outland – heroic, simple, quixotic, idealist – is being turned into a pretence, an imitation.

So the novel is full of shams, replicating that central substitution. St Peter had a 'show study' downstairs in the old house, 'but it was a sham'. [PH, p.16] The wire and wooden forms in his (real) study are sham women, 'fooling' you into an anticipation of softness and warmth. Plain Augusta, not one for shams, is congratulated by St Peter on her fine head of hair: '"You'll never need any of this false hair that's in all the shop windows."' [PH, p.23], which she agrees is a disgrace. Sham characters in the outside world populate the edges of the novel: St Peter's rival at the university, with his false teaching of history and his pseudo-English manners, who 'looked like a short cut' to the country students; [PH, p.56] Homer Bright, the 'greatest bluffer' of all St Peter's students, who has grown up to be Dr Crane's shyster lawyer; the civil servants Tom Outland meets in Washington who spend their life 'trying to keep up appearances'; [PH, p.232] the false Roddy Blakes, impostors who have responded to the advertisement for Tom's lost friend. [PH, p.63] In modern America, St Peter reflects at the end of the novel, even the coffins are padded with 'sham upholstery': 'Just the equivocal American way of dealing with serious facts.' [PH, p.272]

The Professor's relation to the modern world of false substitutions is itself equivocal. His alienation is in large part self-inflicted: intent on keeping true things separated from shams, he has walled himself in, cut himself off. The cultivation of his 'walled-in' French garden in an American city, like the cultivation of his intellect and sensibility in a material world, makes him something of a spiritual snob. It would be possible to dislike St Peter (as it is possible to dislike Cather) for his fastidious aloofness from other people's compromises: Lillian makes this sympathetically clear in her criticism of his intolerance. He cultivates separatism on principle.[19] His idea of Tom is that he kept 'affection and advancement far apart, as if they were chemicals that would disintegrate each other'. [PH, p.172] Likewise, he refuses to have his friendship with Tom 'translated into the vulgar tongue' of money and possessions. His memory of Tom must remain 'outlandish', separate from the world as it is. To be 'integrated' with that world is to lose integrity.

This insistence is part of a general tendency to think in terms of separate categories, illustrated by the Professor's lecture to his students, which laments the impoverishing substitution of science for art and religion. As in the reference to Tom's keeping 'affection and advancement' apart like chemicals, science is identified with separations. It is no accident that in St Peter's ironic conversation with Augusta, when he asks her what people would think if he and Lillian were living in separate houses, he calls 'separation' a 'good scientific term'. [PH, p.20]

Science is opposed to art in the Professor's mind, and art is always referred to in terms of composition, wholeness, design, as in the images of the Bayeux tapestry or the Magnificat. Yet even when his mind dwells on visions of wholeness and composition – analogues for his writing – these visions are separated from the rest of his life. This is especially true of the 'key' memory of his youth, a sailing trip round the south coast of Spain, within sight of the high mountains of the Sierra Nevada. There has been an anticipatory glimpse of this scene when St Peter is at the opera with Lillian. Softened by the courtship memories which *Mignon* evokes, he confides in her that he regrets their adult life together: they should have been 'picturesquely shipwrecked' when they were young. But when he imagines this picturesque shipwreck, he thinks of that Spanish sea-voyage, in sight of the 'agonizingly' high, gleaming snow peaks. Lillian is not in this picture: nobody is in it except himself and 'a weather-dried little sea captain from the Hautes-Pyrénées.' [PH, p.95] It is a strange, suggestive moment in the novel. St Peter's fantasy of an early death is separated from his feelings for his wife and attached to the sea-journey he made as a young man with an all-male crew; the vision of the mountains on that journey is then used as an image for the design of his book. Death, freedom, adventure and space (all qualities of Tom's mountain journey too) are thus divorced from the Professor's sexual and domestic life, and attached to his youth and his writing. And this is fundamental to the idea of separation in the whole novel.

Godfrey St Peter does not die young; it is Tom Outland who dies young. But in the novel's coda, we discover that in his deepest feelings it seems to him he *has* died young. It is, after all, not Tom's loss he is mourning, but his own. In the final substitution of the book, Tom turns into 'another boy': 'the original, unmodified Godfrey St Peter'. [PH, p.263] He recognizes that this boy has had 'the realest of his lives'. 'All the years between had been accidental and ordered from the outside.' A division is posited (Cather had recently been getting irritably interested in Freud)[20] between the 'primitive' 'instinctual' self of childhood, and 'the secondary social man'. So the theme of separation comes to its climax. It is himself he is separated from.

> His career, his wife, his family, were not his life at all, but a chain of events which had happened to him. All these things had nothing to do with the person he was in the beginning.
> [PH, p.264]

The 'secondary social man' is the sexual adult: he has been shaped 'by all the penalties and responsibilities of being and having been a lover'. The primitive self is presexual, solitary, and in wordless communication with nature.[21]

This final recognition explains the Professor's earlier, bitter references to Augusta's 'forms' as 'terrible women', evidence of 'cruel biological necessities'. Her sham women represent the forces which have separated him from his true self. It is tempting to interpret this true self as a homosexual feeling for Tom, since Tom stands in for his own lost primitive nature, Tom's friendship has alienated him from his wife, and all St Peter's Arcadian visions of freedom are scenes of male companionship. (And the great work which was inspired by the Spanish and Southwestern American journeys, his *Spanish Adventurers*, is a chronicle and celebration of male pioneering.) St Peter, like his Spanish adventurers, is no priestly ascetic: his pleasure in good food and drink, his lean energetic attractive body, his Spanish good looks, his classical figure swimming in the lake ('his head looked sheathed and small and intensely alive, like the heads of the warriors on the Parthenon frieze in their tight, archaic helmets' [PH, p.71]) all suggest an erotic male potency which finds no satisfactions in indoor marital life. Connections with Cather's sexual nature are plausible: Doris Grumbach's view that the novel is a story of 'private, unconfessed, sublimated' homosexual love,[22] and that Tom's loss is a projection of

Isabelle's, has a good deal of point. Yet it doesn't quite accommodate the novel's obscure sense of spiritual dislocation. The book not only evokes sexual loss. Cather insists, after all, that the 'primitive', 'real' self is *pre*-sexual. More profoundly, it describes a loss of self, of a sense of one's own reality.

The Professor's study is awkwardly lit and heated. He has written his great work by the light of a 'faithful kerosene lamp', but when it is empty, to avoid going down 'through the human house' to fill it, 'he jammed an eyeshade on his forehead and worked by the glare' of a 'tormenting pear-shaped bulb'. 'It was hard on eyes even as good as his.' [PH, p.27] The 'rusty, round gas stove with no flue' has to be kept on full and the window left open, or the gas might blow out and asphyxiate him. These are functional details, illustrating the makeshift adjustments of his life, and carefully setting up the conditions for his possible suicide. But they work more strongly than that, too. In the end the study becomes his purgatory. After the long summer in which he has been left alone to read Tom's story, he hears that his family is coming back from their European tour: Rosamond is to have a child. But he feels he can no longer live with them: he has fallen 'out of his place in the human family', and his mind dwells gratefully on the thought of 'eternal solitude'. A storm comes up, the air darkens. He lights the stove, and falls asleep watching the 'flickering pattern of light on the wall'. [PH, p.276] In the night he half-wakes, to find the room 'pitch-black and full of gas'.[23]

St Peter is rescued from his passive suicide by Augusta, who fetches him back into the human family, her grim virtues of stoic endurance, held in reserve in the novel, coming into their own at the last. But Cather has it both ways: a death *has* taken place, the death of 'ardour' and 'delight'. The conditions for this death – asphyxiation in the dark, a live burial, the 'house' become a grave – are symbolically opposed to the life-force at the centre of the book.

When the window opens onto Tom Outland's story, a great rush of light and air pours into the book. Obviously, the inset narrative makes a powerful contrast in other ways too. Youth is opposed to age, action to contemplation, aspirations to memory. Tom's improvised male family, with Roddy as a substitute brother/husband, and old Harry and Father Duchene as his mother and father, provide a (preferable) alternative to the Professor's female domestic ties. Tom's story is mostly outdoor, St Peter's indoor. His discovery is of a native, aboriginal history, the Professor's is of European colonizers and exploiters. But the most sensational substitution is of articifial for natural light, and of 'airlessness' [PH, p.150] for space.

The revelation of the mesa and its secret city is one of Cather's most beautifully contrived and most natural-seeming artefacts. This is partly due to the contrast with what surrounds it, partly to the paradox of eloquent testimony given to a simple speaker. But essentially it arises from her intense feeling for what she was describing. All the great visionary sightings of her earlier work – Alexandra's celebration of the unformed land, Thea's rapture of self-realization in the canyon, Jim's momentary epiphany of the plough on the horizon – culminate in the central irradiation of this novel. And here, unlike those earlier climactic moments, there is no end to the describing, no sense that the landscape will ever give up all its meaning. It keeps changing as it is approached, and has to be written over and over again. As Tom gets deeper into the mesa, the light becomes more intense; his journey into prehistoric time thus takes him into the heart of light, as St Peter's journey into his own, personal, past time takes him into the heart of darkness. So the descriptive writing of Tom's story has a strongly sacramental quality.

At first the mesa seems 'tantalizingly' impenetrable. It hangs over Tom and Roddy, a solid inaccessible mass, metamorphosing in different lights:

Some mornings it would loom up above the dark river like a blazing volcanic mountain. It shortened our days, too, considerably. The sun got behind it early in the afternoon, and then our camp would lie in its shadow. After a while the sunset colour would begin to stream up from behind it. Then the mesa was like one great ink-black rock against a sky on fire.

No wonder the thing bothered us and tempted us; it was always before us, and was always changing. [PH, pp.192–3]

As Tom finds his way in, the colours become less threatening and more intimate. When the city has been discovered, and they are setting up camp there, they drink the water of the spring, which seems to metamorphose back into light. The priest is the celebrant of this mystery.

Father Duchene . . . always carried a small drinking-glass with him, and he used to fill it at the spring and take it out into the sunlight. The water looked like liquid crystal, absolutely colourless, without the slight brownish or greenish tint that water nearly always has. It threw off the sunlight like a diamond. [PH, p.209]

When Tom comes back to the mesa, after his disillusioning sojourn under the sad Washington sunsets, the descriptions are resumed, and once more, the elements are merged, so that a transfiguration seems to take place.

When I pulled out on top of the mesa, the rays of sunlight fell slantingly through the little twisted pinons – the light was all in between them, as red as a daylight fire, they fairly swam in it. Once again I had that glorious feeling that I've never had anywhere else, the feeling of being *on the mesa*, in a world above the world. And the air, my God, what air! – Soft, tingling, gold, hot with an edge of chill on it, full of the smell of pinons – it was like breathing the sun, breathing the colour of the sky. [PH, p.240]

As Tom finally takes possession of the mesa and the cliff city, and becomes its only inhabitant, the sun seems to give him its 'solar energy' 'in some direct way'. [PH, p.251] Light is turned into pure, almost overwhelming, life-force:

At night, when I watched it drop down behind the edge of the plain below me, I used to feel that I couldn't have borne another hour of that consuming light, that I was full to the brim, and needed dark and sleep. [PH, pp.251–2]

The cumulative metamorphoses of light into air into fire into colour into water seem to stream onto the page. And through this marvellous writing, a theory of natural laws – not unlike the nineteenth-century American transcendentalists' belief in a ubiquitous, protean 'Oversoul' – is implied. The essence of nature, endlessly self-renewing and energetic, is the direct solar energy. In its essence, it cannot be perceived or described, it can hardly be 'borne'. Tom gets as close to the source of life and light as a human being can. But the pure source constantly adopts different shapes, forms, designs, colours: 'always before us, and always changing'. It's that process which Cather's writing emulates, translating nature's metamorphoses into endlessly resourceful, energetic figurative language.

But, after all, Tom's 'story' is words on a page, signs for things. And at the centre of his natural landscape is a man-made artefact, the cliff-city. From the beginning to the end of Cather's work, the making and reading of signs is all-important. The fundamental desire of her writing is to transpose the forms and designs of the natural world, as perceived and shaped through human action, imagination and memory, into words. And these words, by means of a strenuous, concealed battle for simplicity and inevitability, are made to seem as true as possible to the natural forms, whether these are the marks left by the river on the islands of 'The Enchanted Bluff', or the order of bird flight contemplated by Old Ivar. Very often, an implicit analogy is drawn between the pioneering attempts of human beings to make their own mark on the natural world – the traces of the wheels of the 'Forty-Niners' wagons in *The Song of the Lark*, the faint sign of the Indian circle in *My Ántonia,* and now the cliff-city – and the action of the novelist, ordering her own design. These human orderings are always perceived as ancient vestiges, sympathetically recognized through a long vista of time. So they are made to suggest the immortality of the art-work – more particularly, of the native American art-work, which thus takes on classical dignity. By analogy, Cather seems to be ensuring, or hoping for, the long future of her own designs.

By the time we get to Tom's cliff-city, we have already had a sophisticated indoor version from St Peter of the way in which art can improve on nature. He sounds very like Henry James here, preferring the 'sublime economy' of art to life's 'splendid waste'.[24]

> It struck him that the seasons sometimes gain by being brought into the house, just as they gain by being brought into painting, and into poetry. The hand, fastidious and bold, which selected and placed – it was that which made the difference. In Nature there is no selection. [PH, p.75]

When, in his reactionary, anti-modernist lecture, he opposes science to 'art and religion', he emphasizes this process of selection as the key to the Church's nourishment of the soul through its 'gorgeous dramas' and 'imaginative acts'. It is 'The Novel Démeublé' again, with more insistence on the sacramental function of art:

> The Christian theologians went over the books of the Law, like great artists, getting splendid effects by excision. They reset the stage with more space and mystery, throwing all the light upon a few sins of great dramatic value . . . [PH, p.69]

But St Peter can no longer find the connection between 'composition' and spiritual nourishment, either in the personal 'house' of his life, or in the wider 'house' of his time. Hence, the dislocations, discomfort and asphyxiation in his narrative. The essential point of the split stories is that Tom finds, in the light, what St Peter loses in the dark.

The cliff-city, Tom's find, is an art-work waiting for readers. Very like Keats's Grecian urn – the similarity has often been noticed[25] – it gives out its silent message to future generations. We approach it by way of closer and closer readings. On its first magically silent and sudden appearance, it is described in terms of 'composition':

> Far up above me, a thousand feet or so, set in a great cavern in the face of the cliff, I saw a little city of stone, asleep. It was as still as sculpture – and something like that. It all hung together, seemed to have a kind of composition: pale little houses of

stone nestling close to one another, perched on top of each other, with flat roofs, narrow windows, straight walls, and in the middle of the group, a round tower.

It was beautifully proportioned, that tower. . . . The tower was the fine thing that held all the jumble of houses together and made them mean something. . . . It was more like sculpture than anything else. [PH, pp.201–2]

Tom senses that 'a people with a feeling for design' [PH, p.204] must have built it. As the city is entered and examined, the life of this people is characterized in increasing detail and their pioneering qualities are replicated in the bold discovery and painstaking exploration of the ruins by the two boys and old Henry.

Father Duchene's authoritative commentary on their findings is in contrast with the Professor's history lecture. The Professor laments the substitution of art and religion for science in an impoverished civilization; the priest describes a civilization which integrated science, art and religion. Scientific methods are now seen as agents, not negations, of imaginative understanding. Tom, the future inventor, classifies his finds like 'specimens', and when he finally takes possession of the place it seems to come together in his understanding 'as a series of experiments do when you see where they are leading'. [PH, p.250] To establish the age of the settlement, Duchene cuts down an old cedar in the middle of one of the trails, which could only have grown up after the tribe was destroyed, and 'counted the rings under his pocket microscope'. [PH, p.218] The cliff-dwellers themselves were scientists. They 'experimented with dyes', they used the tower for 'astronomical observations', and among their relics is a bag of surgical instruments: 'a stone lancet, a bunch of fine bone needles, wooden forceps, and a catheter'. [PH, p.212]

Pre-commercial science is one of the 'arts of peace' which Duchene describes as the product of 'an orderly and secure life', and the mark of 'a superior people'. These people were craftsmen who 'developed' their arts, 'improved' their conditions, 'built themselves into this mesa and humanized it'.

Their culture is as close to nature as possible – it would not
have come into being without the setting – but it is not
natural in the sense of barbaric or primitive. Duchene's
formal, reasoned, elegiac celebration of their civilization
insists on 'composition'.

> I see them here, isolated, cut off from other tribes, working out
> their destiny, making their mesa more and more worthy to be a
> home for man, purifying life by religious ceremonies and
> observances, caring respectfully for their dead, protecting the
> children, doubtless entertaining some feelings of affection and
> sentiment for this stronghold where they were at once so safe
> and so comfortable, where they had practically overcome the
> worst hardships that primitive man had to fear. They were,
> perhaps, too far advanced for their time and environment. [PH,
> pp.220–21]

The language sounds like a translation of a classical text –
Duchene is Tom's Latin teacher – and it presents the culture
as the American classical age. To underline this, a resemblance is noted between the designs of the cliff-dwellers'
jugs, and those on 'early pottery from the island of Crete'.
[PH, p.220] Tom reads his Virgil on the mesa, and, in his
memory, superimposes the scenes from the *Aeneid* onto the
cliff-city. This is both like, and mournfully unlike, Jim
Burden's application of Virgil to Nebraska. Like the
Nebraskan pioneers, the Indian cliff-dwellers have composed
and humanized an immensely daunting landscape. But to re-
find that native pioneering tradition, Cather now has to
resort to an exterminated, ancient people.

There is a bitter contrast, then, between the indigenous
folk history of the cliff-city, and the later history of America.
Duchene deduces that the tribe was wiped out, when they
were down in their summer camp, by a barbarian nomadic
'horde', on the rampage for loot. The story of the troll garden
is reinvoked – the envious 'children of the forest' destroying
the enclosed civilization – and provides a paradigm for a
history of the world seen as a succession of tribal conflicts.
The book is full of illustrations of this history. Tom reads his
Caesar while he is minding cattle; when he walks into the

Professor's garden, he starts to recite Aeneas's account of the sack of Troy to prove his knowledge of Latin. When the Professor talks about ritual to his students, he instances Moses, freeing his people through 'ceremonials' from their slave mentality under the Egyptians. St Peter's concealed first name, Napoleon, is derived from the great-great-grandfather who 'came out to the Canadian wilderness to forget the chagrin of his Emperor's defeat'. [PH, p.270] That foiled attempt at world conquest is anticipated by the Spanish imperialist explorers in the New World, the subject of St Peter's book, and the crusaders, represented in a pageant in which his sons-in-law play Saladin and Coeur de Lion.[26]

This succession of conquering tribal imperialists, taking over less powerful tribes in their search for loot and fame − Egyptians, Greeks, Romans, Christians, Spaniards, French − culminates in the modern American republic (which has often been compared to the Roman Empire), now, in the post-war, pre-Depression years, at its most spendthrift and expansionist. So Rosamond's shopping trip to Chicago for her 'painted Spanish bedroom set' is compared by her father to 'Napoleon looting the Italian palaces' [PH, p.154], and the Marselluses plan, like the old European adventurers, to 'pick up a good many things' [PH, p.159] on their trip to France, and to ship them back free of duty from Marseilles to Mexico. The vestiges of this tribal culture, it is implied, would not have much value. If a Tom Outland and a Father Duchene were to excavate it in hundreds of years, what they would dig up would be imports, imitations, and stolen goods.

But Cather's theory of history is not simply of decline and fall. More interestingly, it is of recurrence. So (as with all her classical pastorals) the cliff-city is no prelapsarian idyll. Pain and horror are concealed inside it, tellingly associated with sexuality. In *The Song of the Lark*, the shapes of the caves and the artefacts of the cliff-dwellers inspired Thea to a sense of female potential. But now, into an all-male 'happy family', substituting for unsatisfactory heterosexual female relations, the female body makes an ominous appearance, as a reminder of betrayal. The boys discover a woman's corpse – a 'terrible woman' to match Augusta's 'forms' – and, grimly joking, nickname her Mother Eve. She has been murdered – for adultery, Duchene surmises – and 'her face, through all those years, had kept a look of terrible agony.' [PH, p.214] Mother Eve 'refuses to leave them': when the artefacts are carried away, she falls to the bottom of the canyon, and cannot be salvaged. Cather leaves us to make what we like of this, but strongly suggests the inescapable nature of 'cruel biological necessities'.

Tom only escapes these necessities by dying young; his romances are all with men, and, more intensely, with the mesa and the city. As so often, Cather transposes her own sexual temperament into an idea of active male companionship. Tom appears, both in St Peter's version of him and in his own, as Cather's exemplary hero: young, questing, self-reliant, asexual, full of 'ardour', serious, active, imaginative. Metaphorically speaking he has 'never handled things that were not the symbols of ideas'. [PH, p.260] This – like the direct light of the sun – would be rather too much to bear, if Tom's relationships were perfect. But it is one of the novel's fine subtleties that all Tom's friendships are fallible, and that betrayal exists in his story as well as in St Peter's.

When Tom tells the story of his friendship with Roddy to the little girls, they turn him into the hero of a romantic Western: '"He liked to be free, and to sit in his saddle all day and use it for a pillow at night. . . . Noble, noble Roddy!"' [PH, p.124] Grown-up Kathleen compares their broken friendship to the story of 'Amis and Amile', the devoted chivalric friends of a twelfth-century metrical romance, who sacrifice themselves for each other.[27] Roddy may be the heroic cowboy of Western tradition, but his relationship with Tom is more realistic and vivid than Tom's with St Peter. That friendship takes place mostly at a distance, in a succession of silent scenes played through St Peter's memory. The friendship with Roddy Blake gets closer to Cather's sense of the sadness of unspoken, suppressed homosexual love. It is not, of course, described in those terms. But from the beginning, when Tom rescues Roddy from the gaming-table and Roddy nurses him through his illness, to the final quarrel, when there is 'an ache' in Tom's arms to 'reach out and detain him', [PH, p.247] tender love feelings – as in the popular tradition of American 'buddy buddy' stories and films – are latent in the rugged outdoor relation. 'He ought to have had boys of his own to look after', says Tom of Roddy, adding very revealingly: 'Nature's full of such substitutions, but they always seem to me sad, even in botany.' [PH, p.186] This is, I think, Cather's most direct reference to homosexual feeling in her fiction, as a 'natural' but sad deviation, and it is a melancholy remark.

Like Tom, Roddy is a democratic American hero, a self-reliant working man with no life except what he makes for himself. But Cather is careful to make him less competent, less intelligent and less sensitive than Tom. He believes in education, but as 'some kind of hocus-pocus that enabled a man to live without work'. [PH, p.188] He wants to get rich, and completely fails to understand Tom's feelings about the sanctity of the cliff-city. When Tom sends discouraging reports back from Washington, and Roddy sells off the Indian remains to a visiting German for $4,000, he does it for Tom's benefit ('that money's in the bank this minute, in your name, and you're going to college on it' [PH, p.243]) and is baffled by his outrage.

It looks as if Roddy is set up simply as a foil to Tom, to show his unique aloofness from the profit motive: 'There never was any question of money with me, where this mesa and its people were concerned.' [PH, p.244] Roddy appears to Tom as a traitor to the national inheritance, who has sold what '"belonged to boys like you and me, that have no other ancestors to inherit from"'. [PH, p.242] He seems to join the novel's other traitors: the Congressmen and staff of the Smithsonian, more interested in good lunches and trips to Europe than in 'dead and gone Indians' [PH, p.235], or the German dealer who smuggles the Indian 'curios' onto a French boat out of Mexico, thus avoiding customs in exactly the same way as the Marselluses will on their return journey from Europe. The cliff-dwellers have been sold, as St Peter will allow Tom to be sold: everything 'comes to money in the end'.

But Roddy's betrayal is not quite so moralistically simple. He is an unusual figure in Cather's work, a radical working man. (A more political novelist would have made him a 'Wobbly'.) His favourite book is *Gulliver's Travels* – presumably for its satires on government – and when he and Tom are living together they have 'long arguments' about what they read in the newspapers. Roddy is a staunch defender of the Chicago Anarchists and of Dreyfus. Tom believes in Dreyfus's guilt, and cites him in the heat of their quarrel:

'You've gone and sold your country's secrets, like Dreyfus.'
'That man was innocent. It was a frame-up,' Blake murmured. It was a point he would never pass up. [PH, p.243]

And he goes on to throw Swiftian scorn on Tom's 'Fourth of July talk' and on Tom's treatment of him as 'a hired man'. Given Cather's growing sympathies with Catholicism, her tinges of anti-semitism and her feeling for national pride, one might suppose Roddy's support of Dreyfus to be a black mark against him. In fact not: in 1899 Cather wrote a stirring tribute to Zola's defence of Dreyfus, speaking of 'the courage of the hand that penned *J'Accuse*.'[28] There is no evidence that she changed her mind. Roddy, like Dreyfus, is being wrongly accused: there is betrayal on both sides. His personal tenderness has led him, in Forster's phrase, to betray his country rather than his friend; Tom's idealism makes him betray his friend in the interests of his country. The sense of mutual damage is intensified by Roddy's last words: '"I'm glad it's you that's doing this to me, Tom; not me that's doing it to you."' [PH, pp.247–8] Both young men are 'punished': Roddy disappears forever into the limbo of the modern nomadic American west, the world of railroads and newspapers; and Tom tells himself that 'anyone who requites faith and friendship as I did, will have to pay for it'.

[PH, p.253] He is, indeed, 'called to account', in the catastrophic betrayal of all 'youth' and of Time itself, the Great War.

It seems, then, by the end, that all is lost. The split in the narrative mimics the unassuaged betrayals, separations and substitutions of the whole book. And when we return to the Professor after Tom's 'ardour', we see that he is suffering the symptoms of a well-known medieval condition called 'accidie': spiritual sloth or indifference. He feels 'a diminution of ardour', a sense of being 'flattened out and listless', [PH, p.153] an alienation from his own life, and, to sum up – it is almost his last word – 'apathy'. [PH, p.283] Tom's active story is replaced by his negations. St Peter did not go back to France with Tom, he did not develop the patent of Tom's invention, he does not want to move house, he did not want to go to Europe with his family, he does not read his family's letters, he does not even seem to finish editing Tom's diary. His attempted suicide is itself a negative act; he does not stop himself from being gassed. All that is left for him is the bitter stoicism of Augusta.

But that is not all we are left with. *The Professor's House*, strangely enough, is not a depressing book, though because of its title character's dejection it has usually been read so.[29] Certainly it is full of longing for death and a painful sense of fracture and bereavement. Yet it has an unaccountable element of happiness, and this is because the novel is not so much about dying as it is about writing.

The Professor's House has two kinds of language, two ways of writing about memory. St Peter's is sophisticated, metaphorical and contemplative. His parts of the novel are all about the inspiration, the design and the execution of his book. He makes self-conscious use of linguistic terms, as when he refuses to have his relationship with Tom 'translated into the vulgar tongue', [PH, p.62] or jokingly tells Augusta that her use of 'the bust' as the name for one of her dressmaker's forms is an example of 'a natural law of language, termed, for convenience, metonymy'. [PH, p.18] (Metonymy is a feature of his language, the 'house' standing in for his life and his death, Tom's 'hand' representing to St Peter his whole character.) His writing circles back and forward in time, as opposed to Tom's linear chronology. It is third as opposed to first person, and so appears inward-looking and ironical. Since Tom's death, St Peter has had no one to talk to, and (like James's Dr Sloper or Jane Austen's Mr Bennet) has to take a sardonic pleasure in being misunderstood.

St Peter's style, privileged, involuted, self-referential, is in a tradition of highly mannered Europeanized American writing of which James, Cather's old mentor, is the prime example. (St Peter cites James at one point, apologizing for his family's behaviour like a character in *The American*.) Phyllis Rose, writing very well about *The Professor's House*, finds this manner 'strained – overly didactic, underlining all points, the dialogue forced'.[30] But the strain is the point: Cather needs to set a Europeanized, literary language against a native, democratic American speech. The contrast between St Peter's style and Tom's belongs to a long-running American conflict, pinpointed by Philip Rahv,[31] as that between 'palefaces' (James, Wharton, Eliot) and 'redskins' (Whitman, Twain). Cather is unusual in making both languages interpenetrate.

Tom's is also a written memory. But its eloquence is in strong contrast to St Peter's. Like Huckleberry Finn, Tom is the native plain speaker, talking directly to us in the first person, who doesn't think of himself as articulate. Both Huck Finn and Tom Outland insert paradoxical disclaimers into their most lyrical passages:

> Everything was dead quiet, and it looked late, and *smelt* late. You know what I mean – I don't know the words to put it in.[32]

> I wish I could tell you what I saw there, just *as* I saw it . . . [PH, p.201]

> I can't describe it. It was more like sculpture than anything else. [PH, p.202]

As part of the pretence of inarticulacy, Tom Outland's speech makes frequent use of the tough, jokey understatements that are a feature of Western American male speech. The account of poor old Henry's death, for instance, is made up of simple sentence structures and matter-of-fact colloquialisms: 'We lost old Henry. . . . We'd been a little bothered by rattlesnakes. . . . We had got them pretty well cleared out. . . . We caught sight of a little bunch of ruins. . . . We almost made it. . . . A snake struck him square in the forehead. . . . He was so crazy it took the two of us to hold him. . . . We were so cut up that we were almost ready to quit. . . . He got our minds off our trouble.' [PH, pp.216–17] When this 'ornery' folk speech slides into something more literary, its tropes are almost always similes, as in the descriptions of the mesa and the city (like a diamond, like sculpture, and so on). The effect is sequential and explanatory, in contrast with the Professor's use of metaphor and metonymy, non-linear substitutions which carry more than one meaning at once.

Tom's 'simple' eloquence must ring true: it is essential that we believe in the integrity of his language, so that it can stand against shams and dis-integrations. Cather guarantees this by making him not only unconfident of his own articulacy (unlike Louie Marsellus's supremely confident fluency), but unwilling to speak at all. His story is always being withheld. After he arrives at the Professor's house he 'never took up the story of his life again'; instead, he tells it to the little girls, keeping them in some suspense too: '"Oh, Tom, *tell* us . . ." He would whisper: "Pretty soon."' [PH, p.125] Only after four years does he tell St Peter 'the story he had always kept back'. [PH, p.176] And he tells Roddy about his feelings too late, because 'it was the kind of thing one doesn't talk about directly'. [PH, p.239]

The preliterate Indians left behind them a composition as close to nature as possible; Cather wants Tom's language to be a natural speech, imitating that silent testimony. But Tom is not 'dumb', in either sense (and he is to blame for concealing his feelings from Roddy). He is educated, unlike Huck Finn, and literate. His narration is, in part, a process of naming things: 'We began to call it Cow Canyon'; [PH, p.198] 'Cliff City, as we already called it'; [PH, p.203] 'Henry named her Mother Eve, and we called her that.' [PH, p.214]

And it involves references to reading and writing. When Tom memorizes long passages of Virgil's *Aeneid*, he recognizes, in his own feelings, 'a religious emotion', 'the filial piety' of 'the Latin poets'. [PH, p.251] Once again, Cather is applying an oral tradition of classical poetry to an American landscape. So she deliberately blurs the distinction between the written and the spoken. St Peter plans to 'edit and annotate' Tom's diary 'for publication'. The inset story, however, seems not to be that diary, but Tom's spoken narrative, told to St Peter on another long-ago summer. After his spoken story ends (with 'and the rest you know'), the Professor's narrative resumes with his consideration of Tom's written record. His editorial commentary on it amalgamates and reconciles the spoken and the written:

> To St Peter this plain account was almost beautiful, because of the stupidities it avoided and the things it did not say. If words had cost money, Tom couldn't have used them more sparingly. The adjectives were purely descriptive, relating to form and colour, and were used to present the objects under consideration, not the young explorer's emotions. Yet through this austerity one felt the kindling imagination, the ardour and the excitement of the boy, like the vibration in a voice when the speaker strives to conceal his emotion by using only conventional phrases. [PH, pp.262–3]

Tom's classical narrative confirms the Professor's beliefs about restraint and excision in art. In fact it teaches St Peter to 'excise' his own narrative: after he meets him, his book becomes 'more simple and inevitable' than it was before. [PH, p.258]

So the novel is an epitome of all Cather's writing, in which she divides herself between two 'writers': Tom as the instinctual explorer and the Professor as the conscious reviser. Looked at in this way, negativeness, which seemed to be just an element in the Professor's 'accidie', turns out to be a saving virtue. When Tom takes possession of the cliff-city, 'he does not go for his record': 'I was afraid that I would lose the whole for the parts'. It is only by abandoning words and losing the objects he has labelled that it becomes possible for him to 'co-ordinate and simplify'; it brings with it 'great happiness'.

Co-ordinate and simplify describes the design of the cliff-city, Tom's narrative, and the novel itself. In a mysterious parallel process at the end of the book, St Peter gives up on reading, writing, speech and social relations, and also finds it possible to 'co-ordinate and simplify'. Withdrawing into dream-states and reverie, he rediscovers his 'original ego' and his connection with nature.[33] Only words of one syllable will do for this regressive 'recognition'.

> He seemed to be at the root of the matter; Desire under all desires, Truth under all truths. He seemed to know, among other things, that he was solitary and must always be so; he had never married, never been a father. He was earth, and would return to earth. When white clouds blew over the lake like bellying sails, when the seven pine-trees turned red in the declining sun, he felt satisfaction and said of himself merely: 'That is right'. Coming upon a curly root that thrust itself across his path, he said: 'That is it.' When the maple-leaves along the street began to turn yellow and waxy, and were soft to the touch, – like the skin on old faces, – he said: 'That is true; it is time.' All these recognitions gave him a kind of sad pleasure. [PH, pp.265–6]

This climactic recognition of a primitive, instinctual self brings Cather extraordinarily close to some of her contemporaries. In this great novel, published at the height of the modernist movement, Cather, for all her isolationism and conservative nostalgia, is involved in the modern quest to find, in the instinctual, the primitive, and the mythological, 'elemental and enduring truths'.[34] The connection with Lawrence, particularly striking in this novel, is more than coincidental. Cather met the Lawrences in New York early in 1924, when she was writing it. This was the year of *Studies in Classic American Literature*, which diagnosed the fatal split in the modern American psyche between instinctual, sensual knowledge ('the true centrality of the self')[35] and 'civilized', heightened, neurotic consciousness. After his meeting with Cather, which both writers enjoyed,[36] the Lawrences went to New Mexico. Cather followed them a year later; like the Lawrences, who had by then moved to a ranch outside Taos, she was a wary guest of Mabel Dodge Luhan. Cather paid them a visit, they 'got on famously', [37] and she sent them a copy of *The Song of the Lark*.

The overlap of experiences and interests is remarkable. For all Cather's negative remarks about Lawrence in 'The Novel Démeublé', their responses to the Indian Southwest had a good deal in common. Among the writings of Lawrence which came out of that place and time – 'New Mexico', 'The Woman Who Rode Away', *Birds, Beasts and Flowers* – the essay 'Pan in America', written in 1924, is perhaps closest in feeling. Lawrence rhapsodizes over the pine-tree in the Rockies that 'interpenetrates' his life, expressing 'raw earth-power and raw sky-power'. He identifies the 'silent' Pan-spirit with the tree and the Indians, in opposition to modern America, and laments the personal loss resulting from that split:

> What can a man do with his life but live it? And what does life consist in, save a vivid relatedness between the man and the living universe that surrounds him? Yet man insulates himself more and more into mechanism, and repudiates everything but the machine and the contrivance of which he himself is master, god in the machine.[38]

The tone is quite different, but the preoccupation is connected to Godfrey St Peter's.

There is, also, a striking, if coincidental, similarity of tone between the end of *The Professor's House* and the last section (written at much the same age) of Virginia Woolf's *The Waves* (1931). Bernard, the writer, feeling his youth 'over and done with' ('The moving was over and done'), shocked by the young death of Percival, his Tom Outland, into seeing 'things' without 'pretence and make-believe and unreality', is an elderly man facing his mortality. Moving towards silence and solitude, he turns away from a lifetime of phrase-making, and regresses to a 'little language' – 'I need a howl, a cry' – that will describe 'the world seen without a self'.

Thin as a ghost, leaving no trace where I trod, perceiving merely, I walked alone in a new world, never trodden; brushing new flowers, unable to speak save in a child's words of one syllable. . . .

But how describe the world seen without a self? There are no words. Blue, red – even they distract, even they hide with thickness instead of letting the light through. How describe or say anything in articulate words again? . . . But for a moment I had sat on the turf somewhere high above the flow of the sea and the sound of the woods, had seen the house, the garden and the waves breaking. The old nurse who turns the pages of the picture-book had stopped and had said, 'Look. This is the truth.'[39]

The quest for a true language is common to all three writers. In the end, the Professor's house is the book itself: Cather has written a writer's autobiography. As another fine American woman writer, Eudora Welty, says of it: [40] 'A work of art is the house that is *not* the grave. An achievement of order, passionately conceived and passionately carried out, it is not a thing of darkness.'

12

THE GOLDEN LEGEND

The New World presses on us all; there seems no end to it –
and no beginning. So too with him. . . . To me there is a world
of pleasure in watching just that Frenchman. . . . Watching,
keeping the thing whole within him with almost a woman's
tenderness – but with such an energy for detail – a love of the
exact detail – . . . . This is the interest I see. It is this man. This
– me; this American . . .

William Carlos Williams,
In the American Grain, 1925

THE PROFESSOR'S HOUSE and *My Mortal Enemy* were
paradoxical triumphs, masterpieces written out of depression
and unease. They appear to have had, momentarily, the
effect of a catharsis. The next two years, 1925 and 1926,
were a period of relative contentment. Of course this sort of
biographical generalization sweeps over the very fluctuations
of mood and phases of emotion to which Cather's own
writing was so responsive. But it does seem as if, after 1927,
in her late fifties and sixties, things did not go well for her.
Losses, anxieties, illnesses and disenchantments came to
dominate the last part of her life. The years of *Death Comes for
the Archbishop* were her last 'best years', and they produced
the most appeased and celebratory of all her novels. *Death
Comes for the Archbishop* does not have the childhood landscape and folktale of the Nebraskan pastorals, or the deep
personal feeling of *My Ántonia* or *A Lost Lady*. It doesn't give

itself away emotionally in the manner of *The Song of the Lark* or *One of Ours*; it stays above the complicated tensions of *The Professor's House* and *My Mortal Enemy*. For readers like myself who admire that dark phase of Cather's writing above all the rest, its calm, hagiographical, legendary narrative may be less involving. Something ferocious and unreconciled, that goes right back to the dark primitive troll-self of the hero of her first novel, is placed at arm's length, outside the characters, in a symbolic landscape. *Death Comes for the Archbishop* is secure, ritualized, and impersonal. The 'thing not named' works in it not as a troubling pressure, but for a sense of serene accomplishment. We are being told, the book seems to say, exactly what we need to know, and in the best possible way. Explanations (of motive, relationships, psychological ambiguities) are minimalized. The effect on us is like the influence on Cather of the New Mexican mission churches, which, with their 'moving reality', are, she said, 'their own story'.[1]

The phrase is a reminder of Cather's methods: to build a narrative shape which, as a church is intended to do, incarnates its meanings. This is no new departure. We recognize Cather's insistence on truthfulness as simplicity of form, from Alexandra's 'white book' to Tom Outland's withheld narrative. But now her visionary pastoral has been Christianized; we have moved from B.C. to A.D. Cather's acknowledgement, in 1922, of her links to the Episcopal church (which led in later years to a pious, indeed somewhat sickly correspondence with the Bishop of Red Cloud) had preceded the first signs of interest in orthodox religion in the fiction of the mid 1920s: as a form of art and authority in *The Professor's House*, as a consolation for death in *My Mortal Enemy*. But in these novels, the religious material, though a far cry from her earlier robust satires on Christian hypocrisy, was used equivocally and indirectly. Now, by making her beliefs historical and objectified, she was able to express them fully. Cather's first 'new testament' works supremely well, by virtue of the kind of 'miracle' that is repeatedly accounted for, in the novel, as the combined operation of destiny, love and attention. This 'miracle' never quite recurs. *Shadows on the Rock* has its own charm and interest, but is much quieter. Apart from some perfectly achieved late stories of retrospection, 'Two Friends', 'Neighbour Rosicky' and 'Old Mrs Harris', Cather's work would never again strike the same confidence, depth and joy, like the sound of the Spanish bell which Father Joseph finds in an old adobe church in Santa Fé: 'Full, clear, with something bland and suave, each note floated through the air like a globe of silver.' [DA, p.43]

My Mortal Enemy was written quickly, in the spring of 1925, as soon as *The Professor's House* was finished. That summer she and Edith set out again for the Southwest. In July, Cather was in New Mexico, correcting the proofs of *The Professor's House* (which came out in September to better reviews than she expected) at the San Gabriel Ranch in Española, north of Santa Fé. After that she made her wary visit to the rich, eccentric, bohemian American hostess Mabel Dodge Luhan, on her Taos estate. Cather greatly admired Mabel's silent, impressive-looking Indian husband Tony Luhan, who acted as a chauffeur and guide, and provided a model for the Archbishop's Indian friend Eusabio. But she kept clear of what Lawrence (now miles away with Frieda and Dorothy Brett at the Del Monte Ranch, where Cather paid her respects) spitefully called 'Mabeltown'. She stayed in the Pink House, set apart from Mabel's social round, and she did not stay long.[2]

Her next stop was Santa Fé, still, at that time (for all the American building of the 1880s which her Bishop would deplore), a characteristically New Mexican town, full of adobe houses, set among 'carnelian-coloured hills' which 'closed about it like two encircling arms'. [DA, p.255] The town was dominated by its golden, French Romanesque cathedral of St Francis, the 1880s work of the French Jesuit Archbishop Lamy, whose bronze statue Cather had often admired. Her feeling for French culture and architecture went back, of course, to her early reading and her first visit to

Europe. And her interest in the New Mexican mission priests was an old one too: like most of her subjects, it had been saved up for years. Reconstructing her sources for *Death Comes for the Archbishop*, she remembered her meeting with a Belgian priest in 1912, in 'the beautiful old church at Santa Cruz, New Mexico', 'where he raised fancy poultry and sheep and had a wonderful vegetable and flower garden'.[3] This knowledgeable farmer-priest was of use in *The Professor's House* as Father Duchene. And, just as her feeling for the mesas and the ancient Indian culture was saved, used, and then re-used, so her interest in the mission priests persisted. She told E.K. Brown in 1946 that she had once sat up by the Martyr's Cross, east of Santa Fé, watching the Sangre de Cristo mountains colour in the sunset (a colour which the Bishop startlingly but characteristically compares to liquefying blood of old saints and martyrs) and realized suddenly that the real story of the Southwest was the story of the missionary priests from France, with their cultivated minds, their large vision, and their noble purpose.[4] Now, in this summer of 1925, a chance discovery clinched her feeling for the Southwest and her interest in the missions. She came across a Jesuit biography, by a Father Howlett, of Archbishop Lamy's right-hand man in New Mexico, Joseph Machebeuf, who later became Bishop of Denver. As the story of Richard Wetherill had done for Tom Outland's story, it unlocked her subject, and enabled her to graft a historical narrative onto her private religious feelings.

The stay in Santa Fé was followed, that summer, by dramatic journeys to the Indian pueblo on the great rock mesa of Acoma, west of Albuquerque (via an enforced stay at a filthy hotel in Laguna, where they were trapped by rainstorms.) The drive (they hired a chauffeur: Cather never learned to drive a car)[5] took them past the Enchanted Mesa, the rock on which an Indian tribe had once built their village and been destroyed. Nearly twenty years before, Cather's mid-Western boys had told each other this story in 'The Enchanted Bluff'; now it would be told to the Bishop, for him to make into a spiritual parable of 'the rock', as 'the

utmost expression of human need'. Translated thus, from
fiction to fact to fiction again, altered in its use from
Turgenevian, impressionistic pastoral to a formal Christian
trope, and appropriated from aboriginal American history
into a modernist American narrative, the 'rock' now settles
into the centre of Cather's landscape.

As she left New Mexico, all the materials for *Death Comes
for the Archbishop* – Mexican, French, American, Christian,
Indian – were falling into place. After a meeting with Roscoe
and his family in Denver, and then (as usual in the summers
of the 1920s, and as usual without Edith) a visit to Red Cloud
to see her parents and her brother James's and sister Jessica's
families, she went back to Jaffrey and started to write the
novel. The autumn was interrupted by two lectures at
Chicago University and the Women's City Club at Cleveland
on 'The Tendency of the Modern Novel' – the kind of
appearances Cather undertook reluctantly but carried out
efficiently. (She gave short shrift to a Cleveland reporter who
tried to find out about her next novel, but who elicited one
revealing remark: 'America works on my mind like light on a
photographic plate'.)[6] By March 1926, when *My Mortal
Enemy* was published (to a puzzled and lukewarm reception),
she was well under way; she was to describe the writing of
Death Comes for the Archbishop as 'a happy vacation from life',
a source of daily pleasure.[7]

In May she went back to its setting – for the last time, as it
turned out – visiting the dramatic site of the Canyon de
Chelly, in Navajo reservation land (a long car and horse ride
from Gallup), and the strange landmark nearby, a high rock
shaped like a ship. This finale to her Southwestern travels
was fitted, like a coda, into the last part of the novel. Back in
Taos, Cather took advantage again, briefly, of the Luhans'
hospitality, and also of the Californian novelist Mary Austin's
offer of her house in Santa Fé. (When Austin, in her mystical
and self-regarding 1933 autobiography, *Earth Horizon*, boas-
ted that Cather wrote all of *Death Comes for the Archbishop* in
her house, and at the same time criticized its Francophile
enthusiasm for the cathedral which had been 'a calamity' for

the local Spanish culture, Cather was not pleased.[8]) In the autumn, she made a short and uncharacteristic stay at a writer's colony in New Hampshire, where she was not remembered for conviviality,[9] then travelled up to Grand Manan, the wild Maine island she had fallen in love with in 1921, to oversee the start of the cottage that she and Edith were having built there. For the rest of the autumn she was back at the Shattuck Inn in New Jaffrey, finishing the novel, as she wrote wistfully a year later, 'in a lovely place'.[10] By Christmas *Death Comes for the Archbishop* was finished, and serialization began in January.[11]

Death Comes for the Archbishop is marked out and moved along by the mission priests' enormous, adventurous, arduous journeys, the novel's substitutes for a sustained plot. These huge journeys were true to the history of the pioneering priests: the biographies of Bishops Lamy and Machebeuf are full of them. But they also drew Cather to their lives through a sense of affinity. The writing of *Death Comes for the Archbishop* was, she said, a reflection of her pleasure in wandering and riding through the Southwest over many years.[12] When, in a letter of 1925 from Santa Fé, she compared the pleasure of writing to the pleasure of a pack trip through desert and mountain country,[13] she was not just playing the outdoor, un-genteel, anti-intellectual American writer: this novel really was an attempt to make these pleasures correspond. It enacted, though, not only her pleasant adventures in the Southwest, but the formidable long-distance travels almost annually entailed by family claims and her pursuit of remote writing retreats. She divided these experiences between her two hero-priests. Father Joseph Vaillant (the novel's name for Joseph Machebeuf) has her stoical energy and appetite for travel; Father Jean Latour (Archbishop Lamy) her aesthetic and historical feeling for what she sees.

Cather explains her choice of these two historical figures, and of a narrative to suit them, in a fascinating open letter of 1927 to the editor of *The Commonweal*. Like all the public statements on her aesthetics, it insists, misleadingly, on the natural inevitability of her writing, while revealing a complex process of appropriation and selection. Cather gives a long list of sources for the story: her travels in the Southwest, the Belgian priest and his garden, the New Mexican mission churches with their wooden statues of saints ('a direct expression of some very real and lively human feeling'), her growing curiosity about the distinguished figure of Archbishop Lamy, the discovery of Howlett's book, the frescoes of the life of St Geneviève by Puvis de Chavannes (painted on the nave of the Pantheon in Paris in the 1870s), the 'Golden Legend' (a medieval collection of saints' lives), the language of Father Machebeuf's letters, some conversations with a priest in Red Cloud, and Holbein's 'Dance of Death', mentioned in passing as the inspiration for the title. The use she made of this mixture of personal, literary, oral and painterly materials is brought together in the passage on Puvis de Chavannes and the 'Golden Legend', a marvellous (and much-quoted) exposure of the deliberate strategies behind her seeming unartfulness:

> My book was a conjunction of the general and the particular, like most works of the imagination. I had all my life wanted to do something in the style of legend, which is absolutely the reverse of dramatic treatment. Since I first saw the Puvis de Chavannes frescoes of the life of Saint Geneviève in my student days, I have wished that I could try something a little like that in prose; something without accent, with none of the artificial elements of composition. In the Golden Legend the martyrdoms of the saints are no more dwelt upon than are the trivial incidents of their lives; it is as though all human experiences, measured against one supreme spiritual experience, were of about the same importance. The essence of such writing is not to hold the note, not to use an incident for all there is in it – but to touch and pass on. I felt that such writing would be a kind of discipline in these days when the 'situation' is made to count for so much in writing, when the general tendency is to force things up. In this kind of writing the mood is the thing – all the little figures and stories are mere improvisations that come out of it.[14]

The 'conjunction of the general and the particular' was not a new departure: nor was the grafting of specific styles of art onto personal materials. But, for the first time, Cather was translating historical particulars into fiction. It is a long way from Father Howlett's pious hagiography of the Right Reverend Joseph P. Machebeuf, via de Chavannes, Holbein, and the 'Golden Legend', to the 'something without accent' that Cather made of it; and it is extremely interesting to see how she transformed her historical source into 'the style of legend'.[15]

Father Howlett used Machebeuf's letters to his sister, a nun in a provincial French convent, to tell a chronological story of a young Jesuit seminarian, son of a baker in the Auvergne, who in 1839 broke away from his family, with his friend and fellow-priest Jean Baptiste Lamy, and ran away to the Seminary of Foreign Missions in Paris. Both young priests were sent out as missionaries to Ohio, where they worked for ten years. (In 1844, Machebeuf went to Europe and had an audience with Pope Gregory XVI.) In 1850 Father Lamy was appointed Bishop Apostolic of the newly annexed American territory of New Mexico, and took Machebeuf with him as his Vicar General, as 'part of the agreement we made', (Machebeuf said) 'never to separate'. (An agreement which would be set aside, to Lamy's sadness, when in 1860 Machebeuf was transferred to Denver, to become a notable pioneer priest in the rough goldmining districts of Colorado, until his death in 1889, a year after Lamy's.) Their early days in the Southwest were dominated by their dramatic confrontations with the suspicious, anti-American native Mexican clergy (some of whose lives, according to Machebeuf, were 'scandalous beyond description'), their reconsolidating of a Catholic faith in decline and mission churches in disrepair, and their political programme of 'detaching the church in New Mexico from its Mexican affiliations, and making it dependent upon conditions in the United States'. Howlett complacently attributes to the influence of such Catholic priests the 'elevation of the New Mexican to his present conditions of comparatively intelligent, honest and moral civilization'.[16]

Nothing could be further from Cather's impartial, apolitical tone. Her appropriation of this, the latest of her male authorities, is all in the direction of suggestiveness and evocation, away from propaganda and orthodoxy. Obviously, she switches heroes, making Howlett's background figure of Lamy (a thoughtful scholar-priest) into her central character, and giving Machebeuf, the homely man of action, a second place. To make the shift more conclusive she altered the order of their deaths, so that Lamy/Latour can include, in his last retrospections, the funeral of his old friend. Their names, too, are adapted to her special needs. Latour's tower (of strength? ivory?) contrasts with 'Vaillant' as pilgrim-knight-priest. There is a reminder of Professor St Peter in his attic room (or tower) musing on the valiant Tom Outland. And the meaningful names make a strong gesture, in this Catholicized narrative, towards the great Nonconformist text which so much infuenced Cather, Bunyan's *The Pilgrim's Progress*.[17]

So that Vaillant's valour would not dominate the novel, Cather carefully toned down or omitted all Howlett's stories of Machebeuf's courageous exploits. His public confrontations with the recalcitrant native priests, for instance, are passed over; instead the emphasis is placed on their picturesque, allegorical qualities. Padre Martínez, a formidable embodiment of cunning, primitivism and sensuality, is connected with the sombre rites of the 'Penitentes' at Abiquiu (there is no mention of this in Howlett), and Lucero, his companion in revolt, is given a wonderfully extravagant, Browningesque miser's deathbed scene. The legendary American scout Kit Carson, who in Howlett actively supports Lamy and Machebeuf against Martínez, figures in the novel only in glimpses. He is a friend to Latour and to the native culture (he has a Mexican wife, and is a highly intelligent man who cannot read – 'he had got ahead of books' [DA, p.75]) but plays no active part until the very end, when his 'misguided' war against the Indians surprisingly comes into focus. But mostly he slips through the book as a scout should, providing essential information, turning up when needed, and making himself scarce.

Cather's improvisation on themes provided by Howlett's 'Life and Letters' are as revealing as her suppressions. Latour becomes her kind of hero:[18] delicate and distinguished, chivalric, aesthetic, sympathetic (especially to the Indians, for whom Howlett has no time at all), nostalgic for France, in love with order and tradition, patient to the point of passivity, vulnerable, self-doubting, and in need of Vaillant's support. (Their close friendship was a historical fact – Lamy recalls Machebeuf from Arizona, Howlett records, only because 'he wanted to see him'[19] – but Cather makes the most of it.) Machebeuf, similarly, is developed from every detail offered by his energetic letters into a characterization of an ugly, stoic, zealous Frenchman in the New World, with a love of good food and a talent for begging for the Church, a lack of pride, a democratic gregariousness, and a sentimental faith in the Virgin Mary. Some phrases in his letters, like his jovial complaint that Lamy always sends him to do the dirty work ('à fouetter les chats') [DA, p.162] are simply lifted, others give her the handle for a whole vivid scene. A mention of his love of olive oil and salads is expanded into his first appearance, cooking a French Christmas dinner for Latour and complaining of the lack of ingredients: '"How can a man make a proper soup without leeks, that king of vegetables?"' [DA, p.39] Machebeuf's reference in a letter to his begging two mules from a rich Mexican with the words 'Bishop Lamy needs a mule as badly as I do'[20] becomes, in the section called 'The White Mules', a self-contained story illustrating Vaillant's mixture of candour and ruthlessness. In a bustling, high-coloured, comical narrative which fits its subject, Father Joseph briskly brings the Christian sacraments to Manuel Lujon's benighted household of servants ('"No, I tell you, Lujon, the marriages first, the baptisms afterwards; that order is but Christian"'); [DA, p.55] makes sure, to the amazement of his host, that his lamb for dinner is roasted *seignant* and not stewed with chillis; and wheedles the two mules, for the glory of God, out of the generous but reluctant Lujon. In the next scene, an obvious contrast, Vaillant and Latour, riding those same mules, are looking for shelter in the rain on a lonely stretch of the road to Mora; this time their host is a sinister American, a would-be assassin, with a terrified Mexican wife, who warns them away and escapes after them. There is no climax and no comment in either the jovial or the ominous episode, but a meaning is saved up from each of them: the mules become a touching symbol for the two men's friendship, and the criminal's wife, Magdalena, rescued by the priests, turns into Mary Magdalene.

The mules, stolen from history for Cather's own purposes, as Vaillant steals them from Manuel Lujon for his, set the pace of the book; she once said that she saw *Death Comes for the Archbishop* as a narrative, hardly a novel at all, which moved along on two white mules that were not in a hurry.[21] Howlett's history is transformed into a stylized narrative which avoids chronology and three-dimensionality. There is a plot — the two men make their long journey to New Mexico, they subdue the opposition of the native priests, they bring spiritual order to their terrain over long hard years, Vaillant goes to Colorado and Latour builds his cathedral. But that is not how we see it. We start with some subtle European dignitaries of the Church hearing from a missionary priest, over a very civilized Roman dinner, of the religious needs of the new territories. Then, as though walking through a frame into a different light (another version of the technique of *The Professor's House*) we see a series of significant illuminated pictures. Here is the young Bishop lost and thirsting in the desert, praying in front of a juniper tree shaped like a cross which has 'miraculously' appeared in his path; now here is the Bishop, having been rescued and taken to a Mexican settlement, tellingly called 'Agua Secreta', sitting in the afternoon sun by the banks of the 'life-giving stream', reflecting on this village as 'his Bishopric in miniature':

'hundreds of square miles of thirsty desert, then a spring, a village, old men trying to remember their catechism to teach their grandchildren.' [DA, p.32]

Evidently Cather is working in close imitation of her sources. This process has been much admired and discussed, in analyses of her debt to Puvis de Chavannes' fake-medieval frieze of the quiet holy stories of St Geneviève (its monumental, static quality, the soft light in which the figures seem to be suspended 'outside time', the lack of perspective)[22] and to 'The Golden Legend'. A suggestive comparison has been made with Auerbach's definition, in *Mimesis*, of medieval narrative as 'paratactic', working through complete scenes set side by side: 'a series of loosely related "pictures", each of which captures a gesture from a decisive moment in the subject's life'.[23] Cather's best critics[24] find in her use of this method not a retreat into the *faux-naif*, but a sophisticated version of symbolism, a modernist refusal of naturalism. As in more sensational contemporaneous modernist works, shaped by quite opposite feelings of uncertainty and scepticism – *The Waste Land* or *To the Lighthouse* or *The Sound and the Fury* – the narrative method *is* the meaning. The point, Cather says in her commentary on the novel, is to make it seem that everything is being seen and understood at once – as though God were telling the story. Like the great modernist texts, but with a different intention from most of them, this redistributed narrative makes its centre a conception of time, not as linear accumulation, but as a conjunction of 'timeless moments'.

To this end, a sustained chronology is carefully subverted, and many crucial events, which Howlett narrates in their proper order (such as Latour's encouragement of Vaillant when the two young men are running away from home) are saved up till very near the end of their lives. 'In their end is their beginning.' Instead of a cumulative plot the nine books of the novel have sections with titles, each of which starts again, like the separate anecdotes of saints' lives in the 'Golden Legend' ('In a tyme ther was a man' . . . 'In a tyme

also a man ther was' . . . 'And another tyme he was in his
medytacyons' . . .),[25] with no direct connection to what
preceded it: 'One afternoon in the autumn of 1851'; 'The
Bishop and his Vicar were riding through the rain in the
Truchas mountains'; 'Bishop Latour, with Jacinto, was riding
through the mountains on his first official visit to Taos'.
'Memorable occasions' [DA, p.140], such as the building of
the new cathedral, are anticipated or recalled, but not
enacted. Dates are withheld, and sometimes work back-
wards, so that at the start of the final book, a letter from
Latour dated 1888, a few months before his death, is
followed by a reference to the arrival of his young assistant in
1885, then by a return to the building of the cathedral in
1880, and finally by a recollection of his journey to the
Navajo country in 1875.

The main narrative is punctuated by a number of inset
stories. Some of these are remembered events which have
been 'passed over' at the time, to emerge later. In one of
these, Vaillant tells of an encounter with an Indian who
showed him a cave with, long buried inside it, the chalice
and other objects for the celebration of the Mass. This story
has been 'buried' until it is needed as a parable for Vaillant's
plea that he should be sent to Arizona to discover the 'buried
treasure' of lost Catholic souls. Others of these 'buried', inset
stories go back into history and legend: they invoke the
miracle of Our Lady of Guadalupe in 1531, or the momen-
tous 1680 rebellion of the Indians.

The effect is partly to make the whole story, told in the
twentieth century of the nineteenth, feel like a medieval
legend. (It is often hard to remember that the historical
period of *Death Comes for the Archbishop*, 1848 to 1880, closes
as the period of *O Pioneers!* and *My Ántonia* is beginning. The
later novel seems to be set much earlier in time.) But it is also
to remove irony and suspense, the usual characteristics of
historical narrative. When the Bishop watches his friend's
preparations for the move to Denver, 'he seemed to know, as
if it had been revealed to him, that this was a final break; that
their lives would part here, and that they would never work

together again'. [DA, p.252] No dramatic distinction is made between what is 'revealed' to him, and what to us. Everything can be read, everything is 'revealed' at the same time.

At the end of the book this way of reading is 'revealed' as the novel's subject as well as its method. The Bishop on his deathbed observes 'that there was no longer any perspective in his memories': all his 'states of mind' are 'within reach of his hand, and all comprehensible'. Everything is placed together in 'the great picture of his life'. [DA, p.290] The native prehistory of the ancient New World (which at times he has felt in ominous, antediluvian resistance to his European habits of mind), the historic period 'accomplished' in his lifetime, and the moments of his own existence, are ordered − as the scenes of this narrative have been ordered − from the viewpoint of immortality. It is a reconciled version of the more ominous predestined returnings to the past, which have turned out to be movements towards death, in all her novels. That death 'comes' for the archbishop is simply another scene in the 'great picture', another act in the continuing present tense. As in the Holbein sequence, death does not make an unexpected appearance; he comes, is there, all the time. '"I shall not die of a cold, my son,"' the Bishop says to his young assistant, without anxiety, '"I shall die of having lived."' [DA, p.269]

If history in the eye of God (or the archbishop) is a series of pictures all seen, in stasis, at the same time, the narrative has to make its meanings not out of slowly developing psychological states or complex political entanglements, but out of gesture, appearance, colour and light. What Rebecca West, in a strong essay on *Death Comes for the Archbishop*, calls its 'amazing sensory achievements',[26] its intense, brilliant visualizations, is a performance of prodigious virtuosity. Cather insisted that she had avoided 'dramatic treatment' in this novel, and, in terms of plot, so she did. But in another way, her description of it as an exercise in restraint and simplicity is misleading. In its 'mood' ('the mood is the thing'),[27] *Death Comes for the Archbishop* is sensationally dramatic. Of course Cather has always been able, in Conrad's words, 'to make you hear, to make you feel . . . before all, to make you *see*.'[28] But there are two new developments.

One is that, for the first and last time, the Southwest *is* the novel. In the past – in 'The Enchanted Bluff', or *The Song of the Lark*, or *The Professor's House* – the desert and mesa country had been seen in contrast with, or through the frame of, a more subdued environment. Now, the subdued frame-landscape – here, the fondly remembered grey streets and chestnut trees of the Auvergne, which, when at last he returns to them, Latour finds sad and enervating – has become the background. *Death Comes for the Archbishop* is flooded with colour and space, with light which shifts and fluctuates, written up again and again in imitation of the mesa country, where each rock has its reduplicated cloud-shape 'like a reflection' above it:

> The desert, the mountains and mesas, were continually re-formed and re-coloured by the cloud shadows. The whole country seemed fluid to the eye under this constant change of accent, this ever-varying distribution of light. [DA, p.96]

The language of composition – 're-formed', 'change of accent', 'distribution' – makes plain the parallel she intends between her improvisation as a novelist, and the improvisations of the maker of this astounding scene. 'Let there be light' is a phrase common to both.

That takes us on to the other difference between the 'amazing sensory achievements' of *Death Comes for the Archbishop* and the earlier novels. All this light and colour and landscape *means*: it is there to be read. *Death Comes for the Archbishop* is not full of luxurious description just because she wanted a lot of atmosphere; what is seen (as in the venerable tradition of American philosophers of landscape, Emerson, Thoreau and Frost) is meant to be translated. The distinction between this and the plough on the horizon in *My Ántonia*, or the ridges on the sandbanks in 'The Enchanted Bluff' is that, now, the readings are sacramental. Bishop Latour habitually makes theological translations of the scene – it's part of his Jesuit training. On his first appearance, he shuts his eyes against the unreadable 'geometrical nightmare' of the repetitious desert, and opens them to find a juniper tree he can read – 'living vegetation could not present more faithfully the form of the Cross'. [DA, p.19] The sun glittering on the rain after the storm puts him in mind of the first morning of the Creation; [DA, p.99] the Sangre de Cristo mountains remind him of the dried blood of saints. [DA, p.273]

Latour's Jesuitical interpretations are condoned by the author's typological[29] readings. The priests' gardens, for instance (Christianized versions of the Professor's French garden) obviously symbolize the European qualities of order and good housekeeping their mission brings with it, and much play is made throughout with souls as seeds that need watering. Cather takes particular pleasure in 'reading' the desert plants, which seem to come alive under observation: the patches of wild pumpkin that look 'less like a plant than like a great colony of grey-green lizards, moving and suddenly arrested by fear'; [DA, p.88] the ancient, twisted cottonwoods with bursts of delicate leaf-growth at the very tip of their huge branches. [DA, p.222] By implication, their energetic growth in the teeth of unpromising conditions represents the priests themselves.

But there are different kinds of readings. The illiterate Kit Carson makes a practical reading of the landscape which prints 'a reliable map' of it in his brain; the Indians, his adversaries, make a quite different translation of landscape which the Bishop comes to understand (as he would learn a new language) as a theology equal in complexity to his own. There are variations, too, within the Catholic reading of landscape. Latour appreciates the New Mexican tamarisk tree for its aesthetic suitability: it seems to him 'especially designed in shape and colour for the adobe village'. [DA, p.202] Vaillant, by contrast, loves it because it has been 'the companion of his wanderings' and seems to him 'the tree of the people'. [DA, p.202]

This difference in readings, one more aesthetic and aloof,

the other more personal and humane, extends to the two
priests' views of miracles, a crucial subject which contains a
form of commentary on the way the book works. Vaillant, a
more naive and credulous reader than Latour, believes in
miraculous interventions. 'His dear Joseph' (thinks Latour)
'must always have the miracle very direct and spectacular,
not with Nature, but against it'. [DA, p.29] To corroborate
that reading, several such miracles are given as inset legends,
always told through sympathetically simple voices, like the
humble old Father Escolastico's faithful rendering of the
story of Our Lady of Guadalupe (whose appearance to a
poor Mexican in 1531 was authenticated by the roses she
told him to gather in December and by the miraculous
portrait of herself imprinted on his robe). Latour appreciates
this form of belief. But for him, a miracle is simply an
intensified version of perception:

> 'Where there is great love there are always miracles,' he said at
> length. 'One might almost say that an apparition is human
> vision corrected by divine love. I do not see you as you really
> are, Joseph; I see you through my affection for you. The
> Miracles of the Church seem to me to rest not so much upon
> faces or voices or healing power coming suddenly near to us
> from afar off, but upon our perceptions being made finer, so
> that for a moment our eyes can see and our ears can hear what
> is there about us always.' [DA, p.50]

'To make you hear, to make you feel . . . before all, to make
you *see*.' Clearly Latour's edict on miracles is also a writer's
credo, which transposes the belief Cather has had, from her
earliest writing days, that art is a form of religion, to its
inverse belief (like the cloud over the mesa) that religion is a
form of art.

Latour's speech applies 'miraculous' perception to people,
not landscape; but in this book above all, Cather makes an
indissoluble connection between the reading of the animate
and the inanimate. Her passionate relish for physical detail –
rooms, clothes, food, physique, facial appearances – is not
just for realistic colouring. Characters are speaking pictures,

like the violent sensual face of the old priest of Taos. Latour takes an aesthetic pleasure in the looks of this man, who is his adversary, which mimics the author's (and, by analogy, God's) perception: to look closely is to understand. Rebecca West observes that in connecting Vaillant's eagerness to baptize the Mexicans and to have his lamb cooked properly, Cather is sympathetically invoking the Roman Catholic Church's insistence that 'man must take the universe sensibly'. West contrasts this (favourably) with Puritan asceticism.[30] But, while drawn to Catholic sensationalism, ritual and tradition, Cather also has a strong feeling for the puritan cast of thought, whereby the universe is translated typologically and the people in it (as in Bunyan) represent states of grace.

It is often remarked[31] that the characters in *Death Comes for the Archbishop* play allegorical roles. 'The legend of Fray Baltazar', for instance, tells the story of the seventeenth-century Spanish priest at Acoma who tyrannized over the local Indians so that his garden and his cookery would be of the best. (There's an obvious contrast with our priests' moderate pleasure in *their* gardens and cooking.) For fifteen years he cultivates his 'little kingdom' on the rock, until the day he invites some priests to an 'extravagant' banquet. Unfortunately, the Indian boy waiting at table slops the precious sauce onto one of the priests; Baltazar leaps up and strikes him, and he falls dead. The other priests run away, and at nightfall the Indians come for justice, and throw Baltazar off the cliff: 'So did they rid their rock of their tyrant, whom on the whole they had liked very well. But everything has its day', [DA, p.113] comments the narrator, with marvellously sardonic *insouciance*. Her impersonal, unmoralizing tone, matching the gleeful comic relish with which the whole story has been told, lets her get away with a formal parable against greed, pride, and wrath.

No explanation for this parable is needed. Appearances and actions are not deceptive; indeed, physical signs are insisted on with extreme emphasis, so that, in some of these 'parables', an uncensored display of prejudices about bodies spills out over the requirements of the story. The murderer on the road to Mora doesn't stand a chance in Cather's physiognomical court-of-law:

> He was tall, gaunt and ill-formed, with a snake-like neck, terminating in a small, bony head. Under his close-clipped hair this repellent head showed a number of thick ridges, as if the skull joinings were over-grown by layers of superfluous bone. With its small, rudimentary ears, this head had a positively malignant look. [DA, p.67]

The powerfully sensual Padre Martínez, the priest from Taos, has (it is hinted) an illegitimate son, known as his 'student'. This minor character, Trinidad, has physical abuse heaped on him with almost hysterical relish. He is repulsively fat, greedy, greasy, slothful and imbecilic, with a 'thick, felty voice' [DA, p.164] and a face with 'the grey, oily look of soft cheeses'. [DA, p.145] In the procession of the 'Penitentes' at Abuquiu (a native tradition for which Cather cannot disguise her revulsion) he has himself hung on a Cross and whipped in imitation of Christ, but he is so heavy and weak that the Cross falls down and he faints under the whipping. The disgusting story makes a grotesque travesty of the novel's pleasure in symbolic gestures.

The physical disgust Cather works out on her allegorical sinners is counterpointed by her physical idealization of the saints. Latour, for instance, has fine, elegant fingers (always a 'good sign' in Cather) with a curious mixture of authority and nervousness [DA, p.209] and a 'special' way of handling sacred, or beautiful, objects. [DA, p.241] Magdalena is ugly when she is brutalized, but after her redemption she becomes beautiful. She even appears, in one of the novel's most unembarrassed (though possibly embarrassing) icono-graphical moments, in a sunlit garden surrounded by doves, coming for 'apple blossoms and daffodils' 'in a whirlwind of gleaming wings.' [DA, p.209] Moments like this, taken out of context, are difficult to accept: the allegorizing looks too prescriptive and secure. But the kind of ambivalence and complexity in Marian Forrester or Godfrey St Peter or Myra

Henshawe is not what is wanted here. Now, the figures don't slip out from under the frieze of attitudes in which they are placed. Latour, looking at a roomful of his friends at a Mexican dinner party (where each of them has been described by their clothes and appearance) reflects 'how each of these men not only had a story, but seemed to have become his story'. [DA, p.183] It is the same phrase that Cather used of the New Mexican churches that inspired the novel: 'They are their own story.'

For people to be their own story requires a specialized narrative language. Cather described it as 'tuning' to the right note, and then keeping the pitch by means of 'time-worn phrases' and 'language a little stiff, a little formal'. The effect is of an old translation, a style which aimed to reconcile all the different languages – American, French, Spanish, Indian – of this vanished historical place and time. In the novel's translationese, Eusabio, Latour's dignified Indian friend, speaks a venerable species of pidgin ('My friend has come' [DA, p.221] . . . 'Men travel faster now, but I do not know if they go to better things' [DA, p.291]), while Latour and Vaillant 'converse' with each other as if 'from the French': 'We must trust to these intelligent beasts' [DA, p.70]; 'It is not expedient to interfere' [DA, p.156]. This manner is picked up by the narrative when, as in Vaillant's letters home, it is giving their version of events:

> There were five sons in the Smith family, fellows of low habits and evil tongues. Even the two younger boys, still children, showed a vicious disposition . . . they came with their lewd companions to rob the young pear trees or to speak filth against the priests. [DA, p.216]

The narrator's language, unlike the Smith family's, shows respect for the cultural differences the novel encompasses. In retreat from what she saw as the obliterations of post-war America, Cather had sought out a time and place where several distinct cultures were alive in the same challenging landscape.[32] Her attitude to her material is the opposite of her source, Howlett's, who welcomes Americanization and is indifferent to Mexican and Indian culture. In Cather's version, the Americans (like the murderer on the road to Mora, or the Smith family) are almost always unpleasant, and speak an inferior language. All the other cultures are carefully celebrated: the French for their order, civilization, domestic arts and graciousness, the Mexicans for their passionate, sensual generosity, their fierce pride or naive religiosity, the Indians as ascetic, ritualistic, dignified, courtly and reserved. Latour even takes pleasure in the possibility of an oriental ingredient in the note of his silver bell or the decorations of the Indian church. His aesthetic sensitivity to cultural strata and diversity is matched by both priests' (but especially Vaillant's) responsiveness to simple lives, 'obscure destinies': how they live, how they talk, what they eat and wear, what they believe.

This cultural specificity has a latent ironic sadness. The French Jesuits are supposed to be reformist, and are balked by the fixed traditions of the Indians and the Mexicans. Yet Latour loves the old: he admires the figure of the decadent Mexican priest Martínez, whom he has come to supersede, as 'something picturesque and impressive, but really impotent, left over from the past.' [DA, p.141] It is Vaillant who is eager to bustle about the vast terrain, converting and improving. One cannot imagine Latour converting anybody; and the new church which is his monument is a nostalgic memorial to the traditions of the French Romanesque. The novel's air of being in translation memorializes the cultural distinctions which Latour sees as they vanish. (In life, Lamy was less sensitive to the native culture.)

But the language does not only serve a cultural purpose. It is a deliberate writer's strategy which is trying to simulate what cannot be written. Cather's manipulation of this paradox is more complicated than it looks. *Death Comes for the Archbishop* is a different proposition from *The Professor's House*, with its contrast between a sophisticated Europeanized 'written' language of reflection, and a native 'spoken' language of action. Here the two are trying to be one. Cather's admiration and longing for an oral culture has to be translated into a writing which will replicate it, through sophisticated means, as closely as possible.

Death Comes for the Archbishop is not an anti-literary book (for all that it starts with a joke about the Spanish Cardinal's romantic idea of America being drawn entirely from the novels of Fenimore Cooper). The Bishop reads St Augustine, Mme de Sevigné and Pascal, and both priests lament the problems of illiteracy in their flock. But it repeatedly shows where words fall short. Making its own 'legend' (in the sense of 'a saint's life'), it is full of orally transmitted legends: Father Escolastico's version of Our Lady of Guadalupe, or the account of the 1680 Indian revolt as told by Martínez, who 'knew his country, a country which had no written histories'.[33] [DA, p.152] Just as the novel's episodic collection of stories simulates these unwritten histories, so its vivid image-making invokes the importance of the image for those who cannot read – like the beautifully lifelike parrot ('a wooden pattern of parrots, as it were') which the superstitious old Father Jesus bought from an old pueblo Indian, for whose ancestors (like the Virgin Mary for good Catholics) the bird had always been an object of 'wonder and desire'. [DA, p.87]

But the book has to translate these images into words. 'Legend' originally means (from 'legere') 'what is read'. There is a continual play between the unwriteable and the written. On his deathbed, the old Bishop wishes that he had written down the 'old legends and customs and superstitions' that were dying out [DA, p.277] and 'arrested their flight by throwing about them the light and elastic mesh of the French tongue'. He hasn't; but his unwritten writing is emulated by Cather's, which tries to be as 'light and elastic' a form of verbal arresting as it can.

A kind of joke is made of this tension between the unwritten and the written, in the matter of 'last words'. In the days (Cather tells us, with the knowing authorial voice she occasionally allows into her legendary narrative) when the coming of death was seen as a 'dramatic climax', last words were important.

> The 'Last Words' of great men, Napoleon, Lord Byron, were still printed in gift-books, and the dying murmurs of every common man and woman were listened for and treasured by their neighbours and kinsfolk. These sayings, no matter how unimportant, were given oracular significance and pondered by those who must one day go the same road. [DA, p.170]

So everyone gathers attentively round the deathbed of the miserly old Mexican priest, Padre Lucero. His mind, however, is not on the next world, but on his old sparring partnership with Padre Martínez (a comic travesty of the Latour–Vaillant relationship).

> After a facial spasm that was like a sardonic smile, and a clicking of breath in his mouth, their Padre spoke like a horse for the last time:
>   'Comete tu cola, Martínez, comete tu cola!' (Eat your tail, Martínez, eat your tail!) Almost at once he died in a convulsion. [DA, p.171]

These last words are instantly turned into legend: Lucero, it is reported, has 'looked into the other world' and seen Padre Martínez in torment. The irreverent story, itself 'like a sardonic smile', grotesquely anticipates the point at which death comes for the Archbishop. Though his last words are intently listened for, his broken murmurs are not understood; 'in reality' he is back in his youth, urging Father Vaillant to leave with him for the New World. Both versions, the ridiculous and the sublime, illustrate the difficulty of writing down any legend that will be true to 'reality', of letting literature have 'the last word'.

Language takes its most problematic shape in Latour's attempt to understand the Indians, which (like all the most satisfactory acts of possession in Cather) is a successful failure.[34] The Indian culture has no written language. Instead, as the Bishop observes, it has 'a strange literalness'. There is no making of metaphors or parables in Indian thought; the white man's mental tendency to translate and allegorize is entirely foreign to them. Their relation to the landscape, both physically and conceptually, is not to 'make it over', but to 'pass and leave no trace.' [DA, p.233] Things, for them, *are* their meanings: 'they had their idea in substance'. [DA, p.98] Their legends are not against nature, like Father Vaillant's miracles, but are contained in natural phenomena, like the legend of the Shiprock, the boat-shaped crag near the Canyon de Chelly which the Navajo Indians believe to be 'a ship of the air' that came bearing their first parents to their destined home. [DA, p.295] Unexpectedly, Latour's last retrospection is not of his church or his ministry, but of this Canyon, and of the Navajo's fight for the land which they knew, from the legend, to be inalienably theirs. Latour's dying optimism on behalf of the Navajos now reads like a piece of wishful thinking on Cather's part. But the placing of this coda is crucial: it gives the Indian story equal weight with the Catholic.

This alternative story makes itself felt most eloquently in the scene where Latour takes a language lesson from his Indian guide, Jacinto, as they make their camp, at sunset, outside the pueblo of Laguna.

> Behind their camp, not far away, lay a group of great mesas. The Bishop asked Jacinto if he knew the name of the one nearest them.
> 'No, I not know any name,' he shook his head. 'I know Indian name', he added, as if, for once, he were thinking aloud.
> 'And what is the Indian name?'
> 'The Laguna Indians call Snow-Bird mountain.' He spoke somewhat unwillingly.
> 'That is very nice,' said the Bishop musingly. 'Yes, that is a pretty name.'
> 'Oh, Indians have nice names too!' Jacinto replied quickly, with a curl of the lip.

Jacinto at once withdraws from his momentary hostility by congratulating the Bishop on his youth; the Bishop responds by asking his age, and whether he has children.

'One. Baby. Not very long born.'

Jacinto usually dropped the article in speaking Spanish, just as he did in speaking English, though the Bishop had noticed that when he did give the noun its article, he used the right one. The customary omission, therefore, seemed to be a matter of taste, not ignorance. In the Indian conception of language, such attachments were superfluous and unpleasing, perhaps.

They relapsed into the silence which was their usual form of intercourse. . . . The whole western sky was the colour of golden ashes. . . . High above the horizon the evening-star flickered like a lamp just lit. . . .

Jacinto threw away the end of his cornhusk cigarette and again spoke without being addressed.

'The ev-en-ing-star,' he said in English, slowly and somewhat sententiously, then relapsed into Spanish. 'You see the little star beside, Padre? Indians call him the guide.'

The two companions sat, each thinking his own thoughts as night closed in about them; a blue night set with stars, the bulk of the solitary mesa cutting into the firmament. The Bishop seldom questioned Jacinto about his thoughts or beliefs. He didn't think it polite, and he believed it to be useless. There was no way in which he could transfer his own memories of European civilization into the Indian mind, and he was quite willing to believe that behind Jacinto there was a long tradition, a story of experience, which no language could translate to him. A chill came with the darkness. . . .

'Many stars,' [Jacinto] said presently. 'What you think about the stars, Padre?'

'The wise men tell us they are worlds, like ours, Jacinto.'

The end of the Indian's cigarette grew bright and then dull again before he spoke. 'I think not,' he said in the tone of one who has considered a proposition fairly and rejected it. 'I think they are leaders – great spirits.'

'Perhaps they are,' said the Bishop with a sigh. 'Whatever they are, they are great. Let us say *Our Father*, and go to sleep, my boy.' [DA, pp.90–93]

No 'language' can translate the Indian story to the European mind, or the other way around. The scene concludes, very beautifully, in tolerant inconclusiveness: the saying of the prayer does not give the Christian language the status of a

superior 'last word', but is felt to be, simply, one possible
language of belief. Yet, even though translation is impossible,
the passage is full of mutual attempts at linguistic understanding: of the Indian name for the mesa, of the Indian use
of pronouns,[35] of the European and Indian names and
meanings for the stars. Silence, their 'usual form of intercourse', is felt to be waiting all the time under the conversation; and silence, in this setting, is attractive too.
(Meanwhile, the quiet language for the coming-on of darkness is a reminder of all human beings' ultimate silence.) But
the gestures towards cultural reciprocity which break the
silence *do* make speech out of what cannot be translated, and
thereby stand as a paradigm for Cather's whole attempt in
this novel to write the unwritable.

The scene anticipates a more sinister version of Indian
untranslatability. Near the dying pueblo of the Pecos Indians,
(Jacinto's tribe), where there are 'dark legends' of a perpetual underground fire, which saps the young men's strength,
and of babies sacrificed to a huge snake, Latour and Jacinto
are caught in a terrifying snowstorm. Jacinto leads him to an
underground cave, which they climb into through 'two great
stone lips'. Inside the cave, the Bishop is immediately struck
by an 'extreme distaste' for the place, and Jacinto expresses
anxiety at having brought him there, explaining that it is
'used by my people for ceremonies'. Latour promises to
'forget'. Jacinto then stops up a mysterious dark hole at the
rear of the cave, lights a fire, and takes Latour to the source
of a humming noise which, when Latour puts his ear to a
'fissure' in the stone floor, proves to be the voice of 'a great
underground river', 'moving in utter blackness under ribs of
antediluvian rock'. In the night, Latour sees Jacinto standing
guard over the covered hole. Ever after, the Bishop remembers the cave with 'horror', and though he seeks information
about it from an old trader who knows the Indians, he gets
nothing but vague statements about ancient superstitions.
Nothing is explained: the episode is 'terrible' [DA, p.130] and
untranslatable.[36]

A powerful feeling of inexplicable and alarming mystery comes out of this scene, which can partly (but only partly) be explained in sexual terms. Latour seems to have crawled through a giant vulva into an unpleasantly 'fetid' dark hole, with a darker smaller hole inside it, and a crack above rushing water – a place associated wth the sapping of male virility, the sacrifice of babies, and a snake.[37] It is as though the underground primitivism of the Indian beliefs allows Cather momentarily to suggest what she covers over else- where. *Death Comes for the Archbishop* is a deliberately chaste book. Sensuality is safely placed on the periphery, in the frieze of sins and vices. Latour has a fastidious detestation of Martínez's sloppily erotic household – he is extremely annoyed to find that what he takes to be a mouse in his room is 'a bunch of woman's hair', the left-over of 'some slovenly female toilet'. [DA, p.149] In his moments of discour- agement he feels 'barren' and lonely. [DA, p.211] But these touches of sexual anxiety do not impinge on the central relationship between Latour and Vaillant. As the more vulnerable of the two, Latour has more feeling: he recalls Vaillant from Arizona because he misses him ('why not admit it?' [DA, p.223]), and grieves to see his eager prepara- tions for his final departure. Even so, this is the most untroubled of Cather's carefully de-sexualized relationships. And the successful sublimation of its underground sexual feeling is centred on a figure, which, in this later stage of Cather's writing, now becomes of great importance: that of the Virgin Mother, Mary. Cather's attraction to Catholicism (which understandably led many readers to suppose that she was a practitioner) is mainly explained by her pleasure in this image of Christianized paganism: 'a goddess who should yet be a woman'. [DA, p.257]

Mary's appropriateness is both social and sexual. In her definitive book on the subject, Marina Warner observes that the worship of Mary grew up as a myth for the illiterate and the deprived: 'When the Virgin appears to Catholics in obscure places, clinging to an old way of life that has come under strain, proof is thereby given that God has not

altogether hidden his face.' The miraculous appearances of
Our Lady of Guadalupe to the poor Mexican, or of the Holy
Family as Mexican shepherds in the desert, answer precisely
to that description of the cult, and are part of Cather's
democratic passion for 'obscure destinies'. Warner also
describes the usefulness of Mariolatry as an aid to priestly
celibacy. 'Bad thoughts' were cured by thinking about the
Virgin. Since Mary could not sin, sinfulness was displaced
onto the figure of Mary Magdalene – thus giving the Catholic
Church, Marina Warner points out, its two models for female
behaviour, virgin/mother and whore.[38] Cather makes use of
this doubling of Mary, placing her saved Magdalena in
Father Vaillant's Mary-worshipping May garden, and letting
him call on her, jokingly, as a consolation for two men who
'grow lonely when they see nobody but each other'. [DA,
p.210]

There is only one, strange, underground threat to the
novel's tranquil sublimation of sexual repression or anxiety
into Mariolatry. Mary, like those 'gods in exile' Cather was
once so interested in, is a Christianized version, she says, of a
pagan 'goddess who should yet be a woman'. Indian religions, then, may have their human goddesses. Cather does
not say that the mythical snake of the Pecos is a female
goddess, but it is clear that the cave of the snake, which
Latour so much dislikes, is a female place. Oddly enough, the
name 'Guadalupe', in 'Our Lady of Guadalupe', may have
come from the Mexican word 'serpent'. Juan, to whom she
appears, 'exposed to Jesuit and Franciscan propaganda about
the Immaculate Conception of the Virgin, had merged her
with the native snake mother goddess of the Indians'.[39] It
seems a long way from Latour's terrible underground cave to
the purity of the May garden and the evening star. But the
power of myth is in what lies below it, 'the thing not named',
underground and antediluvian.

For the most part, though, the novel's Mariolatry has no
dark side, and makes a tender female version of this male
story. It is not just that almost all the priests' encounters
involve a woman – suffering, working, rescued, praying –

but that the priests' own lives combine their stoic pioneering with a female, domestic quality. This insinuation of female life into an apparently male-centred narrative is beautifully illustrated by Vaillant's letters home. In Howlett, Machebeuf writes letters to his sister referring gratefully to the vestments which the nuns at her convent have been making him. Cather picks this up, partly to illustrate Vaillant's lack of interest, 'like the saints of the early Church', in 'personal possessions': [DA, p.227] the vestments are for worship only, his daily wear is 'rough and shabby'. But those offstage nuns, doing their woman's work of reading and sewing, are given a voice. It is the more feminine, empathetic Latour who reflects (retrospectively, as usual) on the nuns' 'destinies':

> When he was visiting Mother Philomène's convent, one of the younger Sisters had confided to him what an inspiration it was to them, living in retirement, to work for the faraway missions. She told him also how precious to them were Father Vaillant's long letters, letters in which he told his sister of the country, the Indians, the pious Mexican women, the Spanish martyrs of old. These letters, she said, Mother Philomène read aloud in the evening. The nun took Father Latour to a window that jutted out and looked up the narrow street to where the wall turned at an angle, cutting off further view. 'Look,' she said, 'after the Mother has read us one of those letters from her brother, I come and stand in this alcove and look up our little street with its one lamp, and just beyond the turn there, is New Mexico; all that he has written us of those red deserts and blue mountains, the great plains and the herds of bison, and the canyons more profound than our deepest mountain gorges. I can feel that I am there, my heart beats faster, and it seems but a moment until the retiring-bell cuts short my dreams . . .'
> . . . Father Latour recalled that moment with the nun in her alcove window, her white face, her burning eyes, and sighed.
> [DA, pp.181–2]

This briefly, intensely imagined character, as thwarted by her sex and as incarcerated in her provincial nunnery as the young Cather in her Red Cloud attic, momentarily becomes the novelist. Cather too has translated the priest's 'long letters' into vivid, coloured pictures, recreated through a

concentrated effort of the imagination. But she has the
advantage of 'the nun in her alcove window' of having been
able to turn the corner into those wide spaces. She has made
herself both pioneer and historian, actor and author, female
and male voice, receiver and rewriter of history.

13

TWILIGHT AND MIRACLES

'N'expliquez pas!'

Shadows on the Rock, 1931

All these details, so completely seen, are so spiritualized by
the unusual light, that they seem to lose their actual
substance, and become things of intellect. Nothing is too
small or too trifling to undergo this change, and acquire
dignity thereby.

Nathaniel Hawthorne, *The Scarlet Letter*, 1850

CATHER ALWAYS had a sense of loss and regret after
finishing a book, as though parting company for ever from a
close friend. This recurrent emotion was exacerbated, in the
four years between *Death Comes for the Archbishop* and her
next novel, by events which made this the most stressful and
dislocated phase of her whole life. Her depression in the early
1920s had had deep sources: loss of Isabelle, post-war
malaise, the onset of what James called 'the middle years'.
Between 1927 and 1930 the upsets were more tangible and
drastic. All her language, in the letters of the time, is of
destabilization: of falling props and disappearing landscapes.[1]
The apartment at Number 5, Bank Street where she and
Edith had lived for fifteen years was to be demolished to
make way for the new subway: a stroke of fate which
seemed to fulfil, with mocking appositeness, Cather's view of
the vandalism of modern America. Coinciding with the

unhappy business of putting her things in store and moving to the Grosvenor Hotel (where, to her dismay, she would still find herself five years later) came news of her father's heart attack. That year she divided her time between Red Cloud, Jaffrey and New York, writing almost nothing. Then, after another attack, Charles Cather, who was once such a sweet Southern boy,[2] died, aged eighty, in March 1928. Cather reached Red Cloud the day after his death, and stayed on, grieving, in the house for some weeks.

That summer she went back to wild, beautiful, lonely Grand Manan (where the cottage she and Edith had had built was now ready) by way of Quebec. This first visit to the city – longer than she had planned because of Edith's opportune bout of 'flu[3] – was the beginning of *Shadows on the Rock*; but there would be a great deal of researching and re-visiting before the book was done. And of painful inter-ruptions: in December, while visiting Douglass at Long Beach, her mother, now seventy-eight, had a stroke which left her paralysed and all but speechless, though *compos mentis*; she would spend the next three years slowly dying in a California sanatorium. Cather went over annually in the spring to help the family look after her. She hated California, and found the spectacle of the illness bitter. Edith described the radical effect of these years.

> She realized with complete imagination what it meant for a proud woman like her mother to lie month after month quite helpless, unable to speak articulately, although her mind was perfectly clear. In Willa Cather's long stays in Pasadena . . . she had to watch her continually growing weaker, more ailing, yet unable to die. It was one of those experiences that make a lasting change in the climate of one's mind.[4]

This difficult mother, who for much of Cather's childhood had been prone to illnesses and depressions, whose conser-vative and demanding character had had a powerful effect on the formation of her life and writing (most plainly illustrated in the relation of Nellie and Myra Henshawe)[5] was now infantilely dependent. Everything Cather wrote in her late fifties and sixties was affected by the close conjunction of

her father's death and her mother's stroke. The fiercely
controlled old ladies in 'A Chance Meeting', *Sapphira and the
Slave Girl*, and 'The Old Beauty', the tribulations of female
family life in 'Old Mrs Harris', and the motherless daughters
and feminine fathers of *Shadows on the Rock* and *Lucy
Gayheart*, all take shape from these painful years of mothering her stricken mother.

Between nursing duties, Cather kept up her professional
and private travels, though she was only writing intermit-
tently. In the summer of 1929 she started work on *Shadows on
the Rock* at Grand Manan, and went back to Quebec so as to see
the place in the autumn and the winter. In May of 1930, she
and Edith sailed to France (on the *Berengaria*, the ship the
family travel on in *The Professor's House*) for a four month stay.
She saw Isabelle and Jan, for the first time in seven years; she
researched the French historical material for the novel; and,
in a hotel in Aix, she had the extraordinary chance encounter,
which took her back into the literary past, with an old lady
who turned out to be Flaubert's niece. Cather came back (with
Edith, no doubt, seasick as usual) by way of the St Lawrence
River to Quebec. In the autumn she was at Jaffrey, writing,
and she finished *Shadows on the Rock* in New York on December 27, 1930. After the proofs came she went to California
(and took two honorary degrees, one at Berkeley and the
other back East at Princeton – where she met the Lindberghs –
the latest in a succession of awards she was beginning to find
more distracting than flattering). *Shadows on the Rock* was published in August; it had extensive but only partly enthusiastic
reviews, and large sales. A month later, her mother died.

Cather had not taken *Shadows on the Rock* with her on her sad
journeys to California. While she was there looking after her
mother, she wrote a few stories which went back to her
childhood and to her mother's life, and which would be
published in 1932 as *Obscure Destinies*. But the novel had
been, she told Elizabeth Shepley Sergeant, a refuge, which
she kept as 'a kind of underground place, to which she could
retire for a few hours of concentrated work', like a Pueblo

Indian withdrawing from his village to an 'underground chamber'.[6] The image evokes Bishop Latour's solitary reflections when he visits his Indian friend and stays alone for three days, 'recalling the past and planning the future'; [DA, p.230] or the Professor's attic study; or her much earlier account of family life as a struggle between the group and the individual. Returning to family pressures in her middle age, Cather felt again the tension between the writer's need for solitude and the attractions of domestic relationships. *Shadows on the Rock*, written to console herself for loss and change, is a meditation on childhood, family security and maternal influence, masquerading as a historical novel. But, like all her novels, it also pulls away towards solitude.

The choice of seventeenth-century Quebec looks like an anomaly. Apart from the battle scenes in *One of Ours*, it was the only one of her novels which used material quite outside her experience, acquired through research. (Lamy and Machebeuf's missions overlapped, after all, with her own long experience of New Mexico.) Though the novel centres on a child, she had not saved up French Canada from her own childhood. Apart from some juvenile romantic stories, she had never gone so far back in time. All the same, it was not as uncharacteristic as it seemed. (There is even a clue to very early interest, in an 1897 review of 'The Seats of the Mighty: A Romance of Old Quebec' by an author famous 'for his vivid stories of old Canadian life', whom she congratulates for 'making the most of Canada's literary possibilities'.)[7] Her explorations of unfamiliar Quebec tapped familiar emotions. Edith records her 'memory, recognition, surmise' at 'the sense of its extraordinary French character, isolated and kept intact through hundreds of years, as if by a miracle, on this great un-French continent'.[8] The place aroused Cather's powerful Francophilia,[9] and her deep interest in pioneering cultures, at the point where inherited European traditions were adapting to the challenge of New World conditions, and before assimilation had set in. Quebec appealed to her particularly for being so *un*-assimilated: 'She likes the French Canadians' (she was quoted as saying in

Louise Bogan's 1931 'profile') 'because they have remained
practically unchanged for over two hundred years. . . .
Quebec would never have changed at all . . . if the American
drunks had let it alone.'[10] (Bogan is clearly quoting accur-
ately: that sounds like Cather.) She could use her recent
pleasure in the Grand Manan, Bay of Fundy seascape (which
she would return to in one of her last and strangest stories,
'Before Breakfast'). She found the Canadian coastal scenery,
and the dramatic setting of Quebec itself, intensely beautiful:
and that feeling fills the book. The novel also allowed her, as
Edith observed, to use up the leftover 'world of Catholic
feeling and tradition in which she had lived so happily for so
long'[11] in the writing of Death Comes for the Archbishop.

Shadows on the Rock might have been expected, in fact, to
be more like Death Comes for the Archbishop than it is. They are
both about Catholics, history, and French pioneers in the
New World. They both use the image of the 'rock' at their
centre. And there are other similarities. Shadows on the Rock,
like Death Comes for the Archbishop, is written in a simplified,
deliberate tone, as if in translation. (This time she allows
herself whole sentences and paragraphs in French, as befits
the unassimilated character of the culture.) It places historical and political events in the background of individual lives,
and it evokes the telling of legend.

Yet the feeling is quite other. Indeed, for readers moving
from one book to the next, Shadows on the Rock may feel
disappointingly muted. A robust, sardonic tone comes into
Death Comes for the Archbishop which is not used here. The
colour scheme, in the move to the far north, had gone from
dazzling primary tones to a muffled, luminous haze (very
like the magical moonlight Hawthorne wanted for his
seventeenth-century historical 'romances').[12] As its title suggests, the book is full of fog and twilight. Cather was
impatient with readers who complained of getting chicken
broth instead of roast beef; they might have trusted her, she
said, to know what she was doing.[13]

At one point in the novel, some French tapestries, representing 'garden scenes', are admired by the child heroine.

'One could study them for hours without seeing all the flowers and figures.' [SR, p.59] Cather brought reproductions of the famous Cluny tapestries of the Lady and the Unicorn back from France, and hung them in her room in the Grosvenor.[14] She told Dorothy that the novel was a little tapestry.[15] This comparison, with its suggestion (again very Hawthornian) of faded, decorative figures at play, set about with plants and animals, is different from the monumental, allegorical friezes of Puvis de Chavannes or Holbein. Cather's descriptions of the making of *Shadows on the Rock* are more modest and secular than for *Death Comes for the Archbishop*. What she had found on 'the rock of Quebec', and tried to replicate, was the persistence of an old feeling about life, 'more like an old song, incomplete and uncorrupted, than like a legend. The text was mainly anacoluthon, so to speak, but the meaning was clear'.[16] Anacoluthon is the change from one grammatical construction to another within a single sentence: something unfinished, shifting.[17] A tapestry, an old song, a syntactical merging: the references suggest a history told through small-scale details and a quiet flow of events. There is no journey through vast spaces and long years towards an ever-immanent destiny which contains all the past within itself. The focus here, as she explains, is 'an orderly little French household', from 'a seat in the close air by the apothecary's fire' – not 'military glory' or 'Indian raids' or 'the wild life in the forests'. At the centre of this difference between her two 'historical' novels (though she does not say anything about this) is that the vantage point is not that of a reflective male adult, but of a female child.

The story of Cécile Auclair, the twelve-year-old daughter of a French apothecary-doctor, begins in October 1697 and ends exactly a year later, with a (characteristic) epilogue set in 1713. We find out at once that Euclide Auclair is a fifty-year-old widower and that he came to Quebec from Paris in 1689 because his father's apothecary shop, on the Quai des Celestins, was next door to Count Frontenac's Paris home, and the Count became his family's patron. Frontenac was

Governor General of Canada from 1672 to 1682, was
recalled to France by Louis XIV, under a cloud of disapproval,
and was sent out again, aged seventy, in 1689. Cather has
the historical Frontenac take the fictional Auclair with him
as his personal physician.

In the course of the novel's year, the factual history of the
colony is carefully pieced into the background of the
tapestry. We learn of the three-way conflicts between the
domineering Frontenac, the ascetic old Bishop Laval and the
Parisian, narcissistic Bishop Saint-Vallier; of the ambivalent
relations between Canada and France; and of the characteristic lives of the colonists: the clergy and the nuns, the
bourgeois tradespeople and the pioneering backwoodsmen
and fur traders, the *coureurs de bois*. In the foreground are the
domestic lives of Auclair and his daughter, and their friendships with a selection of 'types': the cobbler Pommier and his
crippled, lively mother; the cross-eyed 'Blinker', town misfit,
whom Cécile looks after because her mother did; Jacques,
the child of one of the women of the town; St Cyr, a priest
from Sault St Louis, the Jesuit mission and Indian reservation at Montreal; the heroic woodsman Pierre Charron; a
ship's captain from St Malo. These fictional characters are
smoothly interspersed with the historical figures – Laval,
Saint-Vallier, Frontenac, Mother Juschereau, the Mother
Superior of the 'Hospitalières' nuns at the Hôtel Dieu, the
Ursuline sisters – all of whom are brought conveniently into
some relation with Cécile and her father. But 'great matters'
are distanced behind day-to-day 'trifles' – 'trifles dear as the
heart's blood', [SR, p.97] the narrator allows herself to say,
in one of the moments of uncensored sentiment which
makes the mood soft and wistful.

The 'great matters' of male history, though distanced, are
very precisely selected. Cather chose to write, not about the
pioneering beginnings of French Canada in the early seventeenth century – Champlain's founding of Quebec, the
sufferings and martyrdoms of the Jesuit missionaries as told
in their *Relations*, the wars with the Iroquois – but about the
next generation of colonists, for whom these events were

already legend, and who, as Byatt says, 'had had time to put
down roots and build a few meagre traditions', tended like
the parsley which Cécile inherits from her mother, and has
to protect against the winter cold.[18] Laval and Frontenac are
old men; their quarrels have been going on 'ever since Cécile
could remember'. [SR, p.20] Cather wanted to give the sense
of a place that already had its history, its 'shadows', its
traditions, but was not yet (as Cécile is not) quite secure of its
future. The period she chose was one of crisis, which would
determine the future of Quebec. Auclair and Cécile's arrival
in Canada in 1689 coincides with the outbreak of the French
war with England, over their rivalry for commerce in the
New World. The story ends with the peace of Rysvik in 1697
and the death of Frontenac in 1698. During these war years,
there was also a war of policy going on between Frontenac
and the King over western expansionism, which the King
regarded as expensive and dangerously undermining to the
French character of the colony. Cather just touches this in,
when Frontenac confides to Auclair that he had made the
mistake of teaching the King geography: the French court
wanted to think of Quebec as 'isolated, French, and
Catholic'. [SR, p.237]

The passing, and unexplained, reference, is a good example of her submerging of history under the story. Cather's
cunning, economical manipulation of her material is
interesting to watch. Not many dates are mentioned, but
there are constant references to 'eight years ago' or 'for the
next three years'. Names of important off-stage places and
events are mentioned with minimal explanation – Sault St
Louis, [SR, p.136] Ville-Marie, the old name for Montreal,
[SR, p.144] Michilimackinak, the main fur-trading post on
the junction of Lakes Michigan and Huron, [SR, p.168] the
Phips bombardment, when Sir William Phips laid unsuccessful siege to the rock. [SR, pp.63, 94, 183] They occur as part
of Cécile's mental furniture. Every so often a historical
survey is made, by means of a set-piece like the arrival of the
ships, or the return of Saint-Vallier in 1713. There is a
particularly ingenious, and odd, instance of this tactic, when

Cécile visits the cobbler to have shoes made for her protégé, little Jacques. Pommier shows her the wooden lasts which are 'the feet of all the great people'. [SR, p.81] The story of Robert la Salle is invoked through the wooden simulacrum of his foot, the foot that 'went farther than any other in New France'. [SR, p.82] The scene works both as a child's history lesson, with objects as teaching aids, and as a metonymic image for the passing of great men, who leave, as it were, their footprints in the sand. (She would come back to that image in her next novel, *Lucy Gayheart*.) It is characteristically suggestive: we never hear the full story of La Salle, Frontenac's friend, an intrepid and rapacious explorer (like those Spanish adventurers Cather so much admired) who tried to extend the French fur-trading monopoly right down the Mississippi to the Gulf of Mexico, where he was murdered.

Evidently Cather had read the great nineteenth-century New English historian Francis Parkman's books on La Salle, and decided to bury that male pioneering story under Cécile's. As she had done for *Death Comes for the Archbishop* and would do again for *Sapphira and the Slave Girl*, she read widely on the period, putting sources against each other for a balanced view. Parkman's anti-Jesuit histories gave her characters, such as Frontenac's ('full of contradictions . . . as gracious and winning on some occasions as he was unbearable on others'),[19] insights into the quality of Canadian life – the 'feminine' influence of the Catholic church,[20] the mixture of roughness and piety, the taming of the wilderness by means of 'a musket, a rosary, and a pack of beaver-skins'[21] – and vivid visual evocations of exactly the sort Cather needed to corroborate her own impressions:

Let us visit Quebec in midwinter [wrote Parkman of the 1650s]. We pass the warehouses and dwellings of the lower town, and as we climb the zigzag way now called Mountain Street, the frozen river, the roofs, the summits of the cliff, and all the broad landscape below and around us glare in the sharp sunlight with a dazzling whiteness. At the top, scarcely a private house is to be seen; but, instead, a fort, a church, a hospital, a cemetery, a house of the Jesuits, and an Ursuline convent. Yet, regardless of the keen air, soldiers, Jesuits, servants, officials, women, all of the little community who are not cloistered, are abroad and astir.[22]

To set against Parkman's robustly Protestant views, she consulted a life of Laval by Abbé Scott, vicar of a village near Quebec whom Cather went to talk to, the famous *Relations* of the martyr-missionaries,[23] and the records and letters of the pioneering nuns, who were of such importance in the religious and social history of Canada, Marie de l'Incarnation, who founded the Ursuline convent in Quebec, and Mother Juschereau of the Hôtel Dieu.[24] And for the splendours and miseries of the Sun King's regime, she went to Saint-Simon.

Cather prided herself on her historical accuracy,[25] though she distorts her main figures somewhat for her own ends: the grimly puritanical Laval is more benign, the overbearing and violent-tempered Frontenac kinder to his dependants, and the austerely fastidious Saint-Vallier more hedonistic than seems to have been the case. (A pity that the oddest example of the hostilities between the Governor and the priests fell outside her time-scheme, Saint-Vallier's outraged censoring in 1694 of an intended production at the castle of Molière's anti-clerical *Tartuffe*.)[26]

But her acquired knowledge is discreetly evident everywhere. When Auclair and Saint-Vallier disagree on the inevitability of the brandy trade, [SR, p.254] they are rehearsing one of the most bitter areas of dispute between the clergy, who wanted to stop the 'nefarious traffic'[27] which corrupted Indians and traders alike, and the traders and administrators who knew that if they didn't give brandy to the Indians, the Dutch would. When Cécile reflects fondly on her time at the Ursuline convent day-school, she illustrates one of the dominant features of colonial life, the 'training of young girls'[28] by the pioneering orders of nuns whose main function, like the Jesuits', was educational. The character of Auclair himself is scrupulously authentic. Sick people mostly went to the Hôtel Dieu or the General Hospital, where they would be bled or purged; but there were a few doctors in the colony, who were often barbers and herbalists as well. The most notable French physician who came over in 1685, was Michel Sarrazin, a surgeon who was also a distinguished botanist and who compiled, as Auclair seems to be doing, a catalogue of over two hundred Canadian plants, with notes of their pharmaceutical properties.[29]

What Cécile takes in of the history that surrounds her comes in the form of objects and legends – her father's medicinal herbs, Madame Juschereau's stories of her predecessor Mother Catherine de Saint-Augustin, M. Pommier's 'feet'. The transformation of history into legend, Cather's lasting subject, is felt as a recurrent process. Just as Cather has been inspired to make this legendary fiction through her readings of Canadian history, so Cécile has the stories of Brébeuf and Chabanel, of Mother Catherine and Jeanne le Ber, repeated to her. Her acquisition of history as legend denotes the making of a colony into a country:

> Cécile liked to think they did things of their own in Canada. The martyrdoms of the early Church which she read about in her *Lives of the Saints* never seemed to her half so wonderful or so terrible as the martyrdoms of Father Brébeuf, Father Lalemant, Father Jogues, and their intrepid companions. . . . And could the devotion of Sainte Geneviève or Sainte Philomène be compared to that of Mother Catherine de Saint-Augustin or Mother Marie de l'Incarnation? [SR, pp.100–101]

An emotional passage on the force of miracles, which, by being told, become 'a beautiful image', confirms the central idea of this writing, that history in the form of legend becomes an object, 'an actual possession' which can be 'bequeathed to another', [SR, p.135] as Cather bequeaths us this book.

History as a legend for Cécile becomes, then, a child's story. In the process it undergoes a considerable amount of censorship. Quebec in the 1690s was more of a rough-house than the sanctuary of French traditions Cather would have liked it to be. A priest described the town in 1704 as 'an open bordello';[30] edicts against drunkenness and immorality were constantly being issued by Laval and Saint-Vallier. Some of the 'King's Girls', sent over from the 1660s as brides for the soldier-settlers, went to the bad; there were a large number of illegitimate and abandoned children. Just outside the town walls there was a shanty town of beggars.[31] In Montreal, when the *coureurs de bois* came in from living in the woods with the Indian women, they tore the place apart. La Hontan, an officer (one of Cather's minor characters) who wrote some witty, sceptical memoirs of the times, described it vividly:

> You would be amaz'd if you saw how lewd these Pedlers are when they return; how they Feast and Game, and how prodigal they are, not only in their Cloaths, but upon Women. Such of 'em as are married, have the wisdom to retire to their own Houses: but the Batchelors act just as our *East-India*-Men, and Pirates are wont to do; for they Lavish, Eat, Drink, and Play all away as long as the Goods hold out; and when these are gone . . . they are forc'd to go upon a new Voyage for Subsistence.[32]

Cather does not omit any of this. Jacques' mother 'Toinette is one of the 'King's Girls', [SR, p.50] always going off with the trappers and abandoning her child; Pierre Charron, when he is out in the woods, squanders his money on 'drink and women and new guns'; [SR, p.171] the slums inside the city walls are mentioned: 'Respectability stopped with the cobble-stones.' [SR, p.61] But everything is softened and muted, filtered through Cécile's domestic pieties. 'Toinette's child is uncorrupted and religious, and she herself is in awe of the Bishop. Pierre Charron doesn't behave like 'a pig' in Montreal out of respect to his mother. His roughness is thoroughly romanticized, and his (offstage) sexuality turns into protective chivalry with Cécile. Cather has done this kind of idealizing before, with her gallant American soldiers in *One of Ours*. Here the intention is twofold. She wants to be optimistic about the future of the French colony. Everything is directed to making Cécile into a true 'Canadienne'. The plot, such as it is, centres on Auclair's deciding not to go back to France, and (less explicitly) on Pierre's recovering from his loss of Jeanne le Ber so that he can become Cécile's future husband. Both these male stories are instruments of Cécile's destiny, to be the mother of sons who are the 'Canadians of the future'. [SR, p.276] They will inherit both the French traditions Cécile so scrupulously preserves, and Charron's 'romantic' pioneering spirit as 'the free Frenchman of the great forests', with 'the good manners of the Old World, the dash and daring of the New'. [SR, pp.169–70] We don't see this marriage, but we hear of it in the epilogue: Pierre and Cécile, Auclair reports, are living in the Upper Town with their four sons and 'are well established in the world'. [SR, p.276] (No more details are given, but presumably Pierre has given up being a *coureur de bois*, and become, as the colony's administrators wanted the backwoodsmen to become, a solid member of the Quebequois *bourgeoisie*.) As with her earlier desire to ensure a future for rural America out of the maternal legacy of women such as Ántonia[33] and Alexandra ('Fortunate country, that is one day to receive hearts like Alexandra's . . . to give them out again . . . in the shining eyes of youth!' [OP, p.309]), the utopian conclusion has required some historical smoothing-over.

But the gentling of Quebec's history has mostly to do with the novel's theme of childhood. *Shadows on the Rock* is a children's book for adults; hence its modest tone and simplified manner. Though the point of Cécile's story is to show her aptitude for motherhood, we are not to see her grow up. She has to be innocent and presexual, 'a little girl of twelve, beginning to grow tall, wearing a short skirt and a sailor's jersey, with her brown hair cropped like a boy's', [SR, p.9] Pierre Charron's 'petit singe'. [SR, p.11] Cather is reinventing herself as a child at the point when she most needed, as she said, to gather the beginnings of things around her.[34] Though she borrowed little Jacques' childishness from her favourite nephew,[35] she gave a version of her own childhood to crop-headed Cécile, with her gentle home-loving father, and a mother as organized and conservative as Cather's, but, being dead and absent, easier to emulate and to love.

Cather enters with deep pleasure into the creation of a tactile, visual child's world. Cécile delights in *things* which take on magical properties, the Count's 'crystal bowl full of glowing fruits of coloured glass', [SR, p.58] Mother Juschereau's embroidered flowers, the cobbler's wooden lasts. Her pleasure in domestic artefacts emulates her mother's belief that a house made up of 'wood and cloth and glass and a little silver' is 'really' made up of 'fine moral qualities'. [SR, p.25] So Cécile's respect for the fragile parsley and the fine sheets her mother left her to look after, the gooseberries her father enjoys, the wood-doves in lard he lays down in the cellar all winter, are moral emotions. Objects are valued for their usefulness to life; hence Cécile's interest in her father's specialities and prescriptions, his boxes of sugared lemon peel, boiled pine-tops for cough syrup, sassafras tea, saffron flowers for flavouring fish soup, bitumen for curing snow-blindness, foxglove-water for the dropsy, the eucalyptus balls he makes for keeping off mosquitoes. Objects, well looked-after, can cure and repay their owners. When Cécile knows she is not going to leave home, all her things look more secure to her:

> She really believed that everything in the house, the furniture, the china shepherd boy, the casseroles in the kitchen, knew that the herbarium had been restored to the high shelves and that the world was not going to be destroyed this winter. [SR, pp.249–50]

On the other hand, when she goes to stay on the Île d'Orléans with the rough smith's family, the Harnois, she is extremely distressed by the bad housekeeping, the dirty sheets and the greasy food. This is because, as she fully realizes on her return, care taken for things makes 'life itself'. [SR, p.195] Even Bishop Laval's holy water needs 'cooking':

> In winter the old man usually carried a little basin as well as his lantern. It was his custom to take the bowl of holy water from the font in the evening, carry it into his kitchen, and put it on the back of the stove, where enough warmth would linger through the night to keep it from freezing. Then, in the morning, those who came to early Mass would not have a

mere lump of ice to peck at. Monseigneur de Laval was very particular about the consecrated oils and the holy water; it was not enough for him that people should merely go through the forms. [SR, p.104]

Things are not empty forms, they are full of literal meanings which do not need to be explained. ('"N'expliquez pas"', Cécile implores Mother Juschereau after a story about Mother Catherine.) Just as historical legends become objects that can be bequeathed, so objects can have spiritual meanings. The translation of objects into things of the mind is insisted on:[36] Auclair's eyes look as if 'his thoughts were pictures', [SR, p.7] the nuns take with them wherever they go a comfortably ordered universe 'in the world of the mind (which for each of us is the only world).' [SR, p.96] Little Jacques, Cécile's naive protégé, endearingly mild and vague, makes the kind of literal readings of objects which are the equivalent of a belief in miracles. Because Cécile's christening mug, his greatest object of admiration, has her name engraved on it, it is 'peculiarly and almost sacredly hers'. [SR, p.87] Because Madame Pommier has a picture of the Holy Family, he thinks that is why her street is called Holy Family Hill. [SR, p.100]

Cather's own reservations (like Bishop Latour's) about the literal reality of miracles is voiced by Auclair and Charron, but that does not remove sympathy from the children's literal beliefs: that they will be struck by lightning for failing to pay for a candle, or that a sailor could be converted by swallowing a morsel of a martyr's skull. Though the childish viewpoint is not the author's, adults in the book are judged in their relation to children. Old Bishop Laval rescues little Jean from neglect, and feels that the child has been sent to him as a sign. The missionary priest, the sea captain, the woodsman, all express strong feelings for children and families, and the life of the 'rock' is seen as that of a sanctified family, here on its way to midnight mass on Christmas Eve:

> Across the white ledges that sloped like a vast natural stairway down to the Cathedral, black groups were moving, families and friends in little flocks, all going toward the same goal, − the

doors of the church, wide open and showing a ruddy vault in
the blue darkness. [SR, p.112]

Like Auclair's thoughts, this is a picture in the mind.
Cather includes in her text, characteristically, some naif
art-works as pictorial analogues for the literal readings of
childhood: the woodcut which Cécile shows Jacques of the
Infant Jesus appearing to St Edmund, awkward and friendly,
with the figure of Jesus 'treading on the earth, not floating in
the air as visions are wont to do', [SR, p.85] or the paintings
in the town church of St Geneviève as a shepherdess, the
kingdom of heaven as a medieval French castle, and the
Virgin Mary as 'a charming figure of young motherhood'.
[SR, p.65] Like the novel, these literal art-works give the
Christian stories a specifically French-Canadian quality. The
most obvious example of this is Cécile's carefully made
nativity scene (distantly echoing the Burdens' Christmas tree
in *My Ántonia*) to which Jacques, meaning well, adds his
precious possession, a wooden carved Canadian beaver, to
stand with the traditional ox and ass.

The Nativity scene is central to the book. Family life – of
the right kind – re-enacts the life of the Holy Family. Cécile's
distaste for the Harnois family and her strict avoidance of
'Toinette are not meant to be just priggishness (though they
look rather like it): they make emphatically clear that the
literal, everyday life of the family has to maintain a metaphorical sanctity. Cather wants Jacques to suggest the Infant Jesus
and Cécile to stand in for the Virgin Mary,[37] and by sustain-
ing the focus of childhood, she gets away with it. The
Mariolatry of *Death Comes for the Archbishop* gave a chaste and
feminine tone to that male story of religious pioneering.
Here, it subdues a history of priests and hunters, doctors and
governors, under a female story of mothering. Mme
Auclair's shadow fills the book: Cécile learns from her, and
from the nuns, childless mother figures, to be the mother of
the house, and (hence) of the nation.

This sounds tiresomely pious, and there is, I think, a
moralizing and sentimental quality to *Shadows on the Rock*

which weakens it. But it is not such a simple, celebratory, or serene novel as I have been making it sound. Cécile is not sorrowful (even when she thinks she is), [SR, p.93] but her childhood is infiltrated by stories of bitter sadness. The strangest and most ambivalent of these is the story of the recluse, a silent presence at the centre of the novel who takes to its furthest point Cather's lifelong attraction for withdrawal and solitary reflection. Judith Fryer reads Jeanne le Ber as a Sybilline, creative female power, weaving her embroideries out of her own time and space.[38] And certainly the story of the girl who has cut herself off from her grieving family and from an adult sexual life, to spend her life alone in her bitterly cold three-room cell behind the altar of a Montreal chapel, makes a powerful alternative system to Cécile's domestic order. Jeanne turns herself into a legend which (like the work of the woman writer) provides lasting and beautiful images out of her private language.

But what Fryer does not do is emphasize our last sighting of Jeanne. Long after he has given up hope of her, Pierre Charron, her childhood sweetheart, hides in the church to see her come out at night to pray. What he sees is a soul in torment, her voice 'hoarse, hollow, with the sound of despair in it. . . . When she prayed in silence, such sighs broke from her. And once a groan, such as I have never heard; such despair – such resignation and despair!' [SR, p.180] It is the paradox of legends, of course, that consolatory, educative life stories come out of personal suffering. But the bitter resignation of Jeanne le Ber makes a story that is not suitable for children.

That opposition between childhood faith and adult disappointment, suffering and failure, persists throughout. All the 'real' stories that are pieced into the narrative are unhappy: the old Bishop's 'heavy labour', [SR, p.74] the Count's 'life of brilliant failures', [SR, p.237] Saint-Vallier's regrets for his mistakes. [SR, p.269] Life for ordinary people under the tyranny of Louis XIV is evoked by two wretched stories, of Auclair's Paris tenant, old Bichet the knife-grinder, tortured and executed for stealing two pots, and Blinker's history as a

torturer of just such unfortunates. But for those ordinary
men who escaped France for the Canadian wilderness life
could be just as grim. The woodsman Antoine Frichette tells
a terrible story of accident and endurance in the snow. The
sufferings of the Jesuit martyrs are often invoked, and, of all
those stories, Cather chooses to tell the most distressing, that
of Noel Chabanel, a fastidious professor of rhetoric for whom
life among the Hurons was an unmitigated ordeal of revulsion, self-reproach and physical indignity. Chabanel's story,
turned to legend, is, like Jeanne le Ber's, an inspiration to
others. But its awful personal painfulness seems to endorse
Auclair's philosophy of resigned stoicism (drawn from his
reading of the Latin poets), rather than the trusting faith of
nuns and children.

Chabanel was always being baited by the Indians (who in
this book, rather surprisingly after *Death Comes for the Archbishop*, do not inspire much interest), and his most horrible
moment comes when they invite him to 'a feast of flesh':

> After he had swallowed the portion in his bowl, they pulled a
> human hand out of the kettle to show him that he had eaten of
> an Iroquois prisoner. He became ill at once, and they followed
> him into the forest to make merry over his retchings. [SR,
> p.150]

His retchings are an antidote to the novel's good housekeeping. Not all the physical sensations in *Shadows on the Rock* are
pleasant: deformities and distressing sights are frequent.
Blinker has a suppurating jaw; a sinful woman in a story of
Mother Catherine develops 'a loathsome disease' and is
buried in a ditch like an 'unclean animal'. [SR, p.37] Frichette's
brother-in-law dies in the woods of a gangrenous leg;
Frichette is ruptured, and has to give up his livelihood.
Poisoning is a recurrent theme. Auclair makes good medi-
cines, but, misused, they would be the 'poisons' 'Toinette
accuses him of storing. 'Medicine is a dark science', he says,
[SR, p.210] and the 'guardian of the stomach', in pioneering
medical days, has to be both wary and bold. Auclair counters
Cécile's credulous belief in the miraculous effects of the

martyr's skull with a horrible story of a famine in France
when the people ate dried bones and died in agony. [SR,
p.125] Cécile and Pierre and Auclair all love good food
(witness their French dinner with the sea captain, 'a dish
made of three kinds of shell-fish, a *tête de veau* . . . a roast
capon with a salad, and for dessert Breton pancakes with
honey and preserves' [SR, p.214]), but Pierre will boast, too,
of eating dog meat and 'tripe de roche' in the wilderness:

> 'You gather it and boil it, and it's not so bad as it goes down, –
> tastes like any boiled weed. But afterwards – oh, what a
> stomach-ache!' [SR, p.186]

The language used to describe the forest itself is of poisoning,
of being choked by mould and stinging insects, of vegetation
strangling itself 'in a slow agony'. [SR, p.7] (We even
discover that the King's heir has died of poisoning. [SR,
p.274]) Poison and medicine, retching and good eating,
counter each other like faith and despair, hope and bitterness. Cather inclines the balance so that she can keep a
sweet smell in the book, like the 'balmy odours' that blew
out from the Canadian shores from the spruce and pine,
which the early explorers believed to be 'the smell of luscious
unknown fruits, wafted out to sea'. [SR, p.187]

She manages her sweetening and softening of the bitter
material not only by turning it into a child's experience, but
by giving the whole book, as its title suggests, the air of a
dream. Everyone dreams. Jacques' memory of being rescued
by the old Bishop comes back to him 'in flashes, unrelated
pictures, like a dream. Perhaps it was a dream'. [SR, p.69]
When Cécile is sick in bed, her mind is 'dreamily' conscious
of her world encircling her 'like layers and layers of shelter,
with this one flickering, shadowy room at the core'. [SR,
p.156] Towards the end of the book, in a strange and
alarming sequence, the dying Count Frontenac is given a
long and ominous dream. He is a boy at an old country
farmhouse, trying to keep out 'a very tall man in a plumed
hat and huge boots' [SR, pp.241–2], a giant against whom
the house must be made safe. The dream has an uncanny

resemblance to Auclair's childhood memory of the Count's return to his Paris home, when the gates he had never seen opened are dragged inward, and the Count appears next day wearing 'his uniform and such big boots', [SR, pp.18–19] terrifying the boy, who hides under the counter. Like Death coming for Count Frontenac, the Count, also, was to be Auclair's destiny.

The mortal dreaming spreads out into the novel's setting, the rock, the river, the sky, which Cather 'paints' over and over,[39] in different lights and season, with all her eloquence and precision. Diffusing the literal, definite readings of childhood are the hazy, obscuring mists of the far northern city, its autumn fogs, 'rolling vapours that were constantly changing in density and colour; now brown, now amethyst, now reddish lavender, with sometimes a glow of orange overhead where the sun was struggling behind the thick weather', giving the feeling of 'walking in a dream', of 'living in a world of twilight and miracles'. [SR, p.61] In the thaw, 'everything grew grey like faintly smoked glass'. [SR, p.153] At sunset, there is an afterglow, 'the slow, rich, prolonged flowing-back of crimson across the sky', with a 'haze' that makes 'the colour seem thick, like a heavy liquid', and makes Cécile, at twilight, think yet again of miracles and martyrs. [SR, p.230] The most haunting time on the rock is All Soul's Night, when

> the shades of the early martyrs and great missionaries drew close about her. All the miracles that had happened there, and the dreams that had been dreamed, came out of the fog [and] overshadowed the living. . . . Fears . . . and memories . . . hung over the rock of Kebec on this day of the dead like the dark fogs from the river. [SR, pp. 94–5]

Haunted by her own past, just at the point where she was turning towards old age, Cather overshadows her story of childhood faith, enduring loyalty and solid rock with a hazy, mournful duskiness. It makes a muted transition from the strong works of the middle years, to her late lookings back.

14

OBSCURE DESTINIES

Your destination and your destiny's
A brook that was the water of the house . . .

Here are your waters and your watering place.
Drink and be whole again beyond confusion.

Robert Frost, 'Directive', 1946

'"EVERYTHING THAT'S alive has got to suffer,"' says old Mrs Harris to her grandsons. The three stories Cather wrote while her mother was dying could well have been stories of pain and loss. One of them recalls the breaking-up of a friendship, one tells of the death of a Czech Nebraskan farmer during hard times, one enters into the last days of a dispossessed, indigent old woman in a troubled family. The 'destinies' of these mid-Western characters from almost half a century back are 'obscure' in the sense of being ultimately mysterious. 'Everything here seemed strangely moving and significant', the doctor thinks in 'Neighbour Rosicky', contemplating the graveyard, 'though signifying what, he did not know'. [OD, p.70] The characters don't know the 'significance' of their own destinies; what they do know, as Gray reminds us in his Elegy for 'the humble joys and destiny obscure' of the poor, from which Cather took her title,[1] is that 'all await alike th'inevitable hour', that all paths 'lead but to the grave'.

But, in fact, these are not painful or morbid stories. Cather may have had 'Un Coeur Simple' in mind when she wrote

'Old Mrs Harris', but (unlike Gertrude Stein's American improvisation on Flaubert, *Three Lives*), she does not emulate Flaubert's 'coldness'.[2] 'Two Friends', and even more so 'Neighbour Rosicky' and 'Old Mrs Harris', are benign stories, full of an appeasing benevolence and resignation. The 'inevitable hour' comes, as for the Archbishop, when it must. Up to that moment, one's destiny is to be made the best of. It is Euclide Auclair's stoicism again. The stories, returning to Nebraska after many years' fictional absence, reinvoke, but more simply and quietly, the pastoral ethics of *O Pioneers!* and *My Ántonia*: the dignity of labour, and 'the sentiment of deep-rooted, patient affection triumphing over all'.[3]

'Neighbour Rosicky' particularly embodies these sentiments, and as a result the story has been much anthologized,[4] nostalgically welcomed, like the less craftily ambivalent of Robert Frost's 'rural' poems, as a celebration of old-fashioned American agrarian values – immigrant hopefulness in the land of opportunity, self-help, honesty, pleasure in the everyday, domestic order, endurance, and a belief in land-ownership as better for the soul than urban wage-earning. It is ironic that the friendship in 'Two Friends' breaks up because one of the men becomes a supporter of Bryan's Populism, and that political rhetoric is repudiated – as Cather felt the need to repudiate it at the start of the polemical 1930s – as destructive of true feeling. After all, the beliefs expressed in these stories still have their roots in that mid-Western populism for which Cather in her youth felt some sympathy. Though the memory of the pettiness and inferiority of small-town provincial life still irks her, everything really bad – sweated labour, squalid (as opposed to honourable) poverty, political agitation, dead-alive confinement – is felt to come from the big cities. The dignified central figures, 'obscure' but not commonplace – Rosicky, Grandma Harris, the slow, solid cattle-rancher in 'Two Friends', meaningfully named Trueman – stand for a moral ideal of pre-war pastoral America. To have left behind a reminder of that legacy is, as it turns out, their 'obscure destiny'. So the stories are more than ever about memory. Cather explained to her old friend

Carrie that 'Two Friends' was not a picture of the two men, but of her memory of them.[5] And the memories of the characters themselves play in and out of these stories about remembering.

Yet, though they do turn away from the modern world (particularly 'Two Friends', which has a smattering of grumpy remarks about 'today' – motor cars, the loss of independent businessmen and the decline of the theatre), these stories have not been well served by the kind of praise that makes them sound merely escapist and reassuring. In all three, there are delicate and risky negotiations: between the solidity of the remembered figures, and their makeshift, transitory environments; between the feelings of childhood and the feelings of age; and between the eloquent simplicity of the narrative, and the difficulty of true speech. The language of memory is not as secure as it looks: the simplest, Cather said of 'Old Mrs Harris', is always the most difficult.[6]

'Two Friends', though told in a calm masterful way, is about a failure of language which puts at risk the narrator's pleasure in memory. It opens with a passage on the need for memories as 'unalterable realities, somewhere at the bottom of things' which can give one 'courage', [OD, p.193] but this sententious-sounding dictum has become more uneasy by the end, when what needed to be kept as one of those unalterable truths has become 'wasted' and 'distorted'. The story of disillusionment – of the two friends in each other, and of the narrator in their friendship – makes a discomforting paradox out of the process of remembering: how do you look back happily on what now makes you feel sad?

As a child (not sexed, but seemingly boyish like Jim Burden – he plays jacks, goes on errands and sits about the grocery store with the men in the evenings) the narrator hero-worshipped the two friends, Dillon the wealthy, clever Irish banker and store-owner, a devout family man and a Democrat, and Trueman, ten years older, the slow quiet Republican poker-playing cattleman from Buffalo. They were his 'two aristocrats', the outstanding men in the small town. The story moves surely between his remembered feeling for them, and their feelings for each other. This is not a simple emotion: Dillon, the more quick and articulate, given to satire, tolerates his friend's gambling and (rumoured) womanizing, relaxations which give the heavy, melancholy rancher a kind of 'double life'. These idiosyncrasies and reciprocities unfold as the characters are observed, always in the context of their specific environment. We register their special attributes – Dillon's well-built store, even the side-walk outside it more solid than anything else in that 'flimsy' community, the two men's fine shirts and handkerchiefs, their excursions to the city, and above all, their conversation – as qualifications for a local reputation: 'He was, according to our standards, a rich man' [OD, p.195] . . . 'Their excursions made some of the rest of us feel less shut away and small-townish.' [OD, p.202] They stand out from the inferior, provincial setting, she suggests, like planets in the firmament.

Cather enjoys astrological analogies, and she makes this one quite specific, even allowing the two men and the narrator to witness a transit of Venus, which portends the eclipse of their friendship. Their relationship as a planetary 'equilibrium', 'like two bodies held steady by some law of balance, an unconscious relation like that between the earth and the moon', producing a 'mathematical harmony' which is aesthetically pleasing to the observer, [OD, p.227] is established by the story's insistence on order. The men's lives are observed in a seasonal pattern, first on winter nights, playing chequers in the back office of Dillon's store, the pattern on the board reflecting the 'equilibrium' of their friendship, the rings on their hands (flashier Dillon's a diamond solitaire, stoical Trueman's an onyx Roman soldier) shining like stars;[7] then on spring and summer evenings, sitting out on the sidewalk in the office armchairs, talking. The figures stand out in the minutely remembered landscape (right down to the shape of each of the chairs) like solid 'masses'.

At the centre of the story is a passage of strange unexpec-ted beauty, in which the men, sitting out in the bright moonlight, seem 'more largely and positively themselves', and the ugly ramshackle buildings of the street are harmonized:

> These abandoned buldings, an eyesore by day, melted together into a curious pile in the moonlight, became an immaterial structure of velvet-white and glossy blackness, with here and there a faint smear of blue door, or a tilted patch of sage-green that had once been a shutter. [OD, p.211]

Sound, like objects, is transfigured: the white dust on the road seems to 'drink up the moonlight like folds of velvet', and drinks up 'sound, too'; all is 'muffled' by the dust that lay 'like the last residuum of material things – the soft bottom resting-place'. [OD, p. 212] Like *Shadows on the Rock*'s twilit chiaroscuro, this resembles Hawthorne's account of the softening and estranging effects of moonlight on a familiar room. Dillon and Trueman, real and familiar in their lives, are transformed by the 'moonlight' of memory and imagination. Silenced, they become blocks of colour in an impressionist painting (like Lily Briscoe's rendering of Mrs Ramsay in *To the Lighthouse*), part of the deep 'soft bottom' silence of the past. But this aesthetic harmonizing, which turns the two dead men, long turned to 'dust' themselves, into 'composed' figures in a silent landscape, does not obliterate the sounds they made. The interest of this very fine story is in the tension between silence – which we identify with memory, death, the stars, paintings – and language, which belongs to life, conflict, relationships, politics, and writing.

'"Careful of the language around here,"' [OD, p.200] Mr Trueman reprimands his poker-playing friends when they get rowdy; and carefulness of language is what, above all, distinguishes the two friends (as it distinguishes their author) from other people. Their talk is carefully contrasted: Mr Dillon has 'such a crisp, clear enunciation, and could say things so neatly' that 'people would take a reprimand from him . . . because he put it so well'. [OD, p.205] His voice expresses the exact shade of his feeling for the person he is speaking to; his speech is never 'perfunctory' or 'slovenly'.

'When he made a remark, it not only meant something, but sounded like something – sounded like the thing he meant.' [OD, p.206] Trueman, by contrast, has a 'thick', 'low' voice, and is usually silent. But every so often he will tell a long story which is 'sure to be an interesting and unusual one'. [OD, p.205] In spite of these differences, both men are admired by the listener (like Neil Herbert haughtily preferring Captain Forrester's decorums to the Ivy Peters generation) for the superiority of their 'conversation' to the inarticulate slang of the young men of the town. Their formalities, like their addressing of each other by their initials, are relished. When they talk about the plays they have enjoyed on their trips to the city they 'transfer' their experience completely: 'They saw the play over again as they talked of it, and perhaps whatever is seen by the narrator as he speaks is sensed by the listener, quite irrespective of words.' [OD, p.218] The experience mimics that of the story's reader, responding to a language that is attempting to transfer something more than words.

But this linguistic harmony is broken in on by another language. Dillon becomes an avid supporter of William Jennings Bryan after hearing the legendary 'cross of gold' speech, and campaigns for him locally. Trueman is disgusted by his friend's conversion to Populism, for reasons which have everything to do with language: Bryan is a 'windbag' with nothing 'back of' his 'tall talk' but 'unsound theory'. [OP, pp.220–21] The narrator agrees; initially enthusiastic, won over by Dillon's rhetoric, he finds that Dillon's voice changes as he gets more political, and becomes 'unnatural'. [OD, p.223] The friendship is 'distorted' by the imposition of this unnatural speech. The two men lose each other (like *The Professor's House* and *Death Comes for the Archbishop*, this is a chaste love story) and the narrator, like a spectator in the theatre when the curtain has closed, loses their language: 'the old stories . . . the minute biographies . . . the clear, detailed, illuminating accounts' and, most of all, 'the strong, rich, out-flowing silence between two friends', which was itself a form of language. [OD, p.226] The story remembers their dis-membered speech at a time when that very language of traditional narrative seemed to Cather to be under threat from a politically unsympathetic modernism.

'Neighbour Rosicky' is more consoling. As its title suggests, by sounding at once homely and foreign, the story makes a kind of translation: Cather was going back to one of the crucial subjects of My Ántonia. (Of the three stories in Obscure Destinies, this is the closest in feeling to the earlier novels, with Rosicky a rewritten version of Ántonia's Cuzak.) Rosicky has 'translated' himself in several ways: from rural Czechoslovakia to London and New York, from urban to rural America, from a bachelor's to a domestic life, and, above all, from suffering to contentment. He translates his painful past into enjoyable stories, turning memories of deep distress into fairy tales. In the end he is translated into the earth, his life 'completed' in a country graveyard.

The potential for sentimentality is kept under control by a very careful language. The narrative is always reminding us of the need for true speech, accurate translation. Rosicky, a man of delicate manners, is careful to speak American for the doctor and for his American daughter-in-law, and his speech is rendered phonetically (more so than the Czech-American speech in O Pioneers! or My Ántonia) as foreign speech. Putting things into words is a challenge to him: his preferred communication is the dialogue of unspoken agreements and assumptions he has with his wife, and his friendship with his horses, in which he finds 'his way of expressing what he felt'. [OD p.61] His body speaks its own language of history and character, the thickened nail of his right hand, for instance, telling of his past as a tailor. Mary silently reads his face for signs of the 'heart' the doctor has diagnosed; his daughter-in-law Polly, at first unwilling to 'read' the foreign family she has married into, but drawn to Rosicky through kindness, responds, after nursing him through his first heart attack, to the language of his hand, 'so alive and quick and light in its communication'.

> It seemed to her that she had never learned so much about life from anything as from old Rosicky's hand. It brought her to herself; it communicated some direct and untranslatable message. [OD, p.67]

It is the narrator's job to communicate in words the 'direct and untranslatable message' of that hand. Like Dillon, Rosicky 'sounds like the thing he meant'; the translation has to be true to that original.

It was a nice graveyard, Rosicky reflected, sort of snug and homelike, not cramped or mournful, – a big sweep all round it. A man could lie down in the long grass and see the complete arch of the sky over him, hear the wagons go by; in summer the mowing-machine rattled right up to the wire fence. And it was so near home. Over there across the cornstalks his own roof and windmill looked so good to him that he promised himself to mind the Doctor and take care of himself. He was awful fond of his place, he admitted. He wasn't anxious to leave it. And it was a comfort to think that he would never have to go farther than the edge of his own hayfield. The snow, falling over his barnyard and the graveyard, seemed to draw things together like. And they were all old neighbours in the graveyard, most of them friends; there was nothing to feel awkward or embarrassed about. . . .

Well, it was a nice snowstorm; a fine sight to see the snow falling so quietly and graciously over so much open country. On his cap and shoulders, on the horses' backs and manes, light, delicate, mysterious it fell; and with it a dry cool fragrance was released into the air. It meant rest for vegetation and men and beasts, for the ground itself; a season of long nights for sleep, leisurely breakfasts, peace by the fire. This and much more went through Rosicky's mind, but he merely told himself that winter was coming, clucked to his horses, and drove on. [OD, pp.18–19]

The passage is deeply rooted in layers of personal feeling and traditions of pastoral writing. Rosicky's own language ('nice', 'sort of snug', 'looked so good', 'take care of himself', 'awful fond', 'draw things together like', 'all old neighbours') is easily woven into the slow Biblical rhythms of the whole sequence ('A man could lie down' . . . 'And it was so near home' . . . 'And it was a comfort' . . . 'And they were all old neighbours') which builds up, in a 'big sweep', towards the quiet climax of the snow, when it moves, as from earth to air, into more lyrical measures ('light, delicate, mysterious, it fell') before coming back to, and closing with, the mortal rhythms of Rosicky and his wagon-horses.

Cather's genius, as strongly felt here as anywhere in her work, makes a simple language, as close as possible to Rosicky's, out of a controlled, experienced craftsmanship. Other voices are invoked (*Ecclesiastes*, Virgil, Housman, Frost),[8] but they are as deeply buried as the inhabitants of Rosicky's graveyard. The rhythm is brilliantly, and discreetly, manipulated.[9] But she 'draws things together' so that technical skill and literary resonances seem 'merely' natural.

Rosicky likes the graveyard because it is 'snug' and homely (the comedy of his not wanting to be embarrassed in the grave is nicely done) and belongs to the seasonal order of his life. At the same time it is out in space, 'open country'. That pastoral reconciling of contradictions – the homely with the spacious – is, throughout the story, set against the confinement of the 'cities of the dead' [OD, p.71] which nearly buries Rosicky alive. There is nothing else in Cather quite like Rosicky's memories of his appalling destitution in London,[10] and of his years working for a tailor's shop in New York. This is not the cultured New York of Eden Bower or Myra Henshawe. Young Rosicky, sharing his loft over a furniture factory in Vesey Street with a Czech cabinet-maker who plays the flute in the evenings, or sitting in Park Place on a hot Fourth of July afternoon, surrounded by the 'blank buildings' of the business district, all empty 'like the stillness in a great factory when the machinery stops', belongs to the American urban half-life, part grotesque, part nightmarish, of Melville's 'Bartleby the Scrivener'. It has its own energy – there is something attractive about that loft, with the sea winds blowing into it, and about Rosicky's attempts to domesticate and cheer up his life as a wage-earner. But 'real' domesticity can only be found, according to the story's agrarian bias, and the tradition of pastoral writing, in the country home – and the country graveyard.

Rosicky's domesticity is feminine. In his youth in New York, he and the Czech cabinet-maker are like a 'bridal pair'; in Nebraska, he and Mary make a partnership which she thinks of, for all their hard life, as essentially 'gentle' and 'soft'. [OD, p.24] All through the story, food and plants and domestic objects are identified with life-warmth: breakfasts cooked for the doctor on the days Mary gives birth, a special cake baked for Rosicky on the day he learns about his weak heart, Mary's geraniums kept blooming all winter indoors, a feather quilt in the making for Polly (a soft place, eventually, for Rosicky's first grandchild). Rosicky participates in this female world, buying the 'ticking' for Mary's pillows and quilts, washing the dishes for Polly, sitting in the kitchen corner sewing. He stitches the story of his past into the present, just as Mary takes out her darning in order to talk about their life together. Rosicky is not emasculated: he is a tough old survivor of hard times. But because of his double history as a tailor-farmer, his easygoing unassertive character which makes the best of 'what we got', his illness, and above all his capacity for 'loving people', he is tender and gentle, lending his presiding spirit, like a minor deity, to this exceptionally gentle story.

'Old Mrs Harris' is less gentle and more problematic. But it too places unheroic female qualities at its centre. Of course, Cather had had domestic female life before in the corners of her fictions. But until this long story (for which the original title was 'Three Women')[11] it had not been at the centre. The story begins with a woman, 'cross-stitch in hand', looking out of her kitchen window across to her neighbour's yard, impatiently waiting for the mother of the house to go out so that she can rush across with her coffee-cake and talk to the grandmother on her own. The opening takes us into a complicated 'cross-stitching' of women's daily lives, women's work and women's preoccupations. The men are in the background. At the centre of the story are three women admiring a baby; not a spiritualized stand-in for the Infant Jesus, but an extremely human baby:

> She reappeared with the baby, who was not crying, exactly, but making eager, passionate, gasping entreaties – faster and faster, tenser and tenser, as he felt his dinner nearer and nearer and yet not his. . . . The baby fell to work so fiercely that beads

of sweat came out all over his flushed forehead. . . . When he was changed to the other side, Hughie resented the interruption a little; but after a time he became soft and bland, as smooth as oil, indeed; began looking about him as he drew in his milk. He finally dropped the nipple from his lips altogether, turned on his mother's arm, and looked inquiringly at Mrs Rosen. [OD, pp.115–16][12]

In its everyday realism, 'Old Mrs Harris' is more directly autobiographical than most of Cather's writing, and is always used as a literal source-book for the life. (If you go to the 'Cather childhood home', taped quotations from 'Old Mrs Harris' illustrate the visit.) Certainly she made few factual changes. Grandma Harris/Grandma Boak has followed her married daughter Victoria Templeton/Jennie Cather from Tennessee, not Virginia, and she falls ill at the same time that her granddaughter Vickie/Willa goes to college. (In fact she died after Cather left home.) Hillary Templeton/Charles Cather is working for an irrigation project, not a loans and insurance office. Vickie has no sisters, only little twin brothers and baby Hughie. Her ambition is to study fossils at Ann Arbor, and the money needed for her university place is raised by Grandma Harris, who secretly persuades the Rosens to lend it to the Templetons. (In fact Charles Cather borrowed the money from a business associate.)[13] But in essence it is the story of Willa Cather's life in about 1889,[14] and gives off that peculiarly intimate, even painful quality of early life closely remembered, as in *The Mill on the Floss* or *David Copperfield*. The Southern family gone West are her family: the long-suffering, indispensable grandmother, the demanding, attractive mother, an ex-Southern 'belle', the weak charming father, the difficult, clever older daughter, the jolly little boys (endearingly recalled) and the servant girl, all living together in a small rented house, and having to adapt to the 'snappy little democracy' of 'Skyline'. The cultured Jewish Rosen family next door are versions of the Wieners, Willa's refuge from her own family in Red Cloud; and the other nosy and philistine neighbours (an equivocal word for Cather) evoke the 'stupid faces' of *The Song of the Lark*.

But to use 'Old Mrs Harris' only as biographical evidence
is to do a damaging injustice to this extremely beautiful
long story, Cather's last great work. Though there is no
sexual disguise, as with Jim Burden, or fictional displace-
ment, as with Thea's singing, 'Old Mrs Harris' makes an
extraordinary imaginative leap. Cather does not only go
back into her own feelings as a fifteen-year-old – in fact for
most of the story Vickie is seen from the outside, somewhat
coolly, by Mrs Rosen – but into the feelings of the three
older women who surrounded her, in which, at the time,
she had little imaginative interest. Mrs Rosen's spirited
mixture of impatient dislike at the Templetons' habits and
culture, mixed with attraction to their humanness, gives a
lively energetic central focus; and the grandmother is one of
Cather's most impressive and sympathetic figures. But the
truly surprising empathy is, at last, with Cather's mother.
Handsome Victoria's spoilt high-handedness with her
family and neighbours, her jealousy of favours done to
anyone else in the house, her lack of sympathy for her
mother and her daughter, all repel us (as Mrs Rosen is
repelled). But Mrs Rosen also has to warm, as we do, to
Victoria's generous energy – laughing in a snow-storm,
nursing the baby. Very late on, we are allowed inside
Victoria's feelings, at the point when she has discovered she
is pregnant again, and her energy erupts as fury and disappointment:

Now and then Victoria sat upright on the edge of the bed, beat
her hands together softly and looked desperately at the ceiling,
then about at those frail, confining walls. If only she could
meet the situation with violence, fight it, conquer it! But there
was nothing for it but stupid animal patience.
   . . . She was still young, and she was still handsome; why must
she be for ever shut up in a little cluttered house with children
and fresh babies and an old woman and a stupid bound girl and
a husband who wasn't very successful? Life hadn't brought her
what she expected when she married Hillary Templeton; life
hadn't used her right. She had tried to keep up appearances, to
dress well with very little to do it on, to keep young for her

husband and children. She had tried, she had tried! Mrs Templeton buried her face in the pillow and smothered the sobs that shook the bed. [OD, pp.177–9]

The moment is not allowed to dominate; we move away from it, as the cool narrative strategy, imitating life's indifference, turns to other centres of feeling. But its loud crying noise, 'smothered' in the quiet narrative, makes a violent protest against 'confinement' in all senses of the word. The paradox of 'Old Mrs Harris' is that frustration and confinement are its subject, yet its effect is of largeness.

From the moment Mrs Rosen looks out of her kitchen window across to her neighbour's yard, we move through narrow frames of doors and windows into circumscribed corners, limited spaces, makeshift interiors. Characters are framed in doorways, glimpsed through them, as in Dutch paintings, washing or reading. They look out for each other covertly, like Mrs Harris watching for Mr Templeton out of the kitchen window so that she can catch him alone. The interiors of the Templeton house feel scrappy and provisional, but none the less confining for that. The door at which Mrs Harris directs a sad look is 'flimsy', made of cheap 'factory' wood; [OD, p.163] the walls that keep in Victoria are 'frail', and are not sound-proof. Mrs Harris inhabits a makeshift space, more a 'passageway' than a room, cluttered with awkward objects. Everything is improvised, substituted; the table is covered with junk and 'too far away from her corner' [OD, p.89] to be used; a box covered with an oilcloth serves as a washstand, a corner hidden by a cheap cotton curtain makes a clothes-cupboard, and a splint-bottom chair with sawn-off legs alternates as a place to put a tea-tray, a work-basket, or a child. Grandmother's bed has no springs, only a thin cotton mattress and wooden slats. Her night-time 'comforter' is a torn cast-off sweater, given to her by Mrs Rosen. She covers her bed up in the daytime and keeps her towel on its 'special nail behind the curtain', her soap in 'a tin tobacco-box'. 'Mrs Harris and her "things" were almost required to be invisible.' [OD, p.98] When she falls ill, Albert, one of the twins, tries to rearrange her room so that it looks more like a sick-room: he brings down a wooden cracker-box and covers it with a napkin, relaces her tin cup with a glass tumbler, and gives her one of his Sunday-school linen handkerchiefs. These would-be consolatory childish improvisations pitifully bring home the meagreness of what is 'hers'. Other spaces in the house are confined and improvised too: Vickie's attic, 'not much bigger than a closet', [OD, p.91] the messy yard with its ragged ditch which, the little boys explain to the disapproving Mrs Rosen, they like to use 'for building bridges over.' [OD, p.119] Only the parlour, with its Brussels carpet and Protestant paintings, is 'neat and comfortable'. [OD, p.114]

It's not only the layout of the house that embodies the confinement of the three generations of women. So does the time scheme of the story (confined to one hot summer, though the characters range about in time in their minds) and, even, its placing inside a volume of three stories, which gives it the same kind of modest obscurity as its central character. (If 'Old Mrs Harris' had been published separately, as a novella the same length as *My Mortal Enemy*, it would have attracted much more attention.)[15] But this female narrative is placed 'inside' in every sense. There are hardly any outdoor scenes. When there is a move out, to the Methodist lawn party at the Roadmaster's house, the family is confined again, in a tent full of gossipy neighbours. Only the Rosens, on their way to the 'social', catch sight of a freer space ('High above, the rustling tree-tops stirred free in the flood of moonlight'). But then philosophical Mr Rosen (like the nuns in *Shadows on the Rock*) has his own interior space: 'He carried a country of his own in his mind, and was able to unfold it like a tent in any wilderness'. [OD, p.121] For the women, such interior space is harder to come by.

Mr Rosen's freer space is largely cultural, and it's that space Vickie longs to go out into. Her journeys across the yard into Mrs Rosen's much more elegant and stylish domain are crude, early attempts to translate herself into a different element. Her greedy awkward half-comprehending forays into Mr Rosen's collection of German Romantics – Coleridge's translation of Schiller's *Wallenstein* (selected, perhaps, for its insistence on character as destiny), *Faust, Wilhelm Meister* – her admiration of Mrs Rosen's Italianate opera-cloak, her responsiveness to the quotation from Michelet that Mr Rosen gives her as a lucky charm (*'Le but n'est rien; le chemin, c'est tout'*) move her towards the possibility of placing herself in a wider, liberating, flexible history of thought.

Vickie is pleased with herself because her liking for Mrs Rosen's house does not make her dissatisfied with her own. This contradictory touch (she is, of course, intensely dissatisfied as well) points to Cather's careful 'cross-stitching'. She does not write off Vickie's home culture: Mrs Harris's readings to the children of *Tom Sawyer* and *The Pilgrim's Progress* provide as much interior space, in their way, as Schiller and Goethe. And the cultural complexity of the Templeton family, their elaborate feudal and chivalric Southern traditions, in which the older women have positions of power in their daughters' houses, brought up short against small-town Western egalitarianism, are acutely examined. As social history, 'Old Mrs Harris' is one of Cather's most exact, specific works.

But the cross-currents reach down to more obscure places than cultural or social oppositions. The story's resemblance to Cather's famous essay on Katherine Mansfield[16] has often been noticed. The Templeton family acts out the drama which Cather describes in that essay between the group life and the individual self. This is intensely felt in every detail of the interior scenes, especially in the moment of re-joining, when Mrs Harris forgets about her painful feet and lonely nights as the children come running down for breakfast and 'she ceased to be an individual' and became 'part of a relationship', [OD, p.136] or, less happily, when Vickie has to join the family dinner table after her father has told her he can't afford to pay for her university place, and 'everyone could see she had been crying'. [OD, p.162] The house's thinly separated spaces mimic the ironic interplay between the self-absorbed characters (Victoria, Vickie, Mr Templeton) and the watchers (Mandy, Mrs Harris, and outside, Mrs Rosen). '"What were families for, anyway?"' Vickie asks herself, furiously resentful of both her mothers having 'gone and got sick' when she is getting ready to leave. The comically brutal question is remorsefully answered by the story. Families are 'for' this painful clash between the self and the group.

The privileged, humane narrator moves through these confining walls into the secret interiors, and brings out of obscurity the private language that people speak to themselves. At the heart of this is the silent voice of the grandmother, which makes a moral centre in relation to which the other characters are placed. Mrs Harris may be neglected, but she has strong beliefs, high standards for herself and her daughter. She can be fiercely outraged: by the family's inability to accommodate a visiting preacher, or by Victoria's offhand treatment of the death of the cat, or by the lack of money for Vickie's education. She is not taken in; she knows exactly why the neighbours respond to Victoria as they do, and what her son-in-law has done with her money: 'Invested; that was a word men always held over women, Mrs Harris thought, and it always meant they could have none of their own money'. [OD, p.165] That sharp irony goes with an intense pride, recognized only by Mrs Rosen, and, going with that pride, an intense desire not to be of any trouble, recognized only by Mandy. Unlike 'Neighbour Rosicky', this is a stern story, dominated by the old lady's ironic stoicism:

> On winter nights, and even on summer nights after the cocks began to crow, Mrs Harris often felt cold and lonely about the chest. Sometimes her cat, Blue Boy, would creep in beside her and warm that aching spot. But on spring and summer nights he was likely to be abroad skylarking, and this little sweater had become the dearest of Grandmother's few possessions. It was kinder to her, she used to think, as she wrapped it about her middle, than any of her own children had been. She had married at eighteen and had had eight children; but some died, and some were, as she said, scattered.
> After she was warm in that tender spot under the ribs, the

old woman could lie patiently on the slats, waiting for daybreak; thinking about the comfortable rambling old house in Tennessee, its feather beds and hand-woven rag carpets and splint-bottom chairs, the mahogany sideboard, and the marble-top parlour table; all that she had left behind to follow Victoria's fortunes.

She did not regret her decision; indeed, there had been no decision. Victoria had never once thought it possible that Ma should not go wherever she and the children went, and Mrs Harris had never thought it possible. Of course she regretted Tennessee, though she would never admit it to Mrs Rosen: – the old neighbours, the yard and garden she had worked in all her life, the apple trees she had planted, the lilac arbour, tall enough to walk in, which she had clipped and shaped so many years. Especially she missed her lemon tree, in a tub on the front porch, which bore little lemons almost every summer, and folks would come for miles to see it

But the road had led westward, and Mrs Harris didn't believe that women, especially old women, could say when or where they would stop. [OD, pp.95–7]

This measured, humane, unflinching voice invests the fragile domestic details – the torn 'comforter', the undependable cat, the lost lemon tree – with *gravitas*. Mrs Harris, unlike Archbishop Latour, has a meagre life to look back on from her deathbed. But the materials are transformed (like the child improvising a sick-room) into dignified matters. The Christian moral, which makes Mrs Harris after all not so unlike the Archbishop ('Blessed are the poor in spirit; for theirs is the kingdom of Heaven')[17] is, fortunately, not explicit. Instead it is invoked entirely through domestic pictures. When Mrs Harris is seen, framed like a figure in a painting by Courbet or Millet, as 'an old woman in a brown calico dress, washing her hot face and neck at a tin basin . . . in an attitude of profound weariness', [OD, p.77] or having her legs rubbed by the servant girl, who kneels in front of her, the shadowy light of the kitchen lantern falling on the two women engaged in this 'oldest rite of compassion', [OD, p.93] the penury of her life is turned into valuable images. Memory (as the narrator concludes, with mournful insistence) pays the debt.

*

The stability and control of *Obscure Destinies* are the work of a settled personality. In her sixties, Cather had grown somewhat monumental, both in her character and in her literary reputation. Views of her before she became weakened by illness and bereavements and deeply depressed by the war, all emphasize her solidity. Even her weaknesses, her depressions and uncertainties, had settled into negative aspects of strength – truculence, refusals, dismissiveness. She seemed like the rock of her own fictions.

Louise Bogan, sent to do a 'profile' for the *New Yorker* in 1931, gave a vivid, if awe-struck, picture.

> One can see at a glance that she herself has always been that rare accident of Nature, a perfectly natural person. She speaks, without the shadow of a doubt, in the accent she acquired as a child. Her voice is deep and resonant. Her dresses are bright in color; she likes brilliant embroidery, boldly designed materials, and exotic strings of beads. She is of medium height, and of the build best described as stocky. She stands and moves solidly. She sits with an air of permanence. . . . She smokes a cigarette as though she really liked the taste of ignited tobacco and rice paper. Her eyes are fine; gray-blue and set well apart. She has a thorough smile. Her face, when she detects some affectation in another's words or actions, can lose every atom of warmth and become hostile and set. It is impossible to imagine her strong hands in a deprecatory gesture. The remarks 'Oh well' and, 'What does it matter?' have never, in all probability, passed her lips.[18]

The same sense of strong freshness comes out of a striking recollection of Truman Capote's, who as a young man working in the Society Library in New York in the early '40s kept seeing 'this absolutely marvellous-looking woman' with 'a wonderful open, extraordinary face, and hair combed back in a bun', wearing 'soft' but 'rather severe' suits, 'distinguished-looking', with 'amazingly pale blue' eyes. One day, when they were both stuck on the steps in the snow, she asked him to have a hot chocolate with her in a nearby restaurant. Capote, talking about writers and writing, told her that his favourite American writer was Willa Cather. She

led him on for a bit ('Which of her books did I like best?').
'"Well", she said finally, "I'm Willa Cather."'[19]

The anecdote suggests good humour, the affable side of
Cather which Yehudi Menuhin brings out in his recollections
of his friendship, begun in childhood, with his mother's
friend 'Aunt Willa'. Menuhin calls her 'a rock of strength and
sweetness', the 'embodiment' of an older, vanished America,
utterly to be trusted and (so it seemed to him) without 'self
doubt'. But even his affectionate memoir contains a warning
note.

> Her strength had a patience and evenness which did not
> preclude a certain severity. There were abuses and vulgarities
> she refused to tolerate, such as exposure in newspapers or on
> radio. She had a contempt for anything too much owned or
> determined by mobs, reserving admiration for high individual
> endeavour, withdrawing more and more from society even as
> she drew closer to us.[20]

That withdrawal is less gently recalled by Elizabeth Shepley Sergeant, still maintaining an intermittent friendship
with Cather after the war years had estranged them. Elsie
found her famous old friend, in her maturity, taciturn,
intolerant, and increasingly difficult to approach ('She never
had the least little bit of small talk, not an iota of ease and
friendliness with a stranger who seemed intrusive'),[21]
though she still retained, deep down, her enthusiasm and
intimate warmth for old friends.

Cather was returning on herself, in her life as in her late
writing. Though she never went back to Red Cloud after a
final family reunion when her mother had died in 1931, she
wrote more than ever to her few remaining friends there,
and, during the Depression years, sent money and gifts to
Annie Pavelka and the other country families of her past.[22]
(One of her complaints at the end of her life was that she felt
almost entirely estranged from Red Cloud; she had always
had enemies there, the town sounded to her changed
beyond recognition, and she deeply resented her sister Elsie's
having sold the family house.)[23] In the 1930s and 1940s her
long intimacies with friends such as Zoë Akins and Dorothy

Canfield Fisher were revivified through letters. Professionally, she made another recapitulation, supervising the
definitive 'Autograph Edition' of her books for publication
in the late 1930s.[24]

Meanwhile the modern world was being held at bay.
Cather's politics in the 1930s consisted of an antipathy for
Roosevelt and the New Deal, an indignant sympathy for the
Lindberghs, hounded by the press after their baby's kid-
napping,[25] an admiration for Edward VIII's abdication
speech (one of the few events that made her listen to the
radio),[26] and a deliberate detachment from the 'progressive'
movements of the day – economic and social reform, psychoanalysis and Marxism – as ultimately irrelevant to real
life.[27] Clearly, the destruction of equilibrium and friendship
through politics in 'Two Friends' was not just a childhood
memory.

Cather's position was not unlike Virginia Woolf's in the
1930s, struggling in The Years to detach fiction from pol-
emics. But in Cather's case this was joined to an increasing
impatience with 'the new'. Obscure Destinies, Lucy Gayheart
and Not Under Forty did look markedly anomalous in the
period of Dos Passos's 1919, Fitzgerald's Tender is the Night
and Nathaniel West's Miss Lonelyhearts. In counterpoint to
the usual tributes of praise and awards (the Howells medal
for fiction in 1930, the Prix Femina Américaine in 1933,
finally the gold medal of the National Institute of Arts and
Letters in 1944), Cather was beginning to be seen by the New
Critics (in particular Granville Hicks and Lionel Trilling[28] as
snobbish, escapist, narrowly provincial and irrelevant. Of
course Cather very much objected to these judgements.[29]
But they swayed her enough to make her change the title of
Not Under Forty to Literary Encounters, and to dispense with
the essays' grumpily disaffected preface ('the world broke in
two in 1922') in the Autograph Edition. And though the
attacks on her for narrowness and intolerance were themselves narrow and intolerant, it is impossible not to feel
disappointed and impatient with the rock-solid old Cather
for writing off most of her contemporaries, as when we find

her dismissing Cyril Connolly's *The Unquiet Grave* for hopelessness and decadence, or lambasting Elizabeth Bowen's stories *Look At All Those Roses* (1941) for their coldly calculating tricks, and their pathological air of a dissecting room without human beings.[30] Elsie Sergeant, herself closely involved with Jungian analysis and O'Neill's theatre, was exasperated with Cather's rejection of Freud, O'Neill, Cubism, Pound and Stein ('whom she could not take seriously'), and kept trying to remind her that she had cared for Proust and seen *Ulysses* as a landmark, that she read Bergson and liked Virginia Woolf.[31] Sergeant even notes that Cather asked her, after her father's death, whether Elsie thought that psychoanalysis would help her. (She didn't.)[32] But such forays into contemporaneity had become the exception to the rule.

Cather simply did not want to participate. When it came to overtures from academics and publishers, journalists and media people, the responses were ferociously self-protective. Inquiries from importunate researchers on her long-ago meeting with Housman,[33] or her friendship with Sarah Orne Jewett, met with short shrift: she told the abrupt and modern young man wanting information on Jewett that he could call on January 1, 1990.[34] Her response was the same to requests for help with creative writing courses (sheer nonsense),[35] for 'Portable Cather' anthologies (since the war everyone wanted to get by easily),[36] for a bibliography of her writings (she didn't see why she should give her attention to something so foreign to her interests)[37] or for reprints of her early stories.[38] The media was the most distasteful: in 1935 she told Carrie Miner Sherwood of a legal action she had brought against someone who wanted to give biographical details about her on the radio, as a lead into an advertisement for electric refrigerators.[39] She was gleeful at having kept at bay the Hollywood people, who wanted to make her rich by filming *My Ántonia*.[40] The second, 1934, Warner Brothers adaptation of *A Lost Lady*,[41] with Barbara Stanwyck as Marian, and Frank Ellinger as a heroic World War I pilot, so outraged her that she would write a clause into her will in 1943 forbidding

dramatization, whether for the purpose of spoken stage presentation or otherwise, motion picture, radio broadcasting,
television and rights of mechanical reproduction, whether by
means now in existence or which may hereafter be discovered
or perfected.[42]

No Cather videos, in perpetuity.

Towards the end of her life, her obsession over privacy
showed up in continuous warnings to her friends not to
show her letters to anyone,[43] and in the burning of as many
letters as she could recall (the will, of course, attempting to
put the lid on the rest); a 'cremation' which, in the case of
Isabelle's letters, returned by Jan Hambourg, caused Elsie
Sergeant 'a chill of regret and dismay'.[44] Manuscripts, too,
had been regularly destroyed. In 1944 she told Sinclair Lewis
(whose praise of her in 1921 had led to an intermittent,
respectful correspondence) that she had nothing to offer a
manuscript collector. When she was working, she wrote a
first draft in longhand, then typed it up, then gave it to a
professional typist (who used a different colour ribbon to
make stupidities easier to spot). The original longhand drafts,
she said casually, were usually lost. She *had* sold three
handwritten manuscripts to collectors, two to England and
one to France, but she didn't know what had happened to
them. And she had always told Knopf to destroy the final
typed versions. With all her travelling, she had never had
room for old manuscripts.[45] The letter – sad reading for
scholars – is all part of the same process: Cather wanted to
obscure her destiny from the wide-open world. It almost
seems possible to believe in Mildred Bennett's apocryphal
story of Cather and Edith Lewis, that when the two old ladies
went out together in New York, Lewis would walk in front to
fend off possible autograph-hunters.[46]

The policy of retreat did not lead to an altogether enjoyable old age. There is a great deal of unmitigated sadness in
the late letters, which in the writing is more controlled and
negotiated. And there were, inevitably, bereavements and
deprivations. Though Cather moved into a stuffily palatial
apartment in Park Avenue in 1932 (with Josephine Bourda

returning as faithful cook, until her much-lamented final departure for her Pyrenean village in 1935), the Depression affected Cather's finances (as well as those of old friends such as McClure). She wasted some of her time in the 1930s sorting out losses from bad investments.[47] The writing of *Lucy Gayheart* began in the spring of 1933 with feelings of 'deadly tiredness', and was interrupted by a sprain to the tendon of her left wrist.[48] As a result, she over-used her right hand and had to stop writing. This was the beginning of hand trouble which would plague her for the rest of her life. In 1940, after signing 500 copies of a first printing of *Sapphira and the Slave Girl*, she sprained her right hand, and thereafter had to wear it in a brace more or less continuously. As she could not bear to dictate fiction, the injury meant a drastic curtailment of her writing. With these hand injuries came, in 1935, two bad attacks of appendicitis, and, in 1942, at nearly seventy years old, a major operation to remove her gall bladder and her appendix, which left her extremely weak.[49] (She went into hospital under the name 'Miss Lewis', an odd detail in the story of Edith's perpetual usefulness.)

These debilitating ailments were not as destructive to her spirit, though, as the losses she sustained. In the spring of 1935, Isabelle Hambourg came to America to consult doctors, very ill with chronic nephritis (for which at that time there was very little treatment except nursing). Cather went back to Europe with her that summer for the last time; it was both a reunion, and a parting from the person for whom she felt she had written all her books.[50] Isabelle died in 1938, within a few months of Cather's favourite brother Douglass, whose death at fifty-eight was unexpected. Cather never fully recovered from the double blow. Then, in 1941, Roscoe Cather fell ill, and Cather made an arduous westward journey to say goodbye to him. He died of a heart attack in 1945. In this period, Cather was also deprived of her refuges: the woods at Jaffrey were wrecked by a hurricane in 1938, and the cottage at Grand Manan became impractical in the war years. (In her last few summers, she found a satisfactory substitute, further down the wild coast of Maine, in a cottage attached to the Asticou Inn, on the appropriately named Mount Desert Island.)[51] But, above all these personal matters, the darkening of Europe and the onset of the war profoundly affected Cather's imagination. Americans, she wrote to Sinclair Lewis in 1938, have been too gullible and innocent; they have lacked the necessary vision of evil.[52] 'When the French army surrendered, she wrote in her line-a-day' diary, Edith recorded, '"There seems to be no future at all for people of my generation."'[53]

There were some consolations. Though the friendships of Cather's late life were mostly saved up, like her writing, from the past, she entered into a few important new relationships which make a welcome dent in the image of a fixed, backward-facing monument. Her correspondence with Stephen Tennant (whose gushing adulation, decoratively arty life-style and flamboyant pedigree rather unexpectedly attracted Cather)[54] allowed her to give a lot of matronly literary advice as to what Stephen should and should not read, and what he should do about his perpetually unfinished book of drawings and writings on Marseilles, *Lascar*. She drew the line at finding an American publisher for his bawdy drawings, which she had to keep in a locked drawer away from her (post-Josephine) New Orleans Catholic cook.

Cather's letters to Tennant give the strong, energetic side of her monumentalism; they are full of gusto, certainty and good sense. Her sound advice to him was self-revealing: Don't talk about the book but get on with it; there's no point setting out to write a masterpiece and then sinking into self-conscious self-analysis; the only way to do it is to have fun with it, like an exciting game. Until the first writing is done, the explanations will only strangle the initial impulse. After you have *caught* it, you can pick about with tones and colours. But even if it doesn't come off, it isn't the end of the world. Cather matches her own robustness, by implication, with Flaubert's (much in her mind after her meeting with Mme Grout), whom she thinks of as a solid Norman workman. Cather had much enjoyed Mme Grout's telling her that when Turgenev visited Flaubert, they talked about everything *except* their books. The letters return repeatedly to the value of instinct over analysis, of robust realities over fastidious sensibilities, and of the old over the new. When she was ill in hospital, she told him, she read nothing but what Fitzgerald once called the 'Helpers-to-Live'.[55] Her late reading (according to these letters and to Menuhin's and Edith's reports) was Chaucer, Shakespeare and Scott. Evidently the pleasure of the quasi-maternal relationship with Tennant was in acting as a mentor and 'Helper-to-Live': when he arrived in America in the winter of 1935, looking frail, she packed him off to Jaffrey to fatten up.

Giving advice and organizing (like her mother before her) also formed part of her affectionate late relationships with her nieces, particularly with Mary Virginia Auld, her sister Jessica's daughter, who had been a favourite of Cather's ever since she was an undergraduate, and who made herself indispensable to Cather and Lewis when she became a New York neighbour and a regular visitor to Grand Manan. Cather was rather surprised at liking Mary Virginia so much, since she had always found her parents lazy and selfish.[56] But she became very involved with her life, anxious over her illnesses, and upset when she and her husband, a surgeon, left New York in 1942.[57]

Cather as fond aunt makes a more sympathetic figure than Cather as crusty recluse. And there were other, more equal, and more formidable, connections and correspondences. Through her old friends Alfred and Blanche Knopf Cather met one of the living writers she most admired, Thomas Mann, after he came to America in 1939 (though we have no details of their meeting)[58] and, also through the Knopfs, Sigrid Undset, 'that great rock of a Norwegian woman'.[59] Undset, author of historical trilogies of medieval Norway, *Kristin Lavransdatter* and *Olav Audunsson*, which Cather found sympathetic, and of some deeply religious novels of modern Norway, had been outspoken against the Nazis in the 1930s. In 1940, when she was in her late fifties, she fled the country (losing one of her sons, who was killed in a concentration camp) in a dramatic escape to America. The New World

greatly impressed her, especially the mid-West. Like Cather,
she was a strong woman with a deep feeling for people's
spiritual relation to their land and their past; they got on
well. (Indeed, it was Cather's only warm relationship with a
woman writer of her own stature and generation.) Cather,
echoing her feelings for Olive Fremstad, admired Undset's
large, heroic warmth and calm, her truthfulness, her ability
to surmount her losses, and her combination of the artist, the
peasant and the scholar.[60]

Undset connected Cather to suffering Europe. So did
another valuable relationship, through letters, with Tomas
Mazaryk, founder-president of Czechoslovakia, who had
corresponded with Cather for about eight years, until his
death in 1937.[61] Mazaryk had an American wife, and had
visited America in 1918 to raise support for Czech/Slovak
unification. Frustratingly (though we know that Annie
Pavelka had some prints from Czechoslovakia on her wall,
which Mazaryk had given Cather),[62] we have no details of
this interesting connection. Perhaps it began with Mazaryk's
reading Czech translations of Cather's work. But all that has
been sacrificed, presumably, to Edith's bonfire.

These links with Europe were crucial for Cather's later
writing, which, while it returned to memories of Nebraska
and Virginia, also went back, in the essays on Mann and on
Mme Grout, in *Lucy Gayheart* and 'The Old Beauty' and the
last unfinished fragment of a novel set in medieval Avignon,
to strong feelings for European culture and history. Of all
these late links to Europe, the most vital and profound was
with the Menuhin family.

Menuhin understood very well what his family gave
Cather: 'We who had found our American author gave our
author her European family.'[63] They met through Jan Hambourg in Paris in 1930, and the following year, when the
fifteen-year-old prodigy was touring the West Coast, the
friendship was resumed. Cather fell in love with them all: the
tough, idiosyncratic mother, the three brilliantly gifted musical
children. They were her last 'proxy family',[64] and the last great
romance of her life, recapitulating her idealizing passions

for Ethelbert Nevin and for the great singers and actresses, like Helena Modjeska and Olive Fremstad, who had so enthralled her. To Cather, the young Yehudi was, simply, 'beautiful'.[65] The family's visits were like festivals, reminiscent of Myra Henshawe's musical evenings. Menuhin recalled 'parties and birthday luncheons, excursions to the Metropolitan Opera, bunches of flowers and orange trees arriving in snowstorms, and always books and walks in Central Park'.[66] Cather read them Shakespeare and gave him Goethe and Heine; later, she admired Hephzibah for giving up her concerts and dashing off to an Australian ranch,[67] and advised Yehudi on his early marital problems. When Isabelle died, Menuhin came to comfort her;[68] and in the month before her own death, in March 1947, Yehudi and Hephzibah and their children were her last visitors.[69] The friendship brought music back to the centre of her life. The Knopfs gave her a 'phonograph' on which to play Yehudi's records; she and Edith went regularly to operas and concerts, and she saw a good deal of Myra Hess, and of Ethel Litchfield, her old musical friend who had moved from Pittsburgh to New York.[70]

But the Menuhins meant not only youth, music and talent to Cather. They also turned her mind again to the double inheritance of American artists. If they stay always at home, she wrote to him, they miss 'the companionship of seasoned and disciplined minds'. But if they 'adopt Europe altogether' they 'lose that sense of *belonging* which is so important'. 'The things his own country makes him feel . . . are about the best capital a writer has to draw upon.'[71] It is the old dilemma of Henry James, or of the 'lost generation' of self-exiled American writers in France. For Cather, the solution (and the one she recommends to Menuhin for his itinerant career of worldwide music-making) is to 'live two lives'. So, doubleness — America and Europe, youth and age, music and writing — came back to her again as a subject for late work.

15

THE IMMENSE DESIGN OF THINGS

Then, because the picture making mechanism was crushed,
the disturbing visions flashed into black, and Paul dropped
back into the immense design of things.

'Paul's Case', 1905

At any rate; that is happiness; to be dissolved into something
complete and great.

My Ántonia, 1918: quoted on Willa Cather's tombstone

Why tear a man loose from his little rock and shoot him out
into the eternities?

'Before Breakfast', 1944

'IN HAVERFORD on the Platte the townspeople still speak
of Lucy Gayheart'. [LG, p.3] Cather's penultimate novel
begins with a marked sense of *déjà vu*. Like the Haverford
townspeople, Cather is 'still speaking' the same story: still,
the exceptional artistic figure escaping from, and returning
to the small restrictive mid-Western town; still, the division
between family life and professional aspiration, native
American environment and world culture. Everything about
her heroine belongs to the Nebraskan past: her name is
stolen from a girl Cather met in 1896, her combination of
golden-brown eyes, spirited skating and musical talent are
remembered from a long-ago Red Cloud friend called Sadie
Becker.[1] And the novel recapitulates earlier fictions: 'A
Death in the Desert', the 1903 story of the singer who gets

away to Chicago, New York and Europe, falls in love with a composer, and comes back to her family in Cheyenne to 'die like a rat in a hole'; 'The Joy of Nelly Deane',[2] of 1911, with the same bright, golden-eyed, musical young girl destroyed by a brutal marriage and by her small-town incarceration; and *The Song of the Lark*, charting Thea's escape through music from the 'Moonstone' which still remembers her.

But although *Lucy Gayheart*'s reworking of old tunes does point to a falling-off in inventive power, Cather is trying, as in all her books, for a distinctive mood. There is a delicate clue to *Lucy Gayheart*: the footprints of three steps, running across a concrete pavement before the concrete had set, and left there for ever, motion in stasis. The prints are 'light, in very low relief; unless one were looking for them, one might not notice them at all'. [LG, p.226] The narrative is similarly light, and in low relief.

The story has a simple air. Lucy, the attractive, lively younger daughter of the town's easygoing German watch-maker, has gone to Chicago to study music and to be a piano teacher, and has fallen in love with the middle-aged singer Clement Sebastian. Sebastian is using her as his accompanist while his regular partner, the sinister James Mockford, is having an operation. Lucy, in a dream of emotion and music, rejects her home suitor, the young businessman Harry Gordon, hard-headed, confident, and secretly sensitive. But the singer is drowned (with – or perhaps by – Mockford), and Lucy, heartbroken, returns to Haverford and her unsatisfactory family. Harry has hastily married a rich girl, and rejects Lucy's desperate overtures of friendship, leaving her to go, in her turn, to a tragic wintry death by drowning. The rest of his time is to be a 'life sentence' of regret and remembering.

All our associations with Lucy are of lightness and ephem-erality: spring flowers, rapid skating, running through rain or cold, 'a twig or a leaf swept along on the current' [LG, p.75], a 'little boy's kite' [LG, p.117], an arrow catching fire. Fire and ice (as in Robert Frost's ominous poem of that title)[3] are continually opposed. Lucy's 'ardour' (Tom Outland's word again), her impetuosity, her inability to conceal or revoke her feelings, her passionate longings for love and art (or love *as* art) are the fire; but the fire has to vie with the cold. When her 'ardour' is strongest, the fire wins: 'The sharp air that blew off the water brought up all the fire of life in her: it was like drinking fire.' [LG, p.47] But when she returns to the 'real' world without 'ardour' or illusions, her heart is frozen and she feels unable to breathe.[4] Her death in the cold river simply confirms and concludes the competition between fire – exhilaration, aspiration – and ice (numbness, suffocation, expiring).

The language of Lucy's aspiration is always fragile and escapist. Going home from skating with Harry, she salutes the 'first star' of the evening as the signal of 'another kind of life and feeling', in a momentary 'flash of understanding'. [LG, pp.11–12] In her mind's eye, the city of Chicago exists as a dark blur punctuated by 'spots' associated with Sebastian where 'a magical meaning might at any moment flash out of the fog'. [LG, p.25] 'This city of feeling rose out of the city of fact like a definite composition, – beautiful because the rest was blotted out.' [LG, p.24] When she first hears Sebastian singing, her intense revelation of art and life as a 'tragic force' [LG, p.31] is like a spell which blots out everything else. In her first love scene with him, she feels as if 'everything were on the point of vanishing'. [LG, p.87] When Harry comes to Chicago while Sebastian is away, Lucy's longing for what is absent is like the loss of a 'ravishing melody'; without it she 'couldn't breathe'. She wants to become 'nothing but one's desire', to dissolve into pure breath. [LG, p.102] After Sebastian's death, she has a revelation, another momentary 'flash', that he incarnated for her the desire for another world, and that 'it' (the vague word often used for Lucy's longings) could be recaptured without him. But the 'it', when defined, is a 'fugitive gleam', a 'flash of promise', insubstantially evoked as 'flowers and music and enchant-ment and love'. [LG, p.184] Lucy's dedication to the primacy of feeling (she is described as one of those for whom their 'fate is what happened to their feelings and their thoughts') makes for a blurring effect, a Paterian synaesthesia of light, music, colour, air and fire. No wonder that when she and Harry are looking at French Impressionist paintings, they argue over representation, Harry insisting that 'anatomy is a fact' and that 'facts are at the bottom of everything', Lucy preferring, in art as in life, 'the city of feeling' over 'the city of fact'.

Those of Cather's critics who have taken this novel at all seriously have pointed to the dangers of Lucy's choice of romance over realism.[5] She occupies an extreme position in that long debate, which Cather embarked on when she was about Lucy's age. And the novel's soft, fragile, emotional language suggests the perils of the position. Lucy is much more like the self-deluding, pointlessly aesthetic Paul than she is like the ferociously ambitious Thea. And, like Paul's, her aspirations to dissolve into a 'bright star'[6] or 'fade far away' and melt into the aether, are frequently brought back to earth, by a voice (Harry's) 'saying something about lunch', or by her return to Haverford. She is constantly terrified that 'romance' will fall apart into mere insubstantiality. To try to enter entirely into that world, believe it to be more 'real' than the 'city of fact', is to disable oneself from the stoic, level vision of the characters in (for instance) *Obscure Destinies*. So Lucy is sometimes seen as blind, and Harry's memory of her as an arrow is not just as an arrow of fire but also of 'blindness', shooting 'toward whatever end'. [LG, p.221]

For all that, Cather engages very deeply with Lucy's impossible romanticism, and doesn't mean us to be detached from it. She tries to make those yearnings into the literary equivalent of a particular kind of music. Instead of a Wagnerian opera, Cather wanted this time to rewrite a Romantic song cycle.

Lucy's epicurean German father looks like the 'daguerreotype of a minor German poet', [LG, p.6] just the kind whose poems might have been set to music. A temperamental affinity for German romanticism is suggested. And when Lucy hears Sebastian singing Schubert, the effect is immediate and irrevocable. His first song is the seaman's invocation to the heavenly twins, the 'Dioscouri', Castor and Pollux, thanking them for their protection. Then, as the last of a 'group' of five 'melancholy songs', he sings the ominous, strange, and tragic setting of Heine's 'Der Doppelgänger':

Still is the night. The streets are at rest.
Here is the house where my loved one lived;
long it is, since she left the town,
yet the house still stands where it did.

A man stands there too, staring up,
wringing his hands in agony;
horror grips me, as I see his face – ▪
the moon shows me my own self.

Double! Pale companion! ['Du Doppelgänger, du bleicher Geselle!']
Why do you ape the torment of love
that I suffered here
so many a night in time past?[7]

The songs fill Lucy with a 'dark and terrifying' conception of love as 'a passion that drowns like black water'. [LG, p.31] Cather does not specify the other songs in the 'group', but 'Der Doppelgänger' belongs to a cycle written in 1828, the last year of Schubert's life, and published posthumously, after his death at thirty-one, as 'Schwanengesang' ('Swan-Song'). They are songs full of longings and departures, with a great deal of 'black water': 'In der Ferne' ('Far Away': 'greetings from him who is fleeing, going out into the world'), 'Abschied' (Farewell') and 'Am Meer' ('By the sea', with a weeping woman whose tears have poisoned the singer's life and made his soul 'die of longing'). At his next concert, Sebastian is singing *Winterreise*, Schubert's late cycle (to poems by Wilhelm Müller, writer of romantic folk poetry in the 1820s) of the lonely heartbroken wanderer on his winter journey towards death. Lucy entirely identifies the singer and the composer – 'this was the thing itself' – but at the same time is aware that Sebastian is not identifying himself with the 'melancholy youth', but is presenting his sorrow as if it were a memory, with 'a long perspective' between 'the singer and the scenes he was recalling'. [LG, p.38] After she has started to play for him, she practises the *songs from Die Schöne Müllerin*, [LG, p.61] an earlier Schubert/ Müller cycle (a great masterpiece of passionate bliss and bitter sorrow) of the wanderer-lover who loses his beloved miller's daughter to the huntsman, and longs to drown in the friendly brook. And the song she associates with Sebastian more than any other is 'Die Forelle' (the tune well known in its later version in the 'Trout' Quintet). Lucy takes from it 'a joyousness which seemed safe from time or change'; [LG, p.76] but in the song the trout is hooked and killed.

There are other kinds of music in *Lucy Gayheart*, all with specific associations. At the end of his first concert, Sebastian sings 'an old setting' of Byron's 'When We Two Parted', which Lucy takes as an 'evil omen' for her own life:

> Pale grew thy cheek and cold,
>   Colder thy kiss;
>   Surely that hour foretold
>   Sorrow to this.
>   [LG, p.32]

Another 'old English song' reiterates the image of the pale cold cheek: Sebastian sings her a setting of Viola's speech in *Twelfth Night*, 'She never told her love', ('but let conceal-ment, like a worm i' the bud, feed on her damask cheek' [LG, p.94]), and refers the song insidiously to Lucy. When she auditions for him, he tries her out with an aria from Massenet's *Hérodiade*, whose title, '*Vision fugitive*', anticipates the 'fugitive gleam' of her longings. They start work on Mendelssohn's oratorio *Elijah*, a line from which, unfinished when first quoted ('If with all your heart you truly seek Him') is completed after Sebastian's death ('You shall ever surely find Him'. [LG, p.185]) With Harry, Lucy goes to a week of Verdi operas, and to *Lohengrin*, which takes her into 'that invisible, inviolable world' with which Harry has noth-ing to do. All these carefully selected musical references corroborate the novel's unappeased sense of melancholy longing, but none more so than the Schubert *Lieder*.

The German *Lied* of the nineteenth century grew out of German folk song; not unlike Cather's writing, it combined

extreme subtlety with an essential simplicity.[8] Hegel, in his
1820s *Lectures on Aesthetics*, defined the necessities for this
fusion of poetry and music. It required 'an intermediate kind
of poetry', 'true, extremely simple, indicating the situation
and the feeling in a few words', with 'the ring of one and the
same feeling pervading the whole', so that the lyrical music
of the setting could 'express in melody the mood of the
individual soul'.[9] That simplicity, intensity and concentration
on one mood, were the qualities Cather was trying to
replicate. It was a double operation, mirroring the doubles
inside the story: to identify with strong emotional moods (as
in Lucy's response to the *Winterreise*) and to distance them
(as in Sebastian's singing of it) into a sense of long, sad
retrospect.

The great *Lieder* – Schumann, Brahms, Schubert, Wolf and
Mahler settings of Goethe and Heine, Möricke, Schiller,
Müller, and a wealth of lesser known romantic poets –
return again and again to the figure of the lonely (usually
male) outcast-lover, and dwell on moments of intense feeling, sometimes focused on a star or a stream, a linden tree or
a bird song. Key words recur, often as the titles of the songs:
Sehnsucht (yearning), Abschied (parting), Traum (dream),
Heimweh (homesickness), Einsamkeit (loneliness), Wanderer. Lucy appropriates these lyric emotions directly into
her own life; the music is her fate: 'As Lucy had been lost by
a song, so she was very nearly saved by one.' [LG, p.178] Her
most intense moments of feeling – yearning towards the
evening star, or remembering lost love in the apple orchard –
are like self-contained *Lieder* set in a song cycle. She longs for
a world elsewhere, like Goethe's Mignon ('Kennst du das
Land'. . . . 'Nur wer die Sehnsucht kennt').[10] Her sense that
what she pursues is a 'fugitive gleam' she 'could never catch
up with' invokes the Jack O'Lantern ('Irrlicht') or Delusion
('Täuschung') that dances along in front of the wanderer in
Winterreise, and misleads him to his death. And Lucy's last
journey is a female re-enactment of that song cycle. Bereft of
love, alienated from her home, she sets out like Schubert's
protagonist, turning her back on the town, stumbling on the

frozen ground, cold tears on her cheeks ('Pale grew thy cheek and cold') and, after Harry goes past refusing to help her, in a rage which gives her the same kind of bravado as in the song 'Courage' ('Mut'). She goes forward to meet (as in 'Wasserflut' and 'Auf dem Flusse') a torrent of flood-waters under the ice.

But Lucy is an accompanist, not a singer, and she does not encompass all the complex phases of feeling in *Winterreise*. The novel is something more than 'The Ballad of Lucy Gayheart', as there is more in the *Lieder* than tender, fragile yearnings. It is Sebastian who embodies the stranger and more sinister aspects of German romanticism, filling the novel with dark and uneasy feelings which go beyond Lucy's range.

Sebastian's baleful aspect is striking, especially since it is part of his attraction for Lucy. Rosowski reads the whole story as a Gothic novel,[11] a rewriting of Dracula from the point of view of the 'Lucy' victim, whose breath is sucked out and whose blood is made to run cold by her demon lover. The reading makes good sense of their strangely oppressive love scenes, and of the secret, occluded circumstances of their meetings. (Lucy hides at his concert, 'steals' after him into church, secretly watches him leave his house, and feels 'shut away' with him.) When she stops Harry proposing to her by telling him she has gone 'all the way' with Sebastian, she may be technically exaggerating (apart from Eden Bower and Marian Forrester, nobody in Cather is seen going all the way), but we feel she is speaking the psychic truth: Sebastian has penetrated and taken her over. There is a suggestion, too, in Lucy's musical dedication to Sebastian (she only plays what he tells her to) of Svengali and his hypnotized Trilby.[12]

But the Svengali/Dracula approach to Sebastian doesn't suggest how much we are asked to feel for him. The book splits itself, first between Sebastian and Lucy, then between their story and Harry's. The musical analogies belong as much to Sebastian's life as to Lucy's. Like Godfrey St Peter, the middle-aged singer has reached the point of encountering his dead youth ('Du Doppelgänger, du bleicher Geselle!'). He speaks of himself as dead-in-life, a ghost, reading of the death of an old

friend as if he were 'reading his own death notice'. [LG, p.77]
Obituaries and funerals are his only spare-time interests.
Like St Peter, he has a dead marriage, spoilt by past hostilities
over a 'talented boy' [LG, p.79] whom Sebastian once 'took
into their house' and whom he had to send away. '"I had a
nice boy in my house once,"' [LG, p.88], he remarks peculiarly to Lucy, sounding as if he might have 'had' him for
dinner.[13] The boy's name, Marius, invokes the artistic and
spiritual ardour of Pater's young hero, and, also, though
perhaps not intentionally, a Paterian sexual ambivalence.
Lucy, in a characteristically suppressed homosexual suggestion, replaces the dead youth; Sebastian finds her
'boyish'. [LG, p.80]

Cather acknowledged her friend Zoë Akins's shrewd spot-
ting of Ibsen's *The Master Builder* in the mood of *Lucy
Gayheart*.[14] Solness, who 'cannot live without joy', feels
himself 'chained to the dead' through his wife's mourning
for their dead children and through the destruction of
happiness which his life's work as an artist has caused. (Both
Solness and Sebastian are martyrs to their talent, as a passing
reference to 'Saint Sebastian' implies.)[15] Hilde bursts into
Solness's life like youth itself, but also like a 'troll' (one of
Cather's favourite early images, now recalled), responding,
and urging him to respond, to the call of 'the impossible'.[16]
Like the Master Builder, Sebastian is split between his
reduced, disappointed life and his 'troll-like' artist's will. But
as an artist, too, he is fatally split.

His split itself is acted out in the pairing with Mockford,
whom A. S. Byatt rightly compares to 'a Thomas Mann
puppeteer'.[17] Mockford presents the cynical opportunist side
of the artist's talent to enchant. Like the laughing red-headed
singer in 'Death in Venice', or the vile hypnotist in 'Mario
and the Magician', or the red-headed actor who disappoints
the trickster Felix Krull, he is the artist as charlatan, always
sneering, laughing and theatrical. Mockford's brilliant playing of Schubert *Lieder* undermines Lucy's romantic reading
of the songs and suggests that art is only 'make-believe', [LG,
p.61] 'Delusion', 'Täuschung'.

Sebastian and Mockford's performance of 'Der Doppelgänger', early on in the novel, points to Sebastian (more
than Lucy) as the embodiment of the Wanderer, haunted
by himself, a stranger to the world: 'Everything in this
room, in this city and this country had suddenly become
unfamiliar and unfriendly'. [LG, p.78] To Lucy's puzzlement,
Sebastian can be 'not at home' even when he seems to be
there, putting on a professional manner 'so perfected that it
could go on representing him when he himself was either
lethargic or altogether absent'. [LG, p.49] He is, and feels,
'unheimlich', that uneasy word of the alienated self, expli-
cated by Freud as having a double meaning, incorporating
'familiar' and 'unfamiliar', 'known' and 'uncanny'. (Lucy
applies the word 'uncanny' both to Mockford [LG, p.38] and
to Sebastian's intimate valet Giuseppe [LG, p.74]).

In his book on *Doubles*, Karl Miller brilliantly describes the
overlapping associations, in German romantic writing and
thereafter, for the theatrical figure of the alienated 'waif' or
'wraith'. The doppelgänger acts out the repressed or hidden
self. And his split self is almost always an orphan and an
outcast:

> The orphan has many shapes, and many names: outcast,
> outsider, stranger, changeling, foundling, bastard . . . waif,
> wraith, victim, outlaw . . . artist, writer, monster, misfit,
> queer . . . The names and attributes of the orphan warn that he
> is equivocal. So is his favourite activity of flight . . . He is
> engaged in the impossible task of trying to escape from himself,
> or to separate himself from someone whom he can't help
> resembling or repeating.

The duality of the waif/wraith, orphan/outcast, artist/
monster figure in romantic literature means that he is both
dangerous (to himself and to others) and pitiable, at once
transcendent and fatal.[18]

Clearly, Cather is as much 'possessed' by the figure of
Sebastian as Lucy is. He projects the strain she feels between
a hampered socialized self and a secret, troll-like artistic will.
That strain is temperamental and persistent, not just the
product of post-war disenchantment. Sebastian is a late,

sinister version of Alexander, in her very first novel, also a 'master builder' fatally divided and doomed to drown. More obscurely, Sebastian's feeding off Lucy's ardour seems to make covert reference to a profound sexual unease in Cather, as though she feels, at some level, that secrecy or a form of repression has cannibalized her own ardour.

Unsatisfactorily, though, *Lucy Gayheart* refuses to let Sebastian take over. Unlike his predecessors, Alexander or St Peter, he remains glamorously fictive, inert, edged out to leave room for Lucy's less interesting romantic illusions. And the impact of his doubleness is diffused by its becoming a general property. Back in Haverford, it becomes apparent that *everyone* has a split self. Even Pauline, who doesn't seem worthy of a doppelgänger, was,

> so to speak, always walking behind herself. The plump, talk-ative little woman one met on the way to choir practice, or at afternoon teas, was a mannikin which Pauline pushed along before her; no one had ever seen the pusher behind that familiar figure, and no one knew what that second person was like. [LG, p.168]

The powerful old matriarch of Haverford, Mrs Ramsay (surely a deliberate reference to Virginia Woolf?), who would like to be a substitute mother for Lucy but remains ineffectual, is felt by her daughter to be changing in old age into a more compassionate person – the novel's only benign version of a split self. And Harry, duplicitously wearing his 'jocular masks' and burying his 'contrary' feeling for Lucy 'so deep that he held no communication with it', [LG, p.217] is also a double person. (He seems to mirror Sebastian, in his cold marriage to a rich efficient woman, and in his working partnership with an 'accompanist', the anxious cashier Milton Chase.)

Cather repeatedly said that she did not care much for *Lucy Gayheart*, but thought that it improved at the end, after she had killed off all the Gayhearts.[19] As such remarks acknowl-edged, the novel is oddly split between two kinds of story, that of the Europeanized artist in crisis, and that of the

American businessman, hardheaded but capable of passion and weakness. (It was a character she returned to repeatedly, in 'A Gold Slipper', in 'Two Friends', and, later, in 'Before Breakfast'.) The divide here between the native and the European, the commercial and the artistic, romance and realism, is awkwardly managed, but it is revealing and characteristic.

The most obvious difference between the Chicago and Haverford sections is that in the latter there is much more about money. We find out that Lucy's pursuit of her 'fugitive gleam' has cost her family 'more than sixteen hundred dollars' in the first two years. [LG, p.191] Pauline has 'the cheque stubs' to prove it. Cheque stubs don't have much to do with Schubert *lieder*: Lucy, it transpires, has always been indifferent to 'small economies'. 'She never seemed to think about money.' [LG, p.172] Pauline's jealous resentful 'sacrifices' are not allowed sympathy (even her fussy housekeeping is revealed as basically indolent and messy); Mr Gayheart's conviction that Lucy is worth any expense is much more endearing. When Pauline (in the tradition of Alexandra's brothers or Claude Wheeler's father) starts chopping down the old orchard to make room for a profitable onion and potato crop, Lucy's anguish is endorsed. All the same, Lucy's poor returns for expenditure stays with us as a hard fact, like the unreconciled opposition between the rifled till and the fantasy life in 'Paul's Case'. And the narrative's transferring of Lucy's emotional 'account' into Harry's currency is not straightforward.

Harry has been seen throughout as tightfisted and ungenerous; Lucy was his one 'extravagance'. [LG, p.23] But after Lucy's death this is made more complicated. Harry 'pays' for his ungenerousness with a 'life sentence' of guilt and sadness which improves his character (he does some generous war work and is nicer to his wife). At the same time he makes 'a great deal of money' [LG, p.222] and buys lots of land and fast cars. As a form of 'retribution' he becomes filially intimate with old Mr Gayheart, playing chess with him evening after evening (like the 'two friends' playing chequers) and lending

him money from his bank, with a mortgage on his house as
'surety'. In a way, Harry at last takes possession of Lucy, as
Ivy Peters takes possession of the Forrester property. The
Gayheart house becomes his, and he can go into Lucy's
bedroom and see her clothes hanging up (as, in one of the
book's odd echoes, Lucy once saw Sebastian's) and take what
he wants of her remains. The photograph of Sebastian in its
'tarnished' silver frame goes into his pocket; Lucy's music
books go into a safe in his bank.

American materialism destroys romantic art and passion?
Not exactly. Harry is an eccentric businessman; he could
have been more successful than he is, and 'now that land
values are going down' (the coda is set in 1927) he can see
that even his shrewd investments may turn out to be 'rather
a joke on him'. [LG, p.222] Chase, the cashier, has suffered
from Harry's foibles: foreclosing on over-generous terms
with a one-time admirer of Lucy's who accused him of
cowardice for not going to her funeral; letting Mr Gayheart
run up debts in excess of the value of his mortgage; and, at
the last, renting rather than selling the Gayheart property to
Chase, so that he can ensure it will stay as it is in his lifetime.
He even gives a businesslike order to his puzzled cashier, in
the voice of one 'talking about alterations in a garage', to
keep intact the cement paving with the traces of Lucy's
footprints.

There is a disequilibrium in Harry's materialism which
gives this part of the novel its depth. His investment in his
memory of Lucy makes him, by the end, a more interesting
split character than Sebastian. All the same, Lucy escapes
him, in a slighter, less impressive version of Marian Forrester's escape out of the edge of Niel's frame. In the concrete
pavement he owns, her footprints are still running away.

The deepest split in *Lucy Gayheart* is, inevitably, between the
past and the present. Harry, the only one of the main characters to outlive the war, feels that 'the world in which he had
been cruel to her no longer existed'. [LG, p.220] As with Tom
Outland and Claude Wheeler, it's strongly suggested that

those whom the gods loved have died young. The rest of
Cather's work – a few stories and essays, a last novel –
concentrate almost entirely on those who live on into old
age, beyond their 'best years'. But *Lucy Gayheart* is connected
to these late writings by the now-familiar trope of the lost
lady who brings back the past.

The last lost ladies are old ladies: Madame Caroline
Franklin-Grout, Flaubert's niece, described in the essay of
1933, 'A Chance Meeting'; the 'old beauty' of the slightly
later story; Sarah Orne Jewett and Annie Fields, coming back
into Cather's mind when she revised her essays on them for
Not Under Forty; and the formidable Sapphira. (Edith also
refers, tantalizingly, to a novella called 'The Golden Wedding', started in the autumn of 1934 but unfinished.)[20]
Evidently Cather perceived the connection between the
essays and the fictions, telling Elsie when she sent her *Not
Under Forty* that 'these are true stories, told just as they
happened'.[21] It is a characteristically deceptive simple statement. *Sapphira and the Slave Girl* is also presented by Cather
as a true story, based on her family's history just as it
happened, with herself as a child entering the fiction as a
final witness. But its fictiveness creates, by analogy, uncertainty about the 'chance meeting' between life and fiction in
the other 'true stories' of her old age. How much did Cather
idealize her memories of 148 Charles Street? And how much
did she 'make up' about Flaubert's niece? How much, in
turn, had Flaubert's niece 'made up' her Flaubert?

Cather spots 'Caro' first, in the hot summer of 1930, as an
unnamed, distinguished old French woman at the old-
fashioned Grand Hôtel at Aix-les-Bains, actively sketching and
going to concerts and operas in spite of her lameness, and telling her new acquaintance what she should do with her time.
'Seeing things through was evidently a habit with this old
lady',[22] Cather remarks wryly, evading her commands at one
point as if escaping 'from an exacting preceptress'. So even
before Cather has kissed her hand in silent, chivalric tribute to
the amazing discovery that the old lady is the niece who was
brought up by Flaubert and to whom he wrote his famous

letters, she has been made to feel deferential. The old lady's questions are imperious and exacting: 'And by that you mean?' Cather is treated by her in the way that she, at sixty-four, now treats her own disciples. Sharon O'Brien describes Madame Grout, severely, as 'opinionated, selfish, domineering, and even a bit cruel', suggesting that she is the dominant mother from whom the daughter has to escape in order to 'find her tongue'.[23] There is certainly no doubt that Cather is at last, in her late years, writing out the conflict between mother and daughter. But Cather puts a good deal of herself, too, into Madame Grout: this is the kind of difficult old lady she is becoming, or would like to become. And their conversation about Flaubert raises the questions that were increasingly preoccupying her about her own posthumous life as a writer.

The discovery of Madame Grout's identity is made when Cather and her 'friend' (who is unnamed in the essay-story) are talking to her about 'the Soviet experiment in Russia'. Edith (in her one recorded remark in Cather's writing, and this anonymous) says that she is grateful that the great Russian writers such as Tolstoi and Turgenev did not live to see the Revolution. All concur; it is a 'comfortably' ('we talked very comfortably') censorious little moment between the three elderly ladies, which opens a window onto the way Cather and Lewis must have talked about the past to each other, and points to the kinds of exclusions this essay makes. The old lady goes on, to Cather's astonishment, to say that she knew Turgenev very well. Her first mention of Flaubert's name, following on from this revelation, is made 'in a curious tone, as if she had said something indiscreet and were evasively dismissing it'.

The curious tone of discretion and evasion persists. Madame Grout, Cather is at pains to tell us, is just and enlightened, 'not an idealist', capable of admitting the 'qualities Flaubert did not have'. (And an 'artist's limitations', Cather says in this essay, 'are quite as important as his powers'.) Nevertheless, she gives a selective and benign version of her childhood with Flaubert, which on the whole avoids personal information (especially about her adult life).

She does provide some gossip about Turgenev and his position in the Viardot household, but what she really wants to talk about is Flaubert's writing and his characters; she speaks of Madame Arnoux in *L'Éducation Sentimentale*, for instance, 'with warm affection', 'so vividly that it was as if she had entered the room'. The old lady's memories thus replicate the lifelikeness of Flaubert's writings. Cather is returned to these by the encounter, in a re-enactment of her own memories of earlier readings of Flaubert. She relishes the works above all for the feeling they give that (as in her own writing) 'it is something one has lived through, not a story one has read'. The niece who, as a child, lay on a rug in the corner of his room while he was writing (pretending that she was safe in the den of a powerful wild animal), and who received his affectionate letters about her character and her education, provides Cather with a close 'translation' of the very spirit of Flaubert, 'his flavour, his personality'.

And translation is, in a sense, the subject of the essay. Their conversational exchanges between French and English are much concerned with vocabulary and phrasing. Cather reassures Madame Grout that 'lowering' is a 'safe' word to apply to the shortening September days, since it would have been used by 'old-fashioned farmers' in the American South. The old lady comments drily (and, we are presumably supposed to think, in the manner of Flaubert) that 'if the farmers use a word it is quite safe, eh?' When Cather starts speaking to her, stupidly, in 'very simple words', she is impatiently reprimanded; 'Speak idiomatically, please'. Cather admires her speech for its 'qualities of good Latin prose: economy, elegance, and exactness'. And the old lady's 'special feeling for language' is her key to Flaubert; she translates him back into life for Cather, and is herself interested above all in translations: her chief memory of Turgenev is of his helping her with a translation of *Faust*, and one of her chief debts to Flaubert is his 'solicitude' over her English lessons. Their closest moment of accord is in their exchange over 'the splendid final sentence of *Hérodias*' where the fall of the syllables is so suggestive of the hurrying footsteps of John's disciples, carrying away with them their prophet's severed head. . . . *'Comme elle était très lourde, ils la portaient al-ter-na-tive-ment.'*

The syllables suggesting the movement – a language which translates 'life' as closely as possible – are repeated and exchanged by the two women, mutually translating Flaubert back to life.

But it is noticeable that this translation is based much more on the works than on the life: it is an edited translation. Cather is as discreet and evasive as Madame Grout about personal matters, commenting on her account of Turgenev: 'But these were very personal memories, and if Madame Grout had wished to make them public, she would have written them herself.' And Cather retreats from the personal legacy she is being offered; she does not want a 'material reminder' of Flaubert in the form of manuscripts or auto-graphed letters ('It was the Flaubert in her mind and heart that was to give me a beautiful memory'), and she does not, as it turns out, pursue the acquaintance. She never takes up the invitation to the 'Villa Tanit'[24] to 'see her Flaubert collection', the Flaubert letter Madame Grout does send her gets stolen in the post, the correspondence lapses, and the last news of her is her obituary. Unike the old lady, Cather has not 'seen things through', and there is a suggestion of remorse at the end of the essay-story.

Cather has edited Madame Grout for her own purposes. It is noticeable that she turns this active, energetic old lady, interested in modern music and new acquaintances, into a guardian of the sacred flame, 'armoured' 'against a world concerned with insignificant matters'. That editing makes an intriguing parallel with Caro's own editing of Flaubert, a process of appropriation which is, itself, edited out of Cather's version. It is probably going to extremes to say, as Ellen Moers does in a debate on Cather's Francophilia, that Madame Grout was 'the worst bitch in nineteenth-century literature', who 'sucked Flaubert dry': 'took his money, refused to give him affection . . . stood at his funeral haggling with the publishers over the rights to Flaubert's books.'[25] But certainly Caroline censored his letters to her and burnt Louise Colet's letters to him. Julian Barnes gives a judicious account of her editings:

> After Flaubert's death his manuscripts passed to his niece ... who treated them rather as she had treated her uncle in life: with a mixture of affection and greed, possessiveness and irritation. She guarded the family name while tidying up all around it, censoring Flaubert's letters for publication and making him as respectable as possible; she tended the flame while discreetly selling off some of the firewood which fuelled it. She is usualy cast as a semi-villain who failed to treat her uncle and his leavings with the same tender solicitude which those criticizing her would have done in her place; but both her moral disapproving and her literary ethics were those of her period and milieu. Moreover, if Caroline looked back over her life and in particular at the lost years of a first marriage into which her uncle encouraged her, she would have been unnatural not to feel a grudge. The case for Caroline has not yet been fully made. When, in his last years, she urged her uncle to leave his large house in Croisset to help with the family's finances, and he refused, she and her husband nicknamed him 'the consumer'. After his death she made up for his resented extravagance by raising money from his manuscripts.[26]

Noticeably, it is her childhood with Flaubert which Madame Grout happily recalls to Cather; what came later was suppressed.

The connections with Cather are extremely suggestive. Cather, with the posthumous help of the 'friend' who lurks at the edges of this essay-story, would in turn censor her own manuscripts and letters; the essay is, by implication, a defence of such proceedings. It is through the 'mind and heart' of her readers that she wants to live on, not through biographies or letters or collectors' items. The personal material is no one else's concern, and should be suppressed — as Madame Grout's mixed feelings and mixed actions are suppressed by Cather, and as, in turn, Madame Grout suppressed a part of Flaubert.

An unresolved paradox remains, of which Cather must

have been aware: the personal letters from Flaubert to Caro, which she enjoys reading so much, are what makes Madame Grout of interest to her. As so often, but here perhaps most intriguingly of all, the desire to edit and 'de-furnish' pulls against the desire to remember and re-incarnate.

The chivalric gesture in 'A Chance Meeting', the kissing of Madame Grout's hand, is elaborated on, more sentimentally, by the middle-aged American-in-exile of 'The Old Beauty', Mr Henry Seabury, a type like the censorious shipboard bachelor who once met Katherine Mansfield (or like the courteous old gentleman, Mr Longdon, out of place in the 'liberated' world of James's *The Awkward Age*). Returning to Europe from a lifetime of business 'in China', Seabury is in search of 'some spot that was more or less as it used to be'. [OB, p.7] His 'chance meeting' at Aix-les-Bains with Madame de Couçy, whom he gradually recognizes as Gabrielle Longstreet, a once-famous Edwardian beauty, with a·romantic past (picked up from Martinique by an English lord, queen of Edwardian society, divorced, moved to New York and Paris, remarried, widowed by the war) takes him back to 'a society whose manners, dress, conventions, loyalties, codes of honour, were different from anything existing in the world today'. [OB, p.5]

For two months, Seabury divides his time between a touching English family who are visiting their son's war grave, and the old beauty and her companion, Mrs Allison, a cheerful plump lady, once 'Cherry Beamish', music-hall star. Both acquaintanceships fuel his lament over a spoilt world, and between them Seabury and Gabrielle repulse the present with all of Cather's most unpalatable intolerance. Madame de Couçy, a 'grim' 'mirthless' 'personage', travels with her photograph album of dead 'heroes' and believes 'one should go out with one's time'; [OB, p.46] she confirms Seabury's prejudice that the beauties of the past (as opposed to the 'cinema stars' of the present) had 'benefited by a romantic tradition . . . an attitude in men which no longer existed'. [OB, p.25] Their high moment together is a ghostly dance in the hotel ballroom, when they put the enervated young couples to shame by a stylish performance of the 'Blue Danube'. 'The two old waltzers were left alone on the floor', amid comments from the spectators: ' "It's so quaint and theatrical." ' [OB, p.60] Gabrielle's last 'scene' is a trip, arranged by Seabury, to visit the monastery of the Grande-Chartreuse. On the way back from this heavenly high place their chauffeur swerves to avoid two young women driving on the wrong side. The old lady is not hurt, but the rude shock of this brush with modernity actually kills her. She dies in the night, and is buried in Père Lachaise, where 'ladies who once held a place in the world' used to buy burial lots. [OB, p.72]

The two girls who cause the accident are interesting specimens. 'They were Americans; bobbed, hatless, clad in dirty white knickers and sweaters. They addressed each other as "Marge" and "Jim" . . . lit cigarettes and were swaggering about with their hands in their trousers pockets.' [OB, p.66] Madame de Couçy calls them 'those creatures'. Cather is making an explicit comparison between these modern, masculinized female friends and the tender, asexual female companionship of 'Madame' de Couçy and 'Mrs' Allison. But this contrast is complicated by the suppressed sexuality of that companionship. Cherry Beamish, who has a boyish nickname, 'Chetty', used to play 'boy parts' (like the young Cather) at the Alhambra: ' "They wouldn't have me in skirts" '. Seabury remembers her ' "in an Eton jacket, with your hair cropped" '. [OB, p.28] But at that period, theatrical transvestism was quite different from the butch get-up of the 'frightful' motorists: it was an act, with its own style and decorum.

Chetty, though, unsettles the story's fixed glare of nostalgia. She herself doesn't mind the 'young things'; ' "The present . . . is really very interesting" ', she tells her friend, ' "if only you will let yourself think so" '. [OB, p.31] If Gabrielle had ' "a swarm of young nieces and nephews, as I have" ', (and as Cather had) ' "she'd see things quite differently" '. [OB, p.45] Chetty democratizes 'things'. The English father remembers her in a popular 'coster song', and it's she who lets us know that Gabrielle's élitism is based on sound investments: '"Her capital is in British bonds."' [OB, p.43]

And, as Seabury slowly recalls the much-lamented past, it turns out not to have been so romantic after all. His most vivid memory of Gabrielle, from his youth, is a tawdry one. He came upon her one night, visiting her house in New York, in the hands of a 'leech', a banker with a dubious foreign accent who has made some investments for her and is claiming his price. The scene is straight out of a bad melodrama of the period:

> Behind the sofa stood a stout, dark man leaning over her. His left arm, about her waist, pinioned her against the flowered silk upholstery. His right hand was thrust deep into the low-cut bodice of her dinner gown. [OB, p.52]

Like Lily Bart in Edith Wharton's *The House of Mirth*, or like the opera singer in Cather's earlier and equally anti-semitic story, 'Scandal', the 'beauty' on her own is the victim of an exchange rate – sex for financial support – which makes the old world rather less chivalric than Seabury would have it. It doesn't occur to Cather (or to Seabury) to follow this through and ask whether the 'frightful' Marge and Jim, post-war feminists, might have escaped from that trap.

Gabrielle, like an older Myra Henshawe, whom she resembles, is an alarming and equivocal emblem of lost past. The story's strangest moment comes when, at the monastery, she stays by 'the great open well', using a 'little mirror' from her handbag to throw a ray of sunlight over its 'black water'.

> When he glanced back . . . she was still looking down into the well and playing with her little reflector, a faintly contemptuous smile on her lips. [OB, p.64]

The contempt is not only for the world; it is also for her own fatuity in trying to re-illuminate, through her little reflections, 'the dark backward and abysm of time'.

'The Old Beauty' was turned down for publication by the *Woman's Home Companion*,[27] an affront to the old writer which ironically confirmed the story's allegiance to an outmoded style. What followed it, slowly and painfully, over the next four years, was a withdrawal from European to American materials, and, as though this was the only part of America she could now bear to write about, a return still further into the past, as far back as Cather could go. But this journey back to earliest memories (which was how she always described *Sapphira and the Slave Girl*)[28] incorporated her sense of the 'evil' being let loose in the world.[29] She told Viola Roseboro that the novel was about something more elusive than memories: it was a narrative of the *terrible* in domesticated form.[30]

Virginia had been brought back to her mind through Mrs Harris's memories, and according to E. K. Brown she had promised her father on his deathbed that she would set a novel there.[31] In 1938, not having been back there since 1913 (when she disliked the romantic Southern attitude and the cowed Southern male),[32] she made a pilgrimage with Edith, who noted, enthusiastically, her characteristic ability to censor out the present.

> Every bud and leaf and flower seemed to speak to her with a peculiar poignancy, every slope of the land, every fence and wall, rock and stream. . . . The countryside was very much changed. But she refused to look at its appearance; she looked through and through it, as if it were transparent, to what she knew as its reality. Willowshade, her old home . . . had become so ruinous and forlorn that she did not go into it, only stood and looked down at it from a distance. All these transformations, instead of disheartening her, seemed to light a fierce inner flame that illumined all her pictures of the past.[33]

Cather's own account of the return[34] is full of lamentations for the destruction of the Timber Ridge country, particularly the 'Double S' country road winding up from Gore to the top of the ridge, once lush with white dogwood blossom and wild honeysuckle and blue-green locust trees. [SSG, pp.115–7]

The novel eloquently reconstructs that lost landscape. Its ending, she insisted, was a directly autobiographical return to her own childhood.[35] What she did not witness – the pre-Bellum Virginia of 1856 – she inherited from the story-telling matriarchy whose narratives underlie the novel; what she did witness, as a child of five, is told, in a characteristic epilogue, with as much factuality as 'A Chance Meeting'. So, in that it invokes earliest memories, it is a tender and affectionate narrative, which returns happily to pastoral conventions.

But this affectionate tenderness was locked into a 'terrible' paradox, shared by other American writers – Mark Twain, or Ellen Glasgow, Cather's exact contemporary – whose families derived from, and whose fictions evoked, the old South. The family past for which personal nostalgia was felt was the slave-owning past; the affectionate personal retrospect could not indulge the social organization which formed the economic basis of that pastoral. Built into Cather's domestic history of a particular West Virginian family, in the years leading up to the Civil War, was the ambivalence about slavery which her novel re-enacted.

We must go back, as Cather was doing, to her beginnings. In my description of Cather's childhood I mentioned the bitter divisions in her family between supporters of the Union and the Rebel, or Confederate, cause. The Cather family belonged to the part of the South which was itself peculiar in relation to the South's 'peculiar institution'. The back country around Winchester was on the border of what would break away as West Virginia in 1863, and was populated by settlers from Pennsylvania and European immigrants. It was not big plantation country, and had no strong tradition of slave-owning (in 1860 there were only 149 slaves in western Virginia in a population of over 45,000)[36] by comparison with the rich Tidewater area in eastern Virginia, where there were over half a million slaves. In 1832 the Virginia State Legislature (of which Rachel Blake's husband, in the novel, is a member) fiercely debated the issues of emancipation;[37] by the 1840s western Virginia had begun to feel it would be better off as a separate free state; and in 1848 a poll in the *Richmond Southerner* estimated that two-thirds of Virginians opposed slavery. Many of the back-country farmers were against secession. During the Civil War, the area around Winchester is said 'to have changed hands sixty-eight times':[38] it was a key point for the possession of Virginia, and its inhabitants were deeply divided.

Cather's family (and, similarly, the Colbert and the Dodderidge families in the novel) embodied all these divisions. On the Cather side, there was the great-grandfather who voted for secession when he was in the legislature, the grandfather and father who were Unionists, and the great-uncle who served as a doctor in the Union Army. Cather's notable great-aunt Sidney Gore was a Baptist who detested slavery, and looked after the wounded of both sides at Valley Home. But Cather's mother's family, the Boaks, had cousins in Louisiana and were Confederate supporters, and we know how strong Grandma Boak's influence was on Cather. Though Jennie Boak reconciled these divisions after her marriage, she kept till her death the sword which had belonged to her brother, William Seibert Boak, who died fighting on the rebel side. This was the uncle whose middle name Cather appropriated, and for whom she wrote a youthful elegy.[39]

Sapphira and the Slave Girl recreates American history out of these family divisions. Historical facts – the 1850 Fugitive Slave Act, for instance, by which runaway slaves could be recaptured in the North – occur as part of the background. The Civil War is fought in three pages in the Epilogue, in the form of neighbourhood legend and family stories: it 'gave people plenty to talk about'. [SSG, p.275] Cather based her novel on the 'true story' of Nancy, the runaway slave, whose return visit to Virginia, when Cather was five, was her first memory.

True story it may have been, but it invoked many others like it. In her reviewing days, Cather had watched the stage version of Eliza's escape on the ice, in *Uncle Tom's Cabin*, all too often.[40] Beecher Stowe's heartfelt mixture of drama and polemic was not for her. What interested Cather was the everyday life of a family for whom slavery was an existing circumstance, and through whose domestic tensions the weight of history pressed in. So the struggle for survival within family life, which she had written about before, eloquently and often, became in this last novel, in spite of its apparently escapist nostalgia for her earliest childhood, more of a political metaphor. The war is in the household.

Sapphira Dodderidge Colbert, now crippled with dropsy, is a proud, efficient managerial woman from a grander Virginian family who, after her father's illness, astounded her family friends by marrying his Lutheran miller (of Flemish parentage) and moving to the poorer country of 'Back Creek'. She brought her slaves with her, to a part of Virginia where they were not regarded as usual, and maintained her authority against her husband's dislike of the 'institution' and the criticism of her widowed daughter, Rachel Blake. Rachel had escaped from her unsympathetic mother by marrying a Washington politician; but after thirteen years of good society and happy domestic life, her husband and son died of an epidemic on a visit to New Orleans, and she has returned to Back Creek with her two little girls. Her conflict with her mother resumes when Sapphira takes against one of her slaves, the attractive 'yellow' girl Nancy, the daughter of Sapphira's reliable black housekeeper Till, and, possibly, of one of Henry Colbert's loose-living brothers. (Or she may be the daughter of a Cuban painter who came to paint the family portraits, but her paternity is purposely kept vague.) Sapphira becomes jealous of her husband's affection for Nancy, who looks after his room at the mill. She invites her feckless, predatory nephew Martin, the son of one of the 'bad' Colberts, to stay, not quite admitting to herself that she is hoping he will 'ruin' Nancy. The girl's life is made a misery, and she asks for help from Rachel Blake, who secretly arranges for her to escape to Canada via the underground route to the free States. Mother and daughter are estranged, but are reconciled when Rachel's little girls fall ill with diphtheria, and one of them dies. In all this, the miller plays a distressed, equivocating part. His feelings for Nancy are not quite as chaste as he believes, his admiration for Sapphira is mixed with bitterness. In the crisis he lets the women take action, but would rather not know what is happening.

Such evasions and negations characterize the family drama, with Sapphira's obstructive and thwarting figure flanked by the stoical, withdrawn daughter, the conscience-stricken husband and the futile nephew. Colbert leaves his coat by the open window of his mill-room so that his daughter can pick his pocket for Nancy's escape-money without his having to acknowledge her action; Sapphira breaks off relations with Rachel by sending her a formal sealed note asking her not to call; whenever the husband and wife are really discussing Nancy, they talk instead about Bluebell, the 'lazy, lying' daughter of the black cook. The evasion, thinks Sapphira ironically, is 'almost as good as a play'. [SSG, p.199]

These fictional details seem, as always, to have the authenticity of fact. Cather said she had collected so much material about the 'manners and customs' of Back Creek Valley that when she weighed what she left out, 'it came to a good six pounds!'[41] What is put in gives the sense of what was left out. The characters are deeply, minutely embedded in their time and place. A secure pastoral rhythm of seasonal labour and lush vegetable growth encircles the action: the late summer harvest, the smoking of hams and bacon throughout spring and summer, the cherry-picking and canning and gathering of laurels in June, the October nutting. The indoor work of the women – cleaning the house, looking after the sick, making worn-out clothes into 'carpet-rags' for the weaver – goes on side by side with the work of the mill and the farm. The perspective is carefully directed. In the far distance are the Quakers who run the 'underground railway', or the 'bad men' down at Hoag Creek tavern, or Sapphira's grand relatives. In the middle distance are the subsidiary but very vivid characters like the abolitionist postmistress (who has her copy of the New York *Tribune* delivered under plain cover), or the conscientious young schoolteacher from Pennsylvania, or the remarkable Dr Clavenger (a Bishop Latour or Godfrey St Peter in cameo), 'with his peculiar expression of thinking directly behind his eyes'. [SSG, p.263] Close up are the inward, fully known details of the furnishings and clothes of the household: the green shades covering the parlour windows, 'painted with garden scenes and fountains'; the 'chestnut secretary' that doubles as the miller's writing desk and bookcase; the house-servant Washington's striped cotton coat and flapping slippers; Nancy's hat, 'an old black turban of Mrs Colbert's' with a red feather stuck on by Till, Nancy's mother. [SSG, p.231] When Till is dressing Sapphira, we see the cloth slippers and ribbon garters that go on her swollen legs; when Rachel sets off to visit a sick friend, one of the poor whites up on the Ridge, we know what's in her basket: 'bandages and turpentine ointment and arnica . . . also a fruit jar full of fresh-ground coffee, half a baking of sugar cakes, and a loaf of "light" bread'. [SSG, p.118] Some of these carefully selected details are nostalgic, like the recollection of the father in his basement toolroom 'making yellow leather shoes for the front paws of his favourite shepherd dog', [SSG, p.281] or of the stream that ran through the kitchen cellar. But more often they are used, like the incidental anecdotes (the case of the stolen church-plate, or the heartbroken slave) to give a solid ground of verisimilitude. When the occasion arises, we learn that in these parts of rural Virginia before the war, farmers and countrymen used to wear 'heavy shawls, fastened with a large shawl-pin', [SSG, p.53] that notes would be sent folded down, without envelopes, [SSG, p.30, 245] that at every dinner party a servant would walk round the table 'waving a long flybrush made of a peacock's tail', [SSG, p.160] and that to leave a light on in the parlour at night with the front door open was a signal for help. [SSG, p.251]

As in *Shadows on the Rock*, whose methods most resemble this novel's, these authentic descriptive furnishings speak of cultural assumptions in a particular history. The family life of *Sapphira and the Slave Girl* is a double one; two histories co-exist, at once separate and connected, as the title suggests. The doubleness which was a psychological theme in *Lucy Gayheart* here becomes a political one. The very geography of the Mill House is duplicated and divided. At the front it is 'orderly', with a porch and a lawn and a fence; 'behind the house lay another world' of the separated kitchen, the negro cabins, the laundry, the smokehouse, and the backyard littered with 'old brooms, spades and hoes, and the rag dolls and home-made toy wagons of the negro children'. [SSG, pp.20–21] That adjacent-separation persists in the church, with the negroes singing 'in the loft' to the rest of the congregation, [SSG, p.78] and in the graveyard, where the plot is divided into two halves, bespeaking two histories:

> On one side were the family graves, with marble headstones. On the other side was the slaves' graveyard, with slate headstones bearing single names: 'Dolly', 'Thomas', 'Manuel', and so on. [SSG, p.101]

Vegetation is a great leveller: the graves on both sides are 'covered with thick mats of myrtle'. But until this covers up their names, people have to belong to their 'sides', whose proximity, and difference, is one of the novel's subjects.

There is, as usual, a great deal about language in the novel. This is still a predominantly oral culture, where newspapers and letters are important events. Back Creek's damp 'deep woods', enclosed by the 'blue wall' of Timber Ridge and the North Mountain, feels out of the world, and local talk is itself life-blood. Cather celebrates this in one of the novel's subsidiary matriarchs, Mrs Ringer, who finds inexhaustible consolation for her son's deformity (he has a club foot) and her daughters' weaknesses (they have both been 'fooled', and she is bringing up their offspring) in her own kind of communication: the grimness of her life (the novel's most brutal sub-plot involves her son's horror at the vicious bullying of a 'poor white' boy by two local thugs) is transformed into narrative energy:

> Mrs Ringer was born interested. She got a great deal of entertainment out of the weather and the behaviour of the moon. Any chance bit of gossip that came her way was a godsend. The rare sight of a strange face was a treat: a pedlar with a pack on his back, or a medicine-vendor come from across the Alleghenies with his little cart. Mrs Ringer couldn't read or write, as she was frank to tell you, but the truth was she

could read everything most important: the signs of the seasons, the meaning of the way the wood creatures behaved, and human faces. [SSG, p.119]

Local speech, dialect and pronunciation, are 'read' in the book with Mrs Ringer's kind of attentiveness. We learn how both Colbert and Sapphira are criticized by the Back Creek natives for their lack of a Southern accent (which could turn, for instance, the name of an itinerant preacher, Leonidas, into 'Lawndis' [SSG,p.123]). Terminology is remarked on: the blacks call jonquils 'smoke pipes'; the Virginians call the afternoon the evening. In church, Lizzie the black cook appropriates the gospel language she can't read on the page, sounding her 'r's' with 'fervent conviction'. Her sloppy daughter makes a sexier transformation of language, calling the song 'The Gypsy's Warning' 'The Gypsy's Warming'. [SSG, p.183] Of all these linguistic shifts, the most striking is the child Cather's reaction to the Canadianized Nancy's pronunciation of 'History'. And, indeed, the word has a different meaning for each of them.

There are two histories, two family trees, and two languages in the story. One is the history of the white colonizers, settling like the Dodderidges on vast tracts of Indian territory, with grants from the first aristocratic English landowners (Sapphira has a coat-of-arms on her carriage), or coming in from all over Europe to work the land, like the Colberts. This is a family tree which can be drawn and dated, going back to Nathanael Dodderidge, who came out of Virginia with Lord Fairfax in 1747, and going forward to the death of Henry Colbert in 1863 and the birth of the narrator (the inheritor of the line) in the mid '70s. There is 'bad blood' in the Colbert lineage, which has 'come to light' in the miller's brothers and their sons, and which he is afraid of finding in himself. When he searches his conscience over slavery, and over his unwelcome sexual feelings for Nancy, he takes what comfort he can from John Bunyan's *Holy War*, reading of 'the state of the town of Mansoul after Diabolus had entered her gates and taken up her rule there', haunting 'like a Ghost, honest men's houses at night'. Like old Mrs

Harris, Colbert, a good weak man caught in a historical dilemma, is consoled by Bunyan's voice, the voice of 'an honest man, who had suffered much . . . speaking to him of things about which he could not unbosom himself to anyone'. [SSG, p.211] The affinity with Bunyan is touching, but the picture of Mansoul is an alarming one. As so often, Cather finds in her allusion an image of doubleness, self-haunting; but here the self that is haunted is not just the miller's, but the whole of the American South's. Like Faulkner's macabrely haunted houses, the Colbert-Dodderidge dynasty is shadowed by the double family tree that spooks all Southern inheritances through miscegenation. It may be that Colbert is afraid, not just of his own 'bad blood', but of what that might link him to. After all, the slave girl he does not want to be too fond of could be his own niece.

Cather's treatment of her black characters is problematic. That she was unaware of this is suggested by a letter to Dorothy, congratulating herself on her accuracy over the 'darkey' speech in the novel.[42] Her references to Till as not being a 'gay darkey', or to Nancy in the cherry tree indulging 'the foolish, dreamy nigger side of her nature', [SSG, p.178] her caricaturing of Lizzie the cook and her daughter Bluebell as idle, tricksy slaves, in contrast with Till and Nancy, make embarrassing reading. She clearly has more interest in the miller's struggle with his conscience, Rachel's quarrel with her mother and her grief over her sick children, and Sapphira's complicated personality, than in Nancy's intolerable predicament, which keeps getting dissolved into picturesque pastoral scenes: Nancy dangling her legs in the cherry tree, or slipping through the flower garden in the misty dawn. Anyone who has read Toni Morrison's *Beloved* or Alice Walker's *The Color Purple* will find difficulty in tolerating Cather's version of black slavery as anything but a dated historical curiosity. Nevertheless, within the limits of her time and type, Cather was trying to make us aware of a monstrous double history.

There are two great-grandmothers in the novel: Sapphira,

the narrator's, and 'Jezebel', who is Nancy's. Through Jezebel's line, Cather encompasses the hundred-year history of
slavery, from the African trade of the 1780s to the post-war
liberation of the 1880s. Like Sapphira, the ancient Jezebel is
proud, ironical, physically reduced, and still alarming to
others; but their histories are bitterly contrasted. Cather
tells the appalling story, in a tone of historical impersonality, of the capture of Jezebel's cannibal tribe, their
incarceration on the slave-ship, her fiery resistance and
taming ('"Clean her off and put a bridle on her"' [SSG,
p.93]), her sale as a powerful healthy animal ('She opened
her jaws') to the Dutchman who 'breaks her in', and her
transfer to Sapphira, who 'entrusts' her with the gardens.
On her deathbed, Jezebel makes a startling joke about how
she could fancy a '"li'l pickaninny's hand"'. Nancy is
shocked, but Sapphira is unmoved: '"I know your granny
through and through"'. [SSG, p.89] The macabre detail
reflects on Sapphira's likeness to Jezebel (she is a kind of
cannibal herself), but also on the cannibalizing of a whole
people.

Jezebel's daughter, Till's mother, is burnt alive in an
accident. Till, who witnessed her mother's death, is trained
as a good house-servant by Sapphira's Devonshire housekeeper, and married off to what Lizzie the cook calls a
'capon-man': 'Miss Sapphy didn't want a lady's maid to be
"havin' chillun all over de place"'. [SSG, p.43] When Nancy
stands in the parlour admiring the Dodderidge family portraits, and hopes they may be the work of her own father,
the two inheritances are ironically juxtaposed. Nancy's story
continues the history of sexual exploitation. Though Cather
is never explicit, the scenes in which Nancy lies awake at
night outside Sapphira's room, listening for Martin Colbert's
step on the stair, or has to wash his pile of 'soiled linen' [SSG,
p.158], or is caught by him in the cherry tree (he 'drew her
two legs about his cheeks like a frame' [SSG, p.181]), make
the point clearly enough.

The novel provides two exits from this double history of
injustice and cruelty. One is the astonishing return of Nancy,

transformed from the 'yaller gal' of the narrator's childhood legends into the distinguished-looking visitor from Montreal, a 'tall, gold-skinned woman' of forty-four, wearing a long black coat lined with grey fur, a turban over her 'shiny blue-black hair', and a black silk dress with a gold watch chain, speaking in a precise Montreal accent of her household responsibilities to her employers and her marriage to their 'half Scotch and half Indian' gardener. [SSG, p.285] She is a surprisingly new kind of heroine for Cather, fleetingly released out of this juncture between earliest memory and last writing.

The other solution offered is not of transforming but of resignation. Henry Colbert, alone in his mill house (like St Peter in his attic study), searching through Bunyan and his Bible (as so many Southerners of the time were searching) for a justification or a condemnation of slavery, keeps having to fall back on the idea of resignation: that 'all the black slaves would be free' according to God's 'great designs', [SSG, p.111] and that until then, all he can do is to try to act decently and find some virtue in the system: '"Sometimes keeping people in their place is being good to them"'. [SSG, p.268]

The novel's weakness is that it too beats this kind of retreat, and collapses its presentation of the historical dilemma into a simplifying nostalgia. To a worrying extent, being kept in one's place is felt to have been a preferable alternative to the changed American world that followed the Civil War. Cather's distaste for motor-cars and pool-halls gives her an alarming affinity with the pre-Bellum anti-abolitionists, who argued that a benign feudal system was more to the advantage of the labourer than the heartless exploitation of an industrialized free economy. (It is another version of Rosicky's distaste for a wage-earning society.) There were plenty of ominous predictions as to what would become of the freed slaves. This is a typical extract from a long poem by the South Carolinan William Grayson (published in 1856, the year of the action of *Sapphira and the Slave Girl*):

The negro freeman, thrifty while a slave,
Loosed from restraint, becomes a drone or knave;
Each effort to improve his nature foils,
Begs, steals, or sleeps and starves, but never toils;
For savage sloth mistakes the freedom won,
And ends the mere barbarian he begun.[43]

It has to be said that this bears some resemblance to the story of what happens to Tap, Cather's jolly mill boy. After Sapphira's death, Colbert frees all her slaves, but none of them can bear to leave the farm. Tap, more than any of them, 'hadn't been able to stand his freedom': [SSG, p.290] he gets into a fight in the pool-hall at Winchester, kills a man and is hanged.

Tap's cruel little story exposes Cather's regret for the feudal system, which is built into her sentiment for the lost young Virginian heroes, *'like Paris handsome and like Hector brave'*, [SSG, p.275] and for the sight, long vanished, of a handsome girl in a 'close-fitting riding-habit with long skirt, the little hat with the long plume', [SSG, p.278] riding side-saddle on the Winchester road, saluted by Cavalry veterans as she 'flashed by'.

The novel's equivocation between resignation and horror centres on the alarming figure of Sapphira. She is a cruel character in a book about cruelty, but she is not easy to read. Though her actions are coercive, even sadistic – a Fascist in historical costume? – she is elusively presented. In her life and in her place in the novel, she is a positive rendered negative, a forcefield of distorted energy.

Like the women heroes of the earlier novels, Sapphira is a manager: she runs the house, the farm, the slaves, the family. The section titles that have her name in them are proprietary ('Sapphira and her household', 'Sapphira's daughter'). The first sentence in the novel of which she is the subject entitles her to authority: 'The Mistress was served promptly.' But like the old ladies of the later fictions, she has become thwarted by paralysis and isolation, and has to exert the authority from a fixed point – a 'large, cumbersome' walnut chair on castors – issuing plots, orders, summonses and rejections as if spinning a web. Strong words are used for this curtailment of the will: what her illness has done to her is as 'cruel' as what she does to others. It is well in character that her suspicion over Henry's feeling for Nancy is as much a horror of losing control, of being 'befooled, hoodwinked in any way' [SSG, p.106] as it is a sexual jealousy.

Sapphira is very like Myra Henshawe, 'crippled but powerful', with her mocking snake's mouth and tyrannical egotism, 'a witty and rather wicked old woman'. [MME, p.80] The reworking of the character points to Cather's unceasing fascination for dangerous female power. As with Myra, Sapphira's style, her regard for appearances, is always emphasized. It is part of her game to be impenetrable, so surface words are always used for her looks and manners. Her hair and clothes are 'in perfect order', [SSG, p.13] her smiles are 'arch' and 'placid', her speech is 'affable', 'mild', 'bland', 'tolerant', with what Rachel perceives as 'a kind of false pleasantness'. [SSG, p.15] The 'blandness' superficially covers something more 'icy' and malicious. Like Myra, Sapphira enjoys power and entertainment. She is amused by the 'glum and disapproving' [SSG, p.15] side of her more morally responsible husband and daughter, and we too find Sapphira more interesting than the conscientious Lutheran miller and the Baptist widow. She treats the intelligent schoolteacher with 'mocking condescension' [SSG, p.81] because he is a Northerner. She is amused by Martin Colbert, a feckless libertine with east-Virginian attitudes to slavery more brutal than her own: '"The niggers here don't know their place, not one of 'em."' [SSG, p.182] But the arena for Sapphira's social appetites and love of control is a more malign one than Myra Henshawe's. Myra, too, liked to fix relationships, with harmful results. Sapphira's interferences, inside the slavery system – Till's forced marriage to the impotent Jeff, Nancy's persecution – are monstrous.

But, in this somewhat obscure and patchy novel, which leaves its own attitudes to the past disturbingly unresolved, we are never quite sure about Sapphira's motives. Rachel cannot decide whether Sapphira fully intends to let Martin rape Nancy, or was merely 'ready to tolerate anything that might amuse him'. [SSG, p.220] The daughter's attempts to understand her mother's 'shades of kindness and cruelty' [SSG, p.219] are, like her father's, ultimately unsuccessful. After Nancy's escape, Cather shifts the balance of feeling about Sapphira, through her sympathetic and courageous response to the touching sickness of Rachel's children and the death of one of them. In the end, Henry has to admit that her cruelty and her stoicism are indivisible:

> After she was old and ill, she never lowered her flag; not even now, when she knew the end was not far off. He had seen strong men quail and whimper at the approach of death. He, himself, dreaded it. But as he leaned against her chair with his face hidden, he knew how it would be with her; she would make her death easy for everyone, because she would meet it with that composure which he had sometimes called heart-lessness, but which now seemed to him strength. As long as she was conscious, she would be mistress of the situation and of herself. [SSG, p.268]

Sapphira and the Slave Girl reads, in part, like a violent last resistance to a coercive maternal figure. But it also works as a characteristically indirect autobiography. Cather is regis-tering her own cold and passionate desire for authorial control, her own experience of the pain and handicap of old age, and her own desire to maintain a stoic dignity in the face of death.

Cather published nothing after *Sapphira and the Slave Girl*, and, due to illness and exhaustion and her crippled hand, wrote very little in the last seven years of her life. At the end, after some months of weakness, she died, of a cerebral haemorrhage, at half-past four on the afternoon of April 24, 1947. (Her secretary was there, but not Edith, who had seen her earlier and said that 'she was never more herself than on the last morning.')[44] The small private funeral was in New York, the burial of the body at Jaffrey, on the 27th, and there was a memorial service at Red Cloud in November. Among her last papers was the unfinished draft of a novel, to be called *Hard Punishments*, set in fourteenth-century Avignon during the papal reign of Benedict XIV. Lewis took it upon herself to destroy this manuscript, but she gave a summary of the novel to a researcher, George Kates, who in 1956 published a collection of Cather's early travel essays (including her eloquent description of Avignon written in 1902) and a volume of her stories, which included his attempt to piece together what the novel might have been.

The story, Cather told Lewis,[45] was of two boys who had suffered the 'hard punishments' of medieval theocracy. One, Pierre, was a simple peasant boy who had been strung up by his thumbs, the other a high-born intelligent youth who had had his tongue cut out for blasphemy. This boy, André, is saved by his aged confessor, Father Ambrose, from a self-destroying sense of personal dishonour, and turns his life to helping the wretched Pierre. Cather's heavily annotated copy of Thomas Okey's 1926 book *The Story of Avignon* showed that, as for *Death Comes for the Archbishop* and *Shadows on the Rock*, she was attending to details – of the papal palace and gardens, the bridge over the Rhone, the life of the medieval city – which she would fuse with her own memories and bury as the substructure of the novel.

By strange chance, a few pages of the manuscript came to light years later, a scene with Father Ambrose and the two boys at Christmas Mass.[46] It is a sentimental and pious piece of writing, waxing emotional on the wonders of 'wonderment' and 'the power to worship', on the beauties of 'faith, belief, imagination', and on the feelings of the crowd and the boys in response to the music. (She had heard a young man singing in the papal palace on her last visit to Avignon in 1935, and it inspired her.)[47] The subject-matter sounds more interesting than the extract, with its reworking of the male friendship of *One of Ours* and *Death Comes for the Archbishop*, its retreat from historical America to the earlier, more glamorous, but equally cruel history of France (at the time of the French occupation), and, above all, its obsession with crippled and stoical heroism. Cather may herself have been feeling, at this time, that she had had her tongue cut out.

Though *Hard Punishments* did not survive, three late stories were published the year after Cather's death. One of these was the once-rejected 'The Old Beauty'. The second in the volume, 'The Best Years', was a long story written in 1945, a last return to Nebraska, written out of her feeling for Roscoe, who died just as the story was finished. He appears in it as a sensitive young Nebraskan 'Hector'. But essentially 'The Best Years' is a story of women, who, this time, in reaction against Sapphira, are benign and protective towards each other. It begins with the likeable, efficient school superintendent, Miss Evangeline Knightly (a tribute to Cather's helpful Red Cloud schoolteacher)[48] riding through the September Nebraskan countryside, all wide horizons and herds of contented animals, on her school rounds. She visits a young teacher called Lesley Ferguesson – so young, indeed, that with Miss Knightly's collusion she has falsified her age to get the job – and admires her geography lesson. She is teaching the children to 'bound' the States by remembering what lies on their borders; the child who is called on to perform is so nervous that he has an 'accident', but, thanks to Lesley's good instruction, the other children don't laugh. Miss Knightly takes Lesley home to 'MacAlpin' for the weekend, and a heartfelt description ensues of a home life that both is and is not Cather's at Red Cloud.

In detail, the family is different: the mother a practical competent committee-joiner, the father a Bryanite and an eccentric enthusiast for experimental farming, who has called his farm 'Wide Awake Farm' because it is an 'observatory' for watching the signs of the times, [OB, p.103] and who is laughed at by his neighbours. But the children's attic room, the excitement of the great trains arriving at the depot, the affection for the brothers, are personal memories, meant to evoke what had come to seem increasingly important to Cather, 'the clan feeling, which meant life or death for the blood, not for the individual'. [OB, p.113]

Lesley Ferguesson, predictably, only survives as a memory. She is wiped out, by pneumonia, in a terrible blizzard.[49] Miss

Knightly, who has been in Lincoln seeing Julia Marlowe in a play called *The Love Chance* (as Cather did in 1894), learns the story from the railroad conductor. In the usual coda, she returns to MacAlpin twenty years later to find Mrs Ferguesson crippled with a bad ankle, and lamenting, in a sustained pastoral elegy, not only her lost daughter but the loss in the modern world of 'real folks'.

This last attempt to 'bound' the horizon of her past through nostalgic elegy is only a moderate success. When Cather saw Julia Marlowe act in 1894, she compared her beauty to 'certain old pictures and lines from certain old pastorals'.[50] The story reaches back for that 'old pastoral' quality, but feels the need, now, to sentimentalize the picture of 'clan life' which, in earlier versions, was more complex and strenuous. All the same, it has an endearingly wistful tenderness for childhood, which links the mortified little boy peeing in his school knickerbockers, the lively 'little teacher', and the small timid brother who has been named after William Jennings Bryan, and knows that he must live up to it and 'some day stop being afraid of the dark'. [OB, p.100]

The story placed last in the posthumous volume (though written before 'The Best Years') was called 'Before Breakfast', and was the only work of Cather's to be set in Grand Manan. Though the action of the story takes place before breakfast, the title may also be an echo of the White Queen's advice to Alice, to stretch her mind by believing a number of impossible things 'before breakfast'. (According to the favourite niece, Mary Virginia, Cather and Lewis had named parts of Grand Manan after places in the Alice books.)[51] Henry Grenfell, dyspeptic, country-loving, self-made Boston businessman, with a cabin on this remote North Atlantic island, well away from his disappointing marriage and sarcastic, successful sons, is in a bad mood. As he showers, dresses and applies his eye-drops, he sees a big snowshoe hare nibbling the clover, then looks up to see the 'serene, impersonal splendour' of Venus, the morning star. 'The poor hare and his clover, poor Grenfell and his eye-drops!' [OB, p.144] On the boat journey, armed as usual with a Shakespeare play (Henry IV part I), he had fallen into conversation with a geologist professor and his attractive symathetic daughter. The Professor had told him that the island is a hundred and thirty-six million years old, and Grenfell has spent a bad night of 'revelation, revaluation', when under the impact of ths awesome information, everything that was 'shut-up' in his life 'simply broke jail, spread out into the spaciousness of the night, undraped, unashamed'. [OB, p.150]

The erotic metaphor leads him into an 'audit' of his tough childhood and chilly marriage, and to an admission that 'his worst' – his mortal – 'enemy' has been, not his wife, but himself. To get away from his thoughts, he hurries out for a walk through the wood to the sea. On his way, he pulls at a twig of 'grandfather' spruce, the skeleton of a fallen tree long since struck by lightning, its root exposed; but the twig, to his astonishment, 'snapped back at him like a metal spring'. [OB, p.160] Once through the dark wood, he gets to the cliffside and feels, 'like Christian of old', that his burden is left 'at the bottom of the hill'. The islands ancient fundamental rock need not depress him; after all, 'the green surface' goes on flourishing. At the headland, he feels his 'relationship unchanged' to the waterfalls, the cliff walls, the resilient 'stunted beeches' and the old birches with their twisted one-sided growth. Looking down, he sees a human figure: it is the geologist's daughter, setting out for a swim before breakfast in the icy water. As she opens her bathrobe, to reveal a pink bathing suit, she looks like a clam shell 'graciously' opening itself out. Grenfell thinks he will have to rescue her, but she takes a quick and competent swim, and he goes back, by-passing the ancient tree, pleased with what he has seen, and reflecting humorously on the encouraging aspects of evolution.

The story gathers up a number of Cather's obsessions: the unhappy self-made American man with a marriage like St Peter's; the pilgrimage through a dark place, as in Bunyan, or

Robert Frost, similarly finding, in 'Birches', life 'too much like a pathless wood' as a twig lashes across his eye; and the enchanting but distanced figure of the lady, a seaborne Venus, 'unashamedly' spied on in an act of benign voyeurism. In its alternation between pioneering, stoic energy, and the impersonal, unmarked stuff of nature, it provides a last, quirky reflection on the human capacity to make its mark. Grenfell's dismay comes out of a fear of dissolution into the impersonal elements, into time itself:

> What was the use . . . of anything? Why tear a man loose from his little rock and shoot him out into the eternities? All that stuff was inhuman. A man had his little hour, with heat and cold and a time-sense suited to his endurance. If you took that away from him you left him spineless, accidental, unrelated to anything. [OB, pp.148–9]

His resistance to this is exemplified by other forms of resistance in nature, troll-like and fierce in the dead tree's springing twig or the growth of the cliffside birches, young and vigorous in the girl's challenge to the freezing ocean. Cather divides herself between the pioneering girl and the old American to cast a last look back, at once pleased and resigned, at the human effort. 'She hadn't dodged,' he reflects. 'She had gone out, and she had come back. She would have a happy day. He knew just how she felt.' [OB, p.166] And he comes back too, his fear of being dissolved into 'the eternities' appeased, his appetite sharpened, to eat his breakfast.

NOTES

1. JOURNEYS

1. Don Hernando de Soto was one of the sixteenth-century Spanish pioneering explorers of what would be New Mexico, who went in search of the fabulous 'Seven Cities of Gold'. He was followed by Coronado, whose ill-fated expedition to the Southwest inspired Cather's imagination.
2. Letter to Miss Masterson, March 15 1943, RC.
3. Malcolm Bradbury left Cather out altogether of his book on *The Modern American Novel* (Oxford: OUP, 1983); apart from David Daiches' short study of 1951 there is no other book on her by a British writer.
4. Scott Fitzgerald, *The Letters of F. Scott Fitzgerald*, ed. Andrew Turnbull (Harmondsworth: Penguin, 1968) p.204.
5. Walt Whitman, 'Birds of Passage', *Leaves of Grass*. See O'Brien, p.440, on Cather's 'rebellion' against Whitman.
6. Frank Norris, *The Octopus*, 1901, Book 1, Ch. 1.
7. Ole Rölvaag, *Giants in the Earth*, 1927 (New York: Harper & Row, 1964), pp.332–3.
8. Norris, *ibid.*
9. Charles Olson, *Call Me Ishmael*, 1947 (London: Jonathan Cape, 1967), p.15.
10. D. H. Lawrence, *Studies in Classic American Literature*, 1924 (Harmondsworth: Penguin, 1971), p.88.
11. Ralph Waldo Emerson, *Nature*, 1836, Ch. I.
12. Emily Dickinson, Letter to Thomas Wentworth Higginson, July 1862.
13. Scott Fitzgerald, *The Great Gatsby*, 1925.
14. Robert Frost, 'The Gift Outright', in *A Witness Tree* (1942), *The Poetry of Robert Frost* (London: Cape, 1971), p.348.
15. Frederick Jackson Turner, 'The Significance of the Frontier in American History', 1893, in Ray Allen Billington (ed.), *Frontier and Section: Selected Essays of Frederick Jackson Turner* (New Jersey: Englewood Cliffs, 1961). See also Harold Simonson, *The Closed Frontier: Studies in American Literary Tragedy* (New York: Holt, Rinehart & Winston, 1970).
16. D. H. Lawrence, *op. cit.*, and William Carlos Williams, *In the American Grain*, 1925 (New York: New Directions, 1956).
17. Willa Cather, 'Nebraska: The End of the First Cycle', *The Nation*, vol. 117, no. 3035, September 5 1923, pp.236, 238.
18. Frank Norris, 'A Plea for Romantic Fiction', December 18 1901, in *The Literary Criticism of Frank Norris*, ed. Donald Pizer (New York: Russell & Russell, 1964), pp.76, 78.
19. *Courier*, April 8 1899, WP, p.608.

20. The 'emergence' of her 'androgynous' voice as a writer from her early years is the subject of Sharon O'Brien's book.
21. Brown, p.95.
22. Woodress I, p.86.
23. Philip Gerber, *Willa Cather* (Boston: Twayne, 1975), p.41, and Kathleen Byrne and Richard Snyder, *Chrysalis: Willa Cather in Pittsburgh, 1896–1906* (Pittsburgh: Historical Society of Western Pennysylvania, 1980), pp.40–42.
24, Letter from Virginia Faulkner to Helen Southwick, March 14 1980, UNeb.
25. Robinson, p.276.
26. Lillian Faderman, in *Surpassing the Love of Men: Romantic Friendship between Women from the Renaissance to the Present* (New York: Morrow, 1981), writes interestingly on the change in self-consciousness about women living together, from the mid nineteenth century (as in the 'Boston marriage' of Sarah Orne Jewett and Annie Fields) to the 1890–1910 period, when Kraft Ebing and Havelock Ellis had introduced the concepts of inversion and degeneracy.
27. KA, p.392.
28. Adrienne Rich, 'Compulsory Heterosexuality and Lesbian Existence', 1980, in Mary Eagleton, ed., *Feminist Literary Theory* (Oxford: Blackwell, 1986), p.23.
29. Dorothy Lambert, 'The Defeat of a Hero: Autonomy and Sexuality in *My Ántonia*', *American Literature*, vol. 53. no. 4, January 1982, p.676.
30. Bonnie Zimmerman, 'What Has Never Been: An Overview of Lesbian Feminist Literary Criticism', in Elaine Showalter, .ed., *The New Feminist Criticism*, (London: Virago, 1986), p.207.
31. Lambert, op. cit.
32. Jennifer Uglow, *George Eliot* (London: Virago, 1987), pp.78–9, gives a discerning account of this essay.
33. WP, pp.276–7.
34. D. H. Lawrence, 'Hawthorne's *Blithedale Romance*', *op. cit.*, p.111.
35. WP, p.699.
36. Ellen Moers, in *Literary Women* (New York: Doubleday, Anchor Books, 1977), pp.153–60, points out that Cather belonged to the last generation for whom this was a popular children's poem. See also O'Brien, pp.272–4, 278–9, Rosowski, pp.229–30, and Fryer, p.337, on Cather's interest in 'Goblin Market'. KA, pp. 346–9.
37. NOF, p.87.
38. WP, p.694.
39. Sarah Orne Jewett, *Deephaven* (Boston: Osgood & Co., 1877), p.41.
40. Sarah Orne Jewett, Letter to Willa Cather, November 27 1908, in *Letters of Sarah Orne Jewett*, ed. Annie Fields (Boston: Houghton Mifflin, 1911), pp.146–7.

2. HOME

The biographical information in Chapters 2–5 is drawn from Brown, Bennett, Lewis, O'Brien, Robinson, Woodress I and II, from letters, and from interviews collected in Bohlke.

1. Letter to Henry Chester Tracy, June 22 1922, UVA.
2. Interview, *Webster County Argus*, Sept 29, 1921; *New York Times Book Review*, Dec 21 1924. In Bohlke.
3. Letter to Carrie Miner Sherwood, Jan 27 1934, RC.

4. Interview, *New York World*, April 19 1925, reprinted *Nebraska State Journal*, April 25 1925. In Bohlke.
5. Letter to Pendleton Hogan, Feb 5 1940, UVA.
6. Letter to Carrie Miner Sherwood, June 28 1939, RC.
7. Letter to Mr Winter, Nov 5 [n.d.], RC.
8. Letter to Mrs Seibel, Jan 31 [1916], RC.
9. Letter to Carrie Miner Sherwood, April 29 1945, RC.
10. Lewis, p.6.
11. Letter to John Phillipson, Nov 15 1943, RC.
12. Interview, *Lincoln Sunday Star*, Nov 6 1921. In Bohlke.
13. Letter to Carrie Miner Sherwood, Jan 27 1934, RC.
14. Letter to Irene Miner Weisz, Jan 6 1945, Newberry.
15. O'Brien, p.345.
16. Sarah Orne Jewett to Willa Cather, Dec 13 1908, *Letters of Sarah Orne Jewett*, ed. Annie Fields (Boston: Houghton Mifflin, 1911), p.249.
17. 'Katherine Mansfield', 1925, NOF, pp.152–4.
18. O'Brien, quoted p.60.
19. O'Brien, p.12.
20. Woodress I, p.23.
21. Letter to Dorothy Canfield Fisher, April 3 1928, Vermont.
22. Letter from Ann Cather to Franc Cather, July 18 1875, Cather Family Correspondence, NSHS.
23. This detail is given to Thea's mother, SL, p.22.
24. *Nebraska State Journal*, Dec 27 1896.
25. Interview, *The Philadelphia Record*, Aug 9 1913, KA, p.448.
26. SL, p.69; 'Nebraska: The First Cycle', *Nation*, Sept 5 1923, vol. 117, No. 303, p.236.
27. Edwin Fussell, *Frontier: American Literature and the American West* (New Jersey: Princeton University Press, 1965), p.426.
28. Letter to Witter Bynner, June 7 1905, Houghton.
29. Letter, Annie Pavelka, Feb 24 1955, RC.
30. Letter to H. W. Boynton, Dec 6 1919, UVA.
31. Letter to Mariel Gere, Sept 18 1897, NSHS.
32. Letter to Mariel Gere, Oct 19 1945, NSHS.
33. Letter to Elizabeth Shepley Sergeant, Sept 18 1914, Morgan.
34. See O'Brien, p.93.
35. Slote, pp.6, 9.
36. 'The Home Town', *Omaha World Herald*, June 24 1934, p.8. For the University of Nebraska at this time, see MA, p.258.
37. Edward Wagenknecht, Review of Brown and Lewis, *Chicago Sunday Tribune Books*, Mar 8 1953. Professor Sherman appears as Thea's schoolteacher (SL, p.131) who 'got out of real work by inventing useless activities for his pupils'.
38. Slote, p.27.
39. *Nebraska State Journal*, Nov 18 1894, KA, p.259.
40. *Nebraska State Journal*, Oct 23 1895, *Lincoln Courier*, Oct 26 1895, KA, pp.293, 297.
41. Slote, p.27.
42. Letters to Louise Pound, June 15 1892, Aug 6 1892, Duke: to Mariel Gere, Aug 1 1893, NSHS; to Geres, Jan 2 1896, NSHS; to Mariel Gere, Mar 12 1896, NSHS; to Mariel Gere, Aug 1 1893, NSHS; to Elizabeth Shepley Sergeant, June 27 1911, Morgan; to Mariel Gere, May 2 1896, NSHS; to Elizabeth Shepley Sergeant, April 20 1912, Morgan.

43. 'Cather Family Letters', ed. Paul D. Riley, *Nebraska History*, vol. 54, no. 4, p.596, Winter 1973. See Woodress II, p.68 for the Cather family's financial situation in the early 1890s. We do not know if Cather contributed to the family's income when she became a journalist, but she was probably self-supporting for the last two years of her university career.

44. 'The Personal Side of William Jennings Bryan', *The Library*, July 14 1900, WP, p.789. For Bryan, see: 'William Jennings Bryan: The Cross of Gold Speech', ed. Richard Hofstadter in *An American Primer*, ed. Daniel Boorstin (Chicago: University of Chicago Press, 1966); J. Leonard Bates, *The United States 1898–1928* (New York: McGraw Hill, 1976), pp.11, 53; *Nebraska: A Guide to the Cornhusker State*, introduced by Tom Allan, compiled by the Federal Writers' Project of the Works Progress Administration for the State of Nebraska (Lincoln: University of Nebraska Press, 1979), pp.5, 184.

3. WORKING HER WAY OUT

For Cather in Pittsburgh, see Slote; WP; Kathleen D. Byrne and Richard C. Snyder, *Chrysalis: Willa Cather in Pittsburgh, 1896–1906* (Pittsburgh: Historical Society of Western Pennsylvania, 1980); Mildred Bennett, Introduction, CSF. For Europe, see George Kates, *Willa Cather in Europe* (New York: Knopf, 1956) and WP, pp.889–952.

1. *Nebraska State Journal*, Jan 3, 1897, WP, p.393. (Hereafter NSJ.)
2. *Lincoln Courier*, Dec 18 1897, WP, p.522. (Hereafter LC.)
3. LC, Aug 24 1901, WP, p.857.
4. Letter to Will Owen Jones, Jan 15 1897, NSHS.
5. Letter to 'Neddius' (Ellen Gere), n.d. [1896], NSHS.
6. NSJ, Mar 11 1891.
7. LC, Sep 28 1895, KA, p.281.
8. Frank Norris, 'The Decline of the Magazine Short Story', *Wave*, XVI, Jan 30 1897, p.3. In *The Literary Criticism of Frank Norris*, p.28.
9. *Home Monthly*, Jan 1897, WP, p.336.
10. Letter to Louise Pound, Oct 13 1897, Duke.
11. Mildred Bennett, 'How Willa Cather Chose Her Names', *Names*, vol. 10, no. 1, March 1962, p.29–37, suggests that 'Helen Delay' stood for Cather's feelings about Pittsburgh – 'Hell and Delay'.
12. *The Library*, June 23 1900, WP, p.772.
13. NSJ, April 5 1896, KA, p.411.
14. Letter to Mariel Gere, Aug 10 1896, NSHS. See Thea's apprenticeship in Chicago, SL, Part III.
15. NSJ, Mar 29 1896, WP, pp.288–9.
16. LC, July 1 1899, WP, pp.474–6.
17. Bennett, p.247.
18. NSJ, Feb 7 1897, WP, pp.397–400.
19. NSJ, May 23 1897, WP, pp.408–11.
20. LC, Feb 5 1898, WP, p.376.
21. LC, Dec 25 1897, WP, pp.413–14. Thea Kronborg has the same experience. SL, p.251.
22. LC, Oct 30 1897, WP, p.388.
23. LC, Dec 16 1899, WP, p.645.
24. NSJ, Nov 1, Nov 8, 1891, KA, pp.426–36, describes Shakespeare's 'awful loneliness'.

25. NSJ, Oct 14 1894, KA, p.188; LC, Oct 26 1895, KA, pp.294–5.
26. NSJ, June 16 1895, KA, p.117; LC, Sept 21 1895, KA, p.119.
27. *New York Sun*, Feb 11 1898, WP, p.458.
28. LC, Jan 14 1899, WP, p.662.
29. LC, Sept 28 1895, KA, p.282.
30. Henry James, *The Tragic Muse*, 1890 (Harmondsworth: Penguin, 1978) p.211.
31. Cather warily admired *Hedda Gabler* (*Index*, Dec 29 1900, WP, pp.798–801); relished but was irritated by Shaw (*Leader*, Dec 2 1898, WP, p.597); loved *Cyrano de Bergerac* (LC, April 15 1899, WP, p.500) and *Mrs Tanqueray* (LC, July 22 1899, WP, pp.677–8); found Vesta Tilley 'dull and proper' (LC, Mar 19 1898, WP, pp.396–7) but liked Johnstone Bennett, another male impersonator, 'the trimmest tailor-made New Woman of them all' (LC, Feb 4 1899, WP, p.543).
32. NSJ, Oct 21 1894, KA, p.253.
33. LC, Sept 7 1895, KA, p.201.
34. NSJ, Feb 23 1896, KA, pp.202–3, is a scathing review of Oscar Hammerstein's music-hall *Faust*.
35. *The Library*, June 9 1900, WP, pp.769–71.
36. LC, Dec 2 1899, WP, p.683.
37. *Hesperian*, Mar 1 1891, KA, pp.421–5.
38. NSJ, May 17 1896, WP, pp. 296–301.
39. *Home Monthly*, Sept 1 1897, WP, p.355.
40. NSJ, Aug 11 1895, KA, p.323.
41. NSJ, May 24 1896, KA, p.342.
42. NSJ, Jan 19 1896, KA, p.352.
43. NSJ, May 24 1896, KA, p.344.
44. LC, Mar 4 1899, WP, pp.554–61.
45. LC, Dec 18 1897, WP, pp.523–5.
46. See 'The Troll Garden', Ch.4, pp.73–8.
47. *Pittsburgh Gazette*, Nov 17 1901, WP, pp.864–7.
48. LC, Sept 16 1899, WP, p.723.
49. NOF, p.138.
50. NSJ, Feb 2 1896, WP, pp.282–6.
51. Letter to Dorothy Canfield Fisher, April 8 1921, Vermont.
52. O'Brien, pp.241, 244; Woodress II, p.141. The letters are published in Marion Marsh Browne and Ruth Crone, *Only One Point of the Compass: Willa Cather in the Northeast* (Danbury, Conn: Archer Editions Press, 1980), pp.66–9, 79–84. See O'Brien, p.236, on Isabelle's character.
53. NSJ, Jan 10 1897, WP, p.506.
54. William Godwin, *Memoirs of the Author of the Rights of Woman*, 1798 (Harmondsworth: Penguin, 1987), ed. Richard Holmes, p.210.
55. Letter to Dorothy Canfield Fisher, Oct 10 1899, Vermont.
56. Letter to Dorothy Canfield Fisher, April 7, May 3, 1922, Vermont.
57. *April Twilights*, 1903, ed. Bernice Slote (Lincoln: University of Nebraska Press, 1962); Revised Edition, Knopf, 1923. In the new edition she took out some poems and added more western material: native ballads ('The Old West, the old times/The old wind singing through/The red, red grass a thousand miles,/And, Spanish Johnny, you!') and a risible attempt at gritty urban realism in 'Street in Packingtown': 'Twisting a shoestring noose, a Polack's brat/ Joylessly torments a cat'.
58. Hugh Kenner, *The Pound Era* (London: Faber, 1972), pp.127, 174, 181–3.
59. Letter to Dorothy Canfield Fisher, May 11 1903, Vermont.
60. Letter to Will Owen Jones, May 7 1903, UVA.

4. BURIED ALIVE

1. For McClure, see David Mark Chalmers, *The Muckrake Years* (New York: D Van Nostrand, 1974), pp.13–25, 79–82.
2. Letter to Will Owen Jones, May 29 1914, UVA.
3. Letter to Elizabeth Shepley Sergeant, June 4 1911, Morgan.
4. Letter to Elizabeth Shepley Sergeant, May 31 1910, Morgan.
5. Letter to Mr Pinker, Feb 20 1909, UVA.
6. Letter to Elizabeth Shepley Sergeant, April 5 1910, Morgan.
7. Letter to Norman Foerster, July 29 1910, UNeb.
8. Georgine Milmine, *The Life of Mary Baker Eddy* (New York: Doubleday, 1909), pp.15, 21, 29, 31.
9. Henry James, 'Mr and Mrs James T. Fields', *Atlantic Monthly*, vol. 116, no. 1, July 1915, pp.21–31.
10. NOF, p.78. See Ch. 9, p.190.
11. Henry James, Preface, *The Aspern Papers* (1888).
12. O'Brien (p.317) compares Cather's description of Charles Street to a Mary Cassatt painting.
13. NOF, pp.67, 69.
14. Letter to Elizabeth Shepley Sergeant, Nov 19 1913, Morgan.
15. Sergeant, p.16.
16. Lewis, p.154.
17. Letter to Edith Lewis, Oct 5 1936, UNeb.
18. Letters from Edith Lewis to Stephen Tennant, n.d. [1948]; Feb 3 [n.d.]; April 16 1948; June 3 [1952]; June 25 1952. Quoted by permission of Hugo Vickers.
19. Letter to Will Owen Jones, May 29 1914, UVA; Letter to Elizabeth Shepley Sergeant, June 27 1911, Morgan.
20. David Daiches, *Willa Cather: A Critical Introduction* (Ithaca: Cornell University Press, 1951; New York: Collier, 1964), p.14.
21. See Ch. 1, pp.13–14, and see O'Brien, p.274.
22. Charles Kingsley, *The Roman and the Teuton*, vol. 10, *The Works of Charles Kingsley* (London: Macmillan, 1884), p.12.
23. Interview, *Nebraska State Journal*, 25 April 1925. In Bohlke.
24. Aunt Georgiana sounds like Cather's Aunt Franc, but she denied this. See James Woodress, Introduction, *The Troll Garden* (Nebraska: University of Nebraska Press, 1983), p.xxv; Woodress II, pp.178, 181. In revisions of 1920 and 1937 she softened the character.
25. Ezra Pound, 'Hugh Selwyn Mauberley: Life and Contacts', *Selected Poems* (Faber, 1959).
26. O'Brien, p.277.
27. The thwarted artist returns in 'Uncle Valentine' (1925) and 'Coming, Aphrodite!' (1920); the artist who succeeds in escaping from, and making use of her environment is Thea Kronborg.
28. Woodress II, p.179.
29. Letter to Will Owen Jones, Mar 6, 1904, UVA.
30. See Ch. 5, pp.97–101.
31. Sarah Orne Jewett to Willa Cather, Dec 13 1908. See Ch. 2, p.22.
32. Letter to Sarah Orne Jewett, Dec 17 1908, Houghton.
33. Godwin, *op. cit.*, pp.226–7.
34. O'Brien, pp.293–4.
35. Jennifer Uglow, *George Eliot* (London: Virago, 1987), p.45.
36. Sarah Orne Jewett to Willa Cather, Dec 13 1908.

37. Letter to Will Owen Jones, May 20 1919, UVA.
38. 'My First Novels: There Were Two', *Colophon*, Part 6, 1931, WCOW; Letter to H. L. Mencken, Feb 6 [1922?]; Preface to *Alexander's Bridge* (Boston: Houghton Mifflin, 1922).
39. Title as serialized in *McClure's*, Feb–April 1912.
40. See Fryer, p.215.
41. William Carlos Williams, *In the American Grain* (1925; New York: New Directions paperback, 1956), p.157. The idea of the split self would recur, rather mechanically, in some later stories much indebted to Hawthorne as well as James: 'The Profile' (1907), about an artist obsessed by his wife's half-scarred, half-perfect face (a disfigurement repeated, as though he's willed it, on his second wife) and 'Consequences' (1915), about a spoilt New Yorker who kills himself after being haunted by an old man who knows all about him and his dead brother, the unspoilt self he might have been.

5. A WIDE, UNTRIED DOMAIN

1. Letter to Elizabeth Shepley Sergeant, April 20 1912, Morgan. See Thea, SL, p.309.
2. Letters to Elizabeth Shepley Sergeant, April 26, Sept 12 1912, Morgan.
3. Letter to Elizabeth Shepley Sergeant, May 21 1912, Morgan.
4. *Ibid.*
5. Letters to Elizabeth Shepley Sergeant, June 15, May 21 1912, Morgan.
6. O'Brien, p.413.
7. O'Brien (pp.418–19) is illuminating on her references to Balzac's line on the desert: 'Dans le desert, voyez-vous, il y a tout et il n'y a rien – Dieu, sans les hommes'.
8. Letter to Elizabeth Shepley Sergeant, Sept 12 1912, Morgan. See also Brown, pp.173–4, on the probable order of composition and expansion of the parts of OP.
9. Letter to Zoë Akins, Oct 31 1912, UVA; Letter to Elizabeth Shepley Sergeant, Feb 2 1913, Morgan.
10. Quoted by Renato Poggioli, *The Oaten Flute* (Harvard: Harvard University Press, 1975), p.157.
11. William Empson, *Some Versions of Pastoral* (London: Chatto & Windus, 1935, Peregrine, 1966), p.13.
12. Empson, p.19.
13. Harry Levin, in *The Myth of the Golden Age in the Renaissance* (Indiana: Indiana University Press, 1969), pp.6–7, makes this point.
14. See Erwin Panofsky, *Meaning and the Visual Arts* (1955; London; Peregrine, 1970), pp. 340–67, for his brilliant analysis of 'Et in Arcadia Ego'.
15. Levin, pp.7, 46.
16. Levin, p.164: 'It is debilitating to believe too rigidly, with Charles Péguy, that the modern world debases ("le monde moderne avilit").'
17. Leo Marx, *The Machine in the Garden: Technology and the Pastoral Idea in America* (Oxford: OUP, 1964, reprinted 1978), p.7.
18. Panofsky, p.343.
19. See Panofsky, Poggioli, Levin. Also Lovejoy and Boas, *Primitivism and Related Ideas in Antiquity* (Baltimore, 1935); John Chalker, *The English Georgic* (London: Routledge, 1969), pp.100–6.
20. *The Georgics of Virgil*, Book IV, Translated by C. Day Lewis (London: Cape, 1940), p.81.

21. Panofsky, p.346, speaks of Virgil's 'verspertinal mixture of sadness and tranquillity', Leo Marx of his 'unruffled, contemplative, Augustan tone', op. cit., p.31.
22. Rosowski (pp.60–61) describes this as the dominant tone of OP. For Cather and Virgil see also Donald Sutherland, 'Willa Cather: The Classic Voice' in *The Art of Willa Cather*, ed. Bernice Slote and Virginia Faulkner (Lincoln: University of Nebraska Press, 1974), pp.156–79. See further, Ch. 6, p.118.
23. William Hazlitt, *Lectures on the English Poets*, VII, 'On Burns and the Old English Ballads', *Complete Works*, vol. V (London: Dent, 1930), p.141.
24. Marx, p.141, referring to Henry Nash Smith, *Virgin Land: The American West as Symbol and Myth* (Cambridge: Cambridge University Press, 1950).
25. Marx, p.226.
26. Quoted by Marx, p.254.
27. Frank Kermode, *The Sense of an Ending* (Oxford: OUP, 1966), p.39. See further Ch. 8, p.179.
28. *The Georgics of Virgil*, p.37.
29. Marx, p.245.
30. Levin, p.14 ff., Poggioli, p.49 ff.
31. Poggioli, p.9
32. Poggioli, p.161.
33. Helen Cooper, *Pastoral: Medieval into Renaissance* (London: D. S. Brewer, 1977), pp.2–3.
34. Empson, p.25. For the grafting of trees in Cather's pastoral, see MA, p.340.
35. Mark Twain, *The Adventures of Huckleberry Finn* (1885), Ch. 7.
36. Eudora Welty, 'The House of Willa Cather', *The Eye of the Storm: Selected Essays and Reviews* (New York: Vintage, 1979; London: Virago, 1987), p.44.
37. Turgenev, 'Behzin Lea', *Sketches from a Hunter's Album*, translated by Richard Freeborn (Harmondsworth: Penguin, 1967), pp.73–4.
38. Cather was unsure about the merits of 'The Bohemian Girl', but Elsie Sergeant persuaded her that 'this was it' (Sergeant, p.76) and that she should offer it to *McClure's* for publication. Its enthusiastic reception surprised her. See O'Brien, pp.399–400.
39. Cather wrote an exasperated review of *The Devil's Disciple* in 1898 (WP, pp.489–90).

6. WOMEN HEROES

1. O'Brien (p.441) finds more continuity between Mrs Bergson's preserving and Alexandra's orchard and garden.
2. Letter to Elizabeth Shepley Sergeant, April 22 1913, Morgan.
3. Rosowski (p.50) points out that Alexandra is always looking beyond the landscape.
4. See Empson, p.100 for the idea that man controls Nature by delighting in it.
5. Rosowski, (p.47) compares him to Virgil's Silenus.
6. Rosowski (p.54) shows Cather's debt to Keats's 'The Eve of St Agnes' here. For 'eclogue' and 'georgic' in *O Pioneers!* see John H. Randall, 'Willa Cather and the Pastoral Tradition', *Five Essays on Willa Cather: The Merrimack Symposium*, ed. John J. Murphy (North Andover, Mass: Merrimack College, 1974), pp.60–83.
7. See O'Brien (p.439) on the parallel between Alexandra's take-over of the land and Cather's take-over of the American Adamic myth.
8. Rosowski, p.57.

9. Letter to E. K. Brown, Oct 7 1946, UNeb.
10. O'Brien, p.447.
11. Woodress I, pp.168–9, Woodress II, p.273.
12. 'My First Novels: There Were Two', 1931, WCOW, p.96.
13. Preface, SL, Jonathan Cape Traveller's Library, 1932.
14. A. S. Byatt, Introduction, SL (Virago 1986), p.xvi.
15. 'My First Novels: There Were Two', WCOW, pp.96–7.
16. Letter to Elizabeth Shepley Sergeant, Dec 7 1915, Morgan.
17. Letter to Dorothy Canfield Fisher, Mar 15 1930, Vermont.
18. Letter to Dorothy Canfield Fisher, Dec 1 1930, Vermont.
19. For Cather's meetings with Fremstad, see Lewis, pp.91–3; Brown, pp.184–5; Letter to Elizabeth Shepley Sergeant, April 22 1913, Morgan.
20. 'Three American Singers', McClure's, Dec 1913, pp.33–48. Quoted Brown, p.186.
21. Letter to Elizabeth Shepley Sergeant, April 22 1913, Morgan.
22. Letter to Elizabeth Shepley Sergeant, Feb 24 1914, Morgan.
23. Letter to Elizabeth Shepley Sergeant, Mar 2 1914, Morgan.
24. Letter to Elizabeth Shepley Sergeant, Sep 22 1913, Morgan.
25. Letter to Elizabeth Shepley Sergeant, June 23 1914, Morgan.
26. O'Brien (p.410) quoting Ellen Moers, Literary Women (New York: Doubleday, 1976), pp.259–60. O'Brien makes an interesting comparison with other American women artists whose work is inspired by the Southwest, the writer Mary Austin, the photographer Laura Gilpin, and the painter Georgia O'Keeffe. For Mary Austin's comparable story-making out of an 'unstoried' landscape, and her use of pots and vessels as an image for narrative, see David Wyatt, The Fall into Eden: Landscape and Imagination in California (London and New York: Cambridge University Press, 1986), pp.81–91.
27. Rosowski (pp.64–6) compares Thea's 'conversion' process very acutely to Carlyle's.
28. Preface, The Wagnerian Romances, 1925, WCOW, p.62. Cather follows Hall closely in her account of Act I of The Valkyrie.
29. Gertrude Hall, The Wagnerian Romances (London: John Lane, 1907), p.94.
30. Preface, The Wagnerian Romances, WCOW, pp.65–6.
31. See O'Brien (pp.108, 275) on Sieglinde/Siegmund as expressive of Cather's 'repressed' self.
32. NOF, p.50.
33. A letter to Elizabeth Shepley Sergeant, June 27 1915, Morgan, shows how proud she was of getting her music right.
34. See Byatt, Introduction, SL (Virago, 1982), p.xvi.
35. Lincoln Courier, June 10 1899, WP, pp.622–3.
36. George Bernard Shaw, The Perfect Wagnerite, 1898 (London: Constable, 1923), p.90.
37. Letter to Dorothy Canfield Fisher, Mar 15 1916, Vermont.
38. Lionel Trilling in 'Willa Cather', After the Genteel Tradition (New York: Viking, 1937) is scathing on this contradiction. The same gap between an American opera singer and a philistine American audience is described in the story 'A Gold Slipper', 1917, YBM.

7. THE ROAD OF DESTINY

1. Crane, pp.66–7.
2. Letter to Will Owen Jones, May 20 1919, UVA.

3. Letter to H. L. Mencken, n.d. [1922], Maryland.
4. In a letter to Viola Roseboro, Feb 20 1941, UVA, Cather said people had accused it of formlessness.
5. Letter to Will Owen Jones, May 20 1919, UVA.
6. Letter to Elizabeth Shepley Sergeant, Aug 10 1914, Morgan.
7. Letter to Elizabeth Shepley Sergeant, Aug 3 1916, Morgan, and to Dorothy Canfield Fisher, Mar 15 1916, Vermont.
8. NOF, p.54.
9. WCOW, p.96.
10. Sergeant, p.121, quoted O'Brien, p.417.
11. Wallace Stevens, 'The Emperor of Ice-Cream', 1923.
12. Rosowski (p.81) draws attention to this.
13. Eudora Welty, 'The House of Willa Cather', op.cit.
14. Ralph Waldo Emerson, 'Nature', Ch. 1, 1836.
15. Walt Whitman, 'Song of Myself', 1855.
16. Tillie Olsen in *Silences* (Virago, 1980) makes a comparison between Blind d'Arnault and Blind Tom in Rebecca Harding's *Life in the Iron Mills* (1861).
17. Rosowski, pp.89–91, is more distrustful of Jim.
18. Sarah Orne Jewett to Willa Cather, Nov 27 1908, in *Letters of Sarah Orne Jewett*, ed. Annie Fields (Boston: Houghton Mifflin, 1911), p.246.
19. Letter to Will Owen Jones, May 20 1919, UVA.
20. Deborah Lambert, in 'The Defeat of a Hero: Autonomy and Sexuality in *My Ántonia*', *American Literature*, vol. 53, no. 4, January 1982, pp.676–90, makes a simplistic decoding of Cather in terms of her lesbianism. O'Brien writes more subtly on the same theme in 'The Thing Not Named: Willa Cather as Lesbian Writer', *Signs: Journal of Women in Culture and Society*, 1984, vol. 9, no. 4, pp.576–99.
21. *A l'Ombre des jeunes filles en fleurs*, Part Two of *A la Recherche du temps perdu*, was published the year after MA, in 1919. Cather later makes occasional reference to Proust in letters and speeches (e.g. Letter to Dorothy Canfield Fisher, 1 Dec 1930, Vermont).
22. Letter to Helen Seibel, Feb 2 1919, NSHS.
23. Blanche Gelfant, 'The Forgotten Reaping Hook: Sex in *My Ántonia*', *American Literature*, vol. 43, March 1971, pp.60–72, reads the novel in terms of Jim's fear of sex and his inability to accept 'the nexus of love and death'.

8. THE LOST AMERICAN

1. Letter to Dorothy Canfield Fisher, March 15 1915, Vermont.
2. Edith Lewis, Letter to Stephen Tennant, n.d. [1948?], Hugo Vickers.
3. Letters to Carrie Miner Sherwood, July 25 [1929], RC; to Charlotte Stanfield, Sept 4 [1924], UVA; to Helen Macfee, June 24 [1932?], RC.
4. Brown, pp.213–14.
5. See Ch. 4, p.66. The story was first published in censored magazine form, as 'Coming, Eden Bower'. For the changes between magazine and book publication see Marilyn Arnold, *Willa Cather's Short Fiction* (Athens and London: Ohio University Press, 1984), pp.112–19, and Slote, ed., *Uncle Valentine and other Stories* (Lincoln: University of Nebraska Press), 1973, Appendix, pp.177–81.
6. See Ch. 5, pp.88–9.
7. Letter to Dorothy Canfield Fisher, Jan 26 1922, Vermont.
8. Letters to Dorothy Canfield Fisher, Mar 8, Mar 22 1922.
9. Sergeant, p.163; O'Brien, p.359. See Ch. 4, p.70.

10. Letter to Elizabeth Shepley Sergeant, Dec 3 1918, Morgan. See Ch. 4, p.70.
11. Letter to Dorothy Canfield Fisher, Mar 8 1922, Vermont. For Aunt Franc, see Ch. 4, note 24.
12. Interview, *New York Herald*, Dec 24 1922.
13. Letter to Dorothy Canfield Fisher, Mar 1922, Vermont.
14. Brown, p.216.
15. Robinson, p.224.
16. Letter to Viola Roseboro, June 5 1920, UVA.
17. Lewis, p.119.
18. Woodress I, p.195, and II, p.334: 'For the rest of her life [she] had no money problems'. Letter to Dorothy Canfield Fisher, Nov 28 1922, Vermont.
19. Hemingway to Edmund Wilson, Nov 25 1923, in Carlos Baker, ed., *Ernest Hemingway: Selected Letters 1917–1961* (New York: Scribners, 1981), p.105.
20. H. L. Mencken, review of *One of Ours*, *Smart Set*, October 1922, reprinted in James Schroeter, ed., *Willa Cather and Her Critics* (Ithaca: Cornell University Press, 1967), pp.10–12.
21. Coningsby Dawson, *Out to Win* (London: Bodley Head, 1918), pp.50–52.
22. John Dos Passos, *One Man's Initiation: 1917*, 1920 (Ithaca: Cornell University Press, 1969), pp.50, 157–8.
23. Letter to Dorothy Canfield Fisher, May 8 [?], 1922, Vermont.
24. Wendel Beiser, Letter to Willa Cather, Oct 17 1922, RC.
25. Brown, p.214. Letter to Elizabeth Vermocken, Sept 19 1922, Morgan.
26. Letters to Elizabeth Shepley Sergeant, Oct 4 1922, Morgan; to Carrie Miner Sherwood, Sept 1 1922, RC.
27. Letter to Dorothy Canfield Fisher, [1923], Vermont.
28. Letters to Elizabeth Vermocken, Sept 18 and 19 1922, Morgan.
29. John Dos Passos, *One Man's Initiation: 1917*, p.45.
30. *Ibid.*, p.81.
31. Letter to Dorothy Canfield Fisher, Mar 21 1922, Vermont; O'Brien, p.214.
32. David Daiches, *Willa Cather: A Critical Introduction* (Ithaca: Cornell University Press, 1951; New York: Collier Books, 1964), p.54.
33. Letter to Carrie Miner Sherwood, Nov 16 1924, RC.
34. Willa Cather, 'Nebraska: The End of the First Cycle', *The Nation*, vol. 117, no. 3035, Sept 5 1923, pp.236, 238, quoted in Ch. 1, p.8.
35. Letters to Dorothy Canfield Fisher, 1922 and 1923, Vermont; Bennett, pp.120–21; F. T. Griffiths, 'The Woman Warrior: Willa Cather and *One of Ours*', *Women's Studies*, 1984, vol. 11, p.269.
36. Letter to Dorothy Canfield Fisher, Mar 8 1922, Vermont.
37. For the Parsifal theme in *One of Ours* see Rosowski, p.106; Griffiths, *op. cit.*, p.270; Woodress I, p.196.
38. In a letter to Dorothy Canfield Fisher, April 7 1922, Vermont, Cather said she had Siegmund in mind.
39. Woodress I, p.196, II, p.328. Letter to Mr Johns, Nov 17 1922, UVA.
40. See Griffiths, *op.cit.*, pp.271–4, on the Edenic theme of *One of Ours*: 'an unmistakeable parable about losing paradise in the Nebraska narrative, and of revisiting it in France.'
41. Rosowski (p.106) describes the unheroic quality of Claude's death.
42. Stanley Cooperman, 'The War Lover: Claude (Willa Cather)', *World War I and the American Novel* (Baltimore: Johns Hopkins, 1967), pp.129–37.
43. For a brilliant analysis of the 'image' of St Joan see Marina Warner, *Joan of Arc: The Image of Female Heroism* (London: Weidenfeld, 1981). For the Statue of Liberty see Marina Warner, *Monuments and Maidens: The Allegory of the Female Form* (London, Weidenfeld, 1985), Ch. 1.

44. For the 'homoerotic' content in the German officer scene, see Griffiths, *op. cit.*, pp.266–7.

9. THE THING NOT NAMED

1. Letter to Dorothy Canfield Fisher, June 17 [1927], Vermont.
2. See Leon Edel, *Literary Biography* (London. Hart Davis, 1957), pp.61–80 for his theory of a breakdown behind PH. Woodress I attributes her state of mind to the menopause (p.197); Woodress II changes this to 'a midlife crisis' (p.368).
3. Letter to Charlotte Stanfield, June 19 1922, UVA.
4. O'Brien, p.240.
5. Lewis, p.131.
6. Letter to Zoë Akins, Sept 14 1923, UVA.
7. O'Brien, pp.240, 384.
8. Letter to Dorothy Canfield Fisher, April 8[?] 1923, Vermont.
9. Letter to Dorothy Canfield Fisher, Feb 27 1924, Vermont.
10. See James Miller, 'Willa Cather and the Art of Fiction' in *The Art of Willa Cather*, ed. Bernice Slote and Virginia Faulkner (Lincoln: University of Nebraska Press, 1974), pp.127–37, on Cather's debt to James's aesthetic theories, and pp.149–52 for the ensuing discussion on her 'theory of fiction'.
11. Virginia Woolf, 'The Narrow Bridge of Art', 1927, *Collected Essays* (London: Chatto & Windus, 1966), vol. II, p. 219.
12. Letter to Henry Tracy, June 22 1922, UVA.
13. Letter to Mr Graff, July 19 1925, RC.
14. Letter to Elizabeth Shepley Sergeant, 1913, Morgan.
15. Letter to Dorothy Canfield Fisher, Oct 23 [?], 1922.
16. Letter to Elizabeth Shepley Sergeant, Oct 2 1929, Morgan.
17. Letter to Viola Roseboro, June 5 1920, UVA.
18. Interview, May 14 1925, *Christian Science Monitor*. In Bohlke.
19. 'On the Art of Fiction', 1920, WCOW, pp.101–3.
20. 'Stephen Crane's *Wounds in the Rain*', 1926, WCOW, p.70.
21. NOF, pp.47–56.
22. This is very like James's description in his book on *Hawthorne* (1879).
23. NOF, p.152.
24. NOF, p.54.
25. Virginia Woolf, 'Modern Fiction', 1919, *Collected Essays* vol. II, p.106.
26. See Bradbury's exclusion of her (Ch. I, note 3). Julian Symons in 'The American Way of Modernism' in *Makers of the New: The Revolution in Literature 1912–1939* (London: Deutsch, 1987), p.189. mentions her, with Ellen Glasgow and Scott Fitzgerald, as one of those who 'stay on the sidelines' of the modernist movement.
27. O'Brien, p.127, and Phyllis Rose, 'Modernism: The Case of Willa Cather', *Modernism Reconsidered*, ed. Robert Kiely and John Hibidle (Cambridge, Mass., 1983), p.124. See further, on Cather's repudiation of modernism, Ch. 14, pp.328–9.
28. NOF, p.78. See Ch. 4, p.69, and Ch. 15, p.349.
29. NOF, p.150.
30. See Ch. 2, p.23.
31. NOF, p.165.
32. NOF, p.155.
33. O'Brien, pp.127, 218.

10. LOST LADIES

1. Quoted Bennett, p.69.
2. Letter to Mariel Gere, Sept 30 1905, NSHS.
3. Letter to Mrs Gere [1901?], RC.
4. Letter to Irene Miner, Jan 6 1945, Newberry.
5. Letter to Pendleton Hogan, Feb 5 1940, UVA. E. K. Brown (p.248) was told she was a woman Cather had known through Lincoln connections. Woodress II, p.380, tentatively identifies her as Myra Tyndale, sister-in-law of Julius Tyndale, who died of cancer in Seattle in 1903.
6. See Ch. 2, p.21.
7. Interview, *Nebraska State Journal*, 22 April 1925. Brown, p.229.
8. Cf. Mother Cuxsom, in Hardy's *The Mayor of Casterbridge* (1886), Ch. XVIII, reporting on the dead Mrs Henchard: '"And all her shining keys will be took from her, and her cupboards opened; and little things a'didn't wish seen, anybody will see; and her wishes and ways will be as nothing!"'
9. Interview, *Nebraska State Journal*, 22 April 1925.
10. Sonnet 94.
11. I was alerted to this connection by an inspired unpublished lecture on Cather by Alistair Stead.
12. Tennyson, *The Forresters* (1892), Act II, scene i. Cather may not have known Tennyson's play, but she was extremely fond of *Ivanhoe*, where Scott makes use of Robin Hood, and she admired Maurice Hewlett's 'bucolic and pastoral' medieval romance, *The Forest Lovers* (1898), which she compared to *Ivanhoe* and described as 'somewhere between Arcady and Shakespeare's Forest of Arden'. [WP, p.270] She also liked the American Howard Pyle's stories for children, which included a version of Robin Hood.
13. *As You Like It*, Act I, scene i, 115–18.
14. Rosowski, p.14.
15. John Keats, 'Robin Hood', *The Complete Poems*, ed. John Barnard (Harmondsworth: Penguin, 1973), p.224; note, p.591.
16. Mary Ellmann, *Thinking About Women* (Virago, 1979), pp.113–14.
17. Rosowski, pp.128–9.
18. A. S. Byatt, Introduction, *A Lost Lady* (Virago, 1980), p.xiii. See also Diane Cousineau, 'Division and Difference in *A Lost Lady*', *Women's Studies*, vol. 11, 1984, pp.305–22, and Nancy Morrow, '*A Lost Lady* and the Nineteenth-Century Novel of Adultery', *Women's Studies*, vol. 11, 1984, pp.287–303.
19. I owe this idea to a fine unpublished essay on *A Lost Lady* by Portia Dadley.
20. A. S. Byatt, *op. cit.*, p.xiv.
21. Letter to Seibel, Jan 24 [1927], RC. Letter to Elizabeth Vermocken, Oct 27 1926, Morgan. Letter to Pendelton Hogan, Feb 5 1940, UVA.
22. Letter to E. K. Brown, Feb 7 1946, Newberry.
23. David Daiches, *Willa Cather: A Critical Introduction*, p.72; Dorothy Van Ghent, *Willa Cather*, Pamphlets on American Writers no. 36 (Minneapolis: University of Minnesota Press, 1964), p.35.
24. Carl Van Doren in *Willa Cather and her Critics*, ed. James Schroeter (Ithaca: Cornell University Press, 1967), p.23. Cather told Dorothy Canfield Fisher (Letter, October 14 1926, Vermont) that she couldn't like her grim story of blood-ties and inheritance, *My Son's Wife*, any more than she could like *Ethan Frome*. Though she disliked it, she discussed it with Elsie (Sergeant, p.72) as 'a story of stark frustration', and it evidently affected her.
25. Henry James, *The Portrait of a Lady*, Ch. XVIII.

26. *The Complete Notebooks of Henry James*, ed. Leon Edel and Lyall Powers (New York and Oxford: OUP, 1987), p.115, Feb 14 1895.
27. See Slote, pp.97–103. For Cather on Modjeska, see WP, pp.37–8, 194–5, 459–61.
28. 'Ach, meine Liebe selber/Zerfloß wie eitel Hauch!/ Du alte, einsame Träne, Zerfließe jetzunder auch!' Heine, *Selected Verse*, translated by Peter Branscombe (Harmondsworth: Penguin, 1967), p.46.
29. Woodress II, p.257 tells us that Cather bought Fremstad a little orange tree for Christmas 1913. Myra buys Modjeska a holly tree.
30. *Pittsburgh Leader*, July 8 1899, WP, p.698.
31. Letters as in note 21.
32. Rosowski, p.153.
33. Fryer, p.303.

11. TAKING POSSESSION

1. Cather is vague on the details of how Tom's invention can power an engine, but he must, presumably, have discovered a gas that would transform with exceptional rapidity into liquid and back, requiring a lighter engine and a new kind of bulkhead to contain the intense pressure it created. In the corrected edition of 1942, all the references to the 'bulkheaded vacuum' or 'vacuum' were changed to 'Outland engine', 'engine', or 'patent', suggesting some unease over these technicalities.
2. See Doris Grumbach, 'A Study of the Small Room in *The Professor's House*', *Women's Studies*, 1984, vol. II, pp.334–5.
3. Letter to Elizabeth Shepley Sergeant, Sept 21 1915, Morgan.
4. 'Willa Cather's 1916 Mesa Verde Essay: the Genesis of *The Professor's House*', Susan Rosowski and Bernice Slote, *Prairie Schooner*, Winter 1984, vol. 54, no. 4, p.84. All writers on the cliff-dwellings (*c*. 1100 AD) call them 'prehistoric'.
5. Gilbert Wenger, *The Story of the Mesa Verde* (Mesa Verde Museum Association, 1980) p.68 and Frank McNitt, *Richard Wetherill: Anasazi* (Albuquerque: University of New Mexico Press, 1957, 1966), p.34.
6. Woodress II, p.264; Lewis, p.97.
7. Letter to Elizabeth Shepley Sergeant, Sept 21 1915, Morgan.
8. *Denver Times*, August 25 1915.
9. Georgia O'Keeffe would fulfil these conditions; see Phyllis Rose, 'Modernism: the Case of Willa Cather' in *Modernism Reconsidered*, p.140.
10. 'Willa Cather's 1916 Mesa Verde Essay', *op. cit.*
11. *Ibid.*, p.86; c.f. G. Nordenskjold, *The Cliff Dwellers of the Mesa Verde*, 1893 (trans. D. Lloyd Morgan, New Mexico: Rio Grande Press, 1979).
12. Woodress II, p.284.
13. Lewis, p.133; Woodress II, p.353. In PH, Cather synthesizes several cliff-dwellings into one.
14. 'Willa Cather's 1916 Mesa Verde Essay', p.84.
15. WCOW, p.31.
16. See Ch. 4, p.84; Ch.15, p.345.
17. Caroline Commanville, *Selected Correspondence of Gustave Flaubert with an Intimate Study of the Author* (New York & London: M. Walter Dunne, 1904), p.41.
18. See Ch. 2, p.18.
19. Fryer (pp.304–6) describes him as a Cartesian separatist of mind and body.
20. In an interview with the *New York World*, May 21 1923 (in Bohlke), Cather

objects to novelists 'carrying too far' the process of chopping up character 'on the Freudian psycho-analytical plan'. But Rosowski points out (pp.141–2) that 'Cather was not hostile to psychology *per se*', and that in 1925 she had been reading Joseph Collins's book *The Doctor Looks at Literature: Psychological Studies of Life and Letters* (New York and London: Allen & Unwin, 1923). Collins analysed 'psychology' in the fiction of Joyce, Dostoievsky, Lawrence, Proust, Dorothy Richardson, Mansfield and others (including what he called 'Two Lesser Literary Ladies of London', Stella Benson and Virginia Woolf). He is hostile to 'Freudianism' for its denial of a higher spiritual life of the mind and for its dangerous theories of the unconscious. Cather followed his general attitude towards psychology as a useful but inexact tool for understanding people, and his theory that 'mental complexes' are produced by the attempt of 'the primitive mental machinery to adapt to more intricate and varied processes than those with which it was originally intended to cope'. (She must have been pleased that he cited 'Paul's Case' as an 'admirable' example of the novelist as 'practical psychologist'.) (Collins, pp.19–20.)

21. Rosowski (pp.134–5) compares Robert Frost's 'nature' writing.
22. Grumbach, *op. cit.*, p.339.
23. A. S. Byatt neatly points out the link with Tom's gas. Introduction, PH (Virago, 1981).
24. Henry James, Preface to *The Spoils of Poynton*, in *The Art of the Novel* (New York: Scribner's, 1934, 1962), p.120.
25. First by Brown, p.241.
26. Byatt pursues this theme in her Introduction, and notes that the *Berengaria*, the ship on which St Peter's family come home from Europe, was the name of Coeur de Lion's wife. It was also the name of the transatlantic liner on which Cather herself travelled from Europe in 1923. (Woodress II, p.339.)
27. David Laird, 'Willa Cather and the Deceptions of Art', *Interface*, ed. Daniel Royot (University of Montpellier, 1985), p.57, emphasizes Cather's use of this medieval *exemplum*.
28. WP, p.724. Dreyfus was reconvicted in 1899, and his name was partially cleared in 1906.
29. Brown takes St Peter's quotation of Longfellow's translation of the Anglo-Saxon poem 'Grave' ('For thee a house was built/Ere thou wast born;/For thee a mould was made/ Ere thou of woman camest') to show that the novel is about a 'profound unconscious preparation for death, for the last house of the professor' (pp.244–5).
30. Rose, *op. cit.*, p.128.
31. Philip Rahv, 'Palefaces and Redskins', *Image and Idea* (1949, revised 1957, in *American Critical Essays: 20th Century*, ed. Harold Beaver, Oxford: OUP, 1959).
32. Mark Twain, *Huckleberry Finn*, Ch. 7.
33. See Rosowski, pp.133 ff, for an excellent analysis of this passage.
34. Rose, *op. cit.*, p.128.
35. D. H. Lawrence, 'Edgar Allan Poe', *Studies in Classic American Literature* (1924, Harmondsworth: Penguin, 1971), p.83.
36. Woodress II, pp.354, 364. For Lawrence in Taos, see Harry Moore, *The Priest of Love* (London: Heinemann, 1974); Mabel Dodge Luhan, *Lorenzo in Taos* (New York: Knopf, 1932); James C. Cowan, *D. H. Lawrence's American Journey* (Western Reserve University, 1970).
37. Edward Nehls, *D. H. Lawrence: A Composite Biography* (Wisconsin: University of Wisconsin, 1958), vol. II, p.414.

38. D H Lawrence, 'Pan in America', *Phoenix* (London: Heinemann, 1936, 1961), p.27.
39. Virginia Woolf, *The Waves*, 1931 (Harmondsworth: Penguin 1951), p.247.
40. Eudora Welty, *op. cit.*, p.58.

12. THE GOLDEN LEGEND

1. 'On *Death Comes for the Archbishop*', November 23 1927, WCOW, p.5.
2. Woodress II, pp.362–5; Harry Moore, *The Priest of Love*, (London: Heinemann, 1974), p.354.
3. WCOW, p.4. See Ch. 5, p.188.
4. Letter to E. K. Brown, Oct 7 1946, Newberry.
5. Woodress II, p.390.
6. Interview, *The Cleveland Press*, 20 Nov 1925. In Bohlke.
7. WCOW, p.11; Letter to Elizabeth Vermorcken, Sept 27 1927, Morgan.
8. Mary Austin, *Earth Horizon* (New York: Houghton Mifflin, 1932), p.359; Woodress II, p.395.
9. Woodress II, p.395.
10. Letter to Elizabeth Vermorcken, Sept 27 1927, Morgan.
11. When she gave the mss. to Knopf she was confident enough to ask, for the first time, for an increase of one per cent in her fifteen per cent royalties. A month after publication it had sold 30,000; by 1942, 178,000. In 1946 she told Brown that she knew it was 'of course' her best book. (Knopf, *The Art of Willa Cather*, p.210; Letter to Miss Masterson, March 15 1943, RC; Letter to Brown, Oct 7 1946, Newberry.)
12. Letter to Brown, Oct 7 1946, Newberry.
13. Letter to Mr Graff, July 19 1925, RC, see Ch. 9, p.186.
14. WCOW, p.9.
15. See Woodress II, pp.402, 303–4; E. & L. Bloom, 'On the Composition of a Novel', *Willa Cather's Gift of Sympathy* (Carbondale: Southern Illinois University Press, 1962), pp.197–236, and Lewis, pp.140–46, on the other sources for *Death Comes for the Archbishop*.
16. Quotations in this paragraph from Rev. W. J. Howlett, *Life of the Rt. Rev. Joseph Machebeuf* (Pueblo, Colorado, 1908), pp.154, 166, 169, 265.
17. 'Valiant-for-Truth' in *The Pilgrim's Progress*, Part 2, is the fighting pilgrim who, like Father Vaillant, opposes his family in order to set out on his pilgrimage. He sings Bunyan's famous hymn 'To be a pilgrim', and it is for him that 'the trumpets sounded on the other side'. In an introduction to Defoe's *The Fortunate Mistress* (Knopf, 1924), she referred to Bunyan's 'satisfying' scenes 'where little is said but much is felt and communicated.' (WCOW, p.79).
18. For the changes in character between Lamy and Latour see Woodress II, p.401, Joan Younger Dickinson, 'Willa Cather and the Priest', *Impact: Albuquerque Journal Magazine*, August 7 1984, pp.10–13; for Lamy see Paul Horgan, *Lamy of Santa Fé* (New York: Noonday Press, 1975).
19. Howlett, p.257.
20. Howlett, p.217.
21. Letter to Norman Foerster, May 23 1933, UNeb.
22. Clinton Keeler, 'Narrative without Accent; Willa Cather and Puvis de Chavannes', *American Quarterly* 17, 1965, pp.119–26.
23. Mary-Ann and David Stouk, 'Hagiographical Style in *Death Comes for the Archbishop*', *University of Toronto Quarterly*, vol. 41, no. 4, Summer 1972, p.295.
24. Rose, *op. cit.*, p.143; Rosowski, p.171.

25. 'St Nicholas', *The Gilte Legende*, ed. Richard Hamer (Heidelberg, 1978), pp.59, 62; 'St Dunstan', *The Golden Legend*, ed. M. Gürlach (Braunschweig, 1972), p.53.
26. Rebecca West, 'The Classic Artist', *The Strange Necessity*, 1928 (Virago, 1987), p.229.
27. WCOW, p.10.
28. Joseph Conrad, Preface, 'The Nigger of the "Narcissus"', 1899. (Cather had read the story; she mentions it in a letter to Norman Foerster, Jan 14 1931, Morgan.)
29. 'Typology', the theological interpretation of natural 'types' (e.g. roses, thorns) as allegories, or of stories as prophecies (e.g. Old Testament David stories as prophecies of Jesus) was a characteristic way of thinking of the American puritans, and had a powerful influence on authors whom Cather admired, such as Emerson and Hawthorne.
30. Rebecca West, *op. cit.*, pp.218–9.
31. Rosowski, p.169; Stouks, *op. cit.*, p.299.
32. Byatt makes a perceptive comparison with William Carlos Williams' concern with 'the specific, the local, the *name*' in his contemporaneous version of American history, *In the American Grain*. Introduction, *Death Comes for the Archbishop* (Virago, 1981).
33. Just as Cather makes Lamy more tolerant of the natives than he was, so she makes Martínez more primitive. Horgan (*op. cit.*, p. 129) shows that he was a clever man who introduced the first printing press into New Mexico.
34. D. H. Lawrence, 'New Mexico', 1931, *Phoenix*, p.145, makes a similar attempt to understand the Indians.
35. Rose (*op. cit.*, p.142) interestingly suggests that Cather's primitivist, antirealist 'impatience with individuated character' is reflected in the Indians' dropping of the definite article.
36. Rebecca West (*op. cit.*, p.224) says that the difference between Cather and D. H. Lawrence is that Lawrence would have been through the hole in the wall after the snake.
37. O'Brien (p.202) rightly sees the sequence in the cave as disturbingly anomalous.
38. Quotations in this paragraph from Marina Warner, *Alone of all her Sex: The Myth and the Cult of the Virgin Mary*, 1976 (London: Pan, 1985), pp.312, 159, 235.
39. Warner, *ibid.*, p.390, note 4.

13. TWILIGHT AND MIRACLES

1. Letter to Carrie Miner Sherwood, July 25 [1929], RC. Letter to Dorothy Canfield Fisher, Sept 30 1930, Vermont.
2. See Ch. 2, p.26.
3. See Ch. 4, p.71.
4. Lewis, pp.156–7. Quoted O'Brien, p.241. There is a fierce passage in 'The Best Years', a late story, about the 'misery' of old people in California. (OB, pp.135–6.)
5. See O'Brien, especially pp.210–15, 237–9, 241–2.
6. Sergeant, p.240. Quoted Fryer, p.336.
7. WP, p.335.
8. Lewis, pp.153–4.
9. Woodress II, p.426, points out that the French domestic atmosphere of SR owed a good deal to Cather's French cook, Josephine Bourda.

10. Louise Bogan, 'American Classic', *New Yorker*, August 8 1931.
11. Lewis, p.155.
12. See Hawthorne's Introductions and Prefaces to *The Scarlet Letter*, *The Blithedale Romance*, *The House of the Seven Gables* and *The Marble Faun*.
13. Letter to Elizabeth Vermorcken, Aug 14 1931, UVA.
14. Lewis, p.156.
15. Letter to Dorothy Canfield Fisher, June 15/16, 1931, Vermont.
16. WCOW, p.15.
17. A. S. Byatt explains 'anacoluthon' eloquently in her Introduction to SR (Virago, 1984), p.xi.
18. See Byatt, *ibid.*, p.xii.
19. Francis Parkman, *Count Frontenac and New France under Louis XIV*, 1877 (Boston: Little Brown & Co., 1922), p.74.
20. See Byatt, p.x.
21. Parkman, *op. cit.*, p.416.
22. Parkman, *The Jesuits in North America in the Seventeenth Century* (London: Macmillan, 1885), pp.332–3.
23. For another striking fictional use of the Jesuit *Relations*, see Brian Moore's novel *Black Robe* (London: Jonathan Cape, 1985).
24. Woodress II, p.231.
25. Letter to Mr Wilcox, August 10 1931, Morgan.
26. See Parkman, *Frontenac*, pp.340–42; W. J. Eccles, *Canada under Louis XIV, 1663–1701* (McLelland & Stewart, OUP, 1964), pp.230–37.
27. Cornelius Jaenen, *The Role of the Church in New France* (McGraw-Hill Ryerson, 1976) p.77.
28. *Ibid.*, p.104.
29. Brown, pp.285–6; Eccles, *op. cit.*, p.139.
30. Jaenen, *op. cit.*, p.57.
31. *Ibid.*, p.112.
32. Eccles, *op. cit.*, p.68.
33. Brown (p.381) compares SR with *My Ántonia*.
34. Letter to Dorothy Canfield Fisher, June 22 1933, Vermont.
35. Letter to Dorothy Canfield Fisher, June 15/16 1931, Vermont; Woodress II, p.432.
36. See Fryer, p.335.
37. Rosowski (pp.184–7) concentrates on Cécile's resemblance to the Virgin Mary.
38. See Fryer, pp.330–42.
39. Woodress II (p.430) compares it with Monet's paintings of Rouen Cathedral.

14. OBSCURE DESTINIES

1. 'Obscure' is probably not meant to be a reminder of *Jude the Obscure*, as Cather very much disliked the novel (KA, pp.359–66).
2. NOF, p.26.
3. See Ch. 5, p.95, note 23.
4. 'Neighbour Rosicky' has been more anthologized than any of Cather's stories except 'Paul's Case' and 'The Sculptor's Funeral'. (Crane, p.248.)
5. Letter to Carrie Miner Sherwood, Jan 27 1934, RC.
6. Letter to Mrs Mellen, [n.d.], UVA.
7. When I visited Red Cloud I noticed that all the men wore large, showy signet rings with their work-clothes.

8. Rosowski (p. 193) says that it is as if 'from the grave Rosicky describes his continuing contentment'. Oddly, she doesn't note the strong resemblance of this passage to Frost's 'Stopping By Woods on a Snowy Evening', though she thinks that the poem lent something to *The Professor's House* (Rosowski, p.134). There is, too, a presumably coincidental resemblance to the last paragraph of Joyce's 'The Dead', where the snow falls all over Ireland with the same effect of mortality recognized and accepted.
9. See NOF, p.112, on Mann's 'tempo' in *Joseph and his Brothers*.
10. Though she did set a few harsh stories in New York, 'a city full of exiles,/Short marriages and early deaths and heartbreaks' (from 'A Silver Cup', *April Twilights*).
11. Marilyn Arnold, *Willa Cather's Short Fiction* (Ohio University Press, 1984), p.141.
12. This is a re-writing of a scene in 'The Joy of Nelly Deane' (1911) in which three old women dote on the baby of a young mother, Nelly, who died in childbirth. Nelly will reappear in the guise of Lucy Gayheart; this story, which has a narrator who goes away from the small mid-Western town for many years and then returns to hear the news of Nelly's death, was evidently much in Cather's mind at this time.
13. Bennett, p.233, Woodress II, p.63.
14. See Ch. 2.
15. Crane, p.248, gives no reprintings of OMH.
16. See Ch. 2, p.23. OMH has affinities with Mansfield's 'Prelude'.
17. St Matthew, 5:3.
18. Louise Bogan, 'American Classic', *New Yorker*, August 8 1931, In James Schroeter, *Willa Cather and her Critics* (Cornell: Cornell University Press, 1967), pp.131–2.
19. Truman Capote, Interview with Gloria Steinem, *McCall's*, November 1967, p.151. In Woodress II, pp.494–5.
20. Yehudi Menuhin, *An Unfinished Journey* (London: Macdonald & Jane's, 1976), p.129.
21. Sergeant, p.210.
22. Letters to Carrie Miner Sherwood, Dec 14 1933, and from Annie Pavelka to Willa Cather, Nov 8 1937, RC.
23. Letters to Carrie Miner Sherwood, April 29 1945, RC, and to Mrs Lizzie Huffman, June 13 1943, RC.
24. Knopf did not publish complete sets; Scribner's had proposed to Knopf that they do a complete limited edition, but Houghton Mifflin would not release their rights to Cather's first four novels. Hence, Houghton Mifflin issued the edition, which began appearing in 1937, in 12 volumes, with *Sapphira and the Slave Girl* added in 1940. Cather did not make major changes for the edition. Alfred Knopf, 'Miss Cather', in *The Art of Willa Cather*, ed. Bernice Slote and Virginia Faulkner (Lincoln: University of Nebraska Press, 1974), p.215; Woodress II, p.468.
25. Letter to Helen Sprague, Mar 20 1932, RC.
26. Letter to Stephen Tennant, Jan 6 [1937], Hugo Vickers.
27. Letter to Bernard de Voto, Mar 19 1937, Stanford.
28. Granville Hicks, 'The Case Against Willa Cather', 1933, and Lionel Trilling, 'Willa Cather', in *After the Genteel Tradition*, 1937. Both in Schroeter, *op. cit.*, pp.159 ff.
29. Letter to Zoë Akins, Oct 28 1937, Huntington, Woodress II, p.474.
30. In letters to Stephen Tennant, Oct 20 1941, June 23 1937, Feb 16 1945, Hugo Vickers.

31. Sergeant, pp. 143, 167, 198, 201, 209. See Ch. 9, p.185. Cather lamented Virginia Woolf's death in a letter to Stephen Tennant of April 15 1941.
32. Sergeant, p.238.
33. Letters to Mr Weber, Dec 12 1944, Jan 3 1945, RC.
34. Letter to 'unknown friend' (possibly F. O. Matthiessen) Nov 22 1935, Morgan.
35. Letter to Mr Oliver, Dec 13 1934, Morgan.
36. Letter to Sergeant, Aug 16 1946, Morgan.
37. Letter to Henry Taylor, Jan 16 1933, UVA.
38. Edward Wagenknecht, Review of Brown and Lewis, *Chicago Sunday Tribune Books*, March 8 1953.
39. Letter to Carrie Miner Sherwood, Dec 9 1935, RC. Woodress II (p.559) says that Cather exaggerated the episode. She had merely refused permission to the 'Frigidaire Corporation' to use her name.
40. Letter to Carrie Miner Sherwood, June 9 1943, RC.
41. The first Warner Brothers film version of 1924, with Irene Rich as Marian, was more faithful to the story, though it did have Niel proposing to Marian.
42. Willa Cather's Will, 29 April 1943, County Court, Webster County Nebraska, RC. 'Paul's Case', adapted in 1980 for TV, was first published in 1905 and so fell into the public domain. Crane, p.354.
43. Letters to Irene Weisz, Jan 6 1945, Newberry; to George Seibel, Aug 21 [1932], RC.
44. Sergeant, p.265.
45. Letter to Sinclair Lewis, Mar 22 1944, RC.
46. Mildred Bennett: Personal communication to the author, April 1987.
47. Woodress II, p.437.
48. Lewis, p.173. There is a strange anticipation of the hand trouble in 'Old Mrs Harris', where Vickie has an infected cut in her finger and has to carry her hand in a sling; the 'throbbing finger' is a kind of 'companionship' in her misery (OD, p.155).
49. A gall bladder operation could interfere with the functioning of the bile ducts and frequently led to digestive problems of the kind Cather suffered (Anthony Eden was another patient with the same complaint in 1956).
50. Letter to Irene Weisz, Oct 14 1938, Newberry.
51. Woodress II, p.497, Lewis, pp.193–4.
52. Letter to Sinclair Lewis, Jan 14 1938, Yale.
53. Lewis, p.184.
54. See Ch. 4, p.71, for Tennant's continuing friendship with Lewis after Cather's death.
55. Letters to Stephen Tennant: [n.d.]; Oct 21 1945; Feb 16 1945; [n.d.] postmark Oct 1944.
56. Letter to Carrie Miner Sherwood, Mar 22 1941, RC.
57. Letter to Irene Weisz, Feb 27 1942, Newberry.
58. Brown, p.288.
59. Alfred Knopf, *op. cit.*, p.218. Sergeant, p.273. See *Sigrid Undset: A Study in Christian Realism*, A. H. Winsnes, translated P. G. Foote (London: Sheed & Ward, 1953).
60. Letters to the Miners, May 16 1941, Feb 19 1942, RC.
61. Letter to Irene Weisz, Jan 6 1945, Newberry.
62. Bennett, p.52. Woodress II, p.480, refers mistakenly to Cather's friendship with *Jan* Mazaryk.
63. Menuhin, *op.cit.*, p.130.
64. Sergeant, p.251.

65. Letters to Carrie Miner Sherwood, May 2 1932, Jan 31 1933, RC.
66. Menuhin, *op. cit.*, p.129.
67. Letter to Carrie Miner Sherwood, June 28 1939, RC.
68. Letter to Carrie Miner Sherwood, December 1940, RC.
69. Lewis, pp.171–2.
70. Lewis, p.168.
71. Menuhin, *op. cit.*, p.130.

15. THE IMMENSE DESIGN OF THINGS

1. Letter to Carrie Miner Sherwood, June 28 1939, RC.
2. See O'Brien, pp.373–6, and Rosowski, pp.220–21, on 'The Joy of Nelly Deane' in relation to LG.
3. 'Some say the world will end in fire,/Some say in ice./From what I've tasted of desire/I hold with those who favour fire./But if it had to perish twice,/I think I know enough of hate/To say that for destruction ice/Is also great/And would suffice.'
4. See Blanche Gelfant, 'The Disembodiment of Lucy Gayheart' in *Women Writing in America; Voices in Collage* (Hanover and London: University Press of New England, 1984), pp.321–2, on the importance of 'inspiration and aspiration' in LG.
5. See Gelfant, *op. cit.*, Rosowski, pp.219–31, and David Stouk, *Willa Cather's Imagination* (Lincoln: University of Nebraska Press, 1975), p.214 ff.
6. Gelfant refers to LG's 'Keatsian imagery' as an expression of Lucy's impossible 'Romantic' desire for transformation, p.126.
7. *The Fischer-Dieskau Book of Lieder*, translated by George Bird and Richard Stokes (London: Gollancz, 1976), p.335.
8. S. S. Prawer, *The Penguin Book of Lieder* (Harmondsworth: Penguin, 1964), 'Introduction', p.17.
9. Prawer, *op. cit.*, p.13. G. W. F. Hegel, *Aesthetics: Lectures on Fine Art*, translated by T. M. Knox (Oxford: OUP, 1975), vol. II, pp.941, 946, 950.
10. 'Do you know the land where the lemons bloom'; 'Only he who knows longing/ Knows what I suffer'. Mignon's songs are from *Wilhelm Meister* (Vickie's reading in 'Old Mrs Harris', OD, p.105), and were set by all the great *lieder* composers. See *The Fischer-Dieskau Book of Lieder*, p.270.
11. Rosowski, p.215 ff.
12. Cather loved George du Maurier's *Trilby* (1894) and often referred to it in her 1890s reviews. KA, pp.357, 366, 362–5.
13. See Rosowski on Sebastian as Dracula, p.225.
14. Letter to Zoë Akins, April 19 1935, Huntington. Fryer writes on *The Master Builder* as a source for *Alexander's Bridge* but not for LG.
15. Gelfant, *op. cit.*, p.135.
16. Henrik Ibsen, *The Master Builder*, Act 2, translated by Una Ellis-Fermor (Harmondsworth: Penguin, 1958), p.171.
17. A. S. Byatt, 'Afterword' to LG (Virago, 1985), p.258.
18. Karl Miller, *Doubles* (Oxford: OUP, 1985, 1987), pp.43–7.
19. Letter to E. K. Brown, Oct 5 1946, Newberry; Letter to Carrie Miner Sherwood, Dec 9 1935, RC.
20. Lewis, p.176.
21. Sergeant, p.258.
22. Quotations from 'A Chance Meeting' from NOF, pp.1–45.
23. O'Brien, pp.322, 326.
24. O'Brien, p.324, says that the name of the villa, that of a cruel matriarchal

goddess, intensifies the sense of Madame Grout's oppressiveness. Perhaps; but presumably Cather did not *invent* the name of the villa.
25. *The Art of Willa Cather*, ed. Bernice Slote and Virginia Faulkner (Lincoln: University of Nebraska Press, 1974), p.82.
26. Julian Barnes, 'The Thunderous Presence of *l'homme-plume*', *Times Literary Supplement*, October 7–13 1988, no. 4, 462, p.1090.
27. Woodress II, p.475.
28. Letter to Mrs Ackroyd, Dec 27 1941, UVA.
29. Rosowski, p.244, uses Cather's letter to Sinclair Lewis (January 14 1938, Yale) about the presence of 'evil' in the world as the key to SSG, which she sees as a Gothic exploration of the psychological problem of evil.
30. Letter to Viola Roseboro, Nov 9, 1940, UVA.
31. Brown, p.308.
32. Letter to Elizabeth Shepley Sergeant, Sept 12 1913, Morgan.
33. Lewis, p.182.
34. Letter to Miss Masterson, March 15 1943, RC.
35. Letter to Laura Hills, Nov 8 1940, Morgan.
36. Russel B. Nye, *Fettered Freedom: Civil Liberties and the Slavery Controversy* (Ann Arbor: University of Michigan Press, 1949), p.28.
37. E. I. McKitrick, ed., *Slavery Defended: The Views of the Old South* (New Jersey: Prentice Hall, 1963), p.20.
38. Nye, *op. cit.*, p.28.
39. Cather used the alternative spelling, 'Sibert'.
40. KA, pp.268–70.
41. Stephen Vincent and Rosemary Benet, 'Willa Cather: Very Civilized and Very American', *New York Herald Tribune, Books*, Dec 15 1940.
42. Letter to Dorothy Canfield Fisher, Oct 14 1940, Vermont.
43. William J. Grayson, 'The Hireling and the Slave', 1856, in *Slavery Defended*, p.61.
44. Woodress II, p.504.
45. George Kates, 'Willa Cather's Unfinished Avignon Story', *Five Stories by Willa Cather* (Random House, Vintage Books, 1956), pp.177–214.
46. 'Avignon' manuscript, UVA.
47. Lewis, p.193; Woodress II, p.493.
48. Bennett, pp.217, 257.
49. Mari Sandoz, soon after, also wrote a story of a young schoolteacher trapped in a Nebraskan blizzard: *Winter Thunder* (Lincoln: University of Nebraska Press, 1951, 1954).
50. WP, pp.36–7.
51. Woodress II, p.416.

SHORT BIBLIOGRAPHY

Short titles and abbreviations used in the text and notes are given first. Other works referred to are listed in the notes. For works by Willa Cather, dates are given of first publication and of the editions I have used. The definitive Autograph Edition of her novels was published by Houghton Mifflin between 1937 and 1941. Spellings from the editions I have used have been retained, even where inconsistent.

NOVELS

AB: *Alexander's Bridge*, Boston and New York: Houghton Mifflin, 1912; New York: Bantam Books, 1962.

OP: *O Pioneers!*, Boston and New York: Houghton Mifflin, 1913; Virago, 1983.

SL: *The Song of the Lark*, Boston and New York: Houghton Mifflin, 1915; London: Jonathan Cape, Traveller's Library, 1932. Second Edition: Autograph Edition, Houghton Mifflin, 1937; Virago, 1982.

MA: *My Ántonia*, Boston and New York: Houghton Mifflin, 1918; Virago, 1980.

OOO: *One of Ours*, New York: Knopf, 1922; Virago, 1987.

ALL: *A Lost Lady*, New York: Knopf, 1923; Virago, 1980.

PH: *The Professor's House*, New York: Knopf, 1925; Virago, 1981.

MME: *My Mortal Enemy*, New York: Knopf, 1926; Virago, 1982.

DA: *Death Comes for the Archbishop*, New York: Knopf, 1927; Virago, 1981.

SR: *Shadows on the Rock*, New York: Knopf, 1931; Virago, 1984.

LG: *Lucy Gayheart*, New York: Knopf, 1935; Virago, 1985.

SSG: *Sapphira and the Slave Girl*, New York: Knopf, 1940; Virago, 1986.

All page references in the text are to the Virago editions except for *Alexander's Bridge* and the 1915 *Song of the Lark*.

COLLECTIONS OF STORIES

CSF: *Collected Shorter Fiction, 1892–1912*, edited by Virginia Faulkner, Lincoln: University of Nebraska Press, 1965, revised 1970.
OB: *The Old Beauty and Others*, New York: Knopf, 1948; Vintage Books, 1976.
OD: *Obscure Destinies*, New York: Knopf, 1932; London: Hamish Hamilton, 1965.
TG: *The Troll Garden*, New York: McLure, Phillips & Co, 1905; edited by James Woodress, Lincoln: University of Nebraska Press, 1983.
UV: *Uncle Valentine and Other Stories: Willa Cather's Uncollected Short Fiction, 1915–1929*, edited by Bernice Slote, Lincoln: University of Nebraska Press, 1973.
YBM: *Youth and the Bright Medusa*, New York, 1920; Vintage Books, 1975.

COLLECTIONS OF NON-FICTION

AP: *April Twilights*, Boston: Gorham Press, 1903; New York: Knopf, 1923.
BOHLKE: *Willa Cather in Person: Interviews, Speeches and Letters*, ed. L. Brent Bohlke (Lincoln: University of Nebraska Press, 1987).
KA: *The Kingdom of Art: Willa Cather's First Principles and Critical Statements 1893–6*, edited by Bernice Slote, Lincoln: University of Nebraska Press, 1966.
NOF: *Not Under Forty*, New York: Knopf, 1936.
WCOW: *Willa Cather On Writing*, New York: Knopf, 1949.
WP: *The World and the Parish: Willa Cather's Articles and Reviews, 1893–1902*, edited by William M. Curtin, Lincoln: University of Nebraska Press, 1970.

BIOGRAPHICAL AND CRITICAL WORKS

BENNETT: Bennett, Mildred, *The World of Willa Cather*, Lincoln and London: University of Nebraska Press, 1951,1961.
BROWN: Brown, E. K., *Willa Cather: A Critical Biography*, New York: Knopf, 1953.
FRYER: Fryer, Judith, *Felicitous Space: The Imaginative Structures of Edith Wharton and Willa Cather*, Chapel Hill and London: University of Carolina Press, 1986.
LEWIS: Lewis, Edith, *Willa Cather Living*, New York: Knopf, 1953.
O'BRIEN: O'Brien, Sharon, *Willa Cather: The Emerging Voice*, New York and Oxford: Oxford University Press, 1987.
ROBINSON: Robinson, Phyllis, *Willa: The Life of Willa Cather*, New York: Holt, Rinehart and Winston, 1983.

ROSOWSKI: Rosowski, Susan, *The Voyage Perilous: Willa Cather's Romanticism*, Lincoln and London: University of Nebraska Press, 1986.

SERGEANT: Sergeant, Elizabeth Shepley, *Willa Cather – A Memoir*, Philadelphia: J. B. Lippincott Co, 1953.

SLOTE: Slote, Bernice, Introduction to KA.

WOODRESS I: Woodress, James, *Willa Cather: Her Life and Art*, New York: Pegasus, 1970.

WOODRESS II: Woodress, James, *Willa Cather: A Literary Life*, Lincoln and London: University of Nebraska Press, 1987.

BIBLIOGRAPHY

CRANE: Crane, Joan: *Willa Cather: A Bibliography*, Lincoln and London: University of Nebraska Press, 1982.

CORRESPONDENCE: LOCATIONS OF MAIN
COLLECTIONS

DUKE: William R. Perkins Library, Duke University, Durham, North Carolina.

HOUGHTON: The Houghton Library, Harvard University, Cambridge, Massachusetts.

HUNTINGTON: The Huntington Library, San Marino, California.

MORGAN: The Pierpont Morgan Library, New York City.

NEWBERRY: The Newberry Library, Chicago, Illinois.

NSHS: The Nebraska State Historical Society, Lincoln, Nebraska.

RC: The Willa Cather Pioneer Memorial Museum, Red Cloud, Nebraska.

UNEB: The Love Library, University of Nebraska, Lincoln, Nebraska.

UVA: The Clifton Waller Barrett Library, University of Virginia, Charlottesville, Virginia.

VERMONT: The Bailey/Howe Library, The University of Vermont, Burlington, Vermont.

INDEX

THE SHORT STORIES OF WILLA CATHER

Selected and Introduced by Hermione Lee

Willa Cather is best known for her superb American novels, but she also wrote over sixty short stories. The first of these was written in 1892, when she was nineteen; the last was published in 1948, the year after her death. Yet until now, there has been no substantial collection of these stories.

Cather's tales range from short, vivid sketches to novellas. Some are very closely linked to the novels in their preoccupations and styles. Some tell of the bitter lives of Nebraskan immigrants, and of the pull between provincial America and the cosmopolitan world of art. Some of the most poignant deal with the challenges and dilemmas for the American artist. And in her marvellous late stories, charged with beautifully controlled strong feeling and eloquently describing the tensions and complications of family life, she looks back to her childhood experiences with as much passion and clarity as in any of her novels. But Cather also lets herself go in the stories in ways she did not in the longer fiction, with harsh satires on New York life, chilling glimpses of the supernatural, and strong expressions of sexual feeling. This rich selection, the first to be published in Britain, is drawn from every period of Willa Cather's writing life, and mixes the little-known with the much anthologized. It adds immeasurably to our perception of Cather's range and complexity.

AMERICAN MODERN CLASSICS

DOROTHY BAKER
Cassandra at the Wedding

DJUNA BARNES
Smoke and Other Early Stories

JANE BOWLES
Two Serious Ladies
Everything Is Nice: Collected Stories

KAY BOYLE
My Next Bride
Plagued by the Nightingale
Year Before Last

MARTHA GELLHORN
Liana
A Stricken Field

ELLEN GLASGOW
Barren Ground
The Sheltered Life
Virginia

ELIZABETH HARDWICK
The Ghostly Lover
The Simple Truth
Sleepless Nights

H.D.
Bid Me To Live
Her

ZORA NEALE HURSTON
Their Eyes Were Watching God
Jonah's Gourd Vine

GRACE PALEY
Enormous Changes at the Last Minute
The Little Disturbances of Man

KATHERINE ANNE PORTER
The Collected Short Stories

AGNES SMEDLEY
Daughter of Earth

GERTRUDE STEIN
Blood on the Dining-Room Floor

EUDORA WELTY
Delta Wedding
Losing Battles
The Optimist's Daughter
The Ponder Heart
The Robber Bridegroom

DOROTHY WEST
The Living is Easy

EDITH WHARTON
The Age of Innocence
The Children
The Fruit of the Tree
The Gods Arrive
The House of Mirth
Hudson River Bracketed
Madame de Treymes
The Mother's Recompense
Old New York
The Reef
Roman Fever

ANZIA YEZIERSKA
Hungry Hearts